THE VAMPIRE IN EUROPE

THE VAMPIRE IN EUROPE

MONTAGUE SUMMERS

GRAMERCY BOOKS
New York • Avenel

This 1996 edition is published by Gramercy Books,
a division of Random House Value Publishing, Inc.,
40 Engelhard Avenue,
Avenel, New Jersey 07001.

Random House
New York • Toronto • London • Sydney • Auckland

Printed and bound in the United States

Library of Congress Cataloging-in-Publication Data

The vampire in Europe / Montague Summers.

Vampires—Europe.

QR800.V3S82

95–48833
398.2'09401—dc20   CIP

8 7 6 5 4 3 2 1

CONTENTS

FOREWORD

Ever since the first publication of Bram Stoker's *Dracula* in 1897, the image of the vampire has fascinated the public imagination. In the intervening century the vampire has become one of our most popular monsters, a permanent fixture in our collective consciousness. In fiction, the vampire legend continues to grow and transform itself, as the huge success of Anne Rice's recent quartet of vampire novels has shown. Since F. W. Murnau's silent film masterpiece *Nosferatu* in 1922, it seems not a year goes by without some new adaptation or treatment of the vampire legend coming to the screen. It is a theme with endless variations, ranging from the archetypal and chillingly classic treatment of *Dracula* starring Bela Lugosi in 1931 to the dark and dashingly romantic *Dracula* of Frank Langella in 1979 to the gory and opulently decadent film adaptation of Rice's *Interview with a Vampire* in 1994.

What is it about the vampire that fascinates us so? Why do we love to be frightened by undead creatures who continue their existence by sucking blood from the living? Perhaps we humans project our deepest and darkest desires—which would frighten us if we were truly aware of them—upon our make-believe monsters. There is a certain mystique, something implicitly sexual about the proclivities of the vampire. They inhabit that erotic, forbidden nexus between sex and death—twin desires that the psychiatrist Sigmund Freud believed lurked just below the surface of our consciousness. Blood itself is the substance of life, and there is something primeval and carnal about it, as the novelist D. H. Lawrence well knew when he wrote:

> One lives, knows, and has one's being in blood....This is one half of life belonging to the darkness. When I take a woman, then the blood-precept is supreme. My blood-knowing is overwhelming. We should realize that we have a blood-being....

Vampires, arising from that secret place in the depths of our imaginations, seem to embody our most blood-curdling fantasies. Through them we can guiltlessly revel in evils our conscious selves would be horrified at. But what if these terrifying creatures really exist? Most people believe vampires to be merely imaginary creatures concocted from harmless Slavic folktales. But like all legends, they evidently have some basis in reality. In *The Vampire in Europe* the learned Montague Summers methodically gathers far-flung accounts of purportedly real encounters with vampires. It seems that traces of their existence have always been perceptible just beyond the pale of normal, daily life.

Or so the writer of this book claims. In his day Montague Summers (1880–1947) was, besides an authority on Restoration drama and the Gothic novel, the author or editor of numerous classic volumes on witchcraft, demonology, and related topics. His significant works include *The History of Witchcraft and Demonology*, (1926), *The Geography of Witchcraft* (1927), and *The Vampire, His Kith and Kin* (1928). Summers was also an eccentric and rather mysterious character. He graduated from Trinity College, Oxford, and became an ordained deacon in the Church of England in 1908, although a year later he converted to Roman Catholicism and began to study for the priesthood. However, although he wore full clerical dress and professed holy orders, he never held ecclesiastical employment with the Catholic Church—there is no record of him in their clergy lists. He is also rumored to have been more than a scholarly historian of the black arts. It is said that in his youth he practiced necromancy, which may account for his rather stern public advocacy that the death penalty should be reinstated for anyone caught practicing witch-craft. It becomes clear, as one reads, that Summers truly believed in vampires and supernatural phenomenon in general. He states:

> In the records of witchcraft, magic, or sorcery, as I have stud-ied them throughout the continent of Europe, in Spain and Russia, in England and Italy, one finds oneself confronted, not once or twice, but literally as a whole, systematically and homogeneously, with the same beliefs, the same extraordi-nary happenings, unexplained and (so far as we know) inexplicable.

But are the stories he is re-telling *true*? It is up to the reader to decide, but you should bear in mind his warning, written not long before his rather sudden death: "The cult of evil, however it may differ in non-essential details in various countries and at various times, is precisely the same everywhere, and has at all times been the same, as it is today."

INTRODUCTION

In a previous study, *The Vampire: His Kith and Kin*, it was my endeavour to trace back the dark tradition of the vampire to its earliest beginnings, until indeed it becomes lost amid the ages of a dateless antiquity, for this remarkable and world-wide belief was very present with primitive man, and is notably significant in the daily customs and practice, both tribal and domestic—more especially in the funeral rites and sepulchral houses—of furtherest aboriginal and most savage indigene. Nor, owing (as I believe) to the fundamental truth, which, however exaggerated in expression and communication, essentially informs the vampire-tradition did the legend die. As man marched towards civilization it persisted, losing much that was monstrous but none of the horror, for the horror was part of the truth.

I also essayed to find some explanation of the traits and activity of the vampire, to formulate some sort of hypothesis which may account for these terrible phenomena. In a matter of such difficulty and intricacy it were hazardous indeed to venture to claim that my suggestions cover more than a few cases of the well-known and credibly reported instances of vampirism. None the less I have had the great satisfaction of learning that many earnest scholars and profounder students of occultism are very largely in agreement with what I posit, and I am emboldened to think that perhaps I have at least pointed towards some clearer and more detailed explication.

To the feather-fool and lobcock, the pseudo-scientist and materialist, these deeper and obscurer things must, of course, appear a grandam's tale. *Inconsulti abeunt sedemque odere Sibyllae.*

Although very certainly in tracing the tradition of the vampire it was necessary to the theme that various examples and cases of vampirism should be related these were largely illustrative of some particular point and so in a sense accidental.

The present volume, which may be considered as complementary, collects a number of histories of vampirism in European countries. Naturally these relations have not all the same evidential value. Anecdotes told by peasants and occasionally folk-lore could not be omitted. Again we are confronted with the fact that an instance of vampirism does not lose but very swiftly and surely gains by report. It is needful then to distinguish and discount, and, although I have neither tampered with nor tinkered at any text, I have taken as my rule the standard of that keenly critical and severely judicious chronicler Dom Jean Mabillon, O.S.B., that we shall write down "certainties as certain, falsehoods as false, and uncertainties as doubtful."

That a large number of cases of vampirism must be accounted certain only the most prejudiced will deny.

Even in many other relations which cannot be pressed in detail it seems beyond a doubt that the main facts are true whilst the accessories have been embellished for the sake of the narrative. Such a history is that of the vampire of Croglin Grange. Mr Charles G. Harper, who investigated the exact locality, assures me that Mr Augustus Hare was undoubtedly lavish in his colouring. Actually there is no place styled Croglin Grange. There are Croglin High Hall and Low Hall, the latter of which is probably the house indicated. Mr Harper adds : "But it is at least a mile distant from the church, which has been rebuilt. The churchyard contains no tomb which by any stretch of the imagination could be identified with that described by Mr. Hare." These discrepancies do not, of course, militate against the essential truth of the tale, but it should be borne in mind that a narrator who thus mingles imagination for effect's sake with fact incurs a serious responsibility. He gives a fine opening to the sceptic and of this every advantage fair and unfair will be taken. If a yarn is to be told for the shudder and the thrill, well and good ; let the ruddle be thick and slab. But write the rubric without ambiguity that this is high romance to follow.

Cases of vampirism may be said to be in our time a rare occult phenomenon. Yet whether we are justified in supposing that they are less frequent to-day than in past centuries I am far from certain. One thing is plain :—not that they do not occur but that they are carefully hushed up and stifled. More than one such instance has come to my own notice. In *The Occult Review* for January, 1929, Captain G. A. Hope relates under the title *The Impassable Barrier* a very terrible story of a vampire. There are even vampire animals. The vampire bat all know, and not long since the papers published a brief account of a vampire wolf (as it is supposed) which at night drained the life blood of flocks and even cattle.

Mrs Hayes informs me of a vampiric experience which befell her only some ten years ago, but happily in this case no actual harm was done, perhaps because the evil force (although none the less dangerous in intent) was something old and waning and had not at the time collected a sufficient reserve of that new strength for which it was so eagerly athirst in order that it might manifest itself more potently and with intensely active malice.

In June, 1918, it chanced that Mrs Hayes took a small house at Penlee, South Devon, not far from Dartmouth. She writes : " I had a friend staying with me, but otherwise we were quite alone in the place. One morning we came down to find in the middle of the parquet floor of the sitting-room the mark of a single cloven hoof in mud. The house and windows were very small, so it was quite impossible for an animal to have got in, nor indeed were such the case could it have managed so as to leave one single footprint. We hunted everywhere for a second trace but without success. For several nights I had most unpleasant and frightening experiences with an invisible but perfectly tangible being. I had no peace until I had hung the place with garlic, which acted like a charm. I tried it as a last resource."

In a recent book, *Oddities*, Commander Gould has spoken of the Devil's Footsteps that have from time to time appeared in South Devon, and it might very well be thought that the haunting at Penlee was the evocation of demonism whose energies persist, that formerly Satanists dwelt or assembled on the spot and diabolic rites were celebrated, but the purgation of the house by garlic unmistakably betrays that the horror was due to a definite vampiric origin. I have no doubt that there are many localities similarly infested, and that from time to time the vampire manifests in a greater or less degree, but the exact nature of these molestations is unrecognized and the happenings unrecorded.

It only remains for me to thank for several pregnant suggestions and the encouragement of their warmest interest those friends whom I have more particularly mentioned in my Introduction to *The Vampire: His Kith and Kin.* I am sincerely grateful to many students of the occult and generous correspondents whose compliments I highly appreciate and who have, moreover, been at the pains to give me from their own experiences material that is both valuable and original.

M. Fernand Hertenberger's " La Joyeuse Messe Noire " is included by the kind consent of M. Georges Briffaut. It was drawn for the edition of *Là-Bas* published in the collection " Le Livre du Bibliophile ", Paris, 1926.

I am especially indebted to Mr Charles G. Harper for permission to reproduce as an illustration his sketch of Croglin Low Hall, which first appeared in his well-known work *Haunted Houses.*

In Festo Manifestationis Imaginis B.M.V.

uulgo *Del Conforto.*

1929

THE VAMPIRE IN EUROPE

THE VAMPIRE
IN EUROPE

CHAPTER I

THE VAMPIRE IN GREECE AND ROME OF OLD

ALTHOUGH perhaps, in Greek and Roman authors, it may be
said that, strictly speaking there are—with one possible
exception—no references to, or legends of vampires according
to the exactest definition of the term as given in such standard
works as Webster's *International Dictionary* and Whitney's
Century Dictionary, yet there do occur frequent, if obscure,
notices of cognate superstitions, esoteric rituals, and ceremonial
practice, which certainly prove that vampirism was not
unknown in Italy and in Greece of ancient times. Webster
thus explains the word vampire : " A blood-sucking ghost
or re-animated body of a dead person ; a soul or re-animated
body of a dead person believed to come from the grave and
wander about by night sucking the blood of persons asleep,
causing their death." Whitney interprets a vampire as
" A kind of spectral body which, according to a superstition
existing among the Slavic and other races on the Lower
Danube, leaves the grave during the night and maintains a
semblance of life by sucking the warm blood of living men and
women while they are asleep. Dead wizards, werewolves,
heretics, and other outcasts become vampires, as do also the
illegitimate offspring of parents themselves illegitimate, and
anyone killed by a vampire."

There were certain demons and blood-sucking ghosts of the
most hideous malignancy in Greek and Roman lore, but the
peculiar quality of the vampire, especially in Slavic tradition, is
the re-animation of a dead body, which is endowed with certain
mystic properties such as discerptibility, subtility, and
temporal incorruption. In the ancient world vampirism was
very closely connected with black magic, and among the crew
of Hecate, " Queen of the phantom-world "[1] we find such

monstrous and terrible goblins as the ἐπωπίδες, the silent
watchers of the night, who may have had something in common
with the terrible "Washerwomen of the Night" in Breton
legend, ghouls of most ruthless savagery and cunning.
Lycophron, ὁ σκοτεινός,[2] has a reference which would seem to
imply that the ἐπωπίδες were also known as "the companions,"
and illfare the luckless wight whose society they craved as
satellite and convoy. Morning and evening, in the dark
watches and at fairest noon the spectral shadow was always at
his side; once and again a faint footstep would echo in his
ear; the presence, now stealthy, now hatefully palpable,
would ever be there until the unhappy wretch, driven to
madness and desperation, fell into an early grave.[3]

Other among the attendance of Hecate were Μορμώ (Mormo)
who, originally a hideous and harmful cacodaemon, degener-
ated into a bugaboo to frighten children.[4]   But most stygian
and fiendish of all this horrid train were the Ἐμπούσαι (Empusas),
most fiendish and most evil, in many ways strangely akin to
the vampire.   This foul phantom, which was wont to appear
with racking vertigo in a thousand loathly shapes, is alluded to
by Aristophanes in the *Ranae*, during the dialogue between
Dionysus and Xanthias when they have crossed the Acherusian
Lake.

ΞΑ. καὶ μὴν ὁρῶ νὴ τον Δία Θηρίον μέγα.
Δι. ποῖόν τι;
ΞΑ. δεινόν παντοδαπὸν γοῦν γίγνεται·
  τότε μέν γε βοῦς, νυνὶ δ’ὁρεύς, τότε δ’αὖ γυνὴ
  ὡραιοτάτη τις.
Δι.   ποῦ ’στι; φέρ’ ἐπ’ αὐτὴν ἴω.
ΞΑ. ἀλλ’ οὐκέτ’ αὖ γυνή ’στιν, ἀλλ’ ἤδη κύων.
Δι. Ἔμπουσα τοίνυν ἐστί.

Again in the *Ecclesiazusae* we have the following dialogue,
1054-1057 :

ΓΡΑΥΣ Β. βάδιξε δεῦρο.
  ΝΕ.   μηδαμῶς με περιίδῃς
  ἑλκόμενον ὑπὸ τῆσδ’, ἀντιβολῶ σ.’
ΓΡΑΥΣ Β.   ἀλλ’ οὐκ ἐγώ
  ἀλλ’ ὁ νόμος ἕλκει σ.’
    ΝΕ.   οὐκ ἐμέ γ’, ἀλλ’ ἔμπουσά τις
  ·ἐξ αἵματος φλύκταιναν ἠμφιεσμένη.

Second Hag : Come hither.
Youth (to the Girl).   O my darling, don't stand by,
    And see this creature drag me !
Second Hag :   'Tis not I,
    'Tis the LAW drags you.
Youth :   'Tis a hellish vampire,
    Clothed all about with blood, and boils and blisters.

It will be noticed that in this translation, which is that of Bickley Rogers, the word Ἔμπουσα is actually rendered by " vampire " and this is perhaps, the nearest equivalent although it must always be borne in mind that a vampire is a dead person who is not really dead, but owing to certain circumstances able to lead a horrible corpse-life.

The Empusa was a demon, that is to say a spirit, who was able to assume a body, visible and tangible, but none the less not real human flesh and blood.

The best known and most highly authenticated instance of an Empusa is that which occurs in the *Life of Apollonius of Tyana* by Philostratus,[5] book IV, xxv.   In discussing the pupils of the great philosopher his biographer tells us : " Among the latter was Menippus, a Lycian of twenty-five years of age, well endowed with good judgement, and of a physique so beautifully proportioned that in mien he resembled a fine and gentlemanly athlete.   Now this Menippus was supposed by most people to be loved by a foreign woman, who was good-looking and extremely dainty, and said that she was rich ; although she was really, as it turned out, none of these things, but was only so in semblance.   For as he was walking all alone along the road towards Cenchreæ, he met with an apparition, and it was a woman who clasped his hand and declared that she had been long in love with him, and that she was a Phœnician woman and lived in a suburb of Corinth, and she mentioned the name of the particular suburb, and said : ' When you reach the place this evening, you will hear my voice as I sing to you, and you shall have wine such as you never before drank, and there will be no rival to disturb you ; and we two beautiful beings will live together.'   The youth consented to this, for although he was in general a strenuous philosopher, he was nevertheless susceptible to the tender passion ; and he visited her in the evening, and for the future

constantly sought her company as his darling, for he did not
yet realize that she was a mere apparition.

"Then Apollonius looked over Menippus as a sculptor might
do and he sketched an outline of the youth and examined him,
and having observed his foibles, he said : 'You are a fine
youth and are hunted by fine women, but in this case you
are cherishing a serpent, and a serpent cherishes you.' And
when Menippus expressed his surprise he added : 'For this
lady is of a kind you cannot marry. Why should you ?
Do you think that she loves you ? ' 'Indeed I do,' said
the youth, 'since she behaves to me as if she loves me.'
' And would you then marry her ? ' said Apollonius. ' Why,
yes, for it would be delightful to marry a woman who loves
you.' Thereupon Apollonius asked when the wedding was to
be. 'Perhaps to-morrow,' said the other, 'for it brooks no
delay.' Apollonius therefore waited for the occasion of the
wedding breakfast, and then, presenting himself before the guests
who had just arrived, he said : 'Where is the dainty lady at whose
instance ye are come ? ' ' Here she is,' replied Menippus, and
at the same moment he rose slightly from his seat, blushing.
' And to which of you belong the silver and gold and all the rest
of the decorations of the banqueting hall ? ' 'To the lady,'
replied the youth, 'for this is all I have of my own,' pointing
to the philosopher's cloak which he wore.

"And Apollonius said : 'Have you heard of the gardens of
Tantalus, how they exist and yet do not exist ? ' ' Yes,'
they answered, 'in the poems of Homer, for we certainly
never went down to Hades.' ' As such,' replied Apollonius,
' you must regard this adornment, for it is not reality but the
semblance of reality. And that you may realize the truth of
what I say, this fine bride is one of the vampires, that is to say
of those beings whom the many regard as lamias and hob-
goblins. These beings fall in love, and they are devoted to the
delights of Aphrodite, but especially to the flesh of human
beings, and they decoy with such delights those whom they
mean to devour in their feasts.' And the lady said : ' Cease
your ill-omened talk and begone ' ; and she pretended to be
disgusted at what she heard, and no doubt she was inclined to
rail at philosophers and say that they always talked nonsense.
When, however, the goblets of gold and the show of silver
were proved as light as air and all fluttered away out of their

sight, while the wine-bearers and the cooks and all the retinue of servants vanished before the rebukes of Apollonius, the phantom pretended to weep, and prayed him not to torture her nor to compel her to confess what she really was. But Apollonius insisted and would not let her off, and then she admitted that she was a vampire, and was fattening up Menippus with pleasures before devouring his body, for it was her habit to feed upon young and beautiful bodies, because their blood is pure and strong. I have related at length, because it was necessary to do so, this the best-known story of Apollonius ; for many people are aware of it and know that the incident occurred in the centre of Hellas ; but they have only heard in a general and vague manner that he once caught and overcame a lamia in Corinth but they have never learned what she was about, nor that he did it to save Menippus, but I owe my own account to Damis and to the work which he wrote."

This famous legend is, of course, well known to English readers from the exquisite poem of Keats, *Lamia*.[6] In this he has, either unconsciously or with intention, added one or two touches of vampirism, which are not found in the original story. For example when " the young Corinthian Lycius " is first seen by Lamia she " fell into a swooning love of him," and what even more closely recalls the trance into which the victim of a vampire is thrown, when she is about to depart

> He sick to lose
> The amorous promise of her lone complain,
> Swoon'd murmuring of love, and pale with pain,
> The cruel lady, without any show
> Of sorrow for her tender favourite's woe,
> But rather, if her eyes could brighter be,
> With brighter eyes and slow amenity,
> Put her new lips to his, and gave afresh
> The life she had so tangled in her mesh :[7]

Again the poem concludes thus :

> " A serpent ! " echoed he ; no sooner said,
> Than with a frightened scream she vanished :
> And Lysius' arms were empty of delight,
> As were his limbs of life, from that same night.
> On the high couch he lay !—his friends came round—
> Supported him—no pulse, or breath they found,
> And, in its marriage robe, the heavy body wound.

It is probable that these suggestions are purely accidental but it must be allowed that they are, at least, very striking.

Towards the end of the third century when Paganism was bitterly striving against Christianity and all undone foresaw its own defeat, the partisans of the old heathendom seeking about for some eminent figure they might put forward as a rival to the Founder of the new religion in a kind of despair resolved to set up Apollonius, to whom, as indeed to many others, shrines and oratories had been erected in various parts of Asia Minor, a land always morbidly avid for new objects of veneration. Thereupon Hierocles, a fierce persecutor, who was governor in Bithynia and in Egypt under the Emperor Diocletian,[8] wrote a treatise *The Lover of Truth* (Philalethes) in which he endeavoured to show that the Philosopher of Tyana had been as wise and as holy, as mighty a worker of miracles and as powerful an exorcist as the Messiah of Nazareth. Naturally his work gave great offence, and was answered by many writers, particularly by Eusebius of Caesarea, the "Father of Church History," who in effect had an easy task in disposing of his opponent. Eusebius declares that the thaumaturgy of Apollonius was probably vastly exaggerated, and emphatically what he did achieve is due to black magic.[9] It has been supposed, but quite unwarrantably, that Philostratus intended his *Life of Apollonius* as a counterblast to the Gospels. Nothing could be further from the truth, for Eusebius is particularly careful to point out that until Hierocles issued his blasphemous tractate no Pagan writer had ever thought of advancing Apollonius as the equal and rival of Our Lord. It must be remembered, too, that other philosophers were boasted and profanely vaunted by the early Pagan controversialists as vying with our Saviour, and Lactantius tells us that it was quite common for people to argue that Apollonius had wrought greater miracles than Christ.[10] He continues: "It is extraordinary that they omit to mention Apuleius, concerning whom the most marvellous stories are related." It will readily be remembered that S. Augustine wrote when speaking of the *Metamorphoses* "aut indicauit, aut finxit," either the author was telling a true story or else perchance, it is fiction.[11]

With regard to Menippus and the Empusa, Eusebius comments: "The youth was clearly the victim of an indwelling demon; and both it and the Empusa and the Lamia which is said to have played off its mad pranks on Menippus, were probably driven out of him with the help of a more important demon."[12]

A curious legend is related of a certain Polycrites, who is considered by Colin de Plancy[13] to have been either a vampire or an ogre. There dwelt at Thermon in Aetolia a citizen named Polycrites, whom the people on account of his candour and integrity appointed governor of the country. This dignity he enjoyed for three years, with the good opinion of all, and about the end of this time he married a woman from Locris. Upon the fourth night after his nuptials he died suddenly. His wife, who had conceived, in due time became the mother of a hermaphrodite, whereupon the priests and the augurs prophesied that this androgynous birth portended an internecine war between the Aetolians and the Locri, and the archons decided that both the mother and her ill-omened offspring must be burned alive, the execution, to prevent mishap, taking place beyond the boundaries of Aetolia. The pyre was accordingly prepared, but as they were about to set light to it Polycrites himself appeared, pale and ghastly to see, clad in a long black robe blotched and dabbled with blood. All present took to flight, but the spectre recalled them, bidding them have no fear. In a terrible voice he warned them that if they burned his wife and young nothing could avert the most awful calamity. But seeing that in spite of all remonstrances, the rabble, over-awed by their soothsayers and magicians, would kill the child directly he had vanished from their sight, he suddenly seized it and tore it to pieces with his teeth, seeming to swallow down great gory gobbets of raw flesh. The crowd uttered hideous yells and hurled stones at the phantom, but this did not disappear until only the head of the child was left undevoured. In horror the magistrates and elders cried aloud that an embassy must at once be sent to holy Delphi to inquire the meaning of these prodigies. The head, however, of a sudden spoke and foretold the most terrible misfortunes all of which were surely and swiftly accomplished. Later it was exposed upon a pillar in the public market-place. A day or two after, opening its eyes which glared with fury, it announced in a hoarse voice that craked from the livid lips how the army of the Aetolians which had taken the field against the rough and warlike Acarnanians, had been cut to pieces in a recent battle. And presently this proved to be true.[14]

Among the long list of Spectres of antiquities, given by Louis Lavater in his treatise *De Spectris, Lemuribus, et magnis atque insolitis Fragoribus*,[15] are the following ; " *Maniæ* according to Festus the grammarian, are fearfully deformed or hideous persons.[16]   Much the same are the *Laruæ*, with which nurses are apt to threaten refractory children.

"*Mormo* is a female form of hideous appearance, a *Lamia* ; sometimes considered to be the same as *Larua*, hence μορμολυκεῖον, *terriculamentum*,[17] *Spectrum, larua*.   Nicephorus in his *Ecclesiastical History*[18] says that the name *Gilo* was given to spectres who wandered about at night.

"*Lamiae* were thought by ancient writers to be women who had the horrid power of removing their eyes, or else a kind of demon or ghost.   These would appear under the guise of lovely courtesans who, by their enticing wiles, would draw some plump rosy-cheeked damoiseau into their embraces and then devour him wholemeal.   Philostratus in his *Life of Apollonius* tells us an extraordinary account or legend of a certain Menippus who fell into the clutches of a lamia.   He also says that these *lamiae* are sometimes called *laruae*, and *lemures* are often known as *Empusas* ; and that nurses use these names in order to frighten children.   Dio Chrysostom[19] relates that in Central Africa there are certain fierce beasts which are termed *lamiae*.   They have the countenances of beautiful women, and their bosoms are so white and fair as no brush could paint. These they show very wantonly and thus attract men by lewd deceit, but their victims they cruelly mangle and craunch. So the prophet Jeremiah saith, *Lamentations*, iv. 3 :   ' Even the *lamiae* have drawn out the breast.'[20]   Apuleius tells us that *lamiae* are merely bugbears for naughty children.

"*Lamiae* are also called *Striges*.   They say that *Striges* are birds of ill-omen, which suck the blood of children lying in their cradles, hence the name is also given to witches whom Festus terms sorceresses (*uolaticae*).[21]   The name *Gorgon* is merely invented to frighten naughty children.   The story goes that the *Gorgons* were most voracious, and they seem to be very like the *lamiae*."

Pausanias, II, tells us that at Corinth Medea's children were said after their death to have been in the habit of destroying infants ; (Τὰ τέκνα Κορινθίων τὰ νήπια ὑπ' αὐτῶν ἐφθείρετο) and that they only ceased from thus infesting the city, when the

Corinthians complied with the injunctions of an oracle, by
establishing yearly sacrifices in their honour, and by erecting a
statue, in the shape of a hideous woman, or lamia, over their
tomb. (*Eumenides*, ed. C. O. Mueller, p. 141.)

Ephialtae and *Hyphialtae*, *Incubi* and *Succubi*, are ghosts
which appear at night, or imps and folletti. The medical
writers and physicians say that ill-health and disease cause
these fantasies.[22] The *Empusa* is an apparition or spectre
which suddenly leaps out upon and attacks unfortunate people,
and appears continually to change its form. For the most
part it exhibits itself about noon in the glare of the blinding
sun. More details may be found in Suidas the Lexicographer.

The belief that the spirits of the dead return was just as
common among the Greeks and Romans of the highest civilization as it is amongst us to-day, and as indeed, it is to be found
at all times throughout the whole world. To this we may
truly apply the Vincentian canon : " Quod semper, quod
ubique, et ab omnibus."[23] The Athenians held that at the
great festival of the Anthesteria, the souls of the departed
returned from Hades and went to and fro about the city.[24]
The month Anthesterion was the eighth of the Attic year
answering to the end of February and the beginning of March,
and it was at this time that ghosts wandered abroad. It may
not untruly be said that this was the Solemn Commemoration
of the Dead among the Athenians, their great All Souls Day,
and if, as is the most obvious and natural interpretation of the
name, the word means Festival of Flowers,[25] then it is a
beautiful thought that the departed should return to earth
with the opening of bud and blossom to revisit their homes
when the spirit of nature comes to life again, as it were, with
all the joy of colour, efflorescence, and youth. This festival
in some sort crowned man's hopes and held out to him a
promise of immortality, one of those gracious antepasts, which
we find in all religions, of the first true Easter Day. The festival of the Anthesteria lasted for three days, and although the
details and exact ritual are obscure, there can be no doubt that
it involved some ceremonial representation of the death and
resurrection of Dionysus. Paradoxical as it may seem, it was
a Festival of wine-drinking and wassail as well as of the dead.
It must be remembered that in primitive times the ghosts of
the departed were looked upon as still being members, and

very powerful members of the clan. If they were forgotten merely because they did not happen to be visibly present they were exceedingly apt to resent this neglect, and accordingly they had to be propitiated by offerings of food and drink, which oblations were sometimes permanent, and sometimes temporary, since as the years passed by it was supposed that they had gone away to a very great distance for good and all and were no longer in touch with the tribe, so that if they came again from that far-off land, so long would be the passage that they could only return as babies, and the soul would have no memory of its previous existence.

Yet it were a great mistake to suppose that fear alone inculcated reverence and a care of the dead. Love also played its part, and at the Anthesteria the departed must be made welcome. Accordingly their places must be laid at table, platters heaped with rich meats and dainties, and cups filled to brimming with the choicest wine.

In most countries of Europe similar beliefs with regard to this annual return of the dead find expression upon the 2nd November, All Souls' Day. Should this date fall upon a Sunday the Commemoration of all the Faithful Departed is transferred to the morrow, 3rd November.[26] In the earliest days of Christianity the names of the dead were entered in the diptychs. During the sixth century it was already customary in Benedictine monasteries to celebrate a solemn commemoration of the deceased members of each community at some date about Whitsuntide.[27] In the time of S. Isidore of Seville (*circa* 560-636) in Spain a similar day was observed on the Saturday before Sexagesima or at any rate on a Saturday not later than Pentecost. Widukind, Abbot of Corvey (*circa* 980) tells us that there had long existed a most venerable custom of publicly praying for the dead on 1st October. And it was about this year, 980, that a Solemn Commemoration was approved and instituted by the Church. In 998[28] S. Odilo, the fifth Abbot of Cluny, established All Souls' Day in his own great house and in all its churches, chapels, hermitages and dependencies. Very shortly the celebration was adopted by all other congregations of the Order, and immediately upon their foundation in 1080 by the Carthusians.[29] It would appear that the diocese of Liège was the first to adopt it under Bishop Notger, who died in 1008.

It is found in the Martyrology of S. Protadius of Besançon, 1053-66. Bishop Otricus, 1120-25, introduced the solemnity into Milan, assigning the 15th October as the date upon which it was to be observed. In the Greek rite this commemoration is held on the eve of Sexagesima Sunday, or, on the vigil of Pentecost. The Armenians celebrate the Passover of the Dead on the day after Easter.

Formerly the Office of the Dead, which is recited by all priests, was an extra office, to be said after that in the octave of All Saints, but according to the new rule it is now the office of the day, having all the normal parts. In Spain, Portugal, and Latin America priests were allowed to say three masses, and this by a decree 11th August, 1915, has been conceded to the whole world.[30] A description of the Cappella Papale which was wont to be held on 2nd November, when the Cardinal Grand Penitentiary celebrated the Requiem and the Supreme Pontiff gave the absolutions from the throne may be found in Gaetano Moroni's *Le Cappelle Pontificie*.[31] On the following day a Cappella Papale was held for the anniversary of all deceased Popes and Cardinals, when the celebrated tapestry representing the raising of Lazarus was suspended over the altar in the Sistine Chapel[32]. On this occasion the Cardinal Camerlengo officiated. Originally Alexander IV, who reigned from 1254 to 1261 had appointed 5th September for this Commemoration, but later it was transferred to 3rd November as a more appropriate date.

In Brittany it is believed that on the eve of All Souls the departed will visit the living directly night has fallen. Of all countries Brittany is that where the dead are nearest ; at the Pardon of the Troménie[33] they are even supposed to take part. The festival is celebrated on the second Sunday in July, and although the bells in the church of Locronan ring gaily, a knell is sounded with slow, sad strokes, whilst the prayers for the dead are being intoned. The Troménie, we are reminded, is not only a pilgrimage for the living ; the dead who did not succeed in accomplishing it during life, rise up from the Land of Souls and come to take part in it. Amongst the men and women in their black clothes and old Armorican cloaks are scattered hosts of shadows risen from the churchyards.

It is said that a Breton village church is the loneliest and saddest place in the world, and when Vespers have been chanted on the eve of All Souls, after many a strange dirge and placebo in their own native tongues the folk go home to gather round the fire and talk in hushed tones of those who have gone before, whilst the good housewife covers the table with a spotless white cloth, sets cheese and cider and pancakes hot from the oven thereon, which done the family retire to rest. All night long the dead warm themselves at the hearth and feed upon the viands that have been prepared. There are those who will tell you that on that haunted night they have heard the benches creak and stealthy footsteps crossing the floor like the rustling of dry leaves. According to ancient legends the wild district of the Ménez is where the unhappy dead wander to and fro, whispering and sighing together, longing for the old years that have long since passed utterly away.

In Bruges—Bruges la Morte—the day of All Souls is observed with great solemnity. On the eve candles burn in the houses all night long and the bells toll till midnight or even may be until dawn. At Scherpenheuvel there are few uncurtained windows which have not a candle or lantern set in them so that the departed may find their way back again from the cold churchyard to their homes. A very general custom in Belgium is to bake " soul-cakes " or " soul-bread " on the 1st November, to be eaten upon the following day. This is supposed to benefit the dead in some mysterious manner. Perhaps there was once a superstition that this eating by proxy may refresh and invigorate the ghosts, which might partially at least explain the custom of magnificent funeral feasts, one might almost say rejoicings, that prevails in so many lands. The Esquimaux of Alaska believe that on particular occasions spirits may actually enter the bodies of their relatives and in a certain fashion partake of what the survivors consume. A similar idea must have originated the Irish wakes, where the deceased is the more honoured the more food and drink are dispatched. At Dixmude it is popularly believed that for every cake eaten a soul is released from Purgatory. At Antwerp and in some other towns the bread is baked with a quantity of saffron, and thus it takes a deep yellow hue, which may recall the cleansing fires of that patient land of hope and woe. On All Souls' Day, and indeed, during the whole month of November, old people in

Antwerp will tell you never to bang a door or shut down a window quickly for fear of hurting the ghosts.

Throughout the whole of Southern Germany and Austria similar customs and ceremonies are scrupulously observed. Thus in the district of Lechrain the festival of All Saints has been completely overshadowed by the following day. The country people visit the churchyard on the afternoon of 1st November, and here they offer cakes and a kind of bun to the hungry dead. These cakes are known as " souls," and are made of the finest white flour in a fixed traditional manner. Many of these are offered in the church together with plates of meal, oats and barley.[34] In some districts food is thrown into the fire in large quantities on All Souls' Day, and tables are spread with lighted candles, empty dishes and cups without wine. In the Upper Palatinate cakes which have been kneaded of white flour are baked and distributed to beggars, who thus deputize for the deceased.[35]

In Bohemia the season of the dead is observed with many a hoar ritual and ancient courtesy. On the eve of All Souls each family assembles round the fireside, when not only are the cakes to be eaten but quantities of cold milk[36] must be drunk, since these long draughts will allay the penitential flames.[37] In the villages they believe that as the curfew rings the departed will come back to take their old accustomed places round the hearth and two or three chairs are always left vacant in the circle. Moreover, the graves are decked with flowers and illuminated with numberless candles to light the " poor souls " on their way to their old homes. In the Tyrol bowls of milk and quantities of dough-nuts are left out on the kitchen table all night.[38] Some people even set pitchers of cold water where a thirsty ghost cannot fail to find them.[39]

In Greece is observed a modern feast $\tau\hat{\omega}\nu$ $\psi\upsilon\chi\hat{\omega}\nu$, celebrated in May, and precisely similar practices are observed. A $\kappa\delta\lambda\upsilon\beta\alpha$ is made and set out on a table which has been covered with the best white cloth. A glass of water is also provided, and a tall taper which will burn all night long. Peasants declare that they have actually seen shadowy figures partaking of this modest jentaculum.

It must not be supposed that the custom of baking and distributing soul-cakes is unknown in England even to-day. Although fast dying out, it is still preserved in certain remoter

Shropshire[40] and Herefordshire[41] villages. Not many years ago, indeed, the practice of "souling" was fairly common, more especially in those districts which touch upon the Welsh border. Girls and boys used to go from farm to farm singing immemorial rhymes and tags of folk verse, nor were there many doors at which they did not receive a little cake, not unlike the pre-war farthing bun. The tradition lingered long in various parts of England and George Young, writing in 1817,[42] says that at Whitby it was then usual to make "soul mass loaves" on or about the 2nd November. These were little bannocks, and children used to look forward to a gift of this bread. Old-fashioned people would preserve one or two in the kitchen cupboard from year to year for good luck's sake. I have been told that a century ago, in some parts of England, Wiltshire and Dorset were named, on or just after the feast of SS. Simon and Jude, 28th October, there was made a kind of fairing, buns in the shape of men and women with currants for the eyes,[43] and it seems quite possible that these were the traditional soul-cake. It is worthy of remark that S. Jude, the protector of desperate cases, the son of S. Mary Cleophas, is one of the most mysterious figures in all hagiology. S. Augustine tells us that it is to him we owe that article in the Creed, which has proved to so many not the least difficult to comprehend : "Credo in . . . carnis resurrectionem." J. K. Huysmans spoke of this great saint as "le Saint 'sans autel', . . ce saint Jude qui, je l'avoue, me hante, car tout demeure mystérieux en lui."[44] By some extraordinary accident S. Jude was confounded with the traitor Judas, and was actually invoked by sorcerers and witches. It was even found necessary that this grievous profanity should be rebuked, and the error officially corrected. It is not without significance that S. Simon was often confused with S. Simeon, who in Italy is still regarded as a *folletto* or goblin Saint. "San Antonio[45] and San Simeone cannot be saints," said a *strega* once to Leyland,[46] "because we always perform incantations in a cellar to them at night." The *Libretto di Stregonerie*, a halfpenny chapbook, gives directions precisely how to make a Novena to *Il Buon Vecchio Simeone*, "and it is certain that soon after the Novena, the good old man will appear in some form, and grant the one praying his request ; but what he principally bestows is the good fortune

of lucky numbers in the lottery." Appropriate invocations
are particularly described. These have to be repeated three
nights in succession at the hour of twelve. If this is exactly
done and not a syllable, not a vowel, omitted or mispronounced
the good old man will appear to you. At least, this is what a
reputed witch told Leland. Like Proteus, the Saint may
assume any figure but you must be fearless in immediately
demanding whatever it is you want to know, or some mishap
will assuredly take place. The *Santi folletti* are not to be
invoked and pothered in vain.[47]

The connexion of SS. Simon and Jude, although confused
and erroneous, with these magical practices is indeed remarkable, and perhaps is owing to something more than a mere
superficial similarity of names. It seems that the English
soul-cake, which was made on or about 28th October, must be
associated with the traditions that cluster around All Souls'
Day. These prevail, or at any rate until recently prevailed, as
far north as Aberdeenshire where, according to T. F.
Thiselton Dyer, as late as 1876 " on All Souls' Day, baked cakes
of a particular sort are given away to those who may chance to
visit the house, where they are made. The cakes are called
' dirge-loaf,' "[48] At the beginning of the nineteenth century
this tradition was yet to be found among the far Western
islands of Scotland, for on S. Kilda the good wives were wont
on All Hallows to bake large scones in the form of a triangle,
and these had to be eaten to the last crumb before to-morrow.[49]

Among the Abruzzi in all the towns and villages numbers of
candles and tapers are bought on the 1st November, and when
dusk falls it is the custom for people to light some on the
graves of their relations, whilst others are kept burning in the
windows all night long. This is to show the dead the way back
to their old homes. In every kitchen there must be neatly set
out upon the table a glowing lamp and a repast of bread and
water. At midnight a ghastly procession issues from the
campo santo, the dead are rising from their graves. First
walk the souls of those who lead good and useful lives, and
lastly in hideous and deformed shapes those who were murdered
or are damned. The man bold enough to stand at a cross-
road, if he has performed dark theurgic ceremonies may see
this awful troop go by. Once someone plucked up the courage
to do this. Those who walked in front bade him depart

whilst all was well. He refused to listen to their warning, but
when the wretched wight saw those who came at the end of
this spectral *cortège* he fell to the ground, and next morning
was discovered dead, his eyes glassy and fixed, his face frozen
and contorted with horror.[50]

Not only do the spirits of the good return, but also those
who have wrought evil in their lives and these are ready for
more mischief. So at the festival of the Anthesteria the
Athenians tied ropes round the temple and sacred places
to keep out evil spirits whose presence would profane the
sanctuary ; they fastened branches of Christ's-thorn to their
doors and windows, and daubed the lintels and grunsel with
pitch. Christ's-thorn or buckthorn, *rhamnus*, is translated by
Gabriel Brotier in his Commentary upon Pliny's *Historia
Naturalis*, "le Neprun."[51] The Greeks thought that to
stick twigs of this in a casement prevented witches from entering
a house. In many parts of Europe, even to-day the same idea
prevails and bunches of buckthorn or hawthorn are hung on a
shutter or gate outside the house. In England it is considered
extremely unlucky to bring hawthorn or may into a house,
especially if it be in flower. Should a sprig be by any chance
introduced, even if it is just worn in a button-hole, it must be
thrown out of the front door immediately, and if the blossom
has been placed in a vase or glass this must be at once scoured
with fair water. In many districts of Bosnia when the women
pay a visit of condolence to a neighbour where a death has
taken place, they conceal a small piece of hawthorn in their
coverchiefs, and, on leaving, they throw this away outside in
the road. It is supposed that if the deceased has become a
vampire, he cannot resist the hawthorn, and he will be so intent
upon picking up the briar that he will forget to follow them
and insinuate himself into their homes.[52]

There was an old superstition in the Highlands of Scotland
that tar painted on a door would not allow witches to pass.[53]
And it is remarkable that the Serbians mark crosses with tar
on the doors of their houses and barns to prevent vampires
from entering to harm themselves or their cattle.[54] A similar
custom prevails among the Bulgarians who believe that in this
manner any prowling ghost may be held in check, and the
homestead secured from malignant invasion.[55] In the Isle of
Man at those seasons when sorcerers have especial power there

were few farmers who did not fasten branches of mayflower over their doors to guard their houses from the incursion of witches, kobolds, and other unearthly visitants. In the same way crosses made of rowan with its scarlet berries were fastened in the cattle sheds and byres, for everyone knows that rowan is the most powerful safeguard against warlocks, boggarts, and all such fiendish folk.[56]

As we have seen, at the Anthesteria the ghosts of relatives and those who have been beloved during life were welcomed back and feasted with food and wine, but in the train of the kindly spirits there inevitably came vast numbers of evil phantoms, and it was necessary that these should be dislodged and dismissed. Accordingly, on the last day of the solemnities the mysterious throngs were bidden depart with the formula : " Out of the house with you, out of doors, ye ghosts. The Anthesteria is over and done."

The most characteristic feature of the vampire is its horrid thirst for blood. By blood it sustains and nourishes its own vitality, it prolongs its existence of life in death and death in life. Blood it seeks and blood it must have. In ancient Greece we find that the dead might be seen in bodily form, and also that blood is required by the dead, who hence regain some measure of life and a certain fulfilment of speech.[57] Nay more, the dead, when they thus appear and have been given their meed of blood acquire sufficient energy and human substance to engage in battle, to contest in wrestling, to beget children, and other very material activities, all of which legend attributes to the vampire. But there is one point, and this a most important feature, which sharply distinguishes the fundamental ideas. The vampire is a thing ineffably evil, most hideous and foul. In ancient Greece, almost without exception, it is the happy dead, the blessed ones, Elysian heroes who return and are in this manner nourished with blood to lend them life and strength.

It is this conception which partially, at any rate, explains the world-wide practice of human sacrifice. The victim was supposed in some mystical way by the outpouring of his blood and the devotion of his life to supplement and intensify the life of the god, to energize, as it were, the deities with an accession of vitality, youth and power. It will be seen that this is vampirism regarded from an entirely different angle. In old Greek myth the Thracian Lycurgus, King of the Edonians, was put to death in order that the land which had become arid and barren might recover its richness and fertility.[58] The usual version of the story says that he opposed the vine-god Dionysus and was rent in pieces. That is to say a sacrifice was offered to the spirit of fecundation, and the richer the blood with which the germinating principle could be supplied, the more bountiful the wine-crop and the harvest, accordingly at a time of dearth and great necessity the noblest in the land the King, must be offered as a victim. Precisely similar is the story of Pentheus, King of Thebes, which has been immortalized by Euripides. Here the young and beautiful god, Dionysus, travelling throughout all countries, comes to his own city Thebes :

> Behold, God's Son is come unto this land
> Of Thebes, even I, Dionysus, whom the brand
> Of heaven's hot splendour lit to life, when she
> Who bore me, Cadmus' daughter Semele,
> Died here. So, changed in shape from God to man,
> I walk again by Dirce's streams and scan
> Ismenus' shore. . . .
>   Aye, Cadmus hath done well ; in purity
> He keeps this place apart, inviolate,
> His daughter's sanctuary ; and I have set
> My green and clustered vines to robe it round.
> Far now behind me lies the golden ground.[59]

His own people, nevertheless have not honoured him ; they have refused him worship, wherefore he has compelled them to acknowledge his divinity and filled them with the frenzy of monomania and red delirium. The King, however, Pentheus, with brutal common sense refuses to allow himself to be swayed by the general enthusiasm. He mocks and even imprisons the god. Dire portents follow, and the Maenads under the spell of some haunted glamour turn upon him to tear him to pieces, his own mother Agave being the first to rend him limb from limb. The story is not a moral one ; there is no sympathetic character in the great drama ; it is frankly a savage tale, and Euripides who is utterly dispassionate, does not seek to veil the atrocity or disguise the cruelty of it. It is, indeed, a study of religious fanaticism ; not hostile, hardly critical, merely objective. Perhaps the one human touch throughout the whole is when Agave returns to her senses and realizes that she has slain her child.

Agave. 'Tis Dionyse hath done it ! Now I see.

Cadmus. Ye wronged him ! He denied his deity.

Agave. Show me the body of the son I love.

And later, when Agave appeals to Dionysus, the god has no answer and merely replies with a fatalistic retort, an ugly barren rationalism, which leads nowhere at all.

Agave. Dionysus, we beseech thee ! We have sinned !

Dionysus. Too late ! When there was time, ye knew me not !

Agave. We have confessed. Yet is thine hand too hot.

Dionysus. Ye mocked me, being God : this is your wage.

Agave. Should God be like a proud man in his rage ?

Dionysus. 'Tis as my sire, Zeus, willed it long ago.[60]

Nothing could be more impotent and more significant than this last line. And indeed until we arrive at the higher hope of the Eleusinian Mysteries this helplessness informs all Greek religion. Perhaps Euripides was portraying the blind ruthlessness and unmorality of nature.

It seems almost certain that these old myths preserve the memory of the immolation of human victims. The author of a dialogue often attributed to Plato, the *Minos*, after mentioning the horrid practices of the Carthaginians, adds that similar customs were not unknown even in Greece itself, and there is a reference to such sacrifices taking place on Mount Lycaeus and that the male descendants of Athamas were liable to be slain in this manner.[61] It would seem that the worship of Lycaean Zeus on this Arcadian hill was a continuation of the very ancient cult of Cronus in this place, a primitive ritual which essentially demanded the immolation of a human victim. There are, it may be remarked, clear indications that at Athens the feast Cronia, which was held in the summer,[62] usually took place during the month Anthesterion. This is the view of August Mommsen, and at Olympia the festival of Cronos was undoubtedly celebrated in the spring. At the wizard sanctuary of Mount Lycaeus the mactation of human victims continued regularly even until after the advent of Christianity. It is extremely significant, moreover, that the ceremonies and lore of the Arcadian mountains were closely connected with a number of legends concerning werewolves and often in modern accounts and Slav superstition it is very difficult to distinguish the werewolf from the vampire. There is a very interesting reference to this in Plato's *Republic*, VIII, 565 : " And what are the first steps in the transformation of the champion into a tyrant. Can we doubt that the change dates from the time when the champion has begun to act like the man in that legend which is current in reference to the temple of Lycaean Zeus in Arcadia ?

What legend ?

According to it, the worshipper who tasted the one human entrail, which was minced up with the other entrails of other victims, was inevitably metamorphosed into a wolf. Have you never heard the story ?

Yes, I have."[63]

Pliny also, in his *Historia Naturalis*, XXXIV, 22 (Vol. II, pp. 186-7),[64] speaking of various stories of men changing into wolves,[65] has the following : " Agriopas, the author of a work upon the victors in the Olympic games, tells how Demaenetus, an Arcadian, transformed himself into a wolf, by partaking of the entrails of a boy who had been sacrificed at Mount Lycaeus, since the Arcadians used to offer human victims to Lycaean Zeus, but that after a space of ten years, he recovered his original form, and overcoming all others in boxing, was crowned a victor at the Olympic games."[66] S. Augustine *De Ciuitate dei*, XVIII, 17, " Of the incredible transformations of human beings that Varro believed," repeats this legend, and writes : " Nay, he names one Daemonetus, who tasting of the sacrifices, which the Arcadians offered (killing of a child) to their god Lycaeus, was turned into a wolf, and becoming a man again at ten years' end, he grew to be a champion, and was victor in the Olympic games."[67] S. Isidore of Seville,[68] in his *Etymologiae (Origines)*, VIII, ix, 5, mentions the " sacrificium, quod Arcades deo suo Lycaeo immolabant, ex quo quicumque sumerent in bestiarum formas conuertebantur."[69]

It is evident that magical properties were ascribed to the blood of these victims, and so when ghosts had tasted blood they received an enchanted life. In the *Odyssey*, Book XI, Odysseus who has been advised by the witch Circe to take counsel from the shade of Tiresias, the Theban seer,[70] makes his way to the realms of the Cimmerians, who are for ever shrouded in mists and darkness,[71] a place whither the glad light of the golden sun can never find entrance. Here amid the shades of night he seeks the black poplar groves which are the bourne of the unseen world. It may be remembered that Vergil compares the Golden Bough to the mistletoe and Kerner von Marilian notes "the mistletoe's favourite tree is certainly the Black Poplar (*Populus nigra*). It flourishes with astonishing luxuriance on the branches of that tree."[72] And the Golden Bough was found by Aeneas " ad fauces graueo- lentis Auerni." The poet, *Aeneid*, VI, 201-209, speaks of his mother's doves who have shown the hero the path :

> Inde ubi uenere ad fauces graueolentis Auerni,
> tollunt se celeres liquidumque per aera lapsae
> sedibus optatis gemina super arbore sidunt,
> discolor unde auri per ramos aura refulsit.
> Quale solet siluis brumali frigore uiscum
> fronde uirere noua, quod non sua seminat arbos,
> et croceo fetu teretes circumdare truncos :
> talis erat species auri frondentis opaca
> ilice, sic leni crepitabat brattea uento.

This has been Englished by Conington thus :

> By turns they feed, by turns they fly,
> Just in the range of human eye ;
> Till when they scent the noisome gale
> Which dark Avernus' jaws exhale,
> Aloft they rise in rapid flight :
> Then on the tree at once alight
> Where flashing through the leaves is seen
> The golden bough's contrasted sheen.
> As in the depth of winter's snow
> The parasitic mistletoe
> Bursts with fresh bloom, and clothes anew
> The smooth bare stems with saffron hue :
> So 'mid the oak's umbrageous green
> The gleam of leafy gold was seen :
> So 'mid the sounds of whispering trees
> The thin foil tinkled in the breeze.

Odysseus has arrived at the phantom land, the Limbo which lies between the kingdom of Hades and the living earth. Here the spirit of the dead has the form, the rank, and the occupations, which were those of the living man. But it is a mere shade, a wraith. " The living heart is not in it " (*Iliad*, XXIII, 103), it is " without strength." And so when Odysseus has evoked the shades of the departed he must needs energize them and lend them vitality. A pit is dug, a cubit square, and herein flows the blood of many sheep which he sacrifices to mighty Hades and mystic Proserpine.[73] All around in a swift, silent throng the shadows draw nigh from every quarter, yearning to drink of the blood, but with drawn sword perforce he keeps them at bay until Tiresias shall appear. Even the ghost of the mother who bare him and whose paps he sucked must be warded off from the trench. At last, yet bearing in his hands the golden staff of prophecy, the figure of the Theban mage hovers at the edge of the brimming fosse and bids the hero sheath that glittering glaive, and suffer him to quaff his fill of the blood, in order that he may announce what is soon to come. Once he has drunk the blood he utters his oracle, and he further tells Odysseus that a draught of the blood will confer upon each ghost who tastes it at least some of the faculties of the living and that those who have partaken will at any rate be empowered to hold converse awhile with the hero. Accordingly the dead mother is now able to talk with her son, but when he endeavours to fold her in his embrace it is all vain, he grasps the thin and empty air.[74] It is worth noting that certain lines (368-481) in this long and most interesting passage are considered by many interpreters to be an Orphic interpolation.

Amongst the other ghosts is prominent the shade of Achilles, and in the *Hecuba* of Euripides the phantom of Achilles is represented as demanding the sacrifice of Polyxena upon his tomb. The chorus of captive Trojan women haste to Hecuba with the mournful news.

> Not for lightening of thy pain ; nay, a burden have I ta'en
> Of heavy tidings, herald of sore anguish unto thee,
> For that met is the array of Achæa, and they say
>   That thy child unto Achilles a sacrifice must be.
>
> For thou knowest how in sheen of golden armour seen
>   He stood upon his tomb, and on the ocean-pacing ships
> Laid a spell, that none hath sailed,—yea, though the halliards
>   brailed
>   The sails up to the yards ;—and a cry rang from his lips :
>
> " Ho Danaans ! whither now, leaving unredeemed your vow
>   Of honour to my tomb, and my glory spurned away ? "
> Then a surge of high contention clashed : the spearhost in
>   dissension
> Was cleft, some crying, " Yield his tomb the victim ! "—
>   others, " Nay ! "

Now the King was fervent there that thy daughter they
should spare,
For that Agamemnon loveth thy prophet bacchanal.
But thy sons of Theseus twain, Athens' scions, for thy bane
Pleaded both, yet for the victim did their vote at variance
fall.

" Ye cannot choose but crown with the life-blood streaming
down
Achilles' grave ! " they clamoured—" and, for this
Cassandra's bed,
Shall any dare prefer to Achilles' prowess her—
A concubine, a bondslave ?—It shall never be ! " they said.[75]

In the *Oedipus Coloneus* the mysterious Oedipus foretelling
that the Thebans had suffered a terrible defeat in battle near
his tomb speaks of his cold dead body as eagerly drinking their
warm flowing blood.[76]

A late legend of Odysseus may be found in Pausianas,
Strabo, Aelian, Suidas, and some other writers.[77] In the
course of his wanderings the hero arrived at the town of
Temesa, one of the most ancient Ausionian settlements in the
south of Italy, in Bruttium on the Sinus Terinaeus. Here a
fellow of his company, having ravished a virgin, was stoned to
death by the inhabitants. The ghost of the dead man forthwith
haunted the city in so fearful a way that the inhabitants began
to take measures to vacate the place and make a new
foundation elsewhere. Upon inquiring, however, of the
Delphian oracle they were told that in order to appease the
spirit they must forthwith build him a temple, and yearly
sacrifice on his altar the most beautiful maiden of their people.
A sanctuary was built in accordance with the divine command ;
and access to the sacred precincts was prohibited on pain of
death to all save the priests who served at this haunted altar,
and here on the anniversary of the death a maiden chosen
by the ministers of this dark rite was immolated to appease the
murdered man. This story also is tinged with a certain
vampirism, as the ghoul in some way proves able to prolong
his existence by feeding at intervals upon the blood of another,
and this libation must be rich and red.

We may say that with regard to modern Greece the superstition of the vampire is not Hellenic but Slav, although it is
quite true that a few of the older elements remain, and it

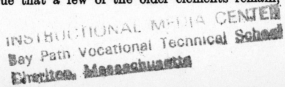

is a mistake to suppose that there was not much in Hellenic lore that was both horrible and harmful.

At Rome, a festival was held in honour of departed spirits on the 9th, 11th and 13th of May. Thus, the Lemuria, closely corresponds with the Greek Anthesteria, but although at first this solemnity may have been intended to propitiate all spirits whether good or evil, there can be no doubt that in later times it was a veneration of fear which sought to ward off the influence of malignant spectres. The cult of the Manes embraced the deified souls of the departed and all good spirits ;[78] the Laralia was a more intimate and domestic celebration in honour of the tutelar Lares whose images stood on the hearth in a little shrine, *aedes*, or in a small private chapel, *lararium*. The Laralia was celebrated on 1st May,[79] and Macrobius speaks of a goddess Mania who is the mother of the Lares, and it would seem that at one time human victims were offered to this deity, for in the *Saturnalia*, I, vii, we read : " In very ancient days they were wont to sacrifice children to the goddess Mania, the mother of the Lares, and human victims were supposed to ensure the safety of the whole clan, but after the expulsion of the Tarquins Junius Brutus, the first consul ordered that these sacrifices should be performed in another fashion . . . so that the guilt of such horrid rights should never again be incurred."[80] In connexion with these dark ceremonies we may remember that although in historical times Mania was considered as the kindly mother of a household, yet it seems as though some occult tradition lingered in the background since, according to Festus, as we have already noted, the word Mania was applied to a deformity. S. Augustine tells us, *De Ciuitate Dei*, IX, xi, Apuleius "says also that men's souls are *dæmones*, and become *lares* if their merits be good ; if evil, *lemures*, goblins ; if uncertain, *manes*. But how pernicious this opinion is to all goodness, who sees not ; for be men never so mischievous, hoping to become *lemures* or *manes*, the more desirous they are of hurt, the worse they turn into, and are persuaded that some sacrifices will call them to do mischief when they are dead, and become such : for these Lares (said he) are evil *dæmones* that have been men on earth."

Ovid gives a full description of the Lemuria, *Fasti*, V, 419-486. He speaks indeed as if the festival was held upon only one day, 9th May, but we know from the inscribed calendars that it lasted three days. Some of the details given by the poet are very curious. He says that when the ninth day of May is come, " then shall the ancient ritual be observed, the ceremonials of the Lemuria which must be performed at night ; these dark hours will present due oblations to the silent Shades . . . it is now the midnight hour, and all nature is wrapped in silence and in sleep ; even the dogs, and the feathered fowl of many a glossy hue slumber and sleep. Then he who is to perform the ancient ceremonies, with awful reverence of heaven's gods rises from his couch ; he dons no sandal, barefoot must he go about this solemn business. Bringing his hands smartly together he knaps his thumb and middle finger, lest haply if all were still some spectre might prevent him at his work. Thrice does he lave his hands in pure spring-water ; he turns his face away and he takes up the black beans in his grasp. Gazing in the opposite direction he casts them over his shoulder, and as he throws them backwards he cries : " With these beans do I pay the ransom for myself and the whole household." This must he say nine times over, nor must he dare to glance behind him. For at his shoulder stands the ghost, who unseen of all gathers up the offering. Again the worshipper shall wash his hands in fair water ; he must strike upon a brazen gong, and at the note he shall beseech the spectres to spare his house. Nine times doth he cry aloud, " O shades of my ancestors, go forth I beseech thee ! " then at last may he look all about him, for now may he truly deem that he has well and duly performed these hallowed mysteries." It was certainly believed that the ghost whom this ceremonial kept at bay would have some unlucky influence in the house, and possibly absorb or seek to absorb the health and vitality of those who dwelt there. This, of course, is a species of vampirism and the psychology of such a belief is far from being untrue. Those who have lived in, or investigated the multiple problems of haunted houses are only too well aware how such influences may feed upon and drain the vitality of persons who unfortunately come under these conditions.

The details of the exorcism are very interesting, and would well repay an exhaustive study, but it must suffice to touch very briefly on just one or two of the chief points. In the first place the worshipper is enjoined to be careful not to lace on his sandals, and we are at once reminded of the passage in

Exodus, iii. 5, where the voice called to Moses out of the burning bush, and said: "Come not nigh hither, put off the shoes from thy feet : for the place whereon thou standest is holy ground." And again when Josue saw the man holding a drawn sword, who stood over against the city of Jericho he cried : " What saith my lord to his servant ? " and S. Michael answered : " Loose, saith he, thy shoes from off thy feet : for the place whereon thou standest is holy. And Josue did as was commanded him." (*Josue* V, 16.) In his mystic ceremonies, Dr. Johannes (l'Abbe Boullan), who died at Lyons in 1893, was clad in robes peculiar to himself, and approached his altar with naked feet.[81]

The knapping of the fingers at the commencement of these rituals may be compared with the Nobertine ceremonial. At the commencement of their High Mass the Premonstratensians clap their hands loudly, an action which is very impressive. The washing of the hands before the commencement of any solemn rite is a natural thought, and is of course common to all religions, and normally has its place in ordinary etiquette. Superstition connected with beans may be found the wide world over from Japan to Peru. On the last night of the year the Japanese observe a ceremony of the expulsion of evil spirits. From various accounts it would seem to be performed in different ways. In some districts the head of the family clad in magnificent robes, takes in his left hand a lacquered box full of beans, and as at midnight he goes to all the rooms, with his right hand he scatters these, uttering the muntra " Go forth ye demons ! Wealth and riches enter ! " Sometimes the right is delegated to a servant, but this is strictly held to be improper, although in the Shogun's palace the ceremony is performed by a priest or some other person of honour especially chosen. The formula is as follows : " *Oni wa soto ! Fuku wa uchi*, Devils go forth ! come in good luck." In a home where the past year has been unhappy members of the household would each collect these beans, picking up one for every year of their life, and one over, and when these have been wrapped up in paper together with a small copper coin which they have rubbed over their hands and faces to transfer the bad luck, the little packet was thrown away as far as it could be flung at a cross road, and this was called "getting rid of misfortune " (*yaku sute*).[82]

Nine is, of course, the mystic number, the multiple of three, and it occurs over and over again in connexion with magical ceremonies in every country, practised by almost every race. In malefic charms when the sorcerer ties a knot in a piece of string or an enchanted thread, this had to be laced nine times to inflict disease and misfortune upon their enemies. In most cases the evil can be sufficiently counteracted merely by loosening the knots, but the difficulty is to find the cord or string. So in a *Commentary* on the Koran we are told that the prophet Mohammed was bewitched owing to the sorceries of a Hebrew mage, who fast tied nine knots in a string and hid it in a well. The prophet was seized with sickness, but the Archangel Gabriel revealed the black spell, and informed him exactly where the charm was concealed. The evil thing was found, and certain incantations recited over it by the holy man. At every rune one of the knots untied itself and the illness was relieved.[83] It is related that in the Orkney Islands a man was actually killed owing to nine knots being tied in a Coventry blue thread.[84] During the celebrated Island-Magee case when a coven of witches were tried at Carrigfergus, 31st March, 1711, before Judges Antony Upton and James Macartney, it was proved that Miss Mary Dunbar, who had come to stay with Mrs. Haltridge, in whose haunted house the mischief began and who had been attacked by strange ailments, had been seized with convulsive fits in which she cried out that three women were tormenting her.[85] It was discovered that one of her aprons had been mysteriously tied up with nine curious knots, and so the curse was launched. The Salic Law inflicted a fine of seventy-two sous and half a golden coin on anyone who fashioned nine knots in a girdle. Among the country folk in Italy to-day *la ghirlanda delle streghe* is well known as one of the most dreaded of charms. A long cord is tightly woven in nine elaborate knots, and it is usual to insert the feathers of a black hen between the strands. This is concealed in some unlikely place with appropriate maledictions and the person at whom the curse is directed will inevitably pine and dwindle most miserably. What is extremely curious—an incident which seems to me very significant as proving that the practice of witchcraft still exists among us—is that in 1886 there was found concealed in the belfry of an English country church a cord tied in nine knots and twisted with a number of feathers

from some black fowl. It had obviously been made quite
recently for the rope was new, and it must have been plaited
for some very definite purpose. An old woman in the village
soon identified it as a "witch's ladder," and when an engraving
had been published in *The Folk Lore Journal* fuller information
was obtained and the whole reason for the horrid charms
came to light. I have already had occasion to mention this
circumstance, which seems to me singularly instructive.[86]
It should be remarked that as the tying of nine knots may
swiftly bring evil upon some unfortunate person, conversely
nine knots have a virtue of healing and protection. Thus a
Scotch charm for a sprained wrist or ankle is to make nine
knots in a coarse black skein and to tie it tightly round the
injured place while you say :

> " The Lord rade,
> And the foal slade ;
> He lighted
> And he righted,
> Set joint to joint,
> Bone to bone,
> And sinew to sinew.
> Heal in the Holy Ghost's name ! "[87]

In the Eighth Eclogue of Vergil, the " Pharmaceutria," the
maiden who is endeavouring to draw Daphnis to her from the
city weaves three knots on each of three strings of different
colours :

> Terna tibi haec primum triplici diuersa colore
> Licia circumdo, terque haec altaria circum
> Effigiem duco ; numero deus impare gaudet.

On Hallow E'en in County Roscommon girls take nine grains
of oats in their mouths, and going forth from the house walk
about until they hear the name of some man casually spoken ;
this is the name of their future husband. Should the maiden
not preserve the most careful silence the charm will have no
effect.[88] In Moravia on Midsummer Eve the maidens gather
flowers of nine varieties and lay these under the pillow when
they go to sleep ; each one will dream of her future lover. A
precisely similar charm is employed in Voigtland, where nine
different kinds of flowers are woven into a garland exactly at
noon on 24th June, and this wreath must be thrown into the

house and not carried in the ordinary way, neither must it come through the door but be cast in at a window, and that evening whoever places it under the pillow is sure to dream of the future spouse.[89] It will be remarked that the mystic number Nine is an integral part of all these charms, and very many more spells of this nature might be similarly described.

He who is performing the ceremonial of the Lemuria must not look behind him. This prohibition against glancing backwards during magical ceremonies or charms is of frequent occurrence, thus in various parts of England when you see the first new moon after mid-summer, go to a lonely stile, turn your back to it, and ask that your lover may appear. His form will come along the path and pass you by, but on no account must you speak or venture to touch him, and if you look back over the stile to see who is coming a misfortune will befall. One can quite understand the temptation some expectant village girl would have to glance over her shoulder, a curiosity almost impossible to resist, and I doubt not that many a time when the charm has failed to operate it has been attributed to this cause. Not merely to refrain from looking backwards but actually walking backwards are essential parts of the " dumb cake " charm, which was usually performed on S. Agnes' Eve. This day, 20th January,[90] was a time of great importance to maidens who desired to know whom they should marry. William Henderson tells us in his *Notes on the Folk-lore of the Northern Counties of England and the Borders*, 1866, " S. Agnes' Fast is practised throughout Durham and Yorkshire : two young girls, each desirous to dream about their future husbands, must abstain through the whole of S. Agnes' Eve from eating, drinking and speaking, and must avoid even touching their lips with their fingers. At night they are able to make together their ' dumb cake,' so called from the rigid silence which attends its manufacture. Its ingredients (flour, salt, water, etc.) must be supplied in equal proportions by their friends, who must also take equal shares in the baking and turning of the cakes, and in drawing it out of the oven. The mystic viand must next be divided into two equal portions, and each girl, taking her share, must carry it upstairs, walking backwards all the time, and finally eat it and jump into bed." It will be remembered that

Keats in his exquisite poem, *The Eve of S. Agnes*, refers to this custom :

> They told her how, upon S. Agnes' Eve,
>   Young virgins might have visions of delight,
> And soft advisings from their loves receive
>   Upon the honey'd middle of the night,
>   If ceremonies due they did aright ;
> As supperless to bed they must retire,
>   And couch supine their bodies, lily white,
>   Nor look behind nor sideways, but require
> Of heaven with upward eyes for all that they desire.

In some cases in the North of England the same charm was used on S. Faith's Day, 6th October, and in other districts, S. Anne's Day, 26th July, was favoured, but these are exceptions, and S. Agnes' Day is the generally accepted time to practise this divination.[91]

With regard to the clanging of a gong in order to drive away spectres the same idea prevailed in some parts of China where ghosts might be expelled by a great clamour, the beating of kettle-drums and the sounding of every kind of discordant instrument, together with shouts and piercing cries. In some districts also, of the same Empire, when an eclipse takes place it is supposed that a huge celestial dragon is swallowing the sun, and the inhabitants of the towns and villages rush out into the streets and fields and make as great a noise as possible with all manners of bells, drums and cymbals to drive away the monster that is trying to devour the light.

It has seemed worth while to inquire into the details of the mystic ceremonies at the Lemuria and to show how nearly they may be paralleled in other lands, since the rite is so closely connected with the idea of malignant ghosts who visit and loiter in a house to absorb and feed upon the vitality of the inhabitants, which is in itself a form of vampirism. The witch Erichtho in Lucan's great poem *Pharsalia* is a hideous conception, but she is a ghoul rather than a vampire.

> Uiuentes animas, et adhuc sua membra regentes.
> Infodit busto : fatis debentibus annos
> Mors inuita subit : peruersa funera pompa
> Rettulit a tumulis : fugere cadauera letum.
> Fumantes iuuenum cineres, ardentiaque ossa
> E mediis rapit illa rogis, ipsamque, parentes

Quam tenuere, facem : nigroque uolantia fumo
Feralis fragmenta tori, uestesque fluentes
Colligit in cineres, et olentes membra fauillas.
Ast ubi seruantur saxis, quibus intimus humor
Ducitur, et tracta durescunt tabe medullae
Corpora ; tunc omnes auide desaeuit in artus,
Immersitque manus oculis ; gaudetque gelatos
Effodisse orbes : et siccæ pallida rodit
Excrementa manus : laqueum, nodosque nocentes
Ore sua rupit : pendentia corpora carpsit,
Abrasitque cruces : percussaque uiscera nimbis
Uulsit, et incoctas admisso sole medullas.
Insertum manibus chalybem, nigramque per artus
Stillantis tabi saniem, uirusque coactum
Sustulit et neruo morsus retinente pependit.
Et quacunque iacet nudum tellure cadauer,
Ante feras, uolucresque sedet : nec carpere membra
Uult ferro, manibusque suis, morsusque luporum
Expectat, siccis raptura e faucibus artus.
Nec cessant a cæde manus, si sanguine uiuo
Est opus, erumpat iugulo qui primus aperto.
Nec refugit cædes, uiuum si sacra curorem,
Extaque funereæ poscunt trepidantia mensæ :
Uulnere sic uentris, non, qua Natura uocabat,
Extrahitur partus, calidis ponendus in aris,
Et quoties sæuis opus est, ac fortibus umbris,
Ipsa facit manes : hominum mors omnis in usu est.
Illa genæ florem primæuo corpore uulsit,
Illa comam læua morienti abscidit ephebo.
Sæpe etiam caris cognato in funere dira
Thessalis incubuit membris : atque oscula fingens,
Truncauitque caput, compressaque dentibus ora
Laxauit : siccoque hærentem gutture linguam
Præmordens, gelidis infudit murmura labris,
Arcanumque nefas Stygias mandauit ad umbras.

It is hardly necessary to insist upon the extreme care with
which antiquity provided for a ceremonial ensepulture of the
departed and the horror with which the cruel profanity of a
dead body lying unburied filled every heart. It is upon this
that that most famous tragedy of Sophocles turns, and because
of the outrage done to the dead, Creon involved his whole house
in sorrow and ruin. Vergil in one of his most famous passages
of his mighty epic, speaks of the souls of persons who have
not received the decent rites of burial and fitting exsequies.
The shades gather fast at the bank of the mystic river, in
number :

Dense as the leaves that from the treen
Float down when autumn first is keen,
Or as the birds that thickly massed
Fly landward from the ocean vast,
Driven over sea by wintry blast
        To seek a sunnier sky.
Each in pathetic suppliance stands,
        So may he first be ferried o'er,
And stretches out his helpless hands
        In yearning for the further shore :[92]

The hero asks his dread companion who are these mighty
throngs. "These," she replies, "are all those whose bodies
lie unburied beneath no mound of earth ; nor may they cross
the holy stream until their bones are laid in some due resting-
place. For a long cycle of one hundred years must they
unquiet and unhappy haunt these dreary and darkling braes
and, then at length when this weary passage of time is o'er
perchance they will be suffered to cross the waters and reach
that bourne for which they yearn in agony of hope deferred."

Sallust,[93] the philosopher, speaks of the ghosts of the dead
which have been seen lingering about their tombs as if loath to
part, and from these apparitions he seeks to prove the doctrine
of metempsychosis. The Rabbi Manasseh says that the Jews
generally believe that after the body of a man has been buried
for one whole year the ghost will continually revisit the tomb,
that it will return frequently from the land to which it has gone,
and that in some mysterious manner it knows all that is passing
round about it, and may even obtain glimpses into futurity.
It was during this year, according to this learned commentator,
that the witch of Endor called up the spirit of the prophet of
Samuel, but that after this period she would have had no
response to her evocations.[94]

Porphyry remarks that the Egyptians believed that if the
spirit of an animal was separated from its body by violence it
did not retire to any great distance but kept hovering near.
The same thing took place with reference to men who met
with a violent death. The soul could not be driven away, so
to speak ; it is bound to the body by mysterious ties of subtlest
and most powerful sympathy. The shades of those whose
bodies have not been decently interred are often seen flitting
near the corpse. This is well known to magicians, and
it is this occult attraction of which they avail themselves, when

having obtained a body or a portion of a body of a dead man they can compel the ghost by their horrid charms to manifest itself to them, and to answer such questions as they may poise, since because of its spirituality it will have a clearer insight into what is to come than can be obtained by those whose faculties are veiled by the grossness of corporeity.[95] It is hardly necessary to say that this necromantic constraint is cruel and unhallowed in the highest degree. It may be remembered that the celebrated Dr. John Dee was commonly reputed, with the help of Edward Kelly, to have forced a dead person to arise from her tomb in order to answer such demands as his curiosity might prompt him to inquire. There is a well-known picture, "Edwd. Kelly, a Magician, in the Act of invoking the Spirit of a Deceased Person." Kelly and Dee are seen in some lone country churchyard beneath the light of a waning moon. They stand within the double circle which is engraven with planetary signs and the mystic names, the archangel Raphael, Rael, Tarniel and the rest. The body, a ghastly apparition, in earth-stained shroud, faces the two wizards.

Demetrius Phalereus says that when the soul of an animal leaves its body the Egyptians held that it acquired extraordinary powers, that it was gifted with reason and could not merely foretell the future but also propound oracles, and he alleges that this was the reason why that nation abstained from eating meat and why they worshipped their gods under the forms of brute beasts.[96]

We have emphasized how all important a decent burial was to the rest and repose of the soul, and there is at least one very striking example of a dead man who refused a grave since he deemed himself unworthy of it. Agathias relates that certain heathen philosophers who in the days of the Emperor Justinian found themselves unable intellectually to accept the Christian doctrine of the Trinity in Unity, resolved that it would be better for them to leave Constantinople and to take up their residence at the court of Chosroes, King of Persia, where they were well assured of a kindly welcome, since this Prince loved the humanities and was everywhere applauded as a munificent patron of Letters. Accordingly, Simplicius of Cilicia, Eulamius of Phrygia, Protanus of Lydia, Hermenes and Philogenes of Phoenicia and the celebrated Neo-Platonist, Isidore of Gaza, betook themselves in one company to the court of Persia, and there they were welcomed with every honour and distinction. After no very long sojourn, however, they found that many things made the land of Chosroes intolerable for them and with quiet deliberation they resolved to retrace their steps to their Byzantine home. Whilst they were on their way they perceived by the roadside an unburied corpse. As in duty bound they caused their servants to dig a grave and give the dead man decent sepulture. During the night this man appeared to one of them in a vision, and in tones of utter misery bade them spare their pains since he was not worthy of a grave, for the earth, the common mother of us all, refused to receive a man who had committed incest with 'his own mother. When the dawn broke, to their horror, they saw that the body had been cast up out of the ground as though, owing to its great sin it deserved nought save supremest dishonour and reprobation.[97] And yet, among the Persians, this commixture was not generally accounted heinous.[98]

Tertullian, *Apologeticum*,[99] says : " Persas cum suis matribus misceri Etesias refert."

Achilles Statius, in the notes to his Catullus (1566), commenting upon XC,[100] writes : " Persas uero ipsos ceteris gentibus odio esse, propter haec nefaria cum parentibus, sororibusque coniugia, ait Eusebius." Muretus, glossing the same passage, has ; " Poeta detestatur nefariam Gellii cum matre libidinem ; aitque ex eorum concubitu Magum aliquem nasci oportere, si Persarum religio uera sit, qui eiusmodi corporum commissiones licitas esse censent : adeoque bonum Magum existere non posse, nisi quem a filio compressa ediderit mater. Xanthus in Magicis narrat magos matribus, filiabus, sororibus commisceri solitos esse, eosque concubitus habuisse legitimos, auctor Clemens libro III. *Stromatum.* Quae ad hanc rem faciunt, ex utriusque linguae scriptoribus studiose collegit Caelius Rhodiginus capite XVIII, libri x.

One of the most detailed and one of the most significant ghost stories in all ancient literature is also the one story which (as I have suggested before) perhaps can truthfully be said to be the story of a Vampire, since the girl actually leaves her tomb in physical form and is living-dead, although she does not suck her lover's blood. It is related by Phlegon of Tralles, the freedman of Hadrian, and the narrator professes to have been an eye-witness of the extraordinary events.[101] Most unfortunately the beginning of the story is missing and accordingly, we cannot be certain why the resuscitated corpse should visit the youth.[102] Wilhelm Xylander (Holtzmann),[103] the celebrated German humanist, in his edition of Phlegon,[104] briefly fills the lacuna as follows : "Narrationis caput deest. Uidetur summa haec esse : Philinnium, Demostrati et Charitus filiam, clam cum hospite Machata etiam uita functam consueuisse, idque nutricem deprehendisse." The story begins abruptly. Philinnion, the daughter of Demostratus and his wife Charito, has been dead and buried rather less than six months. There is staying in the house a young man named Machates, and one night Philinnion's old nurse, noticing a lamp burning brightly in the guest-chamber, peeps through the door to make sure that all is secure and discovers Philinnion lying in bed with the youth. (It is at this point that the narrative as we have it actually begins. . . . εἰς τὸν ξενῶνα προσπορεύεται ταῖς θύραις καὶ καιομένου τοῦ λύχνου καθημένην ἴδεν τὴν ἄνθρωπον παρὰ τῷ Μαχάτῃ.). Beside herself with joy, beholding the girl to all appearances alive, the nurse at once runs to the parents and loudly calls upon them to come and welcome their child who is living and well and has been restored to them by some kindly god. Charito, trembling with fear and joy, swoons away, but upon recovering her senses, she bursts into bitter tears at the thought of her daughter, and crying out that the nurse must be mad, orders her out of the room. The old woman, however, remonstrates very briskly and is certain that she has not been deceived. At last the mother agrees to accompany her, she steals a glance into the room, and there she certainly discerns her daughter and somewhat vaguely recognizes the night-rail, but feeling that at that hour in the morning, when all is dark and still, long before dawn, she could not ascertain the truth without raising the whole house, which naturally in such circumstances she is very loath to do, she resolves to say nothing until the morning, when she will be able to see if her daughter is really in the house, or at any rate she can ask Machates for an explanation of the mystery.

At the break of day it appears that the girl has vanished, whereupon Charito in the greatest distress most earnestly implores Machates to tell her the whole truth and to keep nothing back. The young man, who does not seem to have

been aware that his host had lost a daughter named Philinnion, is greatly distressed, and confesses that an amorous
pigsnie has shared his couch, and that his leman whispered her
name was Philinnion. Moreover, she charged him to keep
their caresses very private. To confirm this story, he produced
a golden ring with which she had presented him, and also a
ribbon from her bosom that had been left behind. No sooner
had Charito seen these two objects than she uttered a piercing
cry, rent her clothes in token of lamentation, tore her hair and
fell fainting to the ground. It was only too true that she
recognized both the ring and the ribbon as having belonged to
her dead daughter and as having been buried in the tomb with
her. Immediately the whole house was thrown into the utmost
confusion and there were shrieks and tears on every side
almost as if a second funeral were taking place. At last
Machates succeeded in quieting them by promising to summon
them during the night should the damsel again visit him.

That night, as may be supposed, nobody slept ; and at the
usual hour Philinnion appeared. The young man himself was
confused and amazed, he did not know what to believe, he
could not think these warm and wanton limbs which he embraced were the cold and rigid members of a corpse, nor was
it possible for a dead woman to eat and pledge him with wine.
Rather he surmised that the gravediggers must have stripped
the body, and sold the ornaments in the town. However, to
the word of his promise, no sooner had she come than he made
a sign to his servant who quietly slipped away and brought the
girl's parents to the room. When they entered Demostratus
and Charito were struck dumb with amazement, but a few
moments afterwards with loud cries they flung their arms
round the figure of their daughter. But Philinnion said in
sorrowing tones : " Oh my mother and father dear, cruel
indeed have ye been in that you grudge my visiting a guest
in my own home for three days and doing no harm to anyone.
But ye will grieve sorely on account of your meddlesome
curiosity. For presently must I return again to the place
that is appointed for me. Do ye also learn that assuredly
it was not contrary to the will of God that I came hither."
Scarcely had she finished these words than she fell back lifeless, and a corpse lay stretched upon the bed in the sight of all.
Charito now uttered the most piercing screams, the unhappy

father lamented aloud, and the whole household could not restrain their grief at the second death (as it were) of one who was so dear to them all. The story was at once bruited throughout the whole town and in an hour or two caused an immense sensation. It seems to have been officially reported to Phlegon, who must have held some high and important position in the city, for he says ταχέως ἔγενετο διὰ πόλεως τὸ πρᾶγμα περιβόητον καί μοι προσηγγελη. Τὴν μὲν οὖν νύκτα ἐκείνην διακατέσχον ἐγὼ τοὺς ὄχλους ἀθροιζομένους ἐπὶ τὴν οἰκίαν. Early in the morning the theatre was crowded with citizens and after the matter had been debated it was decided to open the tomb in order that it might be ascertained whether the body of Philinnion still reposed where it had been laid six months before, or whether her place was empty. Accordingly the family vault was unbarred, and having passed by the bleaching bones of those who had long been deceased, they found upon the bier (ἐπὶ τῆς κλίνης) of Philinnion a ring which Machates had given the lady who had sought his embraces as a love-pledge, as also a parcel-gilt cup with which he had presented her. In great amaze, the magistrates repaired to the house of Demostratus, and then they found the corpse of his daughter laid out where she had fallen on the previous night. At this there was much wonderment and much debate followed until a certain seer and diviner Hyllus by name, who was held in highest honour and esteem, addressing the authorities, bade them by no means to suffer the body of Philinnion to be replaced in the vault but to see that it was forthwith burned to ashes in a remote spot outside the walls of the city. He further enjoined upon them to see that solemn sacrifices were offered Hermes Chthonius,[105] the psychopomp, who conducts the souls of the dead to the underworld ; as also expiatory sacrifices to the Eumenides. Calling Phlegon aside privately he recommended him to sacrifice for the good estate of Caesar and the empire to Hermes, to Zeus Xenios, protector of the rights of hospitality and to Ares, all of which ceremonies were duly performed. The whole town was further ritually cleansed with holy lustrations. Machates, however, for love of his dead leman, slew himself in a kind of despair.

This history is mentioned by Father Richard of Santorini in his work *Relation de ce qui s'est passé de plus remarquable à Sant-Erini* . . . and he considers Philinnion a true vrykolakas.   The fact that she was harmless can be paralleled, for he refers to a shoemaker of Santorini who returned from the grave and so far from being malignant carefully watched over his widow and children.   Again, the intercourse of Philinnion with Machates and their coitus is quite in accordance with popular ideas.   For the Vampire is often violently erotic. He visits his wife and communicates with her ; he even rapes other women in the absence of their relatives ; nay, he has been known to marry and become the father of children.   In ancient Mexico the Ciuateteô, dead women, were the most lascivious of succubi.   These vampires beset handsome young men and compelled them to copulation, sometimes bearing children as a result of this union.

Although the superstition of the vampire was not fully developed in ancient Rome, yet anecdotes such as this of Phlegon, late though they be, all display something more than the germ of the Slav traditions.   It is, of course, very difficult, if not impossible to distinguish between these ghosts who crave for blood, these spectres who batten upon the vitality of others, these malignant apparitions so mysteriously attached to the dead body who may terrify and injure the health of those whom they molest and the vampire of Eastern Europe.   As it is often supposed that vampires in their full life had been persons of exceptional and enormous wickedness, so in Rome after the death of anyone who had earned universal detestation it was not uncommonly believed that a spectre of frightful malignancy, his own evil, in fact, lurked about his tomb. Suetonius relates that after the assassination of Caligula, 24th January, A.D. 41, " His body was carried privately into the Lamian Gardens,[106] where it was half burned upon a pyre hastily raised and then had a small quantity of earth carelessly thrown over it.   It was afterwards disinterred by his sisters upon their return from banishment ; it was decorously cremated and the ashes buried.   Yet before this was done, it was very well known that the keepers of the Gardens were greatly disturbed by horrid apparitions, and not a night passed without some terrible alarm or other, whilst the house in which he had been murdered was suddenly burned to the ground."[107] The Lamian Gardens were on Mount Esquiline, which was so called on account of the oak groves that originally covered it and in whose remotest depths there long lingered many mysterious sanctuaries, "the Chapel of the Oak, and the oratory of Diana at the head of the Slope of Virbius, where Servius Tullius was slain. There can be no doubt that of old the place had been polluted by human sacrifice and the blood shed here would attract the vampire Caligula from his grave.[108] It was upon the haunted Esquiline that, before the wooden statue of Priapus Canidia and Sagana held their sabbat as Horace has described, and even through the Middle Ages this hill long had an evil reputation.

In many countries the oak tree was revered as sacred and the home of a powerful spirit. The old Prussians watered with the red dew of human sacrifice the mighty oak at Romove ;[109] and Lucan tells us that in the Oak Grove of the Druids at Marseilles every tree was sprinkled with the blood of human victims—

Omnis et humanis lustrata cruoribus arbos.[110]

In Scripture we find the worship of the oak tree[111] denounced again and again in the most uncompromising terms. It is plain that cults connected with sacred oaks played so important a part in the popular ideas of religion that even Jehovah was closely connected with them. And indeed the oak tree was sanctified by supernatural appearances. There were oaks in the vale of Mambre where Abram dwelt and built an altar to the Lord : "Mouens igitur tabernaculum suum Abram, uenit et habitauit iuxta conuallem Mambre, quae est in Hebrom : aedificauitque ibi altare Domino."[112] In Christian times the Emperor Constantine erected a church in this sacred spot, and in a letter which has been preserved by Eusebius in his life of the Emperor it is chronicled that " at the Oak of Mambre," which was said to have been defiled by superstitious sacrifices and worse, orders were given that the spot should be hallowed " with the pure building of a basilica."[113] It is recorded that Josue " took a great stone and set it under the oak that was in the sanctuary of the Lord. And he said to all the people : Behold this stone shall be a testimony unto you that it hath heard all the words of the Lord, which he hath spoken to you ; lest perhaps hereafter you will deny it and lie to the Lord your God."[114] This is extremely significant since it would seem from the text that the stone by being placed directly under the oak becomes in some way impregnated with the sanctity of this mysterious tree. That the trees themselves became objects of worship is very clear from various passages in the prophets. Thus Osee says : " They offered sacrifice upon the tops of the mountain, and burned incense upon the hill : under the oak, and the poplar, and the turpentine tree, because the shadow thereof was good : therefore shall your daughters commit fornication, and your spouses shall be adulteresses. I will not visit upon your daughters when they shall commit fornication, and upon your spouses when they shall commit adultery : because themselves conversed with harlots, and offered sacrifice with the effeminate, and the people that doth not understand shall be beaten."[115] The effeminate are the Kēdeshīm, the sacred men and youths, the divine lovers who in Jerusalem were lodged in the walls of the Temple until banished by King Josias who ascended the throne in 637 B.C. " He destroyed also the pavilions of the effeminate, which were in the house of the Lord, for which the women wove as it were little dwellings for the grove " IV, *Kings*, xxxiii, 7. (*A.V.* II, *Kings*, xxiii. 7 : " And he brake down the houses of the sodomites, that were by the house of the Lord, where the women wove hangings for the grove.") Pierre Dufour considers the sacred prostitution as the principal element of the mystical worship and says that the effeminates formed a sect that had its own occult rites and initiations. He continues : " There were beautiful young men without beards, who, with depilated bodies, rubbed down with oils and sweet perfumes, sustained an ignoble commerce in the midst of the sanctuary. The Vulgate calls such debased beings *effeminate ;* in Hebrew they are termed *Kedeschim*—that is to say, *saints* or *consecrated ones.* Their ordinary rôle consisted in the use, more or less active, of infamous mysteries ; they sold their bodies to the adorers of their god and deposited on the altar of the idol the money received from prostitution. . . . In certain ceremonials, celebrated at night in the depths of the forest, when the faces of the beautiful stars were hidden by the foliage of trees or by shame at the filth of mankind, the priests and consecrated ones would attack their own bodies with gashes and slight punctures ; then, heated by vice, excited by their wild instruments of music, they would fall over each other pell-mell, covered with blood."[116] Similar practices prevailed in Ancient Mexico in connexion with their worship, and Bernal Diaz wrote : " Erant quasi omnes sodomia commaculati, et adolescentes multi, muliebriter uestiti, ibant publice cibum quarentes ab isto diabolico et abominabili labore." Eusebius, *Uita Constantini*, III, 55, has an important reference to the wanton rites which even in his day prevailed at Apheca : Γύνιδες γοῦν τινες ἄνδρες οὐκ ἄνδρες, τὸ σέμνον τῆς φύσεως ἀπαρνησάμενοι, θηλείᾳ νόσῳ τὴν δαίμονα ἱλεοῦντο. Nicander in the *Alexipharmaca*, speaking of Cyzicus mentions the underground chambers (θαλάμαι) when the votaries of the goddess Rhea underwent castration, and the place where they celebrated the mysterious rites of Attis (ὀργαστήριον ῎Αττεω). The superb dithyramb of Catullus and the significant description of the lad in such phrases as *tenerum Attin*, *roseis labellis*, *teneris digitis*, must not be forgotten in this connexion.

Ezekiel says : "And you shall know that I am the Lord, when your slain shall be amongst your idols, round about your altars, in every high hill, and on all the tops of mountains and under every woody tree, and under every thick oak, the place where they burned sweet smelling frankincense to all their idols."[117] Isaias also refers to the Israelites of his day as "sons of the sorceress . . . who seek your comfort in idols under every green tree, sacrificing children in the torrents, under the high rocks."[118] There can be no doubt that the human sacrifices which took place in the depths of the oak groves in Palestine were also in ancient days practised on the Esquiline hill, and that the outpouring of human blood attracted both vampires and witches. The psychic atmosphere created by these murderous abominations would have been such from which a spirit like that of the maniac Caligula could have collected stores of energy for its appearance and even, perhaps, for its materialization.

That the ghastly subjects of witches and vampires had taken hold of the popular imagination and were often widely discussed among the Romans as they are amongst us to-day, is proved by the conversation at the dining table of Trimalchio, which Petronius has preserved for us in that immortal fragment of his glorious romance. One of the guests, Niceros has told a werewolf story, and an excellent one it is, but the host proceeds to cap it with his vampire legend. "By the same token," he cries, "I'll tell you myself a horrible story, as strange a thing as if you were to see a donkey prancing upon the tiles of the roof. Whilst I was yet a curly-pated stripling, —and I have been a wanton young Ganymede in my time—our patron's fairest minion died. By Hercules, he was a jewel of a boy, the loveliest of ingles. His poor mother was bewailing his loss, and several of us half heart-broken ourselves, were sympathizing with her in her bitter sorrow. Suddenly outside the witches raised a terrible hullabaloo, you might have thought that a pack of yelping hounds was hunting down a hare. It so happened just then that there was in the house a brawny Cappadocian, a tall plucky fellow, a regular hector, who would have made short work of kicking Jupiter himself off his throne, thunderbolts and levin and all. This young Paladin, wrapping his mantle carefully round his left arm, with his drawn sword in his right hand, unhesitatingly rushed out of doors, and just as it might be here (no harm to what I touch !)[119] ran a woman clean through in a minute. We heard a deep groan ; but the witches themselves—no, I won't tell you a lie—we did not see. At any rate, back came our champion, but only to throw himself swooning on a bed, for he was black and blue all over, covered with bruises just as if he had been beaten from head to foot. There was some devil's work there. We shut the door fast and returned to our business of attempting to console the poor mother. But when she went to embrace the corpse of her son and gathered him in her arms she found nothing else than a mere mawkin, it had neither heart nor anything else, because these vampires had carried off the boy and had left an empty wad of straw in his place. What d'you think of that now ? They are crafty enough, eh ? These night hags who can turn everything topsy-turvey in a second. As for our stout champion, he never recovered but after a few days died raving mad." It will be realized that when stories such as these were accepted, and they won general credence, it became necessary, and not merely a difficult but a dangerous task, to guard the bodies of the dead from these demoniac and vampirish assaults. Considerable light is thrown upon the matter by that marvellous romance, which is one of the most glorious gems of Latin literature spared us by the greedy grasp of time. The *Metamorphoses* of Apuleius has a fascination, perverse and baroque as it may be, which is equalled by few books of any literature. Unbroken is the spell which that decadent mystic has cast upon the ages. His very life was a

romance. Born about the year 125, Apuleius was a native
of Madaura, a city on the borders of Numedia and Gaetulia,
one of those strange towns in Northern Africa where east
meets west, where the newest civilization clashes and coalesces
with the most ancient world. A city of that strange continent
which bears upon it the curse of Cham. Lucius Apuleius
mockingly calls himself a hybrid-semi-Numida and semi-
Gaetulus. In his temperament he combines all the fading
philosophies of the Greeks, all the weary worldliness of the
Roman, all the haunting occultism of the African. *The
Metamorphoses*, his greatest work, was probably written at
Rome whilst he was still a youth in his twenties, shortly after
he had completed his course of study at Athens. In his
superb insolence of premature genius, in his conceit of his own
modish elegance and good looks, in his search for something
new, in his rash assaults upon the supernatural which
colours his whole life, and I would that I could add to his
realization of peace among the mystics of the sanctuary,
Apuleius or Lucius of the *Golden Ass*—for they are one and
the same just as Huysmans was Durtal—is a very modern
type.

That the suggestion of his story is doubtless conveyed from
that same Greek tale whence Lucian had his own witty and
salted version impairs his originality not at all. Apuleius
would have been original had he retold the story of Troy, the
wanderings of Aeneas, or of Ulysses. It is impossible, and it
would be impertinent, here to give any detailed account of
this breviary of magic adventure. Let us be content to
touch upon those few episodes which would seem to have some
connexion with the vampire as he was known to the ancient
world. The romance begins quickly, but not abruptly:
"Thessaliam ex negotio petebam"; —"I had occasion to
visit Thessaly on business." The note is struck in the very
first words. Thessaly, the land of mystery and magic and
marvel. A thousand echoes would awaken. Addressing the
lovelorn swain, Horace cries ;

> Quae saga, quis te soluere Thessalis
> Magus uenenis, quis poterit deus ?

"Can any witch, however skilled, can any mage for all his
Thessalian charms and potions, nay, can heaven itself free thee

from the spell of love ? "[120]   And again, in a yet more famous passage he asks :

> Somnia, terrores magicos, miracula, sagas
> Nocturnos lemures portentaque Thessala rides.

" Do you really laugh at dreams, black magic, strange happenings, witches, midnight apparitions and Thessalian bedevilment ? "[121]   Propertius calls a witch (saga) " Thessala " as a conventional adjective, when he confesses his love, " that passion my oldest friends cannot rid me of, nor a Thessalian enchantress wash from my heart even with all the cleansing flood of mighty ocean."[122] Juvenal speaks of " Thessala philtra," in connexion with " magicos cantus."[123] Lubin paraphrases " magicos cantus " by " necromanticas incantationes," and remarks " Thessalia ueneficiis olim abundabat." This commentator further explains philtron as " poculum amatorium." It will readily be remembered that the brewing of such draughts, whether for love of for hate, was regarded as an integral part of a witch's work and a most heinous offence, since in this way they attempted to interfere with the course of nature.

Almost immediately Lucius meets two travellers, one of whom, Aristomenes relates a story of vampirism and witchcraft, which already contains very many features of later naratives. Aristomenes, who travels through Thessaly, Aetolia, and Boeotia, in cheese, honey, condiments and conserves, arrives at Hypata,[124] the modern Neopatra, one of the principal cities of the district. Here he is disappointed in the purchase of a large consignment of new cheeses, since a rival firm has already made a corner in the market. In order to kill time before he can proceed on his way the following morning, he visits the public baths, and here in the person of a half-starved and wretched tatterdemalion he recognizes a former friend of his, one Socrates, who has for many months been given up as dead. Aristomenes is now determined to befriend an old comrade in spite of his entreaties to be left to perish, and after having plentifully refreshed him he takes him back to dinner at the inn, where he entertains him with good cheer, red wine, and an abundance of amusing gossip. At length the poor fellow is emboldened to tell his tale. Some two years before, or rather more, he was travelling through Macedonia on business, and having had several strokes of good fortune, was already on his way home, his purse full of money, when on the outskirts of Larissa,[125] he was attacked by a band of brigands who stripped him of all he possessed. With great difficulty he dragged himself into the neighbouring town and by chance halted outside a tavern which was kept by one Meroe[126] "admodum scitulam," to whom he related his sad adventures. At first she received him kindly, but after a little while she compelled him to work for her all day as a journeyman tailor, until he was reduced to the utmost destitution.[127] Aristomenes, as was natural, received this confession with considerable indignation, and upbraided his friend for not breaking free from so degrading a bondage. In a moment Socrates turned livid, and cried out, " Hush, hush, fool that you are to abuse a woman skilled in the darkest secrets of goetry. Assuredly so indiscreet a tongue will bring dire vengeance on your head." " In good time, say you so ? " mocking returned the other, " and what kind of woman may this tapstress be, some Caesar's wife or a mighty queen ? " " Saga " inquit, " et diuina, potens caelum deponere, terram suspendere, fontes durare, montes diluere, manes sublimare, deos infimare, sidera extinguere, Tartarum ipsum inluminare." " She is a witch and an enchantress, one whose powerful charms will draw down the very heavens, will silence the earth in the slumbers of death, will harden running waters to cold marble, will dissolve mountains as melting wax, will call forth the shades of the departed from the tomb, yea, will bow the very gods to her will,[128] will extinguish the light of the stars and will relume the murkiest depths of hell." " Oh, come now," cried his friend, "let us drop all this transpontine stuff[129] and talk a little plain common sense." But Socrates proceeds to give a detailed account of this woman's performances, and it is interesting to note that in spite of their extravagances there are certainly points which might be compared with features that occur in the witch trial of the fifteenth and sixteenth centuries. At any rate Aristomenes is so impressed by the narration that he decides the best plan will be for them to make off at earliest dawn, " least by the connivance of her familiar (Numinis ministerii) this witch should find out all that has been said and proceed to avenge herself." Accordingly they bolt and bar the door, and in order to make things more secure, Aristomenes sets his bed against it. Socrates, under the influence of the good wine, to which he has been so long a stranger, is already plunged into a deep sleep on his couch. The hours drawl slowly by, and midnight is barely past when, with a violent noise, the doors hurtle open, striking away with their force the crazy pallet so that it overturns and buries the trembling occupant beneath it. Two hideous women enter the room, the one carries a flaming link, the other a sponge and a naked sword. They take their stand by the side of Socrates, who is still snoring, and the woman who brandishes the sword cries: " Ay, soothly, sister Panthia, this is he, my dear Endymion, my pretty catamite, this is he who is preparing for flight. And I then am to be another Calypso deserted by her Ulysses." And pointing with her hand at the upturned bed, she continued : " And there lies his worthy counsellor, Aristomenes, who put him up to this game and advised him to make good his escape. Well may the wretch tremble with fear, since it shall be my business to see that he repents and full speedily too, of the share he has had in this affair." The second witch proposes that they shall kill him straight away, but Meroe grimly retorts, " Nay, we will let him live if only to cast a handful of earth on the corpse of this vagabond villain." They then seize the unfortunate Socrates by the hair of his head and one of them plunges the sword right up to the hilt through the left side of his throat, whilst the other caught the gushing blood in a small phial with the most extraordinary care so that not a drop fell upon coverlet or pillow. At the same time it seemed as if the poor wretch uttered a deep sigh and poured forth his life with his blood. Panthia instantly pressed the sponge upon the wound muttering : " Oh, sea-born sponge, oh, sea-born sponge, beware lest thou cross running water." His editis (*antequam*) abeunt remoto grabattulo uaricus super faciem meam residentes uesicam exonerant quoad me spurcissimae madore perluerent.

Hardly had they passed over the threshold when the doors closed fast, as it seemed of themselves, whilst bolts and bars returned to their hasps and sockets. Half dead with terror, and trembling in every limb through the fear of being accused of murdering his friend, Aristomenes tied up his bundle as quietly as possible and prepared to slip away unseen. But when he had awakened the porter, this worthy refused to open the doors until daybreak, declaring that the roads were infested with robbers and that travellers must at any rate for their own safety sake tarry till cock-crow. Well-nigh in despair the unfortunate fellow slunk back to his own room and determined to prevent that death to which he was sure he will be condemned by committing suicide. Accordingly he knots an old rope to a beam in the ceiling, and standing upon a stool is about to kick away this support, when the strands of the cord, being thoroughly rotten and untrustworthy, break short, and he is precipitated with some violence on to the couch where his comrade lay. At the noise, the porter, now thoroughly wide awake, dashes in, upon which Socrates leaps up and in a strident voice bawls out that this fellow has crept in to steal something whilst they were asleep. Aristomenes is now half beside himself with joy, but none the less he is anxious to be off as soon as possible. Accordingly, they pay their account and are soon far on the road. Nevertheless, he cannot forbear from stealing a glance now and again at his comrade's neck, but there is no wound, no sign of a cut, no abrasion, nor even a scar, and he realizes that he has suffered from an extraordinarily vivid nightmare, which furnishes an occasion for some highly philosophical remarks upon the necessity for temperance, not only in the matter of wine and strong drink, but also as regards late suppers and rich food, the indigestion resulting from which inevitably breeds those dingy fantasies and maggots of the brain. Socrates laughs merrily at his friend's matutinal homily, and presently confesses that his brisk walk and the shrewd nipping air of dawn have made him not a little hungry. They sit down beneath the shadow of a holt of plane trees, for the sun has already arisen in his strength ; at their feet there runs a little purling brook, clearer than lucent silver or transparent crystal. Humble is their fare, but hearty the appetite. With new bread and an excellent cheese they spread their table, a grassy lawn ; for napery nature provides foliage from the boughs. Having done ample justice to his breakfast, Socrates begins to feel thirsty. He rises, and going to the water-side, bends over to drink. No sooner do his lips touch the stream than a gaping wound bursts open in his throat, the sponge drops out, a small stream of blood trickles down and without a cry he falls a wasted and pinched, a gaunt, emaciated corpse, an atomy of skin and bone upon the river's bank, half

in and half out of the water.   With difficulty his comrade drags
the poor skeleton to land, and trembling lest he shall be observed by some chance wayfarer, scoops out a shallow grave
in the sandy soil, where he lightly covers his unfortunate
friend.   As if he himself had been a murderer, he flies the
accursed place and embracing a voluntary exile, as it were, he
takes up his residence in a town of distant Aetiola, if haply in a
new country he may forget the memory of these horrid events.

It has seemed worth while to give this story in some detail,
for it contains very remarkable features of vampirism.   The
two witches are obviously vampires in the wider acceptance of
the word.   It will be noticed that, although of course they have
not died, they do possess many qualities of the Slav vampire.
They appear shortly after midnight, and in spite of opposing
gates and doors, they are able to effect a supernatural
entry into the chamber of their victim, who remains asleep and
apparently unconscious of their attack, although the next
morning he complains of a certain faintness and languor, and
his comrade notes that whilst he is eating his breakfast he is
pale as boxwood and of a ghastly hue.[130]   Moreover the
vampires draw the blood from the left side of the throat, and
it seems certain that their great care to catch it in the phial or
flask so that not even a drop is spilled is due to the fact
that they wish to preserve this most precious liquor of life
to renew their own vitality.   When they have departed all is
as it was before their forcible irruption, and the man who has
witnessed the proceedings seems to have been thrown into a
kind of trance or torpor so that the next morning he is almost
able to persuade himself that he has been the victim of a
particularly gruesome nightmare, circumstances all of which
are entirely in keeping with the Slav tradition.   The fact that,
so far as we are told, the vampires only make one visit and
drain their victim's blood in one draught so to speak, is a very
minor detail and is quite possibly to be ascribed to literary
convenience rather than to any traditional belief or superstition.

In the course of the romance by Apuleius Lucius arrives at
Hypata, where he lodges with a certain Milo, a skinflint
extortioner, whose wife, Pamphile, is ill-reputed as a most
notorious, but most powerful, sorceress.   As he wanders
through the streets to satisfy his eyes with the reliques of this

town he is met by a lady of high rank and great wealth, an ancient friend of his mother, Byrrhaena, who greets him with the utmost affection, but when she learns where he is lodged, betrays no ordinary anxiety. He is invited to an entertainment at her house, and during the banquet the conversation as is natural, turns upon the beauty and resources of Thessaly, which is praised with considerable eloquence and feeling. Lucius is asked how he is enjoying his visit to Hypata. "If I mistake not," says the lady, "our temples, public baths, and other magnificent buildings are infinitely superior to those which may be seen in any other city of Greece. Here, of all spots on earth, may a man enjoy himself whatsoever his tastes. If you are for business and the crowded mart, in our streets and squares is all the bustle of Rome itself. If you are of a retiring habit and seek peace and leisure, you may find these in the tranquility of our country houses and our villas that stand secluded among their goodly gardens." "All this," frankly acknowledges Lucius "is quite true. But," he goes on to say, "in spite of all the attractions of this delightful town, and the liberty which one enjoys, I am monstrously frightened at the dark mysteries and terrible fascinations of black magic. For it is commonly reported that here in Thessaly not even the graves of the dead are safe, but that invisible hands snatch certain members and remnants of corpses from the tombs, nay, even from the very funeral pyres, and that by their enchantments they afflict the living with dire and deadly misfortune. It is indeed generally said that these witches in their haste and perfervid greed, are sometimes seen to be lurking round the graves even before the mourning cortège arrives at the sepulchre." "All this is true enough," observed one of the guests, "and I can tell you something more, they do not even spare the living. Somebody whom I know—I mention no names—suffered terribly from an attack by these witches, and his face was mutilated in a most unseemly manner." At these words no little laughter arose from the guests, whereupon one of the company rose in high dudgeon and began to make towards the door. The hostess, however, called him back with a gentle speech and begged him to relate the story of his adventure. "Nay, my good Thelyphron," she cried, "I beg you to stay and with your usual good humour relate the accident which happened to you and which has grieved us all so much." After a grumble or two at the incivility of certain of the party, the young man was persuaded to return and relate his mishap to the company. Thelyphron was a young student who, whilst travelling with little thought for the cost of his excursions throughout Thessaly, found himself at Larissa without a penny in his purse, and was sore put to it how to replenish the exchequer. Whilst he was wandering through the market-place he was amazed to hear an old man proclaim in a loud voice : " If anyone will undertake to watch by the side of a dead body he shall be richly rewarded." " What on earth does this mean ? " he asked a bystander. " Are the dead in the habit of running away in this country ? " " You had best hold your tongue," was the somewhat curt reply. " You're a mere slip of a lad, and a green one,'too ; a stranger, I take it, not to know that all over Thessaly witches seek dead bodies in order to use them as ingredients in the confection of the charms." " Yes, but pray tell me in what does this watching of the dead consist ? " He was forthwith informed that anyone who undertook this sad office must remain throughout the livelong night with his eyes fixed steadfastly upon the corpse. He must not suffer his lids to close for a moment of time, since in that very instant whilst he dozed the witches assuming the shape of some animal, would creep in and take him by surprise. They were able to enter the room under the form of small birds, mice, even of flies and vermin, in order that they might, by their spells drown their guardian in sleep and effect their horrid purpose. Such a vigil was dangerous enough in all conscience, and yet for this service no higher reward must be expected than four, or at the most, six pieces of gold.[131] The sting lay in the tail, since by law any person who undertook to watch must, on the following morning, give up possession of the dead body whole and entire, and if any member were missing he was compelled to make good the missing member by an operation on his own person. None the less, the young student was so pressed by his needs that he volunteered for the service and was immediately conducted to a fine mansion where in a darkened bed-chamber was laid out the corpse of the deceased, which he was bidden protect from the abominable Harpies, (a malis Harpyis). Thelyphron believed that the whole thing was some nightmare nonsense, but there entered seven witnesses in whose presence a deposition was made that the body was whole and entire. The watcher was left alone with a large lamp and sufficient oil to keep it burning until dawn, but the wine and food for which he asked were abruptly refused. Night fell, and as the silent hours passed by the shadows grew darker and darker, until the young student who had been bold enough when there were others there, began to feel the horror of the cold crawling minutes. Suddenly he perceived a movement at his feet and saw a little weasel, which had crept into the room, regarding him steadfastly with red baleful eyes. The sight of the creature roused him for a moment, and with a cry he was about to strike it down when, in a flash it whisked round and was out of the door. Almost at the same moment a deep sleep fell upon him, nor did he recover his senses until beneath the window the cocks were crowing lustily to salute the rosy dawn. In a panic he rushed to scrutinize the body, but there appeared no sign of any mark or mutilation. Presently the family entered, the body was carefully examined, and the young man promptly congratulated upon his diligence. He was paid the promised fee, but unluckily, over-excited by his good fortune, he cried to the lady : " You'll find me ready and willing to undertake the same job as soon as you have need of my services," words of the worst possible omen, as prognosticating that another death would shortly take place in the same house, a speech in return to which he was incontinently thrust out of the doors with a hearty curse and a kick.

As he hung about the streets, bitterly regretting his untoward speech, he beheld the funeral appear with all the pomp and trappings of ceremonial woe. The exsequies, however, were interrupted in the most unfortunate manner, as an old man, rushing up, declared that his nephew who lay upon the bier had been poisoned, and that the widow who now feigned to be distraught with grief was the culprit. The crowd at once took sides, and something very like a riot seemed imminent. It was decided to refer the matter to the intervention of an Egyptian necromancer, who agreed to recall by his occult arts the soul to reanimate the lifeless dust so that the dead man himself might testify to his own end. After certain mysterious incantations, to the horror of the bystanders, the corpse stirred, and a hollow voice seemed to issue from its mouth. At the command of the magician the dead man declared he had indeed been cut off through the evil craft of his spouse. A terrible clamour instantly arose, but it was soon evident that a great many considered the whole thing to be witchcraft and that the woman was falsely accused owing to the abominable spells of the wizard who had been bribed for this purpose. However, when silence had been obtained, the dead man said : "I will give you incontrovertible proof that what I declare is true by disclosing a fact known to none other but myself." He then pointed with his cold hand at the trembling Thelyphron and continued : "Last night when that man was diligently keeping watch over my poor mortal frame, the ghouls and witches who were hovering near in order to get possession thereof, finding that they could not cheat his wakefulness, at length by their charms flung him into a deep sleep, and no sooner had his eyelids closed than with runes of potent power they called upon my name, so that my stiffening limbs struggled to obey the command of their incantations.

It so happened that this man bears the same name as myself, and in his trance, hearing himself summoned, he arose and all unconscious walked towards the door. The windows were barred and the door fast locked, but none the less the vampires entered through a crevice and a chink and cut off first his nose and then his two ears. In order that they might for a while conceal their horrid deeds they had fashioned like members in wax, and these models they clapped on the wounds. There he stands, the unfortunate wretch, who has earned, and amply earned his reward, truly not on account of his vigilance but because he has suffered so sore mutilation."

Upon hearing these terrible words Thelyphron instantly put his hand to his nose and to his ears only to find that the story was but too true. Frantic with shame and horror, he fled through the crowds, quickly effecting his escape. His wounds he covered as best he could, to present a decent appearance, but never again did he dare to venture back to his native town, Miletus, and was perforce compelled to earn his livelihood in the city where his misfortunes were known and therefore excited pity and compassion rather than surprise or disgust.

It can, I think, hardly be denied that here we have a legend that is clearly vampirism, and there are several points which in connexion with later superstitions and beliefs deserve some particular attention. In the first place, it is said that the vampire witches who wish to mutilate the dead body, are accustomed to assume the shapes of small animals, and thus to enter the room unsuspected and unseen. De Lancre truly remarks : "Les Démons ont mille moyens pour seduire les seduire hommes and les induire à tétation. Là ou la finesse du serpent ne peut attaindre, il y porte la force du lion, and les souplesses du singe."[132] The entry into the room of mice, flies,[133] or even vermin, which may prove to be a demon or some servant of the demon thus seemingly metamorphosed, may be paralleled with the accounts of the familiars in the English trials for witchcraft. In the seventeenth century there was no more common practice in examinations of this sort than the "Watching of a witch." This was particularly the case in East Anglia during the activities of Matthew Hopkins from 1645 to 1647, a procedure amply described by the Rev. John Gaule in his *Select Cases of Conscience Touching Witches and Witchcraft*, London, 1646. It must be remembered that although Gaule thoroughly disapproved of Hopkins and all his proceedings, nevertheless he was a firm believer in witchcraft and all its operations. He writes : Having taken the suspected Witch, she is placed in the middle of a room upon a stool, or Table, crosse-legg'd, or in some other uneasie posture, which if she submits not, she is then bound with cords ; there is she watched and kept without meat or sleep for the space of twenty-four hours (for they say that within that time they shall see her Imp come). A little hole is likewise made in the door for the Imp to come in at ; and least it might come in some lesse discernable shape, they that watch are taught to be ever and anon sweeping the room, and if they see any spiders or flyes to kill them. And if they cannot kill them, then they may be sure that they are her Impes."

The possibility that a witch or vampire, by a process of dematerialization may enter a room through the merest chink, is commonly believed, and it is undoubtedly connected with that fugitive structure suddenly generated which is known as ectoplasm and which, it is often claimed, possesses the property of the interpenetration of matter. It is recorded that on the occasion of a spiritist séance, 25th November, 1909, with a medium, Eva C., a luminous smoke appeared, which changed into a long white band and shortly condensed into a solid form, although it had streamed through the cabinet in strip like a white creamy substance, sometimes breaking into zig-zags or serpentine waves.[134] A vast number of instances of this dematerialization and subsequent solidification might be cited, but it is sufficient to refer to Schrenck-Notzing's great work *Phenomena of Materialization*.[135] S. Thomas says that although the fallen angels or demons lost in their fall all supernatural gifts, they retained the powers which are integral to their natural existence, and of these not the least is the power to operate upon matter, to transfer it from place to place, to assume a human appearance and to act upon man.[136] Accordingly they are fully able to assist these processes of dematerialization, which brings about that subtlety able to penetrate material objects, and to re-form itself in a tangible and solid body. It is to this power that we must refer the introduction into the experimental room of objects which at the commencement of the proceedings were not originally found there. These are technically knows as "apports." In *Light*, 26th November, 1910, an account is given of these phenomen which occurred at séances with Charles Bailey in Australia. "These apports included an Indian blanket containing a human scalp and tomahawk ; a block of lead said to be found in Roman strata at Rome, and bearing the name of Augustus ; a quantity of gravel alleged to come from Central America, and quite unlike anything seen in Australia ; two perfect clay tablets covered with cuneiform inscriptions and several thousands of years old, and said to have been brought direct from the moulds at Babylon ; and, finally, a bird's nest containing several eggs and the mother bird undoubtedly alive." At the meetings of Messrs. Herne and Williams, fragrant flowers and nosegays were frequently conveyed through the closed doors.

A weasel was a common form assumed by a witch or her familiar. In 1588 an Essex witch confessed all : "Which was this in effect : that she had three spirits : one like a cat, which she called Lightfoot, another like a toad, which she called Lunch, the third like a Weasill, which she called Makeshift . . . the cat would kill kine, the weasill would kill horses, the Toad would plague men in their bodies. There was one olde Mother W. of great T. which had a spirite like a Weasill : she was offended highlie with one H.M. home she went, and called forth her spirite, which lay in a pot of woll under her bed, she willed him to goe plague the man ; he required what she would give him. She said she would give him a cocke, which she did."[137] Of another witch in 1593, it is recorded, " she had three or foure impes, some called them puckrels, one like a grey cat, another like a weasel, another like a mouse." George Giffard, in his *Dialogue concerning Witches* records : " The witches have their spirits, some hath one, some hath more, as two three, foure, or five, some in one likenesse, and some in another, as like cats, weasels, toades, or mise, whom they nourish with milke or with a chicken, or by letting them suck now and then a drop of bloud."

Among the peasantery in certain districts the weasel was regarded with a considerable awe. Thus although the Huzuls of the Carpathians believed that the bite of this animal is poisonous and that it was able to commit serious ravages among the cattle, yet they took the utmost care never to kill a weasel lest the whole tribe should avenge the death of their fellow upon the herds of the murderer. They even celebrated a festival in honour of the weasels, either on S. Matthew's Day, 21st September, or on S. Catherine's Day, 25th November, and whichever festival was appointed throughout the hundred, it must be kept as a holiday, and no work done lest it should offend the weasels and they would then do harm to the flocks and cattle.[138]

Even among the early Christians there seems to have existed an idea that the spirits of the dead had a certain corporeity, and this gave rise to many superstitions and curious practices which were, of course, never officially allowed, but rather checked and repudiated. Possibly it was merely owing to his ignorance of philosophical terminology that Tertullian conceived that all things, pure spirits and even God himself, must be bodies. He certainly goes so far as to say that the human soul was once seen in a vision, as tender, light, and of the colour of air, but none the less having its own particular substantiality. It may be noted that his formal secession from the Church of Carthage took place in 211 (Harnack)[139] and de Labriolle dates the *De Anima* 208-211, so there can be no doubt that it was composed under Montanist influence, although since the new prophecies had not as yet been dogmatically condemned, the author made no open breach with the Church. If, as this long psychological treatise teaches, even God is *corpus*, how much more so are those souls created *ex traduce*.[140] It has, indeed, been remarked, and the observation is in no wise exaggerated, that the doctrine of Tertullian is merely the refined Materialism of the Stoics, supported by paralogistic interpretations of Scripture, whereby owing to the unavoidable objectivity of language, Holy Writ is made to establish a metaphysical but very definite Materialism. In this connexion we must not lose sight of the fact that the influence of the stern African ascetic was immense and endured long flowing through many channels, "*Da magistrum*" S. Cyprian was wont to say when he called for some volume of this great writer to read his daily meditation.[141] S. Irenaeus of Lyons teaches that after death the soul preserves the figure which the body has had in life, and that often it may remain in some sort attached to the body, and that it will preserve a clear memory of all that it has done or left undone during its life on earth. It may be noticed that all this is amply borne out by those who have investigated haunted houses and the phenomena of ghosts and apparitions. It is certain that, under what laws we know not, a spectre is sometimes tangible, an Michael Glycas[142] relates in his *Annals* ($\beta\iota\beta\lambda o\varsigma$ $\chi\rho o\nu\iota\kappa\acute{\eta}$), Part IV, that the Emperor Basil having lost a son whom he dearly loved, applied to a Basilian monk of Santabaren, and this occultist caused the dead boy to appear. The Emperor not only saw, but even spoke to his child, whom he clasped fondly and long in his embrace. This, then, was no ordinary phantom or shadow that this mighty master of necromantic lore had evoked at the bidding of his lord.

In the same way as upon occasion ghosts might be touched and were no mere wraith or hallucination, so on the other hand they were able to leave sensible evidence of their appearance. There are many instances of this but it will serve to quote an occurrence which was reported in the *San Francisco Examiner*, 29th November, 1891. About three weeks before a farmer named Walsingham, and his family had moved to a house on Oakville on the Savanna River. From the very first they were annoyed by the ringing of the door bell at night, the banging of doors and the overturning of furniture. At first they put this down to mischievous neighbours, who perhaps, for some reason or other did not wish the premises to be occupied.

However, the disturbances increased and before a week had passed the house nightly rang with shouts and yells, which would be succeeded by the most hideous laughter and a wailing cry of peculiar horror, long drawn out, which seemed to proceed sometimes from an upper room and sometimes from the garden. One evening, when the daughter of the house, a young lady, was engaged before the looking-glass in changing her toilet, she felt a hand laid gently on her shoulder. Thinking it was her mother, or sister, she glanced in the mirror before her, but was amazed to see no form reflected save her own. Casting her eyes down, she perceived a man's broad hand grasping her arm. Immediately the family rushed in at her screams, but when they reached her the mysterious hand was gone, although her flesh was bruised by the finger marks where it had roughly grasped her. On the next evening, whilst they were seated at the supper table with several guests, a loud groan was heard overhead, and a few minutes later one of the visitors pointed to a stain which was slowly spreading upon the tablecloth, and it was seen that some liquid was pattering onto the table from the ceiling overhead. This seemed so much like the dripping of newly-shed blood that all present rose in horror, whilst Mr. Walsingham and several of his guests ran hastily upstairs and into a room which was directly over the dining parlour. A carpet covered the floor, but nothing appeared to indicate the source of the ghastly dew. The carpet was immediately turned back, only to reveal that the planks were perfectly dry, and even covered with a light dust, yet all the while the floor was being examined those below declared that the red rain never ceased to fall. A hideous stain, the size of a dinner plate, was formed before it finally ceased. Upon the next day this was examined by several skilled chemists under the microscope and they pronounced it undoubtedly to be human blood. The Walsinghams left the house that very afternoon, and although hundreds of persons visited it, only one ventured to remain there after dusk. This was a young man who having foolishly betted that he would spend a night upon the premises, proceeded to carry out his wager. Shortly after dark, he endeavoured to kindle a fire in one of the rooms and also lit a powerful lamp. To his amaze the lamp was instantly blown out, and although he saw nothing, he heard somebody angrily rake out the coals from

the grate and extinguish the smouldering wood. Shortly
afterwards the noises began and lasted for about an hour.
There were other terrible phenomena, and at length, panic-
stricken, he roused himself sufficiently to attempt to fly from
the haunted house. Groping his way in the darkness, he had
nearly succeeded in reaching the door when he found himself
seized by the ankle and violently thrown to the ground.
He was immediately grasped by icy hands which sought to
grip him securely about the throat. He struggled as best he
could against his unseen foe but was speedily overpowered and
choked into unconsciousness. When he was found in the
morning by his friends his throat was black with the marks of
long thin fingers, and covered with scratches made by cruel,
crooked nails. Having been with great difficulty brought out
of his swoon, he lay for many weeks prostrate, confined to his
bed, suffering from shock and nervous prostration. The
doctors expressed themselves unable to account for the extraordinary anæmic condition of his body, although he was a young
man of a particularly full-blooded habit. It is said that no
explanation of these horrors was forthcoming, but it seems
very clear that the house was visited by a vampire, although
since no inquiries were made, the explanation of the phenomena
cannot be precisely ascertained. I believe that shortly after
wards the house was burned to the ground as being the only
way to rid the place of such dangerous manifestations. Here
then, we have a very striking example of a phantom of the
vampire family, which was material enough to extinguish a
lamp, scatter a fire, throw an athletic young man to the ground,
and well-night throttle him to death.

Owing to the prevailing belief that the spirits of the departed
still retain a certain material form and even hunger and
thirst, there grew up in certain dioceses a custom of carrying
food to the tombs and eating it there, since the departed were
supposed, in some way, to be strengthened and comforted by
the collation. This custom was particularly observed at the
shrines of the martyrs and it seems to have been mixed up
with some vague superstition of Pagan sacrifice and oblations
of food and drink to appease the Manes. S. Ambrose particularly prohibited anything of the kind as savouring of
Heathenism, and in the *Confessions*[143] S. Augustine tells us how
S. Monica came to abandon this old custom. " When as my

mother therefore had one time brought unto the oratories erected in memory of the saints, as she was wont to do in Africa, certain cheesecakes, and bread and wine ; and had been forbidden to do it by the sexton : as soon as ever she knew that the Bishop had forbidden this, she did so piously and obediently embrace the notion, that I myself wondered at it, that she should so easily be brought rather to blame her own country custom, than to call the present countermand in question. For no wine bibbing besotted her spirit, nor did the love of wine provoke her to the hatred of the truth, as it doth to many, both men and women, who being a little whittled once, turn the stomach at a song of sobriety, as they would do at a draught of water. But she, when she had brought her basket of these usual junkets, which she meant to eat a little of first, and to give the rest away ; never used to allow herself above one small pot of wine, well allayed with water, for her own sober palate, whence she might sip a mannerly draught. And if there were many oratories of the departed saints, that ought to be honoured in like manner, she still carried the selfsame pot about with her, to be used everywhere, which should only be low allayed with water, but very lukewarm with carrying about and this would she distribute to those that were about her by small sups ; for she came to those places to seek devotion, and not pleasure.

So soon, therefore, as she found this custom to be countermanded by that most famous preacher, and the most pious prelate, Ambrose, yea, forbidden even to those that would use it soberly, that so no occasion of riot might thereby be given to such as loved drinking too well ; and for that these funeral anniversary feasts, as it were, in honour of our dead fathers, did too nearly resemble the superstition of the Gentiles, she most willingly forbare it ever after : and instead of a basket filled with the fruits of the earth, she had now learned to present a breast replenished with purer petitions, at the oratories of the Martyrs ; that she might give away what she could spare among the poor, and that the Communion of the Lord's Body might in that place be rightly celebrated, where, after the example of his Passion, these Martyrs had been sacrificed and crowned."

There is a further allusion to this in the *De Ciuitate Dei*, VIII, xxvii, where the doctor says when speaking of "the honour that Christians give to the Martyrs " ; " wherefore all the religious performances done there, at the Martyrs' solemnities, are ornament of their memories, but no sacrifices to the dead, as unto God, and those that bring banquets thither, which notwithstanding the better Christians do not, nor is this custom observed in most places, yet, such as do so, setting them down, praying over them, and so taking them away to eat, or bestow on those that need : all this they do only with a desire that these meats might be sanctified, by the merits of the Martyrs, in the Name of the God of Martyrs."[144]

Although, of course, the original significance of this custom had been wholly lost and forgotten, in earliest times the carrying of food to the tomb implied a certain feeding of the dead man so that his hunger being appeased, he might not issue forth in vampiric form and prey upon the living.

In Greece to-day a funeral usually concludes with the distribution of meats and wine, and a portion of each must be given to the dead. These feasts at the graveside are called μ ακαρία, and the custom can be traced from the remotest antiquity. Sonnini de Magnoncourt, a French traveller of the seventeenth century in his *Voyages en Grèce et en Turquie*, (II, p. 153), speaks of these banquets taken to the tomb, a spread " wherein they seek to make the dead man participate as well." This custom is not unknown in England as is shown by the following report in the *Daily Express*, Wednesday, 21st March, 1928. Under the heading : " Banquets for the Dead. Ancient Rite leads to a Lawsuit," we have : " The objection of a local council to the placing of food on a grave, a practice which is alleged to be causing scandal, has led to a curious action which is entered on the cause list for to-day. The action comes before Mr. Justice Eve in the Chancery Division.

" The plaintiff in this action is Miss Hoskyns-Abrahall, who is seeking an order from the court to prevent the Paignton Urban District Council from obstructing her in this practice.

" Officials of the Council were in London yesterday waiting for the case to come on. One of them stated in an interview that the grave in question in Paignton Cemetery was that of Mr. Hoskyns-Abrahall, a former Church of England clergyman, who died about ten years ago, and his wife. [Hours in the Vault.] Miss Hoskyns-Abrahall, a relative of the clergyman, had been in the habit of visiting the grave and descending into the vault. There she spent many hours. At every visit she brought provisions—chickens, pigeon-pies, fruit, bread, wine, and various dainties—which she left behind on the grave.

"These had a habit of disappearing, and the position was such that the council had to take action to prevent provisions being left on the grave.

"It is understood that Miss Hoskyns-Abrahall maintains that she is carrying out an ancient rite of the Greek Church.

"An official of the Greek Legation explained yesterday that the custom of placing bread on a grave, a survival from ancient Greek pagan worship, still persists in Greek villages.

"The bread is placed in water on a large plate and left with the body. 'The idea,' he said, 'is that it is thought the soul needs some nourishment, and that it can only find it it the place which the body once inhabited.'"

Some six weeks later the result of the case was known. I quote from the *Daily Sketch*, Friday, 4th May, 1928 :

"Strange rites in a Vault.

"'Distinctly pagan nature,' says Mr. Justice Eve.

"Strange rites in a vault at Paignton cemetery were referred to by Mr. Justice Eve yesterday in the Chancery Division when he gave judgement against Miss Gertrude R. W. Hoskyns-Abrahall, of Torre, who prefers to be called Miss Hoskyns, in her action against Paignton Council.

"Miss Hoskyns, who is a M.A. of Dublin, had the vault built at a cost of £200, and she claimed the right to enter the vault for the purpose of ventilation and in order to perform rites which she said were observed in early Christian times.

"Mr. Justice Eve said that the council had no power to grant Miss Hoskyns a freehold estate in any part of the cemetery. All they could sell was the exclusive right to burial therein, and, as incident thereto, the right to dig a grave and construct a vault for the reception of the body. [Aromatic Gums.] As to the claim to perform alleged Christian rites, it appeared that for the first four years after the construction of the vault she paid an annual visit to the cemetery and entered the vault, carrying with her, as she said, the usual vault furniture, namely, a small chair, a table, a screen, vessels for flowers, and several aromatic gums and deodorisers.

" Throughout 1925-1926 she attempted, by various means, to gain access to the interior of the vault, and on one occasion she succeeded in evading the caretaker and entering the vault.

" She proceeded to light a methylated spirit lamp and several candles, to burn incense, and to cook some meat. [Vault in disorder.] The interior of the vault was in great disorder, broken bottles and paper being strewn about, and for her own safety a police-sergeant superintended her removal from the vault.

" In her statement of claim Miss Hoskyns had stated that she and her mother were members of the Orthodox Greek Church, and that the rites were those of that Church ; but in the witness-box she said that was due to some mistake, and admitted that she and her mother belonged to the Established Church.

" The judge said that he was unable to accept the view that the rites were of Christian origin or character. They appeared to be of a distinctly pagan nature, and certainly not consonant with burial according to the ritual of the Established Church.

" Miss Hoskyns had no right in the vault entitling her to use it for the purposes for which she claimed, and the council was justified in refusing her access and in removing her from the vault. The action failed and would be dismissed with costs."[145]

It was, no doubt, unconscious humour that decided the rights were not " according to the ritual of the Established Church," but it seems a little hard to prohibit these ancient ceremonies.

Pierre Le Loyer in his *Quatre Discovrs, et histoires des spectres*,[146] tells a story of a Pagan vampire, or rather vampire ghost who was able to do harm, although his body had been reduced to ashes, and the explanation may be that some demon was permitted to bring about these misfortunes as a punishment for the heresies of Theodore of Gaza to whose servant they happen. Theodore of Gaza, the celebrated Greek Humanist and translator of Aristotle, was born at Thessalonica early in the fifteenth century, and died in southern Italy in 1478. As early as 1429 he migrated to Italy, where he taught Greek with great applause at the universities of Sienna, Ferrara, and Rome. Having learned Latin from Vittorino da Feltre,[147] he devoted himself to making his version of Aristotle's works in that language and this won him a most favourable reception at the court of Nicholas V (Tommaso Parentucelli), a Pontiff whose name, it has been well said, is never to be mentioned without reverence by every lover of letters. Through the patronage of the famous Cardinal Bessarion, Theodore obtained a small benefice in the Abruzzi, and it was here in those remote districts where Paganism lingered long and where witchcraft held horrid sway that the following events occurred. Attached to the village church as part of the glebe was a small cottage surrounded by vineyards and fertile fields. As parrocco Theodore established here a labourer and his family to work the land. One day, whilst ploughing, the peasant uncovered an urn of dateless antiquity which, upon investigation, proved to contain ashes, doubtless those of incineration. That night, as he slept, there appeared in his dreams a man of harsh and forbidding aspect, who threatened him with the most terrible misfortunes unless he at once carefully reburied the urn in the very spot where he had found it. The man took no notice of the vision, and even mocked at the menaces of the ghost. A few days later, however, his son, a robust young yokel of rudest health, began to complain of lassitude and lethargy, which was put down to laziness or the sullens. A morning or two after the unfortunate boy was discovered dead, lying thin and waxy pale as though every drop of blood had been drained out of his body. The same night the father was again visited by the spectre, who this time appeared, no longer gaunt and thin but portly and in good case, and with words even more imperative and threatening, commanded that the urn should be instantly reburied, adding that if this were not done the second child would speedily dwindle and fall into his grave. In terror, the farmer sought his master at earliest dawn and Theodore hastening to the spot, buried the ill-omened vessel exactly where it had first been found, with, Heathen ceremony and Pagan ritual which were, no doubt, very agreeable to the shade. We note that in this instance there has been what one may call a classical survival of the belief in vampires, or at any rate in spirits which, if they do not, according to the strict Slav tradition, animate a dead body, at least act in a baleful and vampirish manner.

We have in this story the ancient Greek idea of a curse pursuing those who have either not suffered a body to be buried or who have disturbed a tomb, and the reason why the ghost should not actually assume its own dead body, of course lies in the fact that this vehicle has been reduced to ashes, although even as a phantasm it was able to wreak its vengeance upon the living, were it not, as is most probable, and as I have suggested, that Divine Providence allowed a demon full sway in a spot which was fearfully haunted. It will readily be remembered that Satan was permitted to exercise his power to afflict holy Job, and all that the patriarch had was suffered to be in the Devil's hands, so that not only were Job's vast possessions wasted and plundered, reducing him to abject beggary, but his ten children were slain,[143] in the same way as the spectre of the Abruzzi was permitted for some inscrutable purpose to kill the eldest son of the peasant and would also have proceeded to destroy his second child.

That a belief in vampires persisted and was commonly credited throughout the various nations of Europe is very plain. As of more recent date in modern Greece, in Czecho-Slovakia and Jugo-Slavia, the people have taken the matter into their own hands and destroyed the person supposed to be a vampire, so in earlier centuries popular opinion was wont to act without waiting for authority. The Saxons, for example, bore the worst reputation as "devil-worshippers," and when Charlemagne subdued their country, by his "Saxon Capitulary" of 781, he not only obliged every individual to receive Baptism but in view of the excesses to which popular rage might stir up the people against those who persisted in their magical and heathen practices he also inserted in his code the following very significant clause : " Si quis a Diabolo deceptus crediderit secundum morem Paganorum, uirum aliquem aut feminam strigem esse et homines comedere, et propter hoc ipsum incenderit, uel carnem eius ad comedendum dederit, uel ipsam comederit, capitis sententia puniatur."[149]

At the risk of repetition and insistence I would emphasize that the vampiric idea was present among well-nigh all ancient peoples, the one great difference, important enough but not wholly essential, being that whereas the true vampire is a dead body, the vampires of the older superstitions were generally ghosts of spectres, but ghosts that were sometimes tangible and spectres who could do very material harm to living people by exhausting their vitality and draining their blood. The reason why later superstitions demanded as the most prominent element in vampirism the incorruptibility of the dead person and why the Slavonic tradition makes this an essential has already been touched upon in a former volume and is treated at greater length in a following chapter which specifically deals with the modern Greek *vrykolakas*. In the face of the large amount of tradition connected with Greek funereal rites, and the prominence which is given throughout classical literature to their fearful reverence for the departed, it seems impossible to deny that many dark superstitions cognate to the belief in vampires widely prevailed. In Rome, as we have seen, although the tradition may be more mixed, we have a very early, and it might not be exaggeration to say (in primitive times at all events) a very savage cult of the Manes, while the festival of the Lemuria required a ceremonial not very far removed from the rites of black magic. Among Neo-Platonist philosophers and new Christians alike we find curious superstitions connected with the dead, and the belief held by Tertullian and others as to the corporeity of the soul touches nearly the full Slavonic belief in the vampire whose dead body does not return, earth to earth, but remains unnaturally incorrupt. The theosophist and the ecclesiastic no doubt to a very large extent purged their doctrines of offence—the teaching of Tertullian upon the resurrection of the body is excellent—but their psychology could not have been understood by the common folk to whom filtered fragments and aliquot cantles of their indoctrination, and who accepted their ideas in a very gross and materialistic form, so that no mean authorities might serve to bolster up dark superstitions and sanction necromantic practices which were, in truth, forbidden, utterly condemned and accursed.

As Simaetha, Canidia and Erictho had their lineal descendants in Demdike, Jeanne Harvilliers and Renata Saenger, although with great and obvious differentiations, so with certain noteworthy distinctions and varieties the Vampires of the Middle Ages and of to-day, even the Slav vampires, have their ancestry and originals in ancient Greece and classic Rome. It is necessary to emphasize how entirely mistaken was Dom Augustin Calmet when he wrote[150] with reference to the *vrykolakas*. " L'Antiquité n'a certainement rien vû ni connu de pareil. Qu'on parcoure les Histoires des Hébreux, des Egyptiens, des Grecs, des Latins ; on n'y rencontrera rien qui en approche."

NOTES. CHAPTER I.

[1] The name Hecate would seem to be Greek, although some scholars (e.g. Preller and Welcker) incline to believe in a foreign derivation. The earliest references to this mysterious goddess are a quotation in Pausanias from the κατάλογος γουαικῶν attributed to Hesiod, when she is mentioned in connexion with Artemis and Iphigenia; and what is probably the first reference in known Greek literature the noble passage in *The Theogony*. One must remark, however, that Heyne and other commentators consider the " Hymn to Hecate " an interpolation, perhaps the work of Onomacritus. She is twice called μουνογενής, a word from the Orphic poems and mysteries. Goettling distinguishes the hands of two different poets in this passage. Van Lennep argues for the antiquity of these verses, Ἑκάτη may mean " she who stands aloof," " the one who holds herself afar off," but it is very doubtful whether it be connected with ἕκατος, " far-shooting."

[2] Aristotle gives this title also to Heraclitus.

[3] One may compare Sheridon Le Fanu's tale *The Watcher*, which first appeared in a very rare volume, illustrated by Phiz, *Ghost Stories and Tales of Mystery*, Dublin, 1851. It was reprinted as *The Familiar* in a collection *In a Glass Darkly*, 3 vols., Bentley; 1872; also in one volume. There was a modern re-issue of this book, two parts, by Newnes. The latest reprint is Eveleigh Nash and Grayson, London, 1923.

[4] As in Theocritus, xv, 40, where Praxinoa says :

οὐκ ἀξῶ τυ τέκνον· μορμὼ δάκνει ἵππος.

The Scholiast upon Aristides Theodorus (Rhetor), wrote :

ἡ δε Μορμὼ Κορινθία ἦν, ἡ καταφαγοῦσα αὑτῆς τὰ παιδία ἐν ἑσπέρᾳ ἀνέπτη κατά τινα πρόνοιαν· καὶ τοίνυν ὅτε βούλονται τὰ σφῶν παιδία αἱ γυναῖκες φοβῆσαι, ἐπιβοῶσι μορμώ. φησὶ δὲ καὶ Θεόκριτος ' μορμὼ δάκνει.'

[5] The famous sophist was born at Lemnos *circa* 172 A.D. *The Life of Apollonius* was commenced at the suggestion of the Empress Julia Domna, wife of Septimius Severus. The book was given to the world in 217. Philostratus was alive during the reign of Philippus, 244-249.

[6] Written July-September, 1819; published with *Isabella, The Eve of St. Agnes*, and other poems during the first week of July, 1820.

[7] It is true the idea of swooning lovers was a commonplace with the poet, so that he wrote to his own inamorata " all-I can bring you is a swooning admiration of your beauty." Endymion after the vision of Diana is described as having " Swoon'd drunken from pleasure's nipple," (II. ll. 868-9); and he swoons at the thought of Diana's voice when he is in the palace of Neptune (III, 1005-1018). Leigh Hunt in his comments on *The Eve of St. Agnes* points to the fainting of Porphyro at sight of Madeline as the one flaw in the poem, and apologises for it on the plea of the poet's enfeebled health at the time.

[8] Proclaimed emperor by the troops, A.D. 284; abdicated 1 May, 305; died at Salona, 313.

[9] During his life-time Apollonius had been accused of black magic and necromancy by the sophist Euphrates, and a few years after his death by Moeragenes. The orations of Euphrates are lost, and little is known of the work of Moeragenes which was in four books. This was probably the source whence the Byzantine writers, especially John Tzetzes, derived their legends concerning Apollonius. Eusebius points out that Origen *Contra Celsum* has already answered most of the *Philalethes*.

[10] *Diuinarum Institutionum*, V, *De Iustitia :* " Uoluit ostendere Apollonium uel paria, uel etaim maiora [Christo] fecisse. Mirum quod Apuleium praetermisit ; cuius solent et multa et mira memorari." The pagans argued : " Si magus Christus, quia mirabilia fecit ; peritior utique Apollonius, qui (ut describis) cum Domitianus eum punire uellet, repente in iudicio non comparuit ; quam ille, qui et comprehensus est, et cruci affixus."

[11] *De Ciuitate Dei*, xviii, 180, when the Holy Doctor speaks of transformations which seem to happen to human beings, " sicut Apuleius in libris, quos

asini aurei titulo inscripsit, sibi ipsi accidisse, ut accepto ueneno humano animo permanente asinus fieret, aut indicauit aut finxit."

[12] C. xxxi.

[13] *Dictionnaire Infernal*, Sixième Edition, 1863, p. 550. The editio princeps was 2 vols., Paris, 1818. It should be noted that the several editions vary very considerably one from another.

[14] A parallel to the incident of the severed head which spoke may be found in *Les Mille Nuits et Une Nuit*, traduction de Mardrus, "Histoire du Vizir du Roi Iounane et du Médecin Rouaine," Vol. I, pp. 46-65 (ed. 1899). In Michael Maier's *Atalanta Fugiens* there is a symbolic alchemical illustration of a full-grown hermaphrodite being consumed on a pyre.

[15] The first edition is Geneva, 1575. The book was very frequently reprinted: Geneva, 1580; 1670: Leyden, 1659, 1687: Gorichem, 1683. There are French translations; Paris, 1571; Geneva, 1571; Zurich, 1581; German translations; Zurich, 1569, 1578, 1670: and an English translation *Of gostes and spirits walking by night*, by R. M. London, 4to, 1572. Louis Lavater, a Swiss protestant divine, was born at Kyburg, in the canton of Zurich, 1527, and died in 1586. He is the author of various theological and expository tractates.

[16] "Maniae turpes deformesque personae," Festus, ed. Müller, p. 144.

[17] Cf. Aristophanes, *Thesmophoriazusae*, 416-417 :

$$\text{Μολοττικοὺς}$$
$$\text{τρέφουσι, μορμολυκεῖα τοῖς μοιχοῖς, κύνας.}$$

Apuleius, *De Deo Socratis*, has : " inane terriculamentum bonis hominibus."

[18] Edited by Ducaeus, Paris, 1630, 2 vols., folio. Callistus Xanthopolus Nicephorus was born in the latter part of the thirteenth century, and died *circa* 1350.

[19] This famous sophist was born at Prusa in Bithynia about the middle of the first century of the Christian era. Regarded with highest favour by Nerva and Trajan, he died at Rome about A.D. 117. Eighty of his orations are extant, but these are more properly essays on political, moral, and philosophical subjects. Editions by Reiske, Leipzig, 1784, 2 vols.; by Emperius, Brunswick, 1844 ; and by L. Dindorf, Leipzig, 1857.

[20] "Sed et lamiae nudauerunt mammam, lactauerunt catulos suos." *Vulgate.* "Even the sea monsters have drawn out the breast, they have given suck to their young." *Douai.* "Even the sea-monsters draw out the breast, they give suck to their young ones." *A.V.* With marginal note : " Or sea-calves." "Even the jackals draw out the breast, they give suck to their young ones." *Revised Version.*

[21] *s.u.* Strigem. Ed. Müller, p. 314.

[22] ἐφιάλτες ; the night-mare ; Latin, *incubus.*

[23] *Commonitorium*, I, 11.

[24] Hesychius, *Lexicon*, ed. M. Schmidt, Editio Altera ; Jena, 1867. *s.u.* μιαραὶ ἡμέραι· τοῦ Ἀνθεστηριῶνος μηνός, ἐν αἷς τὰς ψυχὰς τῶν κατοιχομένων ἀνιέναι ἐδόκουν. Photius, *Lexicon*, ed. S. A. Naber, Leyden, 1864-1865. *s.uu.* Θύραζε Κᾶρες· οὐκέτ' Ἀνθεστήρια . . . . τινὲς δὲ οὕτως τὴν παροιμίαν φασί· Θύραζε Κῆρες οὐκέτ' Ἀνθεστήρια· ὡς κατὰ τὴν πόλιν τοῖς Ἀνθεστηρίοις τῶν ψυχῶν περιερχομένων. *Id.s.uu.* μιαρὰ ἡμέρα· ἐν τοῖς Χουσὶν Ἀνθιστηριῶνος μηνός, ἐν ᾧ δοκοῦσιν αἱ ψυχαὶ τῶν τελευτησάντων ἀνιέναι, ῥάμνῳ ἔωθεν ἐμασῶντο καὶ πίττῃ τὰς θύρας ἔχριον.

[25] This is the traditional explanation, see Liddell and Scott, *s.u.* Dr. A. W. Verrall's derivation of Ἀνθεστήρια from ἀναθέσσασθαι "to conjure up" is hardly possible. See "The Name Anthesteria," *Journal of Hellenic Studies*, xx (1900), pp. 115-117. Θέσσασθαι, "to seek by prayer" is found in Hesiod (Fr. xxiii, 9) ; Pindar (Nemean, v, 18) ; Archilochus (*apud* Bergk, x) ; Apollonius Rhodius, I, 824 ; and other poets. Hesychius has Θέσσασθαι = αἰτῆσαι. Curtius connects the root Θεσ—with Θεός.

[26] A requiem may be sung by especial permission even on a Sunday, though the privilege is rarely granted. Thus on Sunday, 30 September, 1888, Pope Leo XIII commanded a requiem in all churches.

[27] The various religious families have particular Commemorations of the Deceased belonging to that Order. Thus 13 November is All Monks ;

14 November the Commemoration of All Souls, O.S.B. The Dominicans celebrate All Saints of the Order 12 November and there are four anniversaries for the dead in the course of each year ; 4 February for deceased Parents ; 12 July for those buried in Dominican Cemeteries; 5 September, for Friends and Benefactors ; 10 November for the Brothers and Sisters. The Feast of All Carmelite Saints is 14 November ; 15 November, *Commemoratio omnium Defunctorum Ordinis Carmelitarum*. 13 November the Trinitarians observe All Trinitarian Saints ; on the 14 November is a Solemn Commemoration of the dead of the Order, when the Office of the Dead is sung with a Requiem and the Absolutions *ad tumulum*.

[28] Some authorities incline to a later date, about 1030.

[29] This eremetical Order honours S. Bruno as Founder. It must be remembered that the Office of the Blessed One, *De Beata*, is recited daily as well as the *Agenda Mortuorum*, Matins and Lauds being chanted in midnight choir. The Carthusians have a special *Commemoratio Fratrum nostrorum defunctorum*, 9 November.

[30] S.R.C., 11 August, 1915 (*Acta, Ap. Sedis*, vol. vii, pp. 422-423). The first Mass is the one that was formerly said on All Souls. The second Mass is that for anniversaries, with a new collect, secreta, and post-communion. The third is for the daily Mass for the dead likewise with a new collect, secreta, and post-communion. At each Mass the sequence *Dies irae* is to be recited.

[31] Venice, 1841, pp. 324-326.

[32] The altar was thus appropriately furnished during the "Novendiali" or Nine Days' Obsequies of Pope Leo XIII, who died the death of the just, Monday, 20 July, 1903, at about 4 o'clock in the afternoon. *Sede Uacante*, by Hartwell de la Garde Grissell. Oxford and London, 1903.

[33] The word is a corruption of Trô-Miniky, and signifies "Tour of the Refuge."

[34] Karl Freihher von Leoprechting, *Aus dem Lechrain*, Munich, 1855, pp. 198-200.

[35] F. Schönwerth, *Aus der Oberfalz*, I, 283. In monasteries of the Benedictine Order and, indeed, in most religious houses after the death of a member his place is laid in the refectory and served with meals for thirty days. This food is given to the poor as alms.

[36] Milk has mystic properties, and is connected with many taboos. Among some Caffre tribes of South Africa men who had been wounded or killed an enemy in fight were neither allowed to see the King nor drink milk until they had been ceremonially purified. See Dudley Kidd's *The Essential Kafir*, London, 1904, pp. 309, seq. Among the Nandi of British East Africa a person who has handled a corpse may not drink milk for four days. A. C. Hollis, *The Nandi*, Oxford, 1909, p. 70. The Damaras or Herero of Damaraland in south-western Africa, who have a most elaborate religious ceremonial, pour new milk from the first pail upon the graves of their ancestors during their worship of the dead. Rev. G. Viehe, "Some Customs of the Ovaherero," *South African Folk-lore Journal*, 1879, I, pp. 61, seq. Milk alone will quench the flame of the Hand of Glory ; water makes the evil wicks burn yet more brightly. This thief's talisman was the hand of a man who had been hanged. Sometimes a candle made from the fat of a murderer on the gallows was placed in the hand, but more often the withered fingers were themselves used as Tapers and set on fire. This rendered all persons in the house motionless and plunged them in a trance or deep sleep. Should anyone be able to keep awake one of the fingers would not burn, but once they are lit nothing but milk will extinguish this horrid link.

[37] At the Council of Florence, Cardinal Bessarion in 1438-9 argued against the existence of real purgatorial fire, and the Greeks were assured that the Holy See had never issued any dogmatic decision on the point. However, in the West the belief in some real but mysterious fire is general. S. Augustine, S. Gregory, S. Thomas, and S. Bonaventure would seem to teach this, but perhaps it is better to abstain from over-subtle inquiries.

[38] Ignaz V. Zingerle, *Sitten, Bräuche, und Meiningen des Tiroler Volkes*, Innsbruck, 1871, pp. 176-178.

[39] Christian Schneller, *Märchen und Sagen aus Wälschtirol*, Innsbruck, 1867, p. 238.

[40] Miss G. S. Burne and Miss G. F. Jackson, *Shropshire Folk-lore*, London, 1883, record the old custom.

[41] J. Brand, *Popular Antiquities of Great Britain*, Bohn's edition ; W. Hone, *Year Book* [1832] ; T. F. Thiselton Dyer, *British Popular Customs*, London, 1876 ; Elizabeth Mary Wright, *Rustic Speech and Folk-lore*, Oxford, 1913 ; are a few of the many books which describe the old custom of "souling."

[42] *A History of Whitby and Streonashalth Abbey*, Whitby, 1817, II, 882.

[43] Festus tells us that loaves in the shape of men, called by the Romans *maniae*, were especially made at Aricia. (Ed. C. O. Müller, Leipzig, 1839, pp. 128, 129, 145.) *Et Ariciae genus panni fieri ; quod manici appelletur.* The reading here is slightly uncertain. Delicious little buns are yet made in the shapes of men by old-fashioned bakers, but one rarely sees them (1928). We may compare the gilt gingerbread kings and queens which were a fine feature of rustic wakes and holidays.

[44] Jules Bois, *Le Satanisme et la Magie*, Paris, 1895 : Préface par J.-K. Huysmans, p. xxiv. The following is given as the "Prière au Saint-sans-Autel" ; *Ibid*, pp. 153-4. "Sanctissime Apostole, fidelissime Christi serue et amice, Iuda, qui, ob proditoris nòmen et quorumdam simplicitate in debito tibi cultu desereris, ob tuam uero sanctissimam et apostolicam uitam ubique fere terrarum a uera Ecclesia *specialis calamitosorum et pene desperantium aduocatus inuocaris* et praestissime coleris, ora pro me misero, ut per tua merita in tribulationibus et angustiis meis consolationem recipiam. Tuum auxilium praesertim in praesenti perturbatione et angustia experiar." "O Holy Apostle, most faithful Servant and Friend of Jesus Christ, Saint Jude, thou who on account of thy name being likened unto that of the betrayer and through the folly of the froward hast not received that worship which is due to thee, albeit by the one true Church throughout the whole world thou art venerated and invoked as the especial Patron and Advocate of those who are well-nigh in despair and of the most difficult causes, pray for me miserable sinner that by thy merits I may receive comfort and consolation in my sorrow and my great need. May I experience thy very ready help at this my hour of distress and bitter anguish."

To speak of S. Jude as the "Saint who has no Altar" is a very great mistake. The body of S. Simon and a portion of the body of S. Jude are actually under the centre altar of the three altars in the left transept of S. Peter's. There are important Relics at the Churches of the SS. Dodici Apostoli ; and S. Marco, near the piazza Venezia ; whilst the Feast is kept with great solemnity at these two churches as well as at S. Maria della Pace, piazza della Pace ; and at the S. Cuore al Circo Agonale. One other portion of the Body of S. Jude is at the Church of S. Sernin where it is enshrined in an altar dedicated by Pope Callistus II (Guido of Burgundy), who reigned 1119-1124. Every year the Feast of SS. Simon and Jude is ushered in by a Novena of extraordinary fervour and devotion. On 25 October, 1867, Mgr. le Courtier, Bishop of Montpellier, was obliged to write a letter correcting the confusion which prevailed among the ignorant concerning S. Jude, to whom he had dedicated a church at Béziers, and whose cult he had introduced at Notre-Dame in Paris.

The church of SS. Simone e Guida, which stood near the via dei Coronari, Rome, has been secularized within the last fifty years. In England there are several Protestant churches dedicated to S. Jude.

[45] S. Antony the Great, *Eremita*. But in these charms he is often confused with S. Antony of Padua.

[46] *Etruscan Roman Remains*, p. 238.

[47] If the inquirer is not fearless in asking the Saint will deal him a sound buffet. The sorcerer who constrains spirits to appear safeguards himself with circles and mystic sigils, with occult characters circumscribed upon the ground and the sacred tetragrammaton so that he may be conscious of inviolability.

[48] *British Popular Customs*, p. 410.

[49] M. Martin, "Description of the Western Islands of Scotland," *apud* John Pinkerton's *Voyages and Travels*, London, 1808-1814, III, 666.

[50] Gennaro Finamore, *Credenze, Usi e Costumi Abruzzesi*, Palermo, 1890, pp. 180-182.

[51] Typis J. Barbou, Parisiis, 1779 ; tomus iv, p. 511.   The passage in Pliny, XXIV, lxxvi, runs : " Inter genera ruborum rhamnos appellatur a Graecis, candidior et fruticosior.   Is floret, ramos spargens rectis aculeis, non, ut ceteri, aduncis : foliis maioribus.   Alterum genus est siluestre, nigrius, et quadamtenus rubens.   Fert ueluti folliculos.   Huius radice decocta in aqua fit medicamentum, quod uocatur Lycium.   Semen fecundas trahit.   Alter ille candidior adstringit magis, refrigerat, collectionibus et uulneribus accom- modatior.   Folia utriusque et cruda et decocta illinuntur cum oleo."

[52] F. S. Krauss, " Vampyre im südslavischen Volksglauben," *Globus*, lxi, (1892), p. 326.

[53] J. G. Campbell, *Witchcraft and Second Sight in the Highlands and Islands of Scotland*, Glasgow, 1902, p. 13.

[54] F. S. Krauss, " Vampyre im südslavischen Volksglauben," *Globus*, lxi, 1892, p. 326.

[55] Adolf Strausz, *Die Bulgaren*, Leipzig, 1898, p. 454.

[56] Sir John Rhys, " The Coligny Calendar," *Proceedings of the British Academy*, vol. iv.

[57] The voice of a ghost squeaks and is thin.   Cf. *The Odyssey*, xi, 605-606 :

> ἀμφὶ δε μιν κλαγγὴ νεκύων ἦν, οἰωνῶν ὥς,
> παντοσ᾽ ἀτυζομένων·

In the *Aeneid*, vi, 489-493, at the sight of Aeneas advancing through the shadow of the underworld the Greeks fly in terror :

> At Danaum proceres Agamemnoniaeque phalanges,
> ut uidere uirium fulgentiaque arma per umbras,
> ingenti trepidare metu : pars uertere terga,
> ceu quondam petiere rates ; pars tollere uocem
> exiguam : inceptus clamor frustratur hiantes.

Which Conington turns :

> But Agamemnon's chivalry,
>   When gleaming through the shade
> The hero and his arms they see,
>   Are wildered and dismayed :
> Some huddle in promiscuous rout
>   As erst at Troy they sought the fleet :
> Some feebly raise the battle-shout ;
> Their straining throat the thin tones flout,
>   Unformed and incomplete.

In the *Odyssey*, again, xxiv, 5, τρίζειν, to squeak shrilly, is used of ghosts, ταὶ δε τρίζουσαι ἕποντο.   The same word is immediately applied to the noise made by bats :

> ὡς δ᾽ ὅτε νυκτερίδες μυχῷ ἄντρου θεσπεσίοιο
> τρίζουσαι ποτέονται, ἐπεί κέ τις ἀποπέσῃσιν
> ὁρμαθοῦ ἐκ πέτρης, ἀνά τ᾽ ἀλλήλῃσιν ἔχονται.

Ovid, writing of bats, *Metamorphoses*, 412-13, has :

> Conataeque loqui, minimam pro corpore uocem
> Emittunt, peraguntque leues stridore querelas.

τρίζειν is used by Aristotle of the noise made by young partridges, of the chirp of locusts, or the cry of the ἴυγξ ; by Lucian of the cheeping of swallows ; by Babrius of the squealing of mice.   Horace in his sabbat on the Esquiline, *Sermonum*, I, viii, 40-41, has :

> Singula quid memorem, quo facto alterna loquentes
> umbrae cum Sagana resonarent triste et acutum.

Shakespeare's ghosts " shriek and squeal," *Julius Caesar*, II, 2 : they also " squeak and gibber," *Hamlet*, I, i. I do not know that a thin voice is regarded as a quality of ghosts seen to-day. For the most part they would appear to speak in natural tones. Longfellow, *The Courtship of Miles Standish*, vi, 29-30, tells us

It is the fate of woman
Long to be patient and silent, to wait like a ghost that is speechless
Till some questioning voice dissolves the spell of its silence.

(Nous avons changé tout cela.) And Peter Thyraeus, *De Uariis tam Spirituum quam Uiuorum Hominum Prodigiosis Apparitionibus*, I, xv, ed. Cologne, 1594, p. 52, teaches : " Miscere sermonem cum spiritibus, ex se culpa uacat.

[58] Apollodorus, *Bibliotheca*, ed. R. Wagner, Leipzig, 1894, III, v, 1.

[59] I quote the translation of Sir Gilbert Murray, *et infra*.

[60] ΑΓΑΤΗ. Διόνυσε, λισσόμεσθά σ', ἠδικήκαμεν·
ΔΙΟΝΤΣΟΣ. ὄψ' ἐμάθεθ' ἡμᾶς, ὅτε δ' ἐχρῆν, οὐκ ᾔδετε.
ΑΓΑΤΗ. ἐγνώκαμεν ταῦτ'· ἀλλ' ἐπεξέρχει λίαν.
ΔΙΟΝΤΣΟΣ. καὶ γὰρ πρὸς ὑμῶν θεὸς γεγὼς ὑβριζόμην·
ΑΓΑΤΗ. ὀργὰς πρέπει θεοὺς οὐχ ὁμοιοῦσθαι βροτοῖς.
ΔΙΟΝΤΣΟΣ. πάλαι τάδε Ζεὺς οὑμὸς ἐπένευσεν πατήρ.

[61] The story of King Athamas is told with many variants of detail. His second wife, Ino, being jealous of her two step-children, Phrixus and Helle, secretly persuaded the women of the country to roast the corn before it was sown. When no crop appeared and famine stalked through the land, the King sent to the Oracle at Delphi to inquire the cause thereof, but Ino bribed the messenger to declare that Phrixus and Helle must be sacrificed to Zeus ere the land should obtain peace. But a ram with fleece of gold carried them over the sea. Meanwhile an oracle commanded that Athamas himself should be sacrificed, and as he was wreathed with garlands, about to be immolated, he was rescued by Hercules, some say by his grandson Cytisorus, the son of Phrixus who had reached Colchis and settled there. Helle, as the ram crossed the sea, had fallen from its back and was drowned. But because King Athamas had not been sacrificed it was decreed by heaven that the eldest male of his stock in each generation should be slain on the altar of Laphystian Zeus, and when Xerxes was marching through Thessaly with his host, at the town of Alus he was told that many of the family fled to escape their destiny, but if any one could be caught he was crowned with flowers and led forth in procession to the sacrifice. Very many writers, and amongst other Herodotus (vii, 197), Apollodorus (I, 9), Pausanias (I, xliv, 7 ; IX, xxxiv, 7), Zenobius (iv, 38), Plutarch (*De superstitione*, v), have mentioned this legend.

[62] Upon the twelfth day of the month Hecatombaeon, which closely corresponds to our July, and was formerly the month of Cronos.

[63] I quote the translation of Davies and Vaughan, London, 1898, p. 299.

[64] Typis J. Barbou, Parisiis, 1779.

[65] Homines in lupos uerti, rursumque restitui sibi, falsum esse confidenter existimare debemus, aut credere omnia, quae fabulosa tot saeculis comperimus. Pliny's opinion is at least open to criticism.

[66] Itaque Agriopas, qui Olympionicas scripsit, narrat Demaenetum Parrhasium in sacrificio, quod Arcades Ioui Lycaeo humana etiam tum hostia faciebant, immolati pueri exta degustasse, et in lupum se conuertisse : eumdem decimo anno restitutum athleticae, certasse in pugilatu, uictoremque Olympia reuersum.

[67] Denique etiam nominatim expressit quendam Demaenetum gustasse de sacrificio, quod Arcades immolato puero deo suo Lycaeo facere solerent, et in lupum fuisse mutatum et anno decimo in figuram propriam restitutum pugilatum sese exercuisse et Olympiaco uicisse certamine.

[68] *Circa* 560—4 April, 636.

[69] " The sacrifice which the Arcadians offer to their god the Luycaean, and whereof whosoever taste are turned into the shapes of wild beasts."

[70] The most famous mythical type of prophecy. His tomb was shown hard by the Tilphusian well near Thebes, and likewise in Macedonia.

[71] Cf. Claudian, *In Rufinum*, I, 124-129 :

> Est locus, extremum qua pandit Gallia litus,
> Occani praetentus aquis, ubi fertur Ulysses
> Sanguine libato populum mouisse silentum.
> Illic umbrarum tenui stridore uolantum
> Flebilis auditur questus : simulacra coloni
> Pallidi, defunctasque uident migrare figuras.

Codex Mediceus, II, which is followed by Rottendorf has an inferior reading in line 129, " mugire " for " migrare."

[72] *Pflanzenleben*, 1888, vol. I, pp. 195, 196. Translated by F. W. Oliver as *The Natural History of Plants*, London, 1894-95, I, 204, *sqq.*

[73] ἰφθίμῳ τ' Ἀΐδῃ καὶ ἐπαινῇ Περσεφονείῃ. *Odyssey*, xi, 47.

[74] Cf. *Aeneid*, II, 793-795, when Aeneas endeavours to embrace Creusa :

> Ter conatus ibi collo dare bracchia circum ;
> ter frustra comprensa manus effugit imago,
> par leuibus uentis uoluerique simillima somno.

The lines are repeated *Aeneid*, vi, 700-702.

[75] I quote the translation by A. S. Way, Loeb Classics, *Euripides*, vol. I, p. 257.

[76] *Oedipus Coloneus*. Translated by Thomas Francklin:

> Then buried long in earth, shall this cold corse
> Drink their warm blood, which from the mutual wound
> Frequent shall flow.

[77] A curious illustration of the spectre is given in Beaumont's *Treatise on Spirits*, 1705, p. 18.

[78] Gaius, *Institutiones*, II, 4.

[79] Festus, *De uerborum significatione*, Ed. C. O. Müller. Leipzig, 1839, p. 253.

[80] Cf. also Livy, xvi.

[81] Jules Bois.

[82] W. G. Aston, *Shinto*, London, 1905, p. 309.

[83] *Al Baidaui's Commendary on the Koran*, cxiii, verse 4.

[84] J. G. Dalyell, *Darker Superstitions of Scotland*, Edinburgh, 1834, p. 307.

[85] In the New England trials for witchcraft the " afflicted children " continually complained that the witches, invisible to others, had appeared in the room and were tormenting them. Anne Putman, Abigail Williams, and Mary Walcut declared that on one occasion Rebecca Nurse, who was afterwards executed for sorcery, beat, pinched, bruised and sorely tormented them.

[86] *The Geography of Witchcraft*, London, 1927, p. 179.

[87] R. Chambers, *Popular Rhymes of Scotland*, New edition, p. 349.

[88] H. J. Byrne, " All Hallows Eve and other Festivals in Connaught," *Folk-lore*, xviii (1907), pp. 437, *sqq.*

[89] J. A. E. Köhler, *Volksbrauch, Aberglauben, Sagen und andre alte Ueberlieferungen im Voigtlande*, Leipzig, 1867, p. 376.

[90] The solemnity of S. Agnes falls on 21 January, but technically the Feast commences with the First Vespers.

[91] Burton, *Anatomy of Melancholy*, P. III, s. ii, Mem. 3, sub. 1, writes : " They'll give anything to know when they shall be married—how many husbands they shall have—by cromnyomantia, a kind of divination with onions (His eorum nomina inscribuntur de quibus quaerunt) laid on the altar on Christmas Eve, or by fasting on S. Anne's Eve or night to know who shall be their first husband." The charm by onions was popular in Guernsey and in Derbyshire, in which places S. Thomas' Eve was considered the appropriate time for the experiment. Ben Jonson, *A Particular Entertainment of the Queen and Prince at Althorpe*, 25 June, 1603, says of Queen Mab :

> She can start our Franklin's daughters,
> In her sleep, with shrieks and laughters,
> And on sweet S. Anna's night,
> Feed them with a promised sight—
> Some of husbands, some of lovers,
> Which an empty dream discovers.

S. Faith's day is favoured in the North of England. Three maidens bake a girdle scone of flour, spring water, salt and sugar. Complete silence must be observed during the whole of these operations. It is then put in the oven, each turning it thrice. When it is well browned, it must be divided into three equal parts, and each girl must divide her share into nine pieces, drawing each piece through a wedding-ring which has been borrowed from a woman who has been married exactly seven years. Each girl, whilst undressing for bed, must eat her pieces of cake and recite the following rhyme i

> O good S. Faith, be kind to-night,
> And bring to me my heart's delight ;
> Let me my future husband view,
> And be my visions chaste and true.

[92] Conington's translation.

[93] Περὶ θεῶν καὶ κόσμου. *Fragmenta philosophorum Graecorum.* Ed. F. G. A. Mullach.

[94] Berescith Rabbæ. *c.* 22. See Manasseh *De Resurrectione Mortuorum.* See *The History of Witchcraft*, London, 1926, pp. 176-181.

[95] *De abstinentia* II xcvii. There is an "Animals' Auxiliary Alliance" the members of which are particularly interested in the problems of the continuity of animal life. See *The Occult Review*, March, 1918, p. 164.

[96] IV, 10. But the work may be that of an Alexandrine sophist of the name Demetrius.

[97] Agathias, *Historia.* Ed. B. G. Niebuhr, Bonn, 1828.

[98] In the *Andromache*, 173 *sqq.* Euripides speaks of such connexions as essentially barbaric and opposed to Hellenic ideas :

> τοιοῦτον πᾶν τὸ βάρβαρον γένος·
> πατήρ τε θυγατρὶ παῖς τε μητρὶ μίγνυται
> κόρη τ' ἀδελφῷ, διὰ φόνου δ' οἱ φίλτατοι
> χωροῦσι, καὶ τῶνδ' οὐδὲν ἐξείργει νόμος.

Upon which the scholiast notes : ταῦτα Περσικὰ ἔθη.

[99] Ed. Rigalt, p. 10.

[100]
> Nascatur magus ex Gelli matrisque nefando
> Coniugio, et discat Persicum aruspicium
> Nam magus ex matre et gnato nascatur oportet
> Si ucra est Persarum impia religio.

Strabo, 735, has : τοὺς δὲ Μάγους οὐ θάπτουσιν, ἀλλ' οἰωνοβρώτους ἐωσι· τούτοις δὲ καὶ μητράσι συνέρχεσθαι πάτριον νενόμισται.

[101] Phlegon Trallianus, ΠΕΡΙ ΘΑΥΜΑΣΙΩΝ, apud *Fragmenta Historicorum Graecorum.* Ed. Carolus Müllerus, Parisiis, Didot, 1849, vol. III, pp. 611-613 ; No. 30. Father Richard, *Relation de ce qui s'est passé de plus remarquable à Sant-Erini*, p. 213, knew the story and compares it with an incident that came under his own notice. He is, however, probably quoting from memory as many of his details are incorrect. Mrs. Crowe in her *The Night Side of Nature*, 2 vols, 1848 (Ed. 1857, pp. 372-374) tells this tale, and there is an exceedingly inaccurate version in *The Occult Review*, November, 1924, where the incidents are referred to the fourth century B.C. and said to have taken place during the reign of Philip II of Macedon !

[102] The writer in *The Occult Review* says that Philinnion, who was in love with Machates, had been obliged to marry Craterus, the famous general of Alexander the Great, and died of a broken heart. There is no authority for this ; indeed it involves an error of some four centuries in the dating of these circumstances.

[103] Wilhelm Xylander (Holtzmann) was born at Augsburg, 20 December, 1532. At the age of 26 he obtained the chair of Greek at Hiedelberg, when he died 1576

[104] Basle, 1568.

[105] Horace, *Carminum*, I, x, 17-20 :

> tu pias laetis animas reponis
> sedibus uirgaque leuem coerces
> aurea turbam, superis deorum
> gratus et imis.

[106] The Gens Lamia claimed descent from the mythical hero Lamus, son of Poseidon, the legendary founder of Formiæ. The Gardens were on the Esquiline Hill.

[107] Cadauer eius clam in hortos Lamianos asportatum, et tumultuario rogo seniambustum leui cespite obrutum est : postea per sorores ab exsilio reuersas erutum, crematum, sepultumque. Satis constat, priusquam id fieret, hortorum custodes umbris inquietatos : in ea quoque domo, in qua occubuerit, nullam noctem sine aliquo terrore transactam, donec ipsa domus incendio consumpta sit.

[108] The Esquiline hill seems to have derived its name from the oak trees. The old king of Rome Servius Tullius lived among the oak groves of the Esquiline hill at the head of the Slope of Virbius, and it was here, beside a sanctuary of Diana that he was attacked and slain at the orders of his successor. Cf. Livy, I, 48 ; Dionysius Halicarnasensis, *Antiquitates Romanæ*, IV, 38 *sqq.* (ed. C. Jacoby, Leipzig, 1885-1905) ; Solinus, *Collectanea*, I, 25 (ed. Th. Mommsen, Berlin, 1864). There can be little doubt that the correct reading in Livy is *Urbium Cliuum*, although the older MSS. read *Urbium Cliuum*. The obscure Uirbium, which was not understood, soon became *Urbium*.

[109] Chr. Hartknoch, *Alt und Neues Preussen*, Frankfort and Leipsic, 1684, p. 159.

[110] *Pharsalia*, III, 405.

[111] The sacred tree was sometimes a terebinth. Both the oak and the terebinth are still common in Palestine. Although very different in kind, they are very similar in appearance, and accordingly they were classed together, if not actually confused, by the Hebrews of old, who gave them a like name. Accordingly in some passages of the Old Testament it is not quite clear whether the reference to a Sacred Tree is to an oak or to a terebinth.

[112] *Genesis*, xiii, 18.

[113] Eusebius, *Uita Constantini*, iii, 51-3. (Migne's *Patrologia Graeca*, xx, 1112, *sqq.*).

[114] *Josue*, xxiv, 26-27. Tulit lapidem pergrandem, posuitque eum subter quercum, quæ erat in Sanctuario Domini : Et dixit ad omnem populum : En lapis iste erit uobis in testimonium quod audierit omnia uerba Domini, quæ locutus est uobis : ne forte postea negare uelitis, et mentiri Domino Deo uestro.

[115] *Osee*, iv, 13-14. Super capita montium sacrificabant, et super colles accendebant thymiama : subtus quercum, et populum, et terebinthum, quia bona erat umbra eius : ideo fornicabuntur filiæ uestræ, et sponsæ uestræ adulteræ erunt. Non uisitabo super filias uestras cum fuerint fornicatæ, et super sponsas uestras cum adulterauerint : quoniam ipsi cum meretricibus conuersabantur, et cum effeminatis sacrificabant, et populus non intelligens uapulabit.

[116] Hargraves Jennings, "The Worship of Priapus." Apud, *The Story of Phallicism*, by Lee Alexander Stone, M.D., Chicago, 1927, vol. II, pp. 383-4.

[117] *Ezechiel*, vi, 13. Et scietis quia ego Dominus, cum fuerint interfecti uestri in medio idolorum uestrorum in circuitu ararum uestrarum, in omni colle excelso, et in cunctis summitatibus montium, et subtus omne lignum nemorosum, et subtus uniuersam quercum frondosam, locum ubi accenderunt thura redolentia uniuersis idolis suis.

[118] *Isaias*, lvii, 5. Filii auguratricis . . . Qui consolamini in diis subter omne lignum frondosum, immolantes paruulos in torrentibus, subter eminentes petras. *A.V.*—"Ye sons of the sorceress . . . enflaming yourselves with idols under every green tree, slaying the children in the valleys under the clefts of the rocks." With marginal note on "with idols "; "Or, among the oaks." *R.V.*—"Ye sons of the sorceress . . . ye that inflame yourselves among the oaks, under every green tree ; that slay the children in the valleys under the clefts of the rocks." With marginal note on "among the oaks "; Or, *with idols*."

[119] Saluum sit, quod tango. W. K. Kelly following Burmann explains : " We are to suppose him illustrating his narration by making a feigned thrust at the nearest guest." But Joannes Schefferus in his commentary on Petronius (Amstelodami, 1669, p. 242) prefers to gloss the passage thus : " Formula est eius, qui auertit omen, quod in se ex narratione mali alieni ualere posse pertimescit. Itaque hic parenthesi debet includi. Nam prae-cedens *hoc loco* demonstratiue debet intelligi, quia simul cum his uerbis intenderat digitum in sui propriique corporis eum locum, in quo corpus mulieris fuerat uulneratum." Heinsius added : " Tangebat autem mensam, ut iurantes precantesue solebant." But Burmann says : " Minime hic mensam tangebat, neque suum corpus, sed aliquem conuiuarum proxime ipsi accumbentem, eo loco, quo Cappadox ille mulierem traiecerat, ut solent fere facere, qui sermonibus suis gesticulationes adiungunt. Petit ergo ueniam, quod tangat conuiuæ pectus, uel aliam partem."

[120] Horace, *Carminum*, I, xxvii, 21.

[121] Idem. *Epistularum*, II, ii, 209-210.

[122] IV, xxiv, 10. Recensuit Lucianus Mueller ; Teubner, 1894, p. 90.

[123] VI, 609-10.

[124] The following excerpt is from Murray's *Handbook for Travellers in Greece*, 1900, which I used with great profit during my explorations of Greece. Hypati is an interesting little place, and Murray notices it as follows (p. 575-6) : " *Hypati*, the ancient Hypata, to which name it has reverted from its mediæval name Neópatra (known in Turkish as *Patradjik*). Hypati is finely situated under Mount *Oeta*, the legendary scene of the apotheosis of Heracles. In ancient times it was a town of the district of Phthiotis in Thessaly, and has interest from having been the centre of the military operations carried on in B.C. 323 by the confederate Greeks against Antipater—the so-called *Lamian* war. Some pieces of ancient wall in the masonry of its Spanish Castle are its only antiquities. In the thirteenth century it was the capital of the Principality of Great Wallachia.

During the period when the greater part of continental Greece was subject to the kings of Sicily, Neópatra become a place of importance, and the Sicilian princes were always styled *Dukes of Athens and Neópatra*."

W. M. Leake, *Travels in Northern Greece*, 1835, vol. II, c. 10, has the following description of Neópatra : " Neópatra, by the Turks called Badrajík, stands partly at the head of a long stony slope, similar to that below Mount Katavóthra, and partly upon a ridge which rises at the back of the slope, terminating above in a steep detached summit of a peaked form. On this height are the ruins of a small castle of Lower Greek construction, or perhaps a work of the Franks in the fourteenth century, when Neópatra was conquered from the Greek despot of Western Greece by the Catalans, and became a part of the duchy of Athens under the Spanish sovereigns of Sicily until Thessaly was overrun by the Turks. The ridge is protected on either side by a ravine, in which flows a torrent (ῥεῦμα) ; that on the west has a wide gravelly bed ; the eastern is shaded by plane trees, and waters numerous gardens around a suburb which stands below the ridge on that side. These streams do not fail in Summer, but after turning many mills, irrigate planta-tions of tobacco in the plain. The *Sphercheius*, or Elládha, is diverted from the general course in which it descends to the sea from the westward by the long projection of the hill of Neópatra, which forms a diminishing ridge almost as far as the river's bank."

[125] Murray, *op. cit.* thus mentions Larissa : " Larissa lies in the midst of a fertile plain on the right bank of the *Salamvrias*, the ancient Peneios. Larissa was regarded by the Greeks as a name specially belonging to the " Pelasgi," i.e., it belonged to very early settlers in Greece. When Thessaly was ruled mainly by a few aristocratic families, Larissa belonged to the house of the Aleuadæ, from which, down to 500 B.C., the Tagus, or " General," of Thessaly seems always to have been chosen. It was allied to Athens in the Peloponnesian war ; but in the following century fell under the Macedonian power. Under the Romans it was important, and was the seat of the diet of the Thessalians. It is still the capital of that province, the seat of a

monarch, and the residence of a Greek archbishop. There is an extensive Mohammedan quarter, and a considerable number of Jews.

Like most places which have been continually inhabited, Larissa retains few ancient remains. Several interesting sepulchral reliefs were discovered near the town in 1882, some of which have been removed to Athens ; others are in a small *Museum* to the S. of the principal Square.

5 min. N.W. of the Square, in the direction of a conspicuous Minaret, a bridge of nine pointed arches crosses the river. On the rising ground to the left, close to the bridge, is a Mosque, preceded by a portico, in front of which is an ancient row of columns, including several of handsome *Verde antico*. Nearly 30 minarets, scattered about the Town, recall the days of its Turkish occupation, but most of the Mosques have been converted to other uses.

On the other side of the bridge is a pleasantly shaded Promenade, much frequented by the inhabitants in the evening. Upon an eminence on the right bank stands the Cathedral, occupying the probable site of the ancient Acropolis."

[126] Cf. Ausonius, *Epigrammata*, xx, *In Meroen anum ebriosam* :

> Qui primus MEROE nomen tibi condidit. ille
> Thesidæ nomen condidit Hippolyto.
> Nam diuinare est, nomen componere, quod sit
> Fortunæ, morum, uel necis indicium.
> Protesilæ, tibi nomen sic fata dederunt :
> Victima quod Troiæ prima futurus eras.
> Idmona quod uatem, medicum quod Iapida dicunt :
> Discendas artes nomina præueniunt.
> Et tu sic, Meroe : non quod sis atra colore,
> Ut quæ Niliaca nascitur in Meroe :
> Infusum sed quod uinum non diluis undis,
> Potare immixtum sueta merumque merum.

One may also compare Ovid, *Amores*, VIII, which commences thus :

> Est quædam : (quicunque uolet cognoscere lenam,
> Audiat) est quædam nomine Dipsas anus.
> Ex re nomen habet. Nigri non illa parentem
> Memnonis in roseis sobria uidit equis.

This is thus paraphrased by Sir Charles Sedley :

> There is a Bawd renown'd in *Venus'* Wars
> And dreadful still with honourable scars :   . . .
> *Dypsas*, who first taught love-sick Maids the way
> To cheat the Bridegroom on the wedding day,   . . .
> Each morning sees her reeling to her bed,
> Her native blue o'ercome with drunken red.

Marlowe who endeavours to keep more clearly to the original is rougher :

> There is—whoe'er will know a bawd aright,
> Give ear—there is an old trot, Dipsas hight,
> Her name comes from the thing : she being wise,
> Sees not the morn on rosy horses rise.

[127] One may compare the occupation of Rutilio in *The Custom of the Country* (Beaumont and Fletcher,) folio, 1647, but much earlier, probably composed 1619-1622. Cf. the scenes in the house of Sulpitia, "Mistress of the male-stews."

[128] Following the reading of V(codex Vaticanus). F(codex Florentinus) has "infirmare."

[129] Oro te aulæum tragicum dimoueto et siparium scænicum complicato et cedo uerbis communibus.

[130] Pallore buxeo deficientem uideo. The metaphor *buxeus* is a favourite one with Apuleuis, and in Book IX we have *liuore buxeo fœdatus.*

[131] The *aureus*, the standard gold coin of Rome was first struck in the second Punic war. In was of the value of about 25 denarii or 100 sestertii, weighing

some 120 grains, and being about equal to £1 1s. 1d., the spending value being proportionately greater.

[132] De Lancre. *Tableau de l'inconstance des mauvais anges et démons.* Paris, 1612, p. 2.

[133] It will be readily remembered that Beelzebub, the god of Accaron, was the Lord of flies.

[134] Baron von Schrenck Notzing, *Phenomena of Materialization.* (Translated by Dr. E. E. Fourlier d'Albe). London, Kegan Paul, 1923, p. 4.8

[135] The conclusions reached in this study have been much discussed but they have been by no means disproved.

[136] *Summa Theologica*, P. I, Q. LI, CX, CXI.

[137] George Giffard, *Dialogue concerning Witches.* (Percy Society, VIII. London, 1843).

[138] R. F. Kaindl, *Die Huzulen*, Vienna, 1894, pp. 79, 103 : *id.*, "Viehzucht und Viehzauber in den Ostkartaten," apud *Globus*. lxix, 1906, p. 387.

[139] But the best general work on Tertullian, Monceaux *Histoire littéraire de l'Afrique chrétienne*, I (Paris, 1901), prefers 213.

[140] S. Jerome, *Epistola*, cxxvi, 1, says that "the majority of oriental writers think that, as the body is born of the body, so the soul is born of the soul."

[141] S. Jerome, *De Uiris illustribus*, liii.

[142] The Annals of this Byzantine historian contain the history of the world from the creation to the death of Alexis I. Comnenus, A.D. 1118. There are editions by Bekker, Bonn, 1836 ; and by Migne, Paris, 1866.

[143] *Confessiones*, VI, 2.

[144] "Quæcumque igitur adhibentur religiosorum obsequia in martyrum locis, ornamenta sunt memoriarum, non sacra uel sacrificia mortuorum tamquam deorum. Quicumque etaim epulas suas eo deferunt (quod quidem a Christianis melibribus non fit, et in plerisque terrarum nulla talis est consuetudo)—tamen quicumque id faciunt, quas cum adposuerint, orant et auferunt, ut uesuolunt per merita martyrum, in nomine domini martyrum."

[145] An appeal was lodged by Miss Hoskyns and heard in the Court of Appeal before Lord Justices Scrutton, Greer, and Sankey, as reported in the *Daily Mail*, 8th December, 1928. The appeal was dismissed, as, in the opinion of the Court, these acts of piety were "extraordinary practices . . . out of touch with the habits of modern civilisation." *Daily Express*, 11th December, 1928.

[146] Discours, et histoires des spectres, visions, et apparitions des esprits, anges, demons et ames, se monstrans visibles aux hommes. Divisez en huict livres. Esquels par les visions merveilleuses et prodigieuses apparitions avenuës en tous siecles, tirées et recueillies des plus celebres autheurs tant sacrez que prophanes, est manifestée la certitude des Spectres et visions des Esprits : & sont baillées les causes des diverses sortes d'apparitions d'iceux, leurs effects, leurs differences, & les moyens pour recognoistre les bons et les mauvais & chasser les Demons. Aussi est traicté des extases et ravissemens : de l'essence, nature et origine des âmes, et de leur estat aprés le deceds de leurs corps : plus des magiciens et sorciers, de leur communication auec les malins Esprits. Ensemble des remedes pour se preseruer des illusions et impostures diaboliques. *Paris, Nic. Buon*, 1605, 4to. The first edition is Angers, Georges Nepueu, and Paris, G. Buon, 1586, two parts in one volume, 4to. Second Edition (actually Third Edition) "revue et augmentée," Paris, Nicolas Buon, 4to, 1608.

[147] Born at Feltre, 1397 ; died at Mantua, 1446.

[148] *Job*, Chapters I and II.

[149] *Capitula Caroli Magni pro partibus Saxoniæ*, I, 6.

[150] Calmet *Traité sur les Apparitions des Ésprits* . . . Paris, 1751, vol. II, Preface, p. vi.

CHAPTER II

THE VAMPIRE IN ENGLAND AND IRELAND, AND SOME LATIN LANDS

ALTHOUGH there is some evidence that the Vampire was by no means unknown in England during Anglo-Saxon times, the allusions are accidental and occasional, rather than detailed and direct, that is to say pieces of folk-lore in the remoter countries, half-forgotten oral tradition (now almost entirely dying out), and the persistence of a few old customs, apparently meaningless, which are casually maintained owing to some vague idea of thereby warding off some indefinite ill-luck ; all these, severally petty and paltry in themselves, in their cumulative significance afford evidence of a widespread and deeply-rooted belief in Vampires, even if such manifestations were comparatively few in number, and occurred at long intervals.

The Norsemen no doubt added their quota to the belief, for in ancient Scandinavia the idea that the dead were alive in their burrows gave rise to the fear that they might become un-hallowed monsters of the Vampire breed as may very clearly be seen from the *Grettis Saga*.

William of Malmesbury[1] says that in England it was commonly supposed and indeed certainly known that evil men returned to walk in the world after they are dead and buried, inasmuch as their bodies are re-animated by the Devil, who energizes them and compels them to act as he desires : *nequam hominis cadauer post mortem daemone agente discurrere.*

There are, indeed, some important passages in the *Historia Rerum Anglicarum* of William of Newburgh, which deserve attention. This historian, who was born at Bridlington in 1136, went as a boy to the small and recently founded Priory of Augustinian Canons of Newburgh in the North Riding of

Yorkshire. There he remained to his death in 1198 (or perhaps 1208)[2] as an Austin Canon. His diligence and ability in theological pursuits and the study of history were remarked by Abbot Ernald[3] of Rivaulx and Abbot Robert of Byland, and these prelates, rightly judging of this author's extraordinary talents, both urged him to devote his attention to scholarship and literature. William of Newburgh belongs to the Northern school of chroniclers, who carried on the admirable tradition of the Venerable Bede. This was a spirit entirely opposed to that which inspired Geoffrey of Monmouth who among the pages of his vast *Historia Regum Britanniae*[4] relates the legend of Brut, great grandfather of Aeneas, and the famous romances of King Arthur. In his *Prooemium*, William of Newburgh attacks Geoffrey and his myths with open indignation, not to say a certain acerbity, remarking that " fabulator ille " has " lied most idly and most impudently " concerning King Arthur and the wizard Merlin. This is, no doubt, the correct and impartial attitude, and this striking illustration of his historic integrity won for the good Canon from Freeman the title of " the father of historical criticism." It is, perhaps, impertinent to the point at issue, but it must be pointed out that Geoffrey's " History " has been one of the great influences in English literature, and has made itself felt in the national romance from Layamon to Tennyson. Shakespeare, Milton, Dryden, Pope, Wordsworth and many more have found choicest gold in his legends which still afford us both marvel and delight. Sir Thomas Malory loved them and gave them to us in a new and more exquisite form, whilst what is perhaps Tennyson's most famous poem the poet acknowledged that he drew from " Geoffrey's book, or Malleor's." It were churlish to refrain from honouring Geoffrey of Monmouth as one of the greatest of our story-tellers, although we must not regard him as an historian, but it is with history that we are now concerned. On the other hand there can be no doubt that the character of William of Newburgh well fitted him for the somewhat sterner duties which fall to the lot of a son of Clio. Mr. Hardy, who was no mean judge, says[5]: "His narrative is highly interesting ; the events selected with great judgement. His observations are acute and sensible, and his style is clear and sober." It is well to bear this in mind when we read the following narratives which may be found in Book V

of his Chronicles, Chapters xxii-xxiv.[6] The events are related
sub anno 1196, as having occurred in the reign of Richard I.
The rubric of Chapter xxii runs : *Of the extraordinary happening
when a dead man wandered abroad out of his grave.*

About that time in the county of Buckinghamshire a most
remarkable event took place, and this I first heard of from some
people who lived in that very district, and it was afterwards
told me in fullest detail by Stephen, the highly respected and
most worthily esteemed Archdeacon of that diocese. A
certain man having died, according to the course of nature, was
by the seemly care of his wife and relations decently buried
on the Eve of Ascension Day (29th May). But on the following
night he suddenly entered the room where his wife lay asleep
and, having awakened her, he not only filled her with the
greatest alarm but almost killed her by leaping upon her with
the whole heaviness of his weight and overlying her. On the
second night, also, he tormented the trembling woman in just
the same way. Wherefore in the extremity of dread she
resolved that on the third night she would remain awake and
that then and thenceforth she would protect herself from this
horrible attack by providing a company of persons to watch
with her. Nevertheless, he visited her ; but when he was
driven away by the shouts and cries of those who were keeping
watch, so that he found he could do her no harm, he swiftly
departed. Having been thus baffled and repulsed by his
wife, he proceeded in exactly the same manner to harrass
and annoy his brothers who resided in the same town. But
they, taking pattern from the excellent precautions employed
by their sister-in-law, passed several nights of wakefulness,
surrounded by their household all on guard, and all ready to
receive and repel the onset of the dead man. He made his
appearance, indeed, but it seemed as though he were only
wishful, or only had the power, to molest those who were
asleep, and he was kept at bay by the vigilance and the courage
of any who were on their guard and waking. Next, then, he
roved about and beset animals who were either in the houses
or resting near the houses. This was discovered by the unusual panic and disturbances of the terrified beasts. So
eventually since he proved so terrible and continual a danger
both to friends and neighbours alike, there was nothing for it
save that they should pass their nights in watching and being

continually on their guard.   Accordingly throughout the town
in every house there were certain of the family who kept
awake and mounted guard all night long, whilst everybody was
anxious and fearful lest they should be subjected to some sudden
and unforeseen attack.   Now when for a good while he had
harried people during the night alone, he began to wander
abroad in plain daylight, dreaded by all, although actually he
was seen but by a few.   Very often he would encounter a
company of some half-a-dozen and he would be quite clearly
discerned by but one or two of the number, although all of
them very perceptibly felt his horrible presence.   Well-nigh
scared out of their senses the inhabitants at last determined
that they must seek counsel from the church ; and accordingly
with many piteous lamentations, they laid the whole matter
from first to last before Archdeacon Stephen, whom I have
mentioned above, in his public and official capacity as president
of a diocesan synod which was then convened.   The Archdeacon forthwith wrote a letter to that venerable prelate, His
Lordship the Bishop of Lincoln (S. Hugh),[7] who happened to be
at London.   The screed related all these extraordinary circumstances in regular order, and he requested His Lordship to
give directions as to what must be done to remedy so intolerable an evil, since he felt that the matter should be dealt with
by the highest authority.   When the Bishop heard of this he
was greatly amazed, and forthwith he consulted with a number
of learned priests and reverend theologians, from certain of
whom he learned that similar occurences had often taken place
in England, and many well-known instances were quoted to
him.   They all agreed that the neighbourhood would never
obtain any peace until the body of this miserable wretch had
been disinterred and burned to ashes.   However, such a
method seemed extremely undesirable and unbecoming to the
holy Bishop, who forthwith wrote out with his own hand a
chartula of absolution and sent this to the Archdeacon ordain-
ing that, whatever might be the reason why the man wandered
from his grave, the tomb should be opened, and when the
chartula of absolution had been laid upon the breast of the
corpse, all should be once again fastened up as before.   Therefore they opened the tomb, and the body was found therein
uncorrupt, just as it had been laid upon the day of his burial.
The chartula of episcopal absolution was placed upon his

breast, and after the grave had again been fast closed, the dead man never wandered abroad, nor had he the power to injure or frighten anybody from that very hour.

Chapter xxiii. *Concerning a similar occurrence which happened at Berwick.* It has come to our knowledge that about the same time a similar and no less great wonder took place in the extreme north of England. There is a fine and flourishing town at the mouth of the river Tweed, called Berwick, which comes under the jurisdiction of the King of Scotland. Here then there dwelt a certain man who was indeed surpassing rich in this world's goods, but, as later only too clearly came to light, a most infamous villain. Now, after he was buried, at night he used by the power of Satan, as we may very well believe, continually to issue forth from his grave, and to rush up and down the streets of the town, whilst the dogs howled and bayed in every direction what time this evil thing was abroad. Any citizen who chanced to meet him was distraught with terror, and then just before daybreak he returned to his grave. When this had been going on for some little time nobody dared to step outside his door after nightfall, so terribly did they all dread to meet this fatal monster. Accordingly the authorities, as well as men of poor estate, earnestly discussed what steps had best be taken to rid themselves of so sore a visitation, for even the most thoughtless and irresponsible of them were extremely apprehensive lest, if by some unlucky chance they met this living corpse, they would be fearfully assaulted and injured by the dead man ; whilst those who were more sagacious and far-sighted were afraid lest, unless some speedy remedy were found, owing to the fact that black decomposition of this foul body horribly infected the air with poisonous pollution as it rushed to and fro, the plague or another fatal disease might break out and sweep away many, a disaster which had not infrequently been known to happen in circumstances similar to this. Accordingly they chose them ten young men of singular bravery and strength and bade them exhume this accursed corpse. It was then to be hewn member from member and cut into small pieces, and thrown into a blazing furnace so that it might be entirely burned up and consumed. When this had been done the prevailing panic was calmed, " and the slaughter ceased " (*Psalm* cv. 30). For the monster, while he was roving abroad by the power of

Satan as we have explained, is said to have announced to certain persons whom he encountered that the people should have no rest until his body were consumed to ashes. Therefore, when he had been burned it seemed in truth as though the people had a certain period of rest, but there very shortly broke out a terrible pestilence which carried off the greater part of that town. And nowhere else did the plague rage so fiercely, although, certes about the same time there was an epidemic in several districts of England.

Chapter xxiv. *Concerning certain marvellous events.* It is, I am very well aware, quite true that unless they were amply supported by many examples which have taken place in our own days, and by the unimpeachable testimony of responsible persons, these facts would not easily be believed, to wit, that the bodies of the dead may arise from their tombs and that vitalized by some supernatural power, they speed hither and thither, either greatly alarming or in some cases actually slaying the living, and when they return to the grave it seems to open to them of its own accord. It does not appear that any similar occurrences took place in ancient times, since nothing of the sort is found in old histories, and we know that those writers were always eager to include in their chapters any extraordinary or wonderful event. For we cannot suppose that, inasmuch as they never hesitated to discourse at length about any unusual happening, if circumstances such as these, which are not only most horrible but also most surprising, had taken place in their days they would have been able to refrain from treating them in detail. And yet if I were to set down all the stories of this kind which, as I have ascertained, have taken place in our day, my chronicle would not be merely extremely prolific and diffuse but, I suspect, it would become not a little wearisome to read. Accordingly, in addition to those I have mentioned above, I will only give examples of two quite recent such occurrences, and since the opportunity offers, it will, I make no doubt, be profitable to relate these in the course of our history, for they may well serve as a timely warning to my readers.

Some years ago there died the chaplain of a certain lady of high rank, and he was buried in that stately and magnificent monastery, the Abbey of Melrose.[8] Unfortunately, this priest little respected the sacred vows of his holy order and he passed his days almost as if he were a layman. In particular was he devoted to that idle sport than which scarcely any vanity so cheapens the character and harms the reputation of a priest, whose business it is to minister the Holy Sacrament of the Church, to wit, hunting with horse and hounds, for which he was so notorious that by many he was mockingly nicknamed Hundeprest, that is Dog Priest.[9] And it is quite plain from what happened after his death that he was commonly held in very light esteem, and his guilt was most censurable, nay, even heinous. For several nights he made his way out of his grave and endeavoured to force an entrance into the cloister itself, but herein he failed and he was unable either to injure or even to alarm anybody at all, so great were the merits and the holiness of the good monks who lived there. After that he proceeded to wander further abroad, and suddenly he appeared in the chamber at the very bedside of the lady whose chaplain he had been and uttered the most piercing shrieks and heart-rending groans. When this had taken place more than once, she was almost distraught with fear, dreading that some terrible danger might happen to her, and summoning a senior of the brethren from the monastery she besought him with tears that they should offer special prayers on her behalf since she was tormented in a most extraordinary and unusual manner. When he had heard her story the monk calmed her anxiety, for by her frequent benefactions and charities she had deserved well of Melrose and of all the brethren, and sympathizing with her in her misfortune, he promised that before long a remedy should be found. As soon as he had returned to the monastery he divulged his plan to a prudent and wise monk, and they decided that in company with two stout and brave-hearted young men, they would watch all night in that part of the graveyard where the unhappy priest had been buried. These four, therefore, well armed with spiritual as well as with earthly weapons and secured by their companionship, proceeded to pass the whole night on the spot. Twelve o'clock had already struck, and yet there was no sign of this monster. Accordingly, three of the company withdrew for a while that they might warm themselves by the fire in a lodge near at hand, for the night air nipped sharp and bitter cold, yet the monk who had requested the others to join him resolved not to relinquish his vigil. Now when he was left alone in this place, the Devil, thinking that he had found a fine opportunity to break down the pious man's courage and constancy, aroused from his grave that instrument of his which apparently he had for once allowed to slumber a longer time than usual. When the monk saw the monster close at hand realizing that he was all alone, he felt a thrill of horror ; but in a moment his courage returned. He had no thought of flight, and as the horrible creature rushed at him with the most hideous yell, he firmly stood his ground, dealing it a terrific blow with a battle-axe which he held in his hand. When the dead man received this wound he groaned aloud with a terrible hollow noise, and swiftly turning he fled away no less quickly than he had appeared. But this brave monk followed hard on his heels as he escaped, and compelled him to seek refuge in his grave. This seemed promptly to open to him of its own accord, and when it had sheltered its inmate from his pursuer, it quickly closed over him, the ground appearing undisturbed. Whilst this was going on the three who, shivering from the chill and damps of night, had gone off to warm themselves at the fireside, came running up, a few moments too late, however to see what had taken place. However, when they heard the whole story, they at once decided that at the first break of day they must disinter this accursed corpse and no longer suffer it to remain buried in their churchyard. When they had cleared away the earth and brought the corpse to light they found it marked by a terrible wound, whilst the black blood that had flowed from this seemed to swamp the whole tomb. The carrion, therefore, was carried to a remote place outside the bounds of the monastery, where it was burned in a huge fire and the ashes scattered to the winds. I have related this story quite simply and in a straightforward manner just as it was told to me by the monks themselves.

Another history of the same kind but even more terrible and more fatal, happened in connexion with Alnwick Castle, and this I learned from a very devout old priest of high authority and most honourable reputation, who dwelt in that district, and who informed me that he had actually been a witness of these terrible happenings. A certain man of depraved and dishonest life, either through fear of the law, or else shunning the vengeance of his enemies, left the county of Yorkshire, where he was living and betaking himself to the said castle, whose lord he had long known, settled down there. Here he busied himself in lewd traffic, and he seemed rather to persevere in his wickedness than to endeavour to correct his ways. He married a wife and this soothly proved his bane, as afterwards was clearly shown. For on a day when wanton stories were whispered in his ear concerning his spouse, he was fired with a raging jealousy. Restless and full of anxiety to know whether the charges were true, he pretended that he was going on a long journey and would not return for several days. He stole back, however, that very evening, and was secretly admitted into his wife's bedchamber by a serving wench who was privy to his design. Here he crept quietly up and lay at length upon the roof-trig which ran just over the bed, so that he might see with his own eyes if she violated her nuptial faith. Now when he espied there beneath him his wife being well served by a lusty youth, a near neighbour, in his bitter wrath he clean forgot his perilous position, and in a trice he had tumbled down, falling heavily to the ground just at the side of the bed where the twain were clipping at clicket. The young cuckold-maker beat a hasty retreat ; but his wife, very cunningly concealing her avouterie, hastened to raise him gently from the floor. Anon he comes to himself, and rails at her as a common whore, threatening a speedy punishment. " Ah, my dear," replied the lady, " sign yourself, I pray you, for you are talking wildly ; you rail, and yet this is the result of your lusts, no doubt, for you know not what you say."

Now he was indeed exceedingly shaken from the fall, and being sore bruised and most painfully benumbed over his whole body he became exceedingly ill. The good priest who related this story to me, visited him out of charity and for duty's sake, warning him that he should make a full confession of all his sins, and receive the Blessed Sacrament as Christians use. But he, in answer, related what had happened to him, together with the crafty words of his wife, and he put off fulfilling the timely and pious admonition until the morrow, but on the morrow he was dead. For during that very night this wretched man, who was so great a stranger to God's grace and whose crimes were so many, sank into the sleep of death. And yet, all unworthy as he was, they gave him a Christian burial, which he did not deserve and which profited him nothing. For by the power of Satan in the dark hours he was wont to come forth from his tomb and to wander about all through the streets, prowling round the houses, whilst on every side the dogs were howling and yelping the whole night long. Throughout the whole district then every man locked and barred his door, nor did anyone between the hours of dusk and dawn dare to go out an any business whatsoever, so greatly did each one fear that he might haply meet this fell monster and be attacked and most grievously harmed. Yet even these precautions were of no avail. For the air became foul and tainted as this fetid and corrupting body wandered abroad, so that a terrible plague broke out and there was hardly a house which did not mourn its dead, and presently the town, which but a little while before had been thickly populated, seemed to be well-nigh deserted, for those who had survived the pestilence and these hideous attacks hastily removed themselves to other districts lest they also should perish. The parish priest, the good man from whose mouth I learned this story, was grieved to the heart at this trouble which had fallen upon his flock and at the desolation of his cure. Accordingly upon Palm Sunday he called together a number of wise and devout men who might advise him what was the best course to take in such perilous circumstances, and who might at least console the few wretched souls yet remaining, even if it were with no very high hopes of affording them relief. The ceremonies of the day, therefore, were carried out with especial solemnity, and after he had made a sermon to the people, the good priest invited to his table the devout religious whom he had summoned, together with a number of leading citizens and other honourable men. Whilst they were sat at meat, two young men, brothers, who had lost their father in the recent pestilence, reasoned with one another, thus : " This monster hath slain our father, and if we do not look about he will before long slay us too. Let us, therefore, dare a bold deed which will both provide for our own safety and also avenge the murder of our dear father. There is no one to hinder us, for the chief men of the district are set at meat in the presbytery, and throughout the whole town there is a silence as if it were altogether forsaken and dead. Let us, therefore, exhume this foul pest and let us burn him to ashes with fire." They armed themselves, therefore with sharp spades and betaking themselves to the cemetery, they began to dig. And whilst they yet thought they would have to dig much deeper, suddenly they came upon the body, covered with but a thin layer of earth. It was gorged and swollen with a frightful corpulence, and its face was florrid and chubby, with huge, red puffed cheeks, and the shroud in which he had been wrapped was all soiled and torn. But the young men, who were mad with grief and anger, were not in any way frightened. They at once dealt the corpse a sharp blow with the keen edge of a spade, and immediately there gushed out such a stream of warm red gore that they realized this vampire (*sanguisuga*) had battened in the blood of many poor folk. Accordingly they dragged it outside the town, and here they quickly built a large pyre. When this was in a blaze, they went to the priest's house and informed the assembled company what they had done. There was not a man of these who did not hasten to the spot, and who was not a witness, if future testimony were required, of what had taken place. Now, no sooner had that infernal monster been thus destroyed than the plague, which had so sorely ravaged the people, entirely ceased, just as if the polluted air was cleansed by the fire which burned up the hellish brute who had infected the whole atmosphere.

It will be remarked that in these accounts of the twelfth century the details are in almost every particular similar to those of the Slav and modern Greek histories of vampires. they are in some ways even more terrible, for when a Vampire revisits some unfortunate town or district his ravages are, owing to the appalling fetor of the corpse, in every case apparently followed by an outbreak of the plague.

In that curious but fascinating work, which breathes the very spirit of the Middle Ages, the *De Nugis Curialium* of that even yet more curious person, Walter Map, there are several accounts of Vampires, and this further goes to prove that the tradition was very strong in England about this time. Dr. James places the date of composition of this extraordinary treatise in the years 1181 to 1192 or 1193. Map is now conjectured to have been born in the neighbourhood of Hereford about 1140. His parents were of gentle blood, and they were able to render to King Henry II, both before and after his coronation, such services as ensured that monarch's high regard for their son. He became one of the clerks of the royal household, and obtained considerable ecclesiastical preferment. He was both canon and precentor of Lincoln ; rector of Westbury upon Severn ; prebendary of Mapesbury ; and in later life (1197) Archdeacon of Oxford. In 1199 we find him in France seeking, but in vain, to obtain the Bishopric of Hereford. He seems to have died between 1208 and 1210. That much of the Goliardic Latin satire should have been ascribed to Map is hardly to be wondered at considering his bitter, and one might truly say profane, attacks upon the Cistercians when he does not even spare S. Bernard. This is a serious blemish and something more than a blemish upon his work. The *De Nugis Curialium* (Courtiers' Trifles) is a book of gossip, anecdote, and observation which seems to be put together without any plan or order. It has been said, and probably with some truth, " *Courtiers' Trifles*, all men agree, consists of fragments really written (' by snatches ') by Map, but collected and arranged after his death with little regard to chronology or coherence."[10] Whatever its faults, this book shows that Map was an excellent story-teller, and in the scraps which he has collected, from history, from tradition, from literature, he certainly presents us with a wonderful tapestry of his age woven from the life. " Bardoux has observed very happily that this little collection of tales is not framed in the bright sunlight of the hillside of Fiesole, but belongs, rather, to the dark rooms of a Norman castle, or to the narrow cell of the monk, with the rain and the wind noisy without—but, if these stories lack warmth and colour, they may boast a dramatic fitness and energy."

Map has certainly preserved many curious traditions, and it will seem as though they often have a very sure foundation in fact. Thus Edric Wilde, lord of the manor of North Ledbury, in the reign of Willliam the Conqueror, when one night near a remote and deserted inn (*ghildhus*), peeped through a window and observing a company of many beautiful women, remembers that he has often heard stories of " the wanderings of spirits and how troops of demons appear at night, and to see them is death, and Dictinna (who is identified with Diana) and bands of Dryads and Vampires."[11] It may be remembered that an old decree which was adopted by the canonists such as Regino of Prüm, Ivo of Chartres, Gratian and others spoke of " some wicked women, wholly given over to Satan and caught by the illusions and glamours of demons, believe and profess that they ride abroad at night with Diana on certain feasts, accompanied by an innumerable host of women, passing over immense distances, obeying her commands as their mistress, and evoked by her upon certain nights."

Map also mentions the story of the knight whose wife died and was buried, but he won her back to life again by snatching her from a troop of fairy dancers. After her return she bore him many children. Their posterity survives until this very day, and vast numbers belong to this family who, therefore, are called " Sons of the dead woman."[12]

In the fourteenth chapter of his Second Division, Map tells a strange history of a Vampire-demon. A certain knight who had married a lady of quality, a devout and religious woman, with whom he lived in the utmost happiness, found on the morning after its birth, that his first child, a son, had its throat cut from ear to ear as it lay in the cradle. The same thing happened twelve months later with his second child, and also with his third child in the third year, in spite of the fact that both he himself and his household watched most carefully, for all their diligence proved most lamentably futile. Therefore, when his lady was again pregnant, both he and she spent much time in fasting and in bestowing alms, in prayer and supplication with many tears, and when a fourth boy was born to them they illuminated the whole house and the vicinity with fires, lamps, torches, and and all kept their eyes fast upon the child. Just then there arrived a stranger, who seemed very weary and footsore, as if from a long journey. He sought hospitality in God's name, and was most kindly and religiously welcomed. He determined that he would watch all night with them, and indeed after midnight, when all fell into a most mysterious sleep, he was the only one who was able to keep awake. He suddenly saw bending over the cradle the form of a most worthy and honourable matron, who was seizing the child to cut its throat. He sprang up, wakeful and alert and caught her fast in his grasp until, when all the household had been aroused and gathered round she was recognized at once by many of them, and indeed before long by all, for they declared that she was the noblest of the most respected matrons of that great city, not only by her birth, but by her splendid way of living, as well as owing to her great wealth, and that she enjoyed a high repute and was universally held in the greatest esteem. But when asked her name, and when various other questions were put to her, she obstinately refused to speak. The knight himself, and many others, thought that she remained silent owing to shame at having been detected and they were something minded to let her go. But the stranger refused to give way, for he declared that she was a demon and he continued to hold her tightly in his grasp, whilst with one of the keys of the nearest church he branded her in the face as an open sign of her wickedness. Then he requested them to bring thither as soon as might be the lady whom all thought this creature to be. And whilst he was yet detaining his captive the lady advanced and was seen to resemble her double in every way, even to the mark where she had been branded. Thereupon the stranger addressed them thus as they stood dazed and foolishly lost in astonishment: "There can be no doubt that the lady who has now come is very virtuous and very dear to heaven, and that by her good works she has stirred hell and provoked the anger of devils against her, and so this evil messenger of theirs, this loathsome instrument of their wrath has been fashioned as far as possible in the likeness of this noble lady, that this demon may cause this noble soul to be accused of the guilt of her heinous deeds. And in order that you may believe, see what she will do after I release her." Then the creature flew away through the window howling aloud and screeching terribly. We here have a case of impersonation by a fiend of vampirish qualities, and writers such as Guazzo, Nider, Basin, and the authors of the *Malleus Maleficarum* have discussed this very point, whether it is not possible for demons to assume the form of some noble or saintly person, so that he may be involved in a charge of witchcraft or smirched by some disgraceful scandal.

Fathers Kramer and Sprenger have the following very striking example (*Malleus Maleficarum*, Part II, Question I, XI : " The injury to reputation is shown in the history of the Blessed Jerome, that the devil transformed himself into the appearance of S. Silvanus, Bishop of Nazareth, a friend of S. Jerome. And this devil approached a noble woman by night in her bed and began first to provoke and entice her with lewd words, and then invited her to perform the sinful act. And when she called out, the devil in the form of the saintly

Bishop hid under the woman's bed, and being sought for and found there, he in lickerish language, declared lyingly that he was the Bishop of Silvanus. On the morrow, therefore, when the devil had disappeared, the holy man was heavily defamed; but his good name was cleared when the devil confessed at the tomb of S. Jerome that he had done this in an assumed body."

It does not appear from the history related by Map, who was the stranger by whom the illusion was detected. We may suppose that he was an Angel or a Saint, or if on the other hand he was an ordinary traveller who happened to pass that way, the reason why he was able to keep awake lay in the fact that the household had been cast under a spell to fall asleep at a given time, but as the charm had been confected before his arrival, he was able to remain awake since it was not directed at him.[13] Gervase of Tilbury,[14] in the account he gives of lamias, actually says that they are so called because they lacerate children, " lamiae uel laniae, quia laniant infantes."

Walter Map has other narratives which more nearly resemble the Vampire stories or William of Newburgh, and which show that the idea of a re-vitalized dead man returning to molest the living was regarded as a distinct possibility and a lively danger. In his Second Division, chapter xxvii, he says: The most wonderful thing that I know of happened in Wales. William Laudun, an English soldier, a man of great strength and proven courage, went to Gilbert Foliot,[15] who was at that time Bishop of Hereford, but is now Bishop of London, and said to him, " My lord, I come to thee to ask for counsel. A certain Welsh malefactor recently died in my house, a man who professed to believe in nothing, and after an interval of four nights he has returned each night and has not failed on each occasion to summon forth severally and by name one of his fellow lodgers. As soon as they are called by him they sicken and within three days they die, so that now but a few are left." The Bishop, who was greatly amazed, answered : " Perhaps power hath been given by the Lord to the evil angel of that accursed wretch so that he is able to rouse himself and walk abroad in his dead body. However, let the corpse be exhumed, and then do you cut through its neck sprinkling both the body and the grave throughout with holy water, and so rebury it." This was accordingly done, but none the less the survivors were tormented and attacked by the wandering spirit. Now it happened that on a certain night when only very few were left William himself was called three times by name. But he being bold and active and knowing who it was suddenly rushed out, brandishing his drawn sword. The demon fled fast but he pursued it to the very grave, and as it lay therein he clave its head clean through from the neck. At that very hour, the persecution they endured from this demoniacal wanderer ceased, and since that time neither William himself nor any one of the others has suffered any harm therefrom. We know that this thing is true, but the cause of the haunting remains unexplained.

Chapter xxviii continues : *Another Marvel.* We also know that in the time of Roger, Bishop of Worcester,[16] a certain man who, as it was commonly bruited, died an atheist in his sins, wandered about and was encountered by many who saw him, dressed in a hair-shirt, until he was surrounded in an orchard by all the people of that neighbourhood. And it is stated that he was seen there for three days. We know, moreover, that this same Bishop Roger ordered that a cross should be erected over the grave of the unhappy wretch and that the spirit should be laid. But when the demon had come to the grave, and a great crowd of people followed him, he leaped back in alarm—as we think, at the sight of the cross—and he fled elsewhere. Then the people, acting upon wise advice, removed the cross, and the demon rushed into the grave covering himself with earth, and immediately after the cross was raised upon it again so that he has lain there without causing any disturbance.

In his Fourth Division, No. XII, William Map narrates the well-known story *De sutore Constantinopolitano fantastico,* which may be rendered as " Of an Enchanted Shoemaker of Constantinople," and which certainly claims some connexion with the Vampire tradition. The fable has, indeed, been called a " Monstrous instance of necrophilia." There was no more famous tale in its day ; it is found in the *Otia Imperialia* of Gervase of Tilbury, II, 12, where it is referred to the Gulf of Satalia. It is chronicled by Roger of Hovedon, III, 158 (709, ed. Sevile), an author who derived it from the *Gesta Regis Henrici,* II, 196 ; and it is also told by John Brompton (col. 1216), and by Sir John Mandeville, c. IV. It enters into the Merlin Saga,[17] but it may be remarked that only in Map is the hero a *sutor.*

Map relates that there dwelt at Constantinople a young shoemaker, " about the time when Gerbert was flouringing in fairy
felicity." (*Circiter idem tempus quo Gerbertus fantastica felici-
tate floruerat.* Gerbert was the name of Pope Sylvester II,
who reigned 999-1003, and around whom, owing to his extraordinary learning the most ridiculous legends grew up, reputing
that he possessed occult powers and could work many a magic
feat.) This young shoemaker excelled both in art and in
industry even the masters of his craft, and not only was he able
to do more in one day than all the others could perform in two,
but the results of his haste were infinitely to be preferred to
the results of their study and care. It may be borne in mind
what an elaborate and important article of dress the shoe was
at this time, and how it was often wrought in the most fantastic
devices, a custom which long prevailed, if indeed it can ever
be truly said wholly to have gone out from among us. Dufour,
Histoire de la Prostitution, VI, p. 11, notes : " In the tenth
century shoes *à la poulaine*, with a claw or beak, pursued for
more than four centuries by the anathemas of popes and the
invectives of preachers, were always regarded by mediæval
casuists as the most abominable emblems of immodesty. At
the first glance it is not easy to see why these shoes—terminating in a lion's claw, an eagle's beak, the prow of a ship, or other
metal appendage—should be so scandalous. The excommunication inflicted on this kind of footgear preceded the impudent
invention of some libertine, who wore *poulaines* in the shape
of the phallus, a custom adopted also by women. · This kind
of *poulaine* was denounced as *maudite de Dieu* (Ducange's
Glossary, at the word Poulainia) and prohibited by royal
ordinances (see letter of Charles V, 17th October, 1367,
regarding the garments of the women of Montpellier)."
Chaucer's gay and jolly Absolon had " Powles window corven
on his shoos,"[18] and similar ornature did the young craftsman
fashion for the nobles of Constantinople. Indeed he would no
longer make for any who were not of the highest quality. So
skilful was he that without the measure of his last he could
make a shoe for any bare foot, lame or straight, merely by
glancing at it. Gold in abundance poured to his coffers, and
as he was both a stalwart fellow and handsome, for there was
nobody who could excel him in all the exercises of the arena, in
wrestling and every kind of sport, he was everywhere applauded

as a champion. Now it so happened that one day there came
to his window a very lovely maiden accompanied by a large
retinue, and she, showing him her naked foot, desired him to
fit her with a pair of shoes, and in Rome, it will be remembered
as Dufour says *Histoire de la Prostitution*, II, xviii, "Nudity
of the foot in a woman was a sign of prostitution, and the
brilliant whiteness acted afar as a pimp to attract looks and
desires." But the young man was already entranced with her
beauty, he gazed upon this sight with wide-open eyes, and
after making and selling the shoes, beginning from the foot, he
absorbed the whole woman in his heart,[19] and deep drank in
the deadly evil by which he was utterly lost. A mere serving
man, he sought for dainties from the king's table, and what
ground had he for hope ? In his madness he abandoned his
house, he sold his goods and chattels, yea, even his patrimony,
and he became a soldier so that by the following of arms he
might arise from his lowly condition to the rank of a noble, and
when he sought the lady's hand, if repulsed, he would be at any
rate refused in more courteous phrase. Before he could dare
to unfold his love to his mistress he was determined to make a
name for himself in the field, and indeed through his strength
and valour he soon won that eminence among the chivalry of
knights that he had erstwhile held among the cobblers of the
city. Accordingly he sought the alliance for which he yearned,
and though in truth he deemed himself full worthy he did not
win from her father the lady of his longing. He now blazed
forth into the greatest fury, and he desired nothing so much as
to carry off by force the bride who was refused to him on
account of his lowly birth and poor estate. He joined the
ranks of a mighty squadron of pirates, and so he prepared to
revenge by sea the repulse he had received on land. Before
long he rose to be their general, and he was verily feared both
by land and sea, for success always attended him. Whilst he
was engaged on one of these bloody forays and laying low every
obstacle in his path, news reached him that his lady was dead.
With bitter tears he at once concluded a truce and hastened to
be present at the solemnity of her obsequies. Having assisted
at the funeral, he carefully noted the place where she was
buried, and upon the next night, resorting thither all alone,
he exhumed the dead woman and lay with her, knowing her
just as if she were alive in his embraces. When this dreadful

fornication was over and he rose from the corpse, he heard a
voice bidding him return at the time when she could bring
forth and bear away with him what he had begotten. After
the fitting interval he came back, dug up the grave and received
from the dead woman a human head with the warning that he
must not allow anybody to see it except those of his enemies
whom he wished to destroy. When he had carefully wrapped
this up he placed it deep in a box, and having complete confidence in his power he gave up fighting at sea, and determined
to do battle on the land. To whatsoever cities or towns he laid
siege he displayed this terrible sight of the Gorgon, whereupon
the miserable victims turned to stone since they beheld a horror
as loathly as that of Medusa herself. He was feared by all, and
recognized by all as their lord and master, for men trembled
lest he should cause them to perish suddenly. Nobody, indeed,
understood the cause of this foul plague and instant death. In
one and the same moment they saw and they expired without
a word, without a groan; on the battlements armed men passed
away without receiving any wound. Fortified places, cities,
whole provinces yielded to him, nobody dared to resist ; but
yet everyone was sorely grieved at falling so easily a victim to
so cheap a triumph. Many men thought him to be a sorcerer,
some declared that he was a god ; but whatsoever he sought,
he never met with a refusal.

Among his successes there was one which was certainly
the greatest of them all. Upon the death of the Emperor
of Constantinople this monarch's daughter and heiress was
bequeathed to him. He accepted the legacy ; and who indeed
would have refused such a gift ? After a little while, when she
was conversing with him one day the lady began to question
him concerning the box, and allowed him no rest until she had
learned the whole truth. When she had heard the story, she
resolved to catch him in his own trap, and just as he was waking
from sleep she held the horrible head before his face. Then,
having avenged so many crimes, the princess gave orders that
this Medusa horror should be carried out of the country and
thrown into the midst of the Grecian Sea, together with the
father of this abominable foetus who should share in its utter
destruction. Those who were charged with this business
hastened forth in a galley, and when they had reached the midst
of the ocean they cast the two loathsome creatures into the

depths. As the monsters disappeared beneath the waves the
sea thrice boiled and bubbled, casting up its sandy floor, as
if the ocean had been wrenched and rent to its very depths and
the waters suddenly leaped back, shrinking from the wrath of the
Most High, and just as if the sea, sick with loathing, was trying
to reject what the sick land, recovering from this abominable
birth, vomited into the deep. The waves were raised to the
sky, and leaping forth like a fiery flame, they seemed to storm
the loftiest heights of the air. ["Wast thou angry, O Lord,
with the rivers ? or was Thy wrath upon the rivers ? or Thy
indignation in the sea ? " *Habacuc*, III, 8.] But after a few
days it appeared that the sentence upon these accursed things
was changed, and the waters which had smitten. the very
heaven now rushed downwards and in a mighty maelstrom tore
open a terrible pit. What had been a towering heap was now
an abyss, for the very mud of the depths, unable to bear such an
abomination of horror, was thrown forth, and fell backwards in
sad amaze, gaping with a mighty yawn, opening apart "into
the depths of the sea, in the lowest parts of the deep." (*Job*
xxxviii, 16.) Hence, like Charybdis under Messina, this
whirlpool swallows everything that is poured into its mighty
mouth, and whatsoever falleth therein by chance or is drawn
down by its greedy jaws is lost beyond all redemption. Now
the name of the maiden was Satalia, and so the whirlpool, which
is shunned by all, is called Satalie, or in the common tongue,
Gouffre de Satalie.

The troops of night-wanderers, commonly called Herlethingi
(phalanges noctiuage quas Herlethingi dicebant) who are
mentioned by Map,[20] seem to have been apparitions amongst
whom "there appeared alive many who were known to have
been long since dead," but it is not recorded that they exercised
any vampirish qualities. The account given is exceedingly
curious. "In Brittany there used to be seen at night long
trains of soldiers who passed by in dead silence conducting
carriages of booty, and from these the Breton peasants have
actually stolen away horses and cattle and kept them for their
own use. In some cases no harm seems to have resulted, but
in other instances this was speedily followed by sudden death.
Companies of these troops of night-wanderers, who are commonly called Herlethingi, were very well known in England
even to the present day, the reign of our King Henry II, who is

now ruling over us. These armies went to and fro without let or stay, hurrying hither and thither, rambling about in the most mad vagrancy, all inceding in unbroken silence, and amongst the band there appeared alive many who were known to have been long since dead. This company of Herlethingi was last espied in the Marches of Hereford and Wales in the first year of King Henry II, tramping along at high noon with carts and beasts of burden, with pack saddles and provender-baskets, with birds and dogs and a mixed multitude of men and women. Those who first caught sight of this troop by their shouting and blowing of horns and trumpets aroused the whole district, and as in the manner of those border folk, who are ever on the watch, almost instantly there assembled various bands fully equipped, and because they were unable to obtain a word in reply from this strange host they incontinently prepared to make them answer to a shower of darts and javelins, and then the troop seemed to mingle with the air and forthwith vanished away out of sight. From that day this mysterious company has never been seen by man." So far as I am aware, beyond the suggested connexion with the old story of King Herla, no actual explanation has been offered of this phantom army, but it may be observed that although such an occurrence in England is altogether exceptional it is not entirely unparalleled. Odericus Vitalis, *Ecclesiastical History*, VIII, c. 17, has a history of a priest named Walkelin, who, in January, 1091, saw, at Bonneval in the church of S. Aubri of Anjou, a company of Harlequin (*Herle-Kingi*), a black *cortège* with black horses and black banners, including people of all classes, ladies of quality, knights, ecclesiastics, and many of Walkelin's own former acquaintances and friends. Grimm, *Teutonic Mythology* (Stallybrass), pp, 741 *sqq.*, cites many appearance of these "shades of the dead," and notes that in Gervase of Tilbury's time (*Otia Imperialia*), II, 12) certain haunted woods in Britain rang with "King *Arthur's* mighty hunt."

As Dr. James remarks,[21] "Traces of acquaintance with the *de Nugis Curialium* in contemporary or later mediæval writers are exceedingly scanty" and "No English mediæval library catalogue contains an entry identifiable with the *de Nugis*." The single manuscript is preserved in the Bodleian Library, and here it was examined by Richard James, Camden, and

Archbishop Ussher. It is also mentioned in a letter of Sir Roger Twysden, between 1666 and 1669, which shows that some few scholars were interested in the work, for the writer remarks, "They say there is many stories of good work, fit to bee made publick, in it." But no attention at all was called to the accounts of phantasms and vampires. Indeed, after the twelfth century the vampire tradition seems to have entirely died out of England, and with the rarest exceptions not to have re-appeared until the nineteenth century when there was so marked a revival of interest in occultism. This is the more extraordinary since in all centuries of English history and in all parts of the country traditions of the supernatural are extremely common. It was, of course, generally accepted that witches could make their victims dwindle and pine, and there are many stories of malignant spectres who have power to harm and even to kill those whom they beset. But the tradition of the vampire is hardly to be met with in any quarter, and this fact is the more remarkable when we consider the histories of William of Newburgh and Walter Map and note thence how prominent was the belief in earlier times.

A curious case which was reported in the *Gentleman's Magazine*, July, 1851, belongs to the reign of King Charles I, but this concerns the old idea that a dead body if touched by the murderer will bleed, and cannot strictly be said to be pertinent to Vampirism. Lord Bacon, in his *Sylva*[22] writes : "It is an usual observation that if the body of one murdered be brought before the murderer, the wounds will bleed afresh. Some do affirm that the dead hath opened his eyes."[23] So in Shakespeare's *Richard III*, I, ii, when Gloucester interrupts the funeral, Lady Anne cries :

> O ! gentleman ; see, see ! dead Henry's wounds
> Open their congealed mouths and bleed afresh.
> Blush, blush, thou lump of foul deformity,
> For 'tis thy presence that exhales this blood
> From cold and empty veins, where no blood dwells :
> Thy deed, inhuman and unnatural,
> Provokes this deluge most unnatural.

In Chapman's *The Widow's Tears*, 4to, 1612, Act V, the First Soldier remarks : "The Captain will assay an old conclusion, often approved, that at the murtherer's sight the blood revives again, and boils afresh ; and every wound has a

condemning voice to cry out guilty 'gainst the murtherer."
Drayton in his *Idea, the Shepherd's Garland*,[24] has the following
stanza, xlvi :

> If the vile actors of the heinous deed
>   Near the dead body happily be brought,
> Oft 't hath been prov'd the breathless corpse will bleed.
>   She coming near that my poor heart hath slain,
> Long since departed, to the world no more,
>   The ancient wounds no longer can contain,
> But fall to bleeding as they did before.

King James I in his *Demonologie*, Edinburgh, 1597, has the
following reference to this belief : " As in a secret murder, if the
dead carcass be at any time thereafter handled by the murtherer
it will gush out of blood, as if the blood were crying to the
heaven for the revenge of the murtherer, God having appointed
that secret supernatural sign for trial of that secret unnatural
crime." The instance which occurred in the reign of King
Charles I is so extremely singular that being of no great length
it will, I think, bear quotation in full.

Singular instance of Superstition, A.D. 1629. The Case
or, rather, History of a Case that happened in the County of
Hereford in the fourth Year of the Reign of King Charles the
First, which was taken from a MS. of Serjeant Mainard,[25] who
writes thus :

" I write the evidence that was given, which I and many
others heard, and I write it exactly according to what was
deposed at the Trial at the Bar in the King's Bench. Johan
Norkot, the wife of Arthur Norkot, being murdered, the
question arose how she came by her death. The coroner's
inquest on view of the body and deposition of Mary Norkot,
John Okeman and Agnes, his wife, inclined to find Joan Norkot
felo de se : for they (i.e., the witnesses before mentioned)
informed the coroner and the jury that she was found dead in
the bed and her throat cut, the knife sticking in the floor of the
room ; that the night before she was so found she went to bed
with her child (now plaintiff in this appeal), her husband being
absent, and that no other person after such time as she was
gone to bed came into the house, the examinants lying in the
outer room, and they must needs have seen if any stranger had
come in. Whereupon the jury gave up to the coroner their
verdict that she was *felo de se*. But afterwards upon rumour

in the neighbourhood, and the observations of divers circumstances that manifested she did not, nor according to these circumstances, possibly could, murder herself, thereupon the jury, whose verdict was not drawn into form by the coroner, desired the coroner that the body which was buried might be taken out of the grave, which the coroner assented to, and thirty days after her death she was taken up, in the presence of the jury and a great number of people, whereupon the jury changed their verdict. The persons being tried at Hertford Assizes were acquitted, but so much against the evidence that the judge (Harvy) let fall his opinion that it were better an appeal were brought than so foul a murder should escape unpunished.

"*Anno, paschæ termino, quarto Caroli,* they were tried on the appeal which was brought by the young child against his father, the grandmother and aunt, and her husband Okeman. And because the evidence was so strange I took exact and particular notes of it, which was as followeth, of the matters above mentioned and related, an ancient and grave person, the minister of the parish where the fact was committed, being sworn to give evidence according to custom, deposed, that the body being taken out of the grave thirty days after the party's death and lying on the grave and the four defendants present, they were required each of them to touch the dead body. O's wife fell on her knees and prayed God to show token of their innocency, or to some such purpose, but her very words I forget. The appellers did touch the dead body, whereupon the brow of the dead, which was all a livid or carrion colour (that was the verbal expression in the terms of the witness) began to have a dew or gentle sweat, which reached down in drops upon the face, and the brow turned and changed to a lively and fresh colour, and the dead opened one of her eyes and shut it again, and this opening the eye was done three several times. She likewise thrust out the ring or marriage finger three times and pulled it in again, and the finger dropt blood from it on the grass.

" Hyde (Nicholas), Chief Justice, seeming to doubt the evidence, asked the witness : ' Who saw this beside yourself ? '

"Witness : ' I cannot swear that others saw it ; but my lord,' said he, ' I believe the whole company saw it, and if it had been thought a doubt, proof would have been made of it, and many would have attested with me.'

"Then the witness observing some admiration in the auditors, he spoke further, 'My Lord, I am minister of the parish, I long knew all the parties, but never had any occasion of displeasure against any of them, nor had to do with them, or they with me, but as their minister. The thing was wonderful to me, but I have no interest in the matter, but am called upon to testify the truth and that I have done.'

"This witness was a reverend person as I guess about seventy years of age. His testimony was delivered gravely and temperately, but to the good admiration of the auditor. Whereupon, applying himself to the Lord Chief Justice, he said, 'My lord, my brother here present is minister of the next parish adjacent, and I am assured saw all done as I have affirmed,' whereupon that person was also sworn to give evidence, viz., the sweat of the brow, the change of its colour, the opening of the eye, the thrice motion of the finger and drawing it in again ; only the first witness deposed that a man dipped his finger in the blood to examine it, and swore he believed that it was real blood. I conferred afterwards with Sir Edmund Vowel, Barister at law, and others who concurred in this observation, and for myself, if I were upon my oath, can depose that these depositions, especially of the first witness, are truly here reported in substance.

"The other evidence was given against the prisoners viz., against the grandmother of the plaintiff and against Okeman and his wife, that they lay in the next room to the dead person that night, and that none came into the house till they found her dead next morning, therefore if she did not murther herself, they must be the murtherers, and to that end further proof was made. First she lay in a composed manner in her bed, the bedcloaths nothing at all disturbed, and her child by her in the bed. Secondly, her throat was cut from ear to ear and her neck broken, and if she first cut her throat, she could not break her neck in the bed, nor e contra. Thirdly, there was no blood in the bed, save in that there was a tincture of blood upon the bolster whereupon her head lay, but no other substance of blood at all. Fourthly, from the bed's head on there was a stream of blood on the floor, till it ponded on the bending of the floor to a very great quantity and there was also another stream of blood on the floor at the bed's feet, which ponded also on the floor to another great quantity but no other communication of blood on either of these places the one from the other, neither upon the bed, so that she bled in two places severally, and it was deposed that turning up the matte of the bed, there were clotes of congealed blood in the straw of the matte underneath. Fifthly, the bloody knife in the morning was found clinging in the floor a good distance from the bed. But the point of the knife as it stuck in the floor was towards the bed and the halt towards the door. Sixthly, lastly, there was the brand of a thumb and fore-fingers of a left hand on the dead person's left hand.

"Hyde, Chief Justice : ' How can you know the print of a left hand from the print of a right hand in such a case ? '

"Witness : ' My lord, it is hard to describe it, but if it please the honourable judge (*i.e.* the judge sitting on the bench beside the Chief Justice) to put his left hand on your left hand, you cannot possibly place your right hand in the same posture.'

"It being done, and appearing so, the defendants had time to make their defence, but gave no evidence to that purpose.

"The jury departing from the bar and returning, acquitted Okeman, and found the other three guilty; who, being sever-ally demanded why judgement should not be pronounced, sayd nothing, but each of them said, ' I did not do it '; ' I did not do it.' Judgement was made and the grandmother and the husband executed, but the aunt had the privilege to be spared execution, being with child. I inquired if they confessed anything at execution, but they did not as I was told."

Thus far the sergeant, afterwards Sir John Mainard, a person of great note and judgement of the law. The paper, of which this is a copy, was found amongst his papers since his death (1690) fair written with his own hand. Mr. Hunt of the Temple took a copy of it, gave it me, which I have hereby transcribed.[26]

In 1847 was published *Varney the Vampire ; or, The Feast of Blood*, a very lengthy but well written and certainly exciting romance, which runs to no less than two hundred and twenty chapters, making a book of 868 pages. This was such an "unprecedented success," that it was reprinted in 1853 in penny parts by E. Lloyd, 12, Salisbury Square, Fleet Street, the famous purveyor of " shockers " and " dreadfuls." *Varney the Vampire* is one of the earliest works of Thomas Preskett Prest, one of the most prolific as he was one of the most admired authors of this school. Although the incidents crowd fast upon one another and, one and all, are of the most lurid description, the narrative is very far from being ill-managed, in fact it is told with a certain sombre power and forcefulness which claims our attention, whilst the connexion of this extremely lengthy romance is so adroitly managed that the interest never flags nor fails. Preskett Prest certainly knew his public and his works had an immense circulation. It is the more curious that to-day they are excessively rare and, no doubt, the author himself would be vastly surprised at the prices which are paid for fresh clean copies of his melodrames. He was careful to strike the right note in his very titles, for we have such ultra-transpontine nomenclature as *The Skeleton Clutch ; or, The Goblet of Gore ; Sawney Bean, the Man-Eater of Midlothian*, to which reference has already been made ;[27] *Angelina, or, The Mystery of S. Mark's Abbey*, 1841 ; *Blanche, or, The Mystery of the Doomed House*, 1843 ; *The Black Monk or, The Secret of the Grey Turret*, 1844 ; *The Death Grasp, or, The Father's Curse*, 1844 ; *The Maniac Father, or The Victim*, 1844 ; *The Blighted Heart, or, The Old Priory Ruins*, 1849; *The Miller and His Men, or, The Secret Robbers of Bohemia*, 1852 ; which latter is founded upon the play *The Miller and his Men*, by Isaac Pocock, first produced at Covent Garden on the 21st October, 1813, with Farley, Liston, Mrs. Egerton, and Miss Booth in the cast. The scene is laid on " the Banks of a River on the Borders of a Forest in Bohemia." This proved one of the most popular of sensational pieces, and may be said to have kept the stage until the beginning of the twentieth century. The greatest success of Preskett Prest was undoubtedly his immortal romance *Sweeney Todd, the Demon Barber of Fleet Street*. It was once supposed that Sweeney Todd actually lived, but this extraordinary figure is almost certainly due to our author's fertile imagination. Upon the stage Sweeney Todd has triumphantly endured until the present day, and many dramatists have fitted his adventures for the boards whereon they have never failed to win singularly good applause.

The date of the story of *Varney the Vampire* is about 1730, and Prest definitely states that his romance is founded upon incidents which were alleged to have taken place in England in the last years of the reign of Queen Anne. No such

record has been traced, but if the statement be correct it is
exceedingly interesting to find a case of vampirism in England
at this date where the tradition had almost, if not entirely,
died out, although it may be remarked that it was about this
time that a great deal of notice was being attracted by the
extraordinary events reported from Hungary and Serbia. It
is quite possible, of course, that Prest threw out these suggestions to give his work an extra spice, but, however that may
be, he has certainly studied the Vampire legends and traditions
with some care, and he introduces into his chapters several
telling touches which can be authenticated by parallel circumstances in vampire legends, and these by no means the best
known or the most easily accessible. For all his lurid color-
atura he has made definite researches into authentic and rare
material.

Varney the Vampire is an extraordinarily scarce book, and
it may not be impertinent therefore to give the first chapter
at length both as a specimen of Prest's work and as no mean
description of a Vampire.

> ". . . ' How graves give up their dead,
> And how the night air hideous grows
> With shrieks ! '

"MIDNIGHT.—THE HAIL STORM.—THE DREADFUL VISITOR.

THE VAMPYRE.

"THE solemn tones of the old cathedral clock have announced
midnight—the air is thick and heavy—a strange, death-like
stillness pervades all nature. Like the ominous calm which
precedes some more than usually terrific outbreak of the
elements, they seem to have paused even in their ordinary
fluctuations, to gather a terrific strength for the great effort.
A faint peal of thunder now comes from far off. Like a signal
gun for the battle of the winds to begin, it appeared to awaken
them from their lethargy, and one awful, warring hurricane
swept over a whole city, producing more devastation in the
four or five minutes it lasted, than would a half century of
ordinary phenomena.

" It was as if some giant had blown upon some toy town,
and scattered many of the buildings before the hot blast of his

terrific breath ; for as suddenly as that blast of wind had come did it cease, and all was as still and calm as before.

"Sleepers awakened, and thought what they had heard must be the confused chimera of a dream. They trembled and turned to sleep again.

"All is still—still as the very grave. Not a sound breaks the magic of repose. What is that—a strange pattering noise, as of a million of fairy feet ? It is hail—yes, a hailstorm has burst over the city. Leaves are dashed from the trees, mingled with small boughs ; windows that lie most opposed to the direct fury of the pelting particles of ice are broken, and the rapt repose that before was so remarkable in its intensity, is exchanged for a noise which, in its accumulation, drowns every cry of surprise or consternation which here and there arose from persons who found their houses invaded by the storm.

"Now and then, too, there would come a sudden gust of wind that in its strength, as it blew laterally, would, for a moment, hold millions of the hailstones suspended in mid air, but it was only to dash them with redoubled force in some new direction, where more mischief was to be done.

"Oh, how the storm raged ! Hail—rain—wind. It was, in very truth, an awful night.

*　　*　　*　　*　　*

"There is an antique chamber in an ancient house. Curious and quaint carvings adorn the walls, and the large chimney-piece is a curiosity of itself. The ceiling is low, and a large bay window, from roof to floor, looks to the west. The window is latticed, and filled with curiously painted glass and rich stained pieces, which send in a strange, yet beautiful light, when sun or moon shines into the apartment. There is but one portrait in that room, although the walls seem panelled for the express purpose of containing a series of pictures. The portrait is that of a young man, with a pale face, a stately brow, and a strange expression about the eyes, which no one cared to look on twice.

"There is a stately bed in that chamber, of carved walnut-wood is it made, rich in design and elaborate in execution ; one of those works of art which owe their existence to the Elizabethan era. It is hung with heavy silken and damask furnishing ; nodding feathers are at its corners—covered with dust are they, and they lend a funereal aspect to the room. The floor is of polished oak.

"God! how the hail dashes on the old bay window! Like an occasional discharge of mimic musketry, it comes dashing, beating, and cracking upon the small panes; but they resist it—their small size saves them: the wind, the hail, the rain, expend their fury in vain.

"The bed in that old chamber is occupied. A creature formed in all fashions of loveliness lies in a half sleep upon that ancient couch—a girl young and beautiful as a spring morning. Her long hair has escaped from its confinement and streams over the blackened coverings of the bedstead; she has been restless in her sleep, for the clothing of the bed is in much confusion. One arm is over her head, the other hangs nearly off the side of the bed near to which she lies. A neck and bosom that would have formed a study for the rarest sculptor that ever Providence gave genius to, were half disclosed. She moaned slightly in her sleep, and once or twice the lips moved as if in prayer—at least one might judge so, for the name of Him who suffered for all came once faintly from them.

"She has endured much fatigue, and the storm does not awaken her; but it can disturb the slumbers it does not possess the power to destroy entirely. The turmoil of the elements wakes the senses, although it cannot entirely break the repose they have lapsed into.

"Oh, what a world of witchery was in that mouth, slightly parted, and exhibiting within the pearly teeth that glistened even in the faint light that came from that bay window. How sweetly the long silken eyelashes lay upon the cheek. Now she moves, and one shoulder is entirely visible—whiter, fairer than the spotless clothing of the bed on which she lies, is the smooth skin of that fair creature, just budding into womanhood, and in that transition state which present to us all the charms of the girl—almost of the child, with the more matured beauty and gentleness of advancing years.

"Was that lightning? Yes—an awful vivid, terrifying flash—then a roaring peal of thunder, as if a thousand mountains were rolling one over the other in the blue vault of Heaven! Who sleeps now in that ancient city? Not one living soul. The dread trumpet of eternity could not more effectually have awakened any one.

" The hail continues. The wind continues. The uproar of the elements seems at its height. Now she awakens—that beautiful girl on the antique bed ; she opens those eyes of celestial blue, and a faint cry of alarm bursts from her lips. At least it is a cry which, amid the noise and turmoil without, sounds but faint and weak. She sits upon the bed and presses her hands upon her eyes. Heavens ! what a wild torrent of wind and rain, and hail ! The thunder likewise seems intent upon awakening sufficient echoes to last until the next flash of forked lightning should again produce the wild concussion of the air. She murmurs a prayer—a prayer for those she loves best ; the names of those dear to her gentle heart come from her lips ; she weeps and prays ; she thinks then of what devastation the storm must surely produce, and to the great God of Heaven she prays for all living things. Another flash, —a wild, blue, bewildering flash of lightning streams across that bay window, for an instant bringing out every colour in it with terrible distinctness. A shriek bursts from the lips of the young girl, and then, with eyes fixed upon that window, which, in another moment, is all darkness, and with such an expression of terror upon her face as it had never before known, she trembled, and the perspiration of intense fear stood upon her brow.

" 'What—what was it ? ' she gasped ; ' real, or a delusion ? Oh, God, what was it ? A figure tall and gaunt, endeavouring from the outside to unclasp the window. I saw it. That flash of lightning revealed it to me. It stood the whole length of the window.'

" There was a lull of the wind. The hail was not falling so thickly—moreover, it now fell, what there was of it, straight, and yet a strange clattering sound came upon the glass of that long window. It could not be a delusion—she is awake, and she hears it. What can produce it ? Another flash of lightning— another shriek—there could be now no delusion.

" A tall figure is standing on the ledge immediately outside the window. It is its finger-nails upon the glass that produce the sound so like the hail, now that the hail has ceased. Intense fear paralysed the limbs of that beautiful girl. That one shriek is all she can utter—with hands clasped, a face of marble, a heart beating so wildly in her bosom, that each moment it seems as if it would break its confines, eyes distended and fixed

upon the window, she waits, froze with horror.   The pattering
and clattering of the nails continues.   No word is spoken, and
now she fancies she can trace the darker form of that figure
against the window, and she can see the long arms moving
to and fro, feeling for some mode of entrance.   What strange
light is that which now gradually creeps up into the air ? red
and terrible—brighter and brighter it grows.   The lightning
has set fire to a mill, and the reflection of the rapidly con-
suming building falls upon that long window.   There can be
no mistake.   The figure is there, still feeling for an entrance,
and clattering against the glass with its long nails, that appear
as if the growth of many years had been untouched.   She
tries to scream again but a choking sensation comes over her,
and she cannot.   It is too dreadful—she tries to move—each
limb seems wedged down by tons of lead—she can but in a
hoarse faint whisper cry,—

"'Help—help—help—help !'

"And that one word she repeats like a person in a dream.
The red glare of the fire continues.   It throws up the tall gaunt
figure in hideous relief against the long window.   It shows,
too, upon the one portrait that is in the chamber, and that
portrait appears to fix its eyes upon the attempting intruder,
while the flickering light from the fire makes it look fearfully lifelike.   A small pane of glass is broken, and the form
from without introduces a long gaunt hand, which seems
utterly destitute of flesh.   The fastening is removed, and one-
half of the window, which opens like folding doors, is swung
wide open upon its hinges.

"And yet now she could not scream—she could not move.
'Help !—help !—help !—' was all she could say.   But, oh,
that look of terror that sat upon her face, it was dreadful—a
look to haunt the memory for a life-time—a look to obtrude
itself upon the happiest moments, and turn them to bitterness.

"The figure turns half round, and the light falls upon the
face.   It is perfectly white—perfectly bloodless.   The eyes
look like polished tin ; the lips are drawn back, and the
principal feature next to those dreadful eyes is the teeth—the
fearful looking teeth—projecting like those of some wild
animal, hideously, glaringly white, and fang-like.   It
approaches the bed with a strange, gliding movement.   It
clashes together the long nails that literally appear to hang

from the finger ends. No sound comes from its lips. Is she going mad ?—that young and beautiful girl exposed to so much terror ; she has drawn up all her limbs ; she cannot even now say help. The power of articulation is gone, but the power of movement has returned to her ; she can draw herself slowly along to the other side of the bed from that towards which the hideous appearance is coming.

" But her eyes are fascinated. The glance of a serpent could not have produced a greater effect upon her than did the fixed gaze of those awful, metallic-looking eyes that were bent on her face. Crouching down so that the gigantic height were lost, and the horrible, protruding, white face was the most prominent object, came on the figure. What was it ?--what did it want there ?—what made it look so hideous—so unlike an inhabitant of the earth, and yet to be on it ?

" Now she has got to the verge of the bed, and the figure pauses. It seemed as if when it paused she lost the power to proceed. The clothing of the bed was now clutched in her hands with unconscious power. She drew her breath short and thick. Her bosom heaves, and her limbs tremble, yet she cannot withdraw her eyes from that marble-looking face. He holds her with his glittering eye.

" The storm has ceased—all is still. The winds are hushed ; the church clock proclaims the hour of one : a hissing sound comes from the throat of the hideous being, and he raises his long, gaunt arms—the lips move. He advances. The girl places one small foot from the bed on to the floor. She is unconsciously dragging the clothing with her. The door of the room is in that direction—can she reach it ? Has she power to walk ?—can she withdraw her eyes from the face of the intruder, and so break the hideous charm ? God of Heaven ! is it real, or some dream so like reality as to nearly overturn the judgment for ever ?

" The figure has paused again, and half on the bed and half out of it that young girl lies trembling. Her long hair streams across the entire width of the bed. As she has slowly moved along she has left it streaming across the pillows. The pause lasted about a minute—oh, what an age of agony. That minute was, indeed, enough for madness to do its full work in.

" With a sudden rush that could not be foreseen—with a strange howling cry that was enough to awaken terror in every breast, the figure seized the long tresses of her hair, and twining them round his bony hands he held her to the bed. Then she screamed—Heaven granted her that power to scream. Shriek followed shriek in rapid succession. The bed-clothes fell in a heap by the side of the bed—she was dragged by her long silken hair completely on to it again. Her beautiful rounded limbs quivered with the agony of her soul. The glassy, horrible eyes of the figure ran over that angelic form with a hideous satisfaction—horrible profanation. He drags her head to the bed's edge. He forces it back by the long hair still entwined in his grasp. With a plunge he seizes her neck in his fang-like teeth—a gush of blood, and a hideous sucking noise follows. *The girl has swooned, and the vampyre is at his hideous repast!* "

An exceptionally interesting account of a Vampire was given by Captain Fisher to Mr. Augustus Hare, and is printed in the *Story of My Life*.

"Fisher," said the Captain, "may sound a very plebeian name, but this family is of a very ancient lineage, and for many hundreds of years they have possessed a very curious old place in Cumberland, which bears the weird name of Croglin Grange. The great characteristic of the house is that never at any period of its very long existence has it been more than one story high, but it has a terrace from which large grounds sweep away towards the church in the hollow, and a fine distant view.

"When, in lapse of years, the Fishers outgrew Croglin Grange in family and fortune, they were wise enough not to destroy the long-standing characteristic of the place by adding another story to the house, but they went away to the south, to reside at Thorncombe near Guildford, and they let Croglin Grange.

"They were extremely fortunate in their tenants, two brothers and a sister. They heard their praises from all quarters. To their poorer neighbours they were all that is most kind and beneficent, and their neighbours of a higher class spoke of them as a most welcome addition to the little society of the neighbourhood. On their part, the tenants were greatly delighted with their new residence. The arrangement of the house, which would have been a trial to many, was not so to

them. In every respect Croglin Grange was exactly suited
to them.

"The winter was spent most happily by the new inmates
of Croglin Grange, who shared in all the little social pleasures
of the district, and made themselves very popular. In the
following summer there was one day which was dreadfully,
annihilatingly hot. The brothers lay under the trees with their
books, for it was too hot for any active occupation. The
sister sat in the veranda and worked, or tried to work, for in
the intense sultriness of that summer day, work was next to
impossible. They dined early, and after dinner they still sat
out on the veranda, enjoying the cool air which came with the
evening, and they watched the sun set, and the moon rise over
the belt of trees which separated the grounds from the church
yard, seeing it mount the heavens till the whole lawn was
bathed in silver light, across which the long shadows from the
shrubbery fell as if embossed, so vivid and distinct were they.

"When they separated for the night, all retiring to their
rooms on the ground floor (for, as I said, there was no upstairs in
that house), the sister felt that the heat was still so great that
she could not sleep, and having fastened her window, she did
not close the shutters—in that very quiet place it was not
necessary—and, propped against the pillows, she still watched
the wonderful, the marvellous beauty of that summer night.
Gradually she became aware of two lights, two lights which
flickered in and out in the belt of trees which separated the lawn
from the churchyard, and, as her gaze became fixed upon them,
she saw them emerge, fixed in a dark substance, a definite
ghastly *something*, which seemed every moment to become
nearer, increasing in size and substance as it approached.
Every now and then it was lost for a moment in the long
shadows which stretched across the lawn from the trees, and
then it emerged larger than ever, and still coming on. As she
watched it, the most uncontrollable horror seized her. She
longed to get away, but the door was close to the window, and
the door was locked on the inside, and while she was unlocking it she must be for an instant nearer to *it*. She longed to
scream, but her voice seemed paralysed, her tongue glued to the
roof of her mouth.

"Suddenly—she could never explain why afterwards—the
terrible object seemed to turn to one side, seemed to be going

round the house, not to be coming to her at all, and immediately she jumped out of bed and rushed to the door, but as she was unlocking it she heard scratch, scratch, scratch upon the window, and saw a hideous brown face with flaming eyes glaring in at her. She rushed back to the bed, but the creature continued to scratch, scratch, scratch upon the window. She felt a sort of mental comfort in the knowledge that the window was securely fastened on the inside. Suddenly the scratching sound ceased, and a kind of pecking sound took its place. Then, in her agony, she became aware that the creature was unpicking the lead ! The noise continued, and a diamond pane of glass fell into the room. Then a long bony finger of the creature came in and turned the handle of the window, and the window opened, and the creature came in ; and it came across the room, and her terror was so great that she could not scream, and it came up to the bed, and it twisted its long, bony fingers into her hair, and it dragged her head over the side of the bed, and—it bit her violently in the throat.

" As it bit her, her voice was released, and she screamed with all her might and main. Her brothers rushed out of their rooms, but the door was locked on the inside. A moment was lost while they got a poker and broke it open. Then the creature had already escaped through the window, and the sister, bleeding violently from a wound in the throat, was lying unconscious over the side of the bed. One brother pursued the creature, which fled before him through the moonlight with gigantic strides, and eventually seemed to disappear over the wall into the churchyard. Then he rejoined his brother by the sister's bedside. She was dreadfully hurt, and her wound was a very definite one, but she was of strong disposition, not even given to romance or superstition, and when she came to herself she said, ' What has happened is most extraordinary and I am very much hurt. It seems inexplicable, but of course there is an explanation, and we must wait for it. It will turn out that a lunatic has escaped from some asylum and found his way here.' The wound healed, and she appeared to get well, but the doctor who was sent for to her would not believe that she could bear so terrible a shock so easily, and insisted that she must have change, mental and physical ; so her brothers took her to Switzerland.

" Being a sensible girl, when she went abroad she threw herself at once into the interests of the country she was in. She dried plants, she made sketches, she went up mountains, and, as autumn came on, she was the person who urged that they should return to Croglin Grange. ' We have taken it,' she said, ' for seven years, and we have only been there one ; and we shall always find it difficult to let a house which is only one storey high, so we had better return there ; lunatics do not escape every day.' As she urged it, her brothers wished nothing better, and the family returned to Cumberland. From there being no upstairs in the house it was impossible to make any great change in their arrangements. The sister occupied the same room, but it is unnecessary to say she always closed the shutters, which, however, as in many old houses, always left one top pane of the window uncovered. The brothers moved, and occupied a room together, exactly opposite that of their sister, and they always kept loaded pistols in their room.

" The winter passed most peacefully and happily. In the following March, the sister was suddenly awakened by a sound she remembered only too well—scratch, scratch, scratch upon the window, and, looking up, she saw, climbed up to the topmost pane of the window, the same hideous brown shrivelled face, with glaring eyes, looking in at her. This time she screamed as loud as she could. Her brothers rushed out of their room with pistols, and out of the front door. The creature was already scudding away across the lawn. One of the brothers fired and hit it in the leg, but still with the other leg it continued to make way, scrambled over the wall into the churchyard, and seemed to disappear into a vault which belonged to a family long extinct.

" The next day the brothers summoned all the tenants of Croglin Grange, and in their presence the vault was opened. A horrible scene revealed itself. The vault was full of coffins ; they had been broken open, and their contents, horribly mangled and distorted, were scattered over the floor. One coffin alone remained intact. Of that the lid had been lifted, but still lay loose upon the coffin. They raised it, and there, brown, withered, shrivelled, mummified, but quite entire, was the same hideous figure which had looked in at the windows of Croglin Grange, with the marks of a recent pistol-shot in the leg : and they did the only thing that can lay a vampire—they burnt it."[28]

Of recent years the histories of Vampirism in England are perhaps few, but this is not so much because they do not occur as rather that they are carefully hushed up and stifled. In 1924 the Hon. Ralph Shirley wrote : " It may be doubted, indeed, in spite of the lack of records, whether vampirism in one form or another is quite as absent from the conditions of modern civilization as is commonly supposed. Although we are not to-day familiar with the Slavonic type of vampire that sucks the blood of its victims, producing death in two or three days' time, strange cases come to light occasionally when people are the victims, by their own confession, of something of a very similar nature, the vampire in these cases being an entity in human form who indulges in intercourse with some-one of the opposite sex. Such cases are to-day, generally speaking, promptly consigned to one of our lunatic asylums and do not reach the public ear. I happened, however, quite recently to hear an instance of the kind. The victim had been engaged to a young man, the family, on account of the man's antecedents, not approving of the engagement, but not being actively hostile. The man died suddenly, and the girl was prostrated with grief. Shortly after, however, she recovered her normal cheerfulness, and somewhat later confessed to her mother that she was visited by her former lover in physical form. She subsequently became engaged to another man, but owing to threats, as he said, of her deceased lover, the engagement was broken off. The last time I heard of the young lady in question she was stated to be consumptive. Naturally, these things do not get into the papers, and obviously the ordinary medical man will put down instances of the kind as pure hallucination. Still, if we have any belief in the philosophy of the occultist, they are bound to give us pause and make us hesitate before saying that vampirism is entirely a thing of the past."[29] Such cases, in truth, are happening every day and I have met with not a few instances in my own experience.

It may not be impertinent to notice that during the Salem troubles and the witch prosecutions in New England, which were at their height from 1691-1693, there occur certain details which might be attributed to vampirism but which do not strictly fall into that category. Many of the " afflicted children," as the sufferers were generally known, complained that apparitions presented themselves bruising and tormenting them and seemingly draining their vitality. In particular, the wife and daughter of Thomas Putman, Abigail Williams, and Mary Walcut complained that they had actually been bitten by these phantoms, and they showed the marks of teeth, both upper and lower set, imprinted upon their wrists. It was, of course, a common thing that those who had been overlooked should pine away until they dropped into an early grave, and this is one of the notes of the vampire's malignancy, for, as we should expect, witchcraft and vampirism are very closely allied.

There have, however, occurred in America at a far more recent date incidents which evince a strong belief in the power of the vampire. During the year 1854 the *Norwich Courier* (U.S.A.) reported some remarkable happenings which had taken place at Jewett, a neighbouring town. In 1846-7 a citizen of Griswold, Horace Ray, had died of consumption. Unfortunately two of his children, young men, developed the same disease and followed him to the grave, the younger and last of these passing away about 1852. It was found that yet a third son was a victim to the same fatal disease, whereupon it was resolved to exhume the bodies of the two brothers and cremate them because the dead were supposed to feed upon the living ; and so long as the dead bodies in the grave remained entire the surviving members of the family must continue to furnish vital substance upon which these could feed. Wholly convinced that this was the case, the family and friends of the deceased on 8th June, 1854, proceeded to the burial ground, exhumed the bodies of the deceased brothers and having erected a great pyre, burned them there on the spot.

The Providence Journal in 1874 recorded that in the village of Placedale, Rhode Island, a well-known inhabitant, Mr. William Rose, himself dug up the body of his own daughter and burned her heart, acting under the belief that she was exhausting the vitality of the remaining members of the family. In the following year Dr. Dyer, one of the leading physicians of Chicago, reported a case which came under his own observation. The body of a woman who had died of consumption, was taken from the grave and burned, under the belief that she was attracting after her into the grave her surviving relatives.

It has been stated : "At Waterford, in Ireland, there is a little graveyard under a ruined church near Strongbow's Tower. Legend has it that underneath the ground at this spot there lies a beautiful female vampire still ready to kill those she can lure thither by her beauty."[30] No authority is given for this, which is perhaps hardly surprising when one knows that there is not nor ever was such a tower at Waterford as "Strongbow's Tower." Probably there is some confused reference to "Reginald's Tower," which Strongbow (de Clare, Earl of Pembroke) used as a fortress in 1170, and where King John established a mint, whence it was called Dundory. That great Irish authority, the late Chevalier W. H. Gratton-Flood informed me[31] that there is no legend of a Vampire connected with Reginald's Tower, and probably the following tale has been confused which is related in regard to the capture of Waterford by the Anglo-Normans by Giraldus Cambrensis[32] in his *Topographia Hibernica*. A frog was found in the grassy meadows near Waterford, and was brought alive to Cork before Robert le Poer, the warden of the city (who lived in Reginald's Tower). All were astonished at the sight of the frog, this being the first frog discovered in Ireland. It is said that the frog was solemnly interred in Reginald's Tower. Cambrensis notes that the frog must have been brought over by Strongbow among the baggage of the force he led from England.

In ancient Ireland the Vampire was generally known as *Dearg-dul*, "red blood sucker," and his ravages were universally feared. Irish hagiographical lore vividly portrays various burial customs. To be interred under a cairn of stones is regarded as heathenish, doubtless since such a pile marked haunted places. In a letter ascribed to Theodoret, *Epistle lxxx*, it is said : "Let every one throw a stone on his grave, lest perchance . . . he return to earth," and Geoffrey of Monmouth clearly looked upon sepulture in a howe or barrow as purely pagan : "iussit eum sepeliri et cumulum terrae super corpus eius pagano more apponi."[33] The embalming of a body was so ethnic a practice that the effect thereof must be loosed and undone by saying mass before the remains can be laid in consecrated earth.[34] This, no question, is connected with the idea so prevalent in Greece that a body which does not corrupt in the grave is bound by a curse or excommunication. On the other hand we also find among the histories that incorruption is regarded as a sign of virginal chastity and holiness.   But in *Eyrbyggjasaga*, xxxiv, when the folk were terrified at the "walkings " of the dead Thorolf they go to his cairn, and break it open to find his corpse fresh and undecayed :   " váru allir menn kraeddir vid aptgöngur þórólfs, . . .   foru upp . . . til dysjar hans ; brjóta dysina ok finna þórólf par ófúinn." This is a clear touch of vampirism.

It is worth remark that there are many legends of wolves in Irish saintly legend, and very often these animals appear in a most beneficent and kindly light.   Thus S. Molua (or Lugaid) founded an annual feast on behalf of the wolves[35] ;   Colman Mac Lauchain had a standing covenant with the wolves[36]; miracles are wrought on behalf of wolves[37] ; nay, it was even said that one Saint, S. Ronan, was actually accused of being a werewolf : " Ronanum . . .   aliquando conuerti in lupum, et non solum caedem exercere pecorum, uerum etiam filiorum hominum."   The fact is that he was always attended by a certain wolf, a gentle and loving beast who served him sweetly and courteously, so that even now we say "As gentle as S. Ronan's wolf."   The body of the great Saint lies at Locronan, and there his festival with a thronged Pardon is held on the second Sunday in July.   It is hardly a matter for surprise that, since the wolf is so well spoken of in Irish lore, the vampire who is closely allied to the werewolf should be practically unknown in early legend.

In Ireland to-day, as in England, the Vampire, although records are rare, is by no means unknown, and I quote at length a most interesting and most important case reported by R. S. Breene in *The Occult Review*, October, 1925.[38]

"The following story was told to me many years ago by persons who were supposed to be relatives of the priest who figures in it.   As far as I have been able to find out, I see no reason for doubting that what I am setting down here is approximately a statement of fact.   One consideration would have much weight with me in leading me to accept at least the intention of truth in the narrators.   The incident happened in a county in Ireland where the vast majority of the inhabitants have always been ardent Roman Catholics.   People of this sort would never dream of inventing such a story about an ecclesiastic.   So strong is their veneration for the priesthood, and their belief in the sanctity of their parish clergy, that it is almost impossible to understand how such circumstances as I here narrate could be associated in the popular mind with the name and memory of one who had received Holy Orders. Yet it was from Roman Catholics who described themselves as eye-witnesses that the information was derived. Again I have read that vampirism only appears in countries which are spiritually in a backward condition, as in some areas of Eastern Europe. Now though, as I have said, the people amidst whom these events took place were Roman Catholics, yet they were not of a high type. The country is wild, isolated and mountainous. Even in recent years numerous terrible crimes of violence have been reported from the neighbourhood, some of them of a peculiarly senseless character. I was myself shown, some years ago, a spot marked with a white cross upon a stone by the roadside, where a lad of about twenty years of age had a few nights previously kicked his father's brains out, on no apparent provocation. One would almost have said, on examining the evidence in connexion with the case, that there had been something very like demoniac possession. I have never since been in any part of Ireland where the inhabitants generally seemed to be so conscious of the interpenetration at all times of the things that are not seen with the things that do appear. One felt them to be in touch with a realm of being that we know nothing about in the outer world. They were crude, brave, and, as we would say, superstitious. The element of fear, the fear of the unknown, was always to be felt. The most of the inhabitants of the district were poor, but a number of farmers were able to live in a certain degree of plain comfort. The publicans and the farmers generally gave one son to the Church.

"A member of the family of M——, a farming connexion, had been ordained to the priesthood, and eventually was put in charge of a little hill parish by the local Bishop. He is reputed to have been a quiet, inoffensive man, not given much to the companionship of his flock, and rather addicted to reading and study. His parishioners listened with edification to his sermons, brought their children to him for the rite of baptism, made their confession to him at intervals, and took the sacred bread of the Holy Communion from his hands on Sundays and the greater festivals of the Church. He did not often conduct stations at their houses, as did some of his colleagues in other parishes, who were more gregariously inclined. He was hospitable to strangers, and had frequently placed beds in his little parochial house at the disposal of belated travellers and even tramps. Yet no one in his immediate neighbourhood would have thought of going to see him socially. They went to him on the Church's business, or they did not go at all. He was, in a word, respected, though not greatly liked.

"When he had little more than passed his fiftieth birthday he suddenly fell ill and died, after a brief confinement to his chamber. He was buried with all the simple pomp that surrounds the obsequies of an Irish country priest. His body, I should have said, was removed before the funeral to his mother's house, which was several miles distant from his parish. It was from there that the funeral took place. It was a sad picture when the body came home to the aged mother, whose chief pride in her later years had been her 'boy in the Church,' the priest ; and it was sadder still when the coffin set out once more from the whitewashed farmhouse, to carry its occupant upon his last journey to the rocky graveyard in the hills where all his kin had laid their bones for generations. According to custom, all the male and female members of the connexion accompanied the corpse. The bereaved mother was left to her thoughts for the rest of the day in the house of death. In the afternoon she allowed the maid, who did the rough work about the place, to go across the fields to her own people for a few hours. Mrs. M—— was as brave as any other woman of her class, and in her trouble she wished to be alone.

"Meanwhile the funeral cortege wended its slow way (a long procession of traps, jaunting-cars and spring-carts) towards its destination in the mountains. They did not waste much time in getting their sad task over and done, but they had a long road to traverse, and the sun was already declining in the heavens as they climbed the last succession of hills on the way to the homestead they had left in the morning. It was a priest's funeral, and, both going and coming, they had not cared to halt at the scattered public-houses they had passed on the wayside, as they would most certainly have done, and done frequently, in the case of anybody else's. They were all sober, but many of them, particularly the womenfolk, had fallen asleep. Night was already in the air. The shadows were lengthening below the hill-crests, but upon the white limestone highway everything was still in broad daylight. At the foot of a slope the mourners in the first cars suddenly became aware of a solitary figure coming down towards them walking rapidly. As the distance between them and the pedestrian lessened they were surprised to see that he was a priest. They knew of no priest who could be there at such a time. Those who had taken part in the ceremonies at the grave had not come so far with them on the return journey. They began to speculate as to who the man could be. Remarks were exchanged, and meanwhile the newcomer had met the foremost car. Two men were awake in it. There could be no mistake. *They saw at once, and quite clearly, that they were face to face with the man whom they had laid in his grave two or three hours before.* He passed them with his head slightly averted, but not sufficiently to prevent them from making absolutely certain of his identity, or from noting the intense, livid palour of his skin, the hard glitter of his wide-open eyes, *and* the extraordinary length of his strong, white teeth, from which the full red lips seemed to be writhed back till the gums showed themselves. He was wearing, not the grave-clothes in which he had been attired for his burial, but the decent black frock-coat and garments to match in which they had last seen him alive. He passed down the long line of vehicles, and finally disappeared round the turn in the road. Some one in every loaded trap or car had seen him ; in short, most of those who had been awake and on that side. A thrill of terror passed through the whole party. With hushed voices and blanched cheeks they pushed on quickly, now only anxious to get under some sheltering roof and round some blazing hearth before dread night should fall upon them.

" Their first call was at the M—— farmhouse. In the front was a little porch built round the door, a small narrow window on either side. About this they gathered, and hurriedly decided to say no word of what had happened to the bereaved mother. Then some one knocked, but received no answer. They knocked again, and still being denied admittance, they began to be uneasy. At last some one thought of peeping in through one of the little side-windows, when he saw old Mrs. M—— lying face downward on the floor. They hesitated no longer, but literally broke in, and it was some little time before they were able to bring her round again to consciousness. This, briefly, is what she told them.

"About half an hour earlier, she had heard footsteps on the flags outside, followed by a loud challenging knock. She was surprised that they should have returned so soon, and, besides, she had been expecting the sound of the cars approaching. She decided that it could not be any of the family, and so, before opening, she looked out at the side. There to her horror she saw her dead son standing in the broad daylight much as she had last seen him alive. He was not looking directly at her. But she, too, noted the extraordinary length of his teeth, the cold blaze of his eyes, I might say the wolfishness of his whole bearing, and the deathly pallor of his skin. Her first instinctive movement was to open the door. Then fear swept over her, swamping even her mother love. She felt her limbs giving way under her, and quickly sank into the oblivion in which she lay until they found her.

"This is the story as it was told to me. If there was a sequel, I never heard it. Was this a case of vampirism ? It has not been altogether unknown in Ireland. At any rate I have thought it worthy of record."

I have, I think, seldom met with a more interesting account of a Vampire, and there are not a few points which might be considered in detail. Usefully to do so, however, would necessitate an inquiry into any recent developments which have taken place, any outbreak of vampirism in the particular district. Such investigations could but cause poignant suffering to the living and entail a regrettable publicity. Accordingly it will be more discreet and more kind to leave the history as it stands. It bears the hall mark of truth in every particular, and is indeed a most notable and striking relation.

As in England and in Ireland, in France the records of Vampirism are few ; one might perhaps not untruthfully say designedly few. In *Là-Bas*, xi, J. K. Huysmans speaks of the " vampirism " of Gilles de Rais, but this is to use the modern French word in its most extended signification. Gilles de Rais was a necrophilist, a necrosadist, and tortured with blood-madness, hæmatomania.[39] But, strictly, he was not a vampire, although he had the Vampire's thirst for blood. Huysmans writes : " Gilles et ses amis se retirent dans une champe éloignée du château. C'est là que les petits garçons enfermés dans les caves sont amenés. On les déshabille, on les bâillone ; le Maréchal les palpe et les force, puis il les taillade à coups de dagues, se complait à les démembrer, pièces à pièces. D'autres fois, il leur fend la poitrine, et il boit le souffle des poumons ; il leur oeuvre aussi le ventre, le flaire, élargit de ses mains la plaie et s'assied dedans. Alors, tandis qu'il se macère dans la boue détrempée des entrailles tièdes, il se retourne un peu et regarde par dessus son épaule, afin de contempler les suprêmes convulsions, les derniers spasmes. Lui-même l'a dit : J'étais plus content de jouir des tortures, des larmes, de l'effroi et du sang que de tout autre plaisir. . . . Bientôt ses furies s'aggravèrent ; jusqu 'alors, il avait assouvi sur des êtres vivants ou moribonds la rage de ses sens ; il se fatigua de souiller des chairs qui pantclaient et il aima les morts. . . . Le vampirisme le satisfit, pendant des mois. Il pollua les enfants morts, apaisa le fièvre de ses souhaits dans la glace ensanglantée des tombes ; il alla même, un jour que sa provision d'enfants était apuisée, jusqu'à éventrer une femme enceinte et à manier le fœtus !"

I have heard, by those who personally knew the lady, the original of Madame Chantelouve in *Là-Bas* termed a Vampire. Her presence, her society had the effect of sucking the vitality of those who were with her, and her energies markedly increased, her brilliance shone brighter as their depression and enervation grew more languid and more tired. In his study of Huysmans[40] G. Aubault de la Haulte Chambre tells us that Madame Chantelouve was "une espagnole satanique, autrefois amoureuse de Huysmans et qu'il appelait, dans l'intimité, losqu'il parlait d'elle Doña Sol."[41]

Huysmans continues : "Puis, après ces excès [Gilles] tombait, épuisé, en d'horribles sommes, en de pesants comas, semblables à ces sortes de léthargies qui accablèrent, après ses violations de sépulture, le sergent Bertrand. Mais, si l'on peut admettre qui ce sommeil de plomb est l'une des phases connues de cet état encore mal observé du vampirisme ; si l'on peut croix que Gilles de Rais fût un aberré des sens génésiques, un virtuose en douleurs et en meurtres, il faut avouer qu'il se distingue des plus fastueux des criminels, des plus délirants des sadiques. . . ."

The case of Sergeant Bertrand, who at the time of his trial was throughout France known as "The Vampire" is the classic

example of necrophilia.　On 10th July, 1849, an investigation
was held before a council of war presided over by Colonel
Manselon.　"It is remarked that the court was extremely
crowded, and that many ladies were present."[42]　For many
months various cemeteries in and around Paris had been the
scenes of the most frightful profanations.　The guardians of
Perè la Chaise had noticed, or believed they had noticed, a
shadowy figure flitting by night among the graves, but they
could never succeed in laying hands on him and some began to
suppose it was a phantom.　Graves were found fearfully
desecrated.　The bodies were torn from their resting-places,
violated and scored with hideous mutilations.　When these
events ceased at Père la Chaise they began in a remote suburban
graveyard.　The body of a little girl aged seven who had been
buried one noon was found on the following morning torn from
the earth, the coffin burst open, and the corpse hideously
maltreated.　"Every means were taken to discover the
criminal ; but the only result of the increased surveillance was
that the scene of profanation was removed to the cemetery
of Mont Parnesse, where the exhumations were carried to such
an extent that the authorities were at their wit's ends.　Considering, by the way, that all these cemetries are surrounded
by walls and have iron gates, which are kept closed, it certainly
seems very strange that any ghoul or vampyre of solid flesh
and blood should have been able to pursue his vocation so long
undisturbed."　At length by a trap the guardians of the
cemetery were able to surprise the mysterious visitant who none
the less escaped with severe wounds and leaving a trail of blood
from their shots.　A few scraps of military attire were found,
and when some sappers of the 74th regiment remarked that
shortly after midnight one of their sergeants had returned so
injured that he had been conveyed to Val de Grace, the military
hospital, it was realised that the culprit was found.　At his
examination Bertrand avowed that an irresistible impulse
drove him to disinter and violate corpses, after which he fell
into a sort of trance or coma.　The details of the corpses he
had outraged were of the most horrible nature, and his
mutilations seem to have been wrought in a state of dementia.
The doctors, however, judged him responsible, and he was
sentenced to a year's imprisonment.[43]

The following account of a French vampire is given by Miss

Jessie Adelaide Middleton in her work *Another Grey Ghost Book* :

" A French viscount—de Morière by name—was one of the very few French noblemen who managed to retain their estates through the troublous times of the French Revolution. He was an extraordinary looking man, very tall and thin, with a high, almost pointed, forehead, and protruding teeth.

" Under an air of suave courtesy and kindness he concealed a ferociously cruel disposition, which showed itself when the fires of the great revolution had burned themselves out, and all was once more quiet. To get level, as it were, with the working classes, he sent for his retainers and workpeople one by one, and, after he had interviewed them, cut off their heads. It is not surprising to hear that, in return, he himself met his death by assassination at the hands of some of the peasantry.

"No sooner, however, was the viscount laid in the grave than an appalling number of young children died in the neighbourhood, all of whom bore the vampire marks at their throats. Later on, when he had been buried for some time, and while the tomb was being repaired, there were nine more cases in a single week. The awful slaughter went on until seventy-two years passed away, and the viscount's grandson succeeded to the title.

" Young de Morière, hearing the appalling stories of his grandfather, consulted a priest with the idea of laying his horrible ancestor's ghost, and, after some discussion and delay, it was decided to open the tomb. The services of a man specially successful in such cases were obtained, and the vault was opened in the presence of the authorities.

" Every coffin was found to have undergone the usual process of rotting away, except that of the old viscount, which, after seventy-two years, was perfectly strong and sound. The lid was removed and the body was found quite fresh and free from decomposition. The face was flushed and there was blood in the heart and chest. The skin was soft and natural. New nails had grown on both hands and feet.

" The body was removed from the coffin and a white thorn was driven by the expert through the heart of the corpse, with the ghastly result that blood and water poured forth and the corpse groaned and screamed. Then the remains were burned on the seashore ; and from that day the child-deaths ceased and there were no more mysterious crimes in the neighbourhood.

"The family archives were searched and it was found that the old viscount had come originally from Persia, where he married an Indian wife, and afterwards took up his residence in France, where he became a naturalised subject. The vampiric taint was in his blood."

In Italy, especially among the Abruzzi, the peasants fear "la strega chi succia il sangue." A mother will see her child pine and waste away, and is at her wits' end how to relieve him. She goes to the priest who recites the Holy Gospel over the poor child upon whose head he has laid the broad spade of his stole : she returns home and hangs over the doorway a cross of wax which has been blessed on Ascension Day. She takes a pinch of salt, ties it up in a little linen bag, and hangs this amulet round her child's neck. She cuts off a lock of the sick lad's hair and burns it that the smoke may drive the witch far afield. She sprinkles the hinges of the doors with Holy Water and recites aloud the *Credo* thrice. Then the husband "does the seven nights," that is to say he watches for seven long nights. Perhaps he may catch the hag and be able to seize her fast by her hair.

At midnight the witch anoints her body with the magic salve, she mounts upon a huge he-goat and cries : "Away, away, through snow and storm, carry me to the nut-tree of Benevento."[44] As she is on her way to the sabbat she passes through the houses sucking the blood of the little children, and the babies pine and pine to die at last. Perhaps in some cottage the father, supremely anxious for his babe is "doing the seven nights." An earthen pot turned upside down shrouds a bright light. There in the dark the father takes his stand. If he can but prick the witch with a pin, however gently, she will be discovered. The watcher hears a noise. He quickly uncovers the light. The witch has already fled.

At earliest dawn he goes in search of a wise woman, and begs her to tell him how he may rescue his child from the imminent danger. He is instructed to kill a dog or a cat and lay the body behind the house door. The witch cannot enter unless she has first counted every hair on the dead animal, and whilst she is at her task dawn will break. Then must she fly to her own place, for if she tarry until sunrise she will not be able to escape, and she will be discovered stark naked in the village street.

These details are given by de Nino in his valuable study *Usi e Costumi Abruzzesi*,[45] and it seems probable that this is the source whence Gabriele D'Annunzio derived his material for the following episode which occurs in the *Trionfo della Morte*, IV, " La Vita Nuova," iii. The small son of a peasant woman, Liberata Mannella, is wasting away and near to death. The poor child is lying in its rough little cradle. " La misera creatura nuda, smunta, scarnita, verdastra, metteva un lamento continuo agitando debolmente gli ossicini spolpati delle gambe e delle draccia come per chiedere aiuto." The unhappy mother dazed with grief from time to time mechanically rocks the cradle. " Allora le imagini sacre, i pentacoli, i brevi, di cui l'abete era quasi tutto coperto, ondeggiavano e susurravano, in una pausa momentanea del pianto." Another woman, Candia, relates at length the various methods the parents have employed to dissolve the spell which is killing their child. " Che cosa non avevano fatto ? Ella raccontava tutte le prove, tutti gli esorcismi. Era andato il prete, e aveva proferite le parole del bambino con un lembo della stola. La madre aveva sospesa all'architrave la croce di cera, benedetta nel giorno dell'Ascensione ; aveva asperso d'acqua santa i cardini delle imposte e recitato ad alta voce il *Credo* tre volte ; aveva messo un pugno di sale in un pannolino e chiuso in un nodo l'aveva legato al collo del figliuolo morente. Il padre *aveva fatto le sette notti :* per sette notti aveva vegliato, nell'oscurita, dinanzi a una lucerna accesa coperta da una pentola, attento ad agni rumore, pronto ad assalire la strega per ferirla. Sarebbe bastato anche un sol colpo di spillo per renderla visibile agli occhi dell'uomo. Ma le sètte veglie erano trascorse in vano ! Il figliuolo dimagriva e si consumava d'ora in ora, senza rimedio. E il padre disperato in fine aveva ucciso un cane e aveva messo il cadavere dietro l'uscio, per consiglio d'una maliarda. La strega non avrebbe potuto entrare se prima non avesse contati tutti i peli della bestia morta. . . .[46]

Similar traditions prevail in Sicily. But it is acknowledged that the one infallible remedy is the protection of the Church, and as is the wont of Christian people in a Christian land it is to the benedictions and exorcisms of the Church that they have recourse to defend themselves from the power of evil and to guard themselves against the hosts of darkness and the devil.

NOTES. CHAPTER II.

[1] Born *circa* 1090 ; died *c.* 1143. *Gesta Regum*, II, 4.

[2] Tanner, *Bibliotheca*.

[3] Abbot of Melrose ; elected Abbot of Rivaulx in 1189.

[4] First printed at Paris, 1508. Recent editions are by Giles, London, 1844 and by Schulz, Halle, 1854.

[5] Introduction, *Monumenta Historica Britannica*, p. 8.

[6] pp. 182-190, vol. II, *Historia Anglicana*, ed. H. C. Hamilton, 1856.

[7] S. Hugh who was born about the year 1135, died at London, 16th November, 1200.   He entered the Grande Chartreuse as a novice in 1153, and in 1180 became prior of Witham, the first Carthusian foundation in England.   21st September, 1181, he was consecrated Bishop of Lincoln.   He was canonized twenty years after his death by Hororius III in 1220.   It is not known what became of S. Hugh's Relics under Henry VIII, but for three centuries his magnificent golden shrine in Lincoln Cathedral had been the most celebrated centre of pilgrimage in the North of England, and it was soon robbed by the sacrilegious tyrant.

[8] The historian, no doubt, learned these events from Ernald, sometime Abbot of Melrose, but now Abbot of Rivaulx.   Melrose in Roxburghshire founded in 1136 by David I was the earliest Cistercian Monastery in Scotland.   Its first community came from Rivaulx, the famous Yorkshire house colonized from Citeaux.   Melrose often suffered during the Border Wars and it was burned by the English troops of Henry VIII in 1544.   The ruins were further desecrated by a fanatical mob in 1569.

[9] One cannot but be reminded of Chaucer's Monk :

> A Monk there was, a fair for the Maistrye,
> An out-rydere, that lovede venerye :
> A manly man, to been an abbot able.
> Ful many a deyntee hors hadde he in stable :
> And, whan he rood, men mighte his brydel here
> Ginglin in a whistling wind as clere,
> And eek as loude as dooth the chapel-belle
>
> He yaf nat of that text a pulled hen,
> That seith, that hunters been nat holy men ;
>
> Therefore he was a pricasour aright ;
> Grehoundes he hadde, as swifte as fowel in flight ;
> Of priking and of hunting for the hare
> Was al his lust, for no cost wolde he spare.

[10] *De Nugis Curialium (Courtiers' Trifles)*, Englished by Frederick Tupper and Marbury Bladen Ogle. London, 1924. Introduction, p. xxi.

[11] *De Nugis Curialium*, II, xii. Reading instead of *alares, laruas* as suggested by Tupper and Ogle. The word *alares* is rewritten in erasure in the MSS.

[12] *Id.*, II, xiii. See Liebrecht, *Zur Volkskunde* (1879), 59, 504.

[13] *Id.*, II, xiv.

[14] *Otia Imperialia*, p. 39.

[15] Gilbert Foliot was born early in the twelfth century of an Anglo-Norman family.   He became a monk at Cluny, and in 1147 Bishop of Hereford, whence he was translated to London in 1163.   Unfortunately in the struggle between S. Thomas and Henry II he attached himself to the king's party.   He died at London in 1186.   There is a very full treatment of Foliot's character in L'Hullier's *St. Thomas de Cantorbéry*, 2 vols, Paris, 1891.

[16] Roger, Bishop of Worcester, was a younger son of Robert, Earl of Gloucester.   He was educated with the future king, Henry II, and consecrated Bishop of Worcester by S. Thomas of Canterbury, 23rd August, 1163.   He loyally supported S. Thomas whom he joined in exile, 1167, although the

king had refused him leave. When they met at Falaise in 1170 he sternly rebuked Henry and a reconciliation followed. Had not Bishop Roger interceded with Pope Alexander III, England would have been put under an interdict after the martyrdom of S. Thomas. The supreme pontiff frequently employed him as delegate in ecclesiastical causes, and spoke of him and Bartholomew, Bishop of Exeter, as "the two great lights of the English Church." Bishop Roger died at Tours, 9th August, 1179.

[17] F. Liebrecht in his notes on the folk-lore of the *De Nugis* (*Zur Volkskunde*, Heilbronn) may be consulted.

[18] *Miller's Tale*, 3318 (332).

[19] This seems to point to foot-fetichism, for which see Dr. Havelock Ellis, *Studies in the Psychology of Sex*, vol. V, "Erotic Symbolism," c. 11. Restif de la Bretonne, 1734-1806, was probably the first case of a foot-fetichist whose particular passion is recorded in any detail. "The predominance of the foot as a focus of sexual attraction, while among us to-day it is a not uncommon phenomenon, is still not sufficiently common to be called normal; the majority of even ardent lovers do not experience this attraction in any marked degree. But these manifestations of foot-fetichism which with us to-day are abnormal, even when they are not so extreme as to be morbid, may perhaps become more intelligible to us when we realize that in earlier periods of civilizations and even to-day in some parts of the world, the foot is generally recognized as a focus of sexual attraction, so that some degree of foot-fetichism becomes a normal phenomenon."—Op. cit. ed. 1927, Philadelphia, p. 21.

[20] In Epistle xiv, Peter of Blois speaking of the miseries endured by the courtiers who accompanied Henry II on his progresses calls them *Milites Herlewini*, but this is possibly a coincidence. The story of King Herla will be found in Map, I, xi. This legendary Monarch of Britain was detained in fairyland for two hundred years when he deemed his absence had been but three days. And now "in endless wandering he maketh mad marches with his army without stay or rest." If a man halt or falls out of the ranks he crumbles to dust. Hartland, *The Science of Fairy Tales*, devotes Chapter VII to "The supernatural lapse of time in fairyland."

[21] *De Nugis Curialium*, Oxford, 1914, Preface, p. xiii.

[22] London, folio, 1627, p. 958.

[23] In Richard Whitlock's *Zootomia*, London, 8vo, 1654 (p. 123 and p. 135) we find the expression : "But at the approach of whom must this coarse bleed ? " Robert Heath in his verses *Bleeding at the Nose at Clarastella's Approach* in *Clarastella ; together with Poems, occasional Elegies, Epigrams, Satyrs*, London, 12mo, 1650, has a pretty conceit :

> So at the Murtherer's approach we see
> The corpse weep at its wounds again.

In Otway's *The Soldier's Fortune*, produced at Dorset Garden early in 1680 ; 4to, 1680 ; Act IV, when Sir Davy Dunce approaches the shamming Beaugard, who is supposed to have been killed by the jealous cuckold's orders, Lady Dunce fearful of the trick being discovered interposes with "Oh, come not near him, there's such horrid Antipathy follows all murders, his wounds would stream afresh should you but touch him."

[24] London, 4to, 1593.

[25] A good picture of Serjeant Maynard may be found in the life of Lord Keeper Guildford by the Hon. Roger North (Vol. I, London, 8vo, 1826). This astute old fox lived to a great age and successfully accommodated his elastic principles to the changes of the time whilst seeming to adhere steadily to the revolutionary party. He has been agreeably satirized as "Bartoline, an old corrupt Lawyer," by Crowne in *City Politicks*, produced at Drury Lane in January, 1682-3 ; 4to, 1683.

[26] *The Gentleman's Magazine*, July, 1851.

[27] *Vide*, chapter I.

[28] It should be remarked that Mr. Charles C. Harper in his interesting, if somewhat sceptical study *Haunted Houses* (Revised and enlarged, 1924, p. 86), commenting upon this relation says : "It is to be added from personal

observation, that there is no place called Croglin Grange. There are Croglin High Hall and Low Hall. Both are farmhouses, very like one another, and not in any particulars resembling the description given. Croglin Low Hall is probably the house indicated, but it is at least a mile distant from the church, which has been rebuilt. The churchyard contains no tomb which by any stretch of imagination could be identified with that described by Mr. Hare." This criticism does not seem to affect the story in the slightest. I am bound to say that from the drawing by Mr. Harper of Croglin Low Hall it appears to be exactly Croglin Grange. The vault—since the family was long extinct—may easily have been obliterated. Such a precaution would be obvious after the fearful experience from the attack of the Vampire, and would not be a difficult business. Moreover it would be soon done without attracting notice. It were to be wished that the name of the family had been given so that the history of the Vampire might be traced. Often, however, such records are destroyed from the domestic archives.

²⁹ Occult Review, November, 1924, vol. XI, No. 5, pp. 258-59.

³⁰ Dudley Wright, Vampires and Vampirism. Second edition, 1924, p. 50.

³¹ In a private letter, 4 February, 1928.

³² Gerald de Barry, born circa 1147; died 1216-1220. His many works are reprinted in the Rolls Series edited by Brewer and Dimock. The volumes dealing with Ireland, Topographia Hibernica, and Expugnatio Hibernica (this title is attached as a misnomer by Gratianus Lucius, Dr. Lynch, 1662) are especially famous.

³³ Historia Regum Britanniæ, viii, 7.

³⁴ Felire of Oengus, ed. Whitby Stokes. Henry Bradshaw Society. (1905), p. 241.

³⁵ Uita Sancti Moluæ, xxxiii. Quodam die sanctus pater Molua iuit uidere armentum monasterii sui; et uidit prope uiam inter arbusta lupos esurientes et clamantes in celum. Et motus misericordia, ac[c]ersiuit illos secum, et, collacauit in hospicio, lauit pedes eorum, et fecit uitulum occidi et coqui, et traditus est eis cum omni humanitate. Et tale conuiuium anniuersario more Sanctus Molua faciebat lupis. Postea lupi alacres ceperunt custodire pecora sancti Moluæ ab aliis lupis et a furibus; et erant quasi domestici cum pastoribus Sancti, cognoscentes se inuicem: et multis diebus post obitum Saniti Moluæ hoc illi lupi faciebant.

³⁶ Irish MS. at Rennes, f. 86.

³⁷ Uita Sancti Boecii, xiv. " Qualiter lupus hynnulum pro uitulo occisso sibi adduxit." Uita Sancti Coemgeri, ix; Uita Sancti Fechini, vii; Uita Sancti Finani Abbatis de Cenn Etigh, xxiv; Acta Sanctorum Hiberniæ ex codice Salmanticensi, (ed. de Smedt et de Backer, 1888), ccc., Deux Vies inédites de Saint Malo (ed. Dom F. Plaine et A. de la Borderie, 1884); Breui-arium Aberdonense (2 vols, 4to, 1854), Pars Hicmalis, Propria Sanctorum, f. 26, ve; et sacpissime inter legenda.

³⁸ Vol. XLII, No. 4, pp. 242-245.

³⁹ For a particular study of Gilles de Rais see my Geography of Witchcraft, pp. 389-396; together with the authorities to whom reference is made on p. 459. See also my History of Witchcraft and Demonology, Bibliography, p. 342.

⁴⁰ J.-K. Huysmans (Souvenirs). Paris. [1924].

⁴¹ op. cit., p. 79.

⁴² Reynold's Miscellany, No. 125, vol. V. New Series. For the week ending Saturday, November, 30th, 1850, pp. 293-4. A contemporary article giving many valuable details.

⁴³ The case has been studied in great detail by Dr. Épaulard, Le Vam-pirisme.

⁴⁴ An old walnut tree of dense shade and mighty girth near Benevento was reputed to be the general rendezvous of all the witches in Italy. There is a pamphlet by Peter of Piperno De Nuce Maga Beneuentana which gives in some detail the history of and many curious legends connected with the wizard walnut tree of Benevento. See my Geography of Witchcraft, pp. 546-48.

[45] Vol. I, c. lxiv. pp. 143-45.

[46] The passage has been thus translated by Georgina Harding:

"What have they not done ? Candia told of all the different means they had tried, all the exorcisms they had resorted to. The priest had come and, after covering the child's head with the end of his stole, had repeated verses from the Gospel. The mother had hung up a wax cross, blessed on Ascension Day, over a door, and had sprinkled the hinges with holy water and repeated the Creed three times in a loud voice ; she had tied up a handful of salt in a piece of linen and hung it round the neck of her dying child. The father had ' done the seven nights '—that is, for seven nights he had waited in the dark behind a lighted lantern, attentive to the slightest sound, ready to catch and grapple with the vampire. A single prick with the pin sufficed to make her visible to the human eye. But the seven nights' watch had been fruitless, for the child wasted away and grew more hopelessly feeble from hour to hour. At last, in despair, the father had consulted with a wizard, by whose advice he had killed a dog and put the body behind the door. The vampire could not then enter the house till she counted every hair on its body."

CHAPTER III

HUNGARY AND CZECHO-SLOVAKIA

HUNGARY, it may not untruly be said, shares with Greece and
Slovakia the reputation of being that particular region of the
world which is most terribly infested by the Vampire and
where he is seen at his ugliest and worst. Nor is this common
reputation undeserved. It was owing to a number of extraordinary and terrible occurences towards the end of the
seventeenth century, which visitations persisted into the earlier
years of the eighteenth century, that general attention was
drawn to the problem of the Vampire, that theologians and
students of the occult began to collect data of these happenings
which made sufficient noise to be reported in such journals
as the *Mercure galant* and the *Glaneur Hollandois*. There
followed, such was the universal interest aroused by these
events, very many monographs and academic dissertations to
which attention has already been drawn. It will suffice here
to remind ourselves of just a few of these, such works for
example as Philip Rohr's *De masticatione mortuorum*, Leipzig,
1679; the *Magia posthuma* of Charles Ferdinand de Schertz,
which was published at Olmutz in 1706, and which directly
dealt with a case of vampirism that had come under the
author's notice. This will be treated in detail a little later.
We also have early in the eighteenth century the *De
masticatione mortuorum in tumulis liber* of Michael Ranftius,
Leipzig, 1728; a *Dissertatio de cadaueribus sanguisugis* by John
Christian Stock, Jena, 1732; *Relation von den Vampyren oder
Menschensaugern*, Leipzig, 1732; *Relation von denen in Servien
sich erzeigenden Blutsaugern*, 1732; *Besondere Nachricht von
denen vampyren oder sogennanten Blut-Saugeren*, 1732; *Uisus
et repertus über die sogenannten Vampyren*, Nuremburg, 1732;
*Dissertatio de hominibus post mortem sanguisugis, uulgo dictis
Uampyrea*, Leipzig, 1732, of John Christopher Rohlius and
John Hertelius; *Dissertatio de Uampyris Seruiensibus* of John
Henry Zopfius and Francis van Dalen, 1733; a second work of

Michael Ranftius printed at Leipzig, 1734, *Tractatus von dem Kauen und Schmatzen der Todten in Gräbern, worin die wahre Beschassenheit der Hungarischen Vampyrs oder Blut-Sauger gezeiget, auch alle von dieser Materie bisher edirten Schriften recensiret werden;* nor must we forget the important *Von Vampyren* of John Christian Harenberg, issued in 1739. This list of rare treatises, many of which were published at Leipzig, might be almost indefinitely prolonged, but a sufficient number of names has been given to show the extraordinary attention that was being excited by the problem of vampirism, an attention evoked by actual happenings. In fact one student many years later wrote an article, which seems to have escaped general notice, to which he gave the name *Le Diable à Leipizg.*[1]

In his famous work *An Antidote against Atheism : or, An Appeal to the Natural Faculties of the Mind of Man, whether there be not a God,* 1653 (second edition with Appendix, 1655), the great Cambridge Platonist Henry More[2] relates the following,[3] which are probably the first histories to be recorded concerning Vampires by an English author since the Chroniclers of the twelfth century.

A certain Shoemaker in one of the chief Towns of *Silesia*, in the year 1591, *Septemb.* 20, on a Friday betimes in the morning, in the further part of his house, where there was adjoining a little Garden, cut his own Throat with his Shoemaker's knife. The Family, to cover the foulness of the fact, and that no disgrace might come upon his Widow, gave out, that he died of an Apoplexy, declined all visits of friends and neighbours, in the meantime got him washed, and laid Linens so handsomely about him, that even they that saw him afterwards, as the Parson, and some others, had not the least Suspicion but that he did die of that disease ; and so he had honest Burial, with a funeral Sermon, and other circumstances becoming one of his rank and reputation. Six weeks had not past, but so strong a rumour broke out, that he died not of any disease, but had laid violent hands upon himself, that the Magistracy of the place could not but bring all those that had seen the corps, to a strict examination. They shuffled off the matter as well as they could at first, with many fair Apologies, in behalf of the deceased, to remove all suspicion of so heinous an act: but it being pressed more home to their Conscience, at last they confessed, he died a violent death, but desired their favour and clemency to his widow and children, who were in no fault ; adding also, that it was uncertain but that he might be slain by some external mishap, or, if by himself, in some irresistible fit of phrency or madness.

Hereupon the Councel deliberate what is to be done, Which the Widow hearing, and fearing they might be determining something that would be harsh, and to the discredit of her Husband, and herself, being also animated thereto by some busie bodies, makes a great complaint against those that raised these reports of her Husband, and resolved to follow the Law upon them, earnestly contending that there was no reason, upon mere rumours and idle defamations of malevolent people, that her Husband's body should be digged up, or dealt with as if he had been either *Magician*, or *Self-murtherer*. Which boldness and pertinacity of the woman, though after the confession of the fact, did in some measure work upon the Council, and put them to a stand.

But while these things are in agitation, to the astonishment of the Inhabitants of the place, there appears a *Spectrum* in the exact shape and habit of the deceased, and that not only in the night, but at mid-day. Those that were asleep it terrified with horrible visions ; those that were waking it would strike, pull, or press, lying heavy upon them like an *Ephialtes* : so that there were perpetual complaints every morning of their last night's rest through the whole Town. But the more freaks this *Spectrum* play'd, the more diligent were the friends of the deceased to suppress the rumours of them, or at least to hinder the effects of those rumours ; and therefore made their addresses to the President, complaining how unjust a thing it was, that so much credit should be given to idle reports and blind suspicions, and therefore beseech'd him that he would hinder the Council from digging up the corps of the deceased, and from all ignominious usage of him: adding also, that they intended to appeal to the Emperour's Court, that their Wisdoms might rather decide the Controversy, than that the cause should be determined from the light conjectures of malicious men.

But while by this means the business was still protracted, there were such stirs and tumults all over the Town, that they are hardly to be described. For no sooner did the Sun hide his head, but this *Spectrum* would be sure to appear, so that every body was fain to look about him, and stand upon his guard, which was a sore trouble to those whom the Labours of the Day made more sensible of the want of rest in the night. For this terrible *Apparrition* would sometimes stand by their bed-sides, sometimes cast itself upon the midst of their beds, would lie close to them, would miserably suffocate them, and would so strike them and pinch them, that not only blue marks, but plain impressions of his fingers would be upon sundry parts of their bodies in the morning. Nay, such was the violence and impetuousness of this Ghost, that when men forsook their beds, and kept their dining-rooms, with Candles lighted, and many of them in company together, the better to secure themselves from fear and disturbance ; yet he would then appear to them, and have a bout with some of them, notwithstanding all this provision against it. In brief, he was so troublesome, that the people were ready to forsake their houses, and seek other dwellings, and the Magistrates so awakend at the perpetual complaints of them, that at last they resolved, the President agreeing thereto, to dig up the Body.

He had lain in the ground near eight months, *viz.* from *Sept.* 22, 1591, to *April* 18, 1592. When he was digged up, which was in the presence of the Magistracy of the Town, his body was found entire, not at all putrid, no ill smell about him, saving the mustiness of the Grave-cloaths, his joints limber and flexible, as in those that are alive, his skin only flaccid, but a more fresh grown in the room of it, the wound of his throat gaping, but no gear nor corruption in it ; there was also observed a Magical mark in the great toe of his right foot, *viz.* an Excrescency in the form of a Rose. His body was kept out of the earth from *April* 18, to the 24*th*, at what time many both of the same town and others came daily to view him. These unquiet stirs did not cease for all this, which they after attempted to appease, by burying the corpse under the Gallows, but in vain ; for they were as much as ever, if not more, he now not sparing his own Family : insomuch that his Widow at last went her self to the Magistrate, and told them, that she should be no longer against it, if they thought fit to fall upon some course of more strict proceedings touching her Husband.

Wherefore the seventh of *May* he was again digged up, and it was observable, that he was grown more sensibly fleshy since his last interment. To be short, they cut off the Head, Arms, and Legs of the Corps, and opening his Back, took out his Heart, which was as fresh and intire as in a Calf new kill'd. These, together with his Body, they put on a pile of wood, and burnt them to Ashes, which they carefully sweeping together, and putting into a Sack (that none might get them for wicked uses) poured them into the River, after which the *Spectrum* was never seen more.

As it also happen'd in his Maid that dy'd after him, who appeared within eight days after her death, to her fellow servant, and lay so heavy upon her, that she brought upon her a great swelling of the eyes. She so grievously handled a Child in the cradle, that if the Nurse had not come to his help, he had been quite spoil'd ; but she crossing her self, and calling upon the Name of *Jesus*, the Spectre vanished. The next night she appeared in the shape of an *Hen*, which, when one of the Maids of the house took to be so indeed, and followed her, the Hen grew into an immense bigness, and presently caught the Maid by the throat, and made it swell, so that she could neither eat nor drink of a good while after.

She continued these stirs for a whole month, slapping some so smartly, that the stroke were heard of them that stood by, pulling the bed also from under others, and appearing sometime in one shape, sometimes in another, as of a Woman, of a Dog, of a Cat, and of a Goat. But at last her body being digged up, and burnt, the Apparition was never seen more.

These things being done at *Breslaw* in *Silesia*, where this *Weinrichius* then lived, which makes the Narration more considerable. This concealing the name of the parties, I conceive, was in way of civility to his deceased Towns-man, his Towns-man's Widow, and their Family.

The other Story[4] he sets down he is not the first Pen-man of, (though the things were done in his time, and, as I conceive, some while after what was above related, as a passage in the Narration seems to intimate) but he transcrib'd it from one that not only dwelt in the place, but was often infested with the noisom occursions of that troublesome *Ghost*, that did so much mischief to the place where he dwelt. The Relation is somewhat large, I shall bring it into as narrow compass as I can.

Johannes Cuntius, a Citizen of *Pentsch* in *Silesia*, near sixty years of age, and one of the *Aldermen* of the Town, very fair in his carriage, and unblameable, to men's thinking, in the whole course of his life, having been sent for to the *Mayor's* house (as being a very understanding man, and dexterous at the dispatch of businesses) to end some controversies concerning certain Waggoners, and a Merchant of *Pannonia* having made an end of those affairs, is invited by the *Mayor* to Supper : he gets leave first to go home to order some businesses, leaving this sentence behind him, *It's good to be merry while we may, for mischiefs grow up fast enough daily.*

This *Cuntius* kept five lusty Geldings in his Stable, one whereof he commanded to be brought out, and his shoe being loose, had him ty'd to the next post : his Master with a Servant busied themselves to take up his leg to look on his hoof, the Horse being mad and mettlesome, struck them both down ; but *Cuntius* received the greatest share of the blow : one that stood next by help'd them both up again. *Cuntius* no sooner was up and came to him self, but cry'd out, *Wo is me, how do I burn, and am all on a fire !* which he often repeated. But the parts he complain'd of most, the Women being put out of the room, when they were searched, no appearance of any stroke or hurt was found upon them. To be short, he fell downright sick, and grievously afflicted in Mind, loudly complaining, that his Sins were such, that they were utterly unpardonable, and that the least part of them were bigger than all the Sins of the World besides ; but would have no Divine come to him, nor did particularly confess them to any. Several rumours indeed there were that once he had sold one of his Sons, but when, and to whom, it was uncertain ; and that he had made a Contract with the Devil, and the like. But it was observed, and known for certain, that he had grown beyond all expectation rich, and that four days before this mischance, he being witness to a Child, said, that that was the last he should be ever witness to.

The night he dy'd, his eldest Son watched with him. He gave up the Ghost about the third hour of the night, at what time a black Cat, opening the Casement with her nails, (for it was shut) ran to his bed, and did so violently scratch his face and the bolster, as if she endeavoured by force to remove him out of the place where he lay. But the Cat afterwards suddenly was gone, and she was no sooner gone, but he breathed his last. A fair Tale was made to the Pastor of the Parish, and the Magistracy of the Town allowing it, he was buried on the right side of the Altar, his Friends paying well for it, No sooner *Cuntius* was dead, but a great Tempest arose, which raged most at his very Funeral, there being such impetuous Storms of Wind with Snow, that it made men's bodies quake, and their teeth chatter in their heads.   But so soon as he was interred, of a sudden all was calm.

He had not been dead a day or two, but several rumours were spread in the town of a *Spiritus incubus*, or *Ephialtes*, in the shape of *Cuntius*, that would have forced a Woman. This happen'd before he was buried.   After his burial, the same *Spectre* awaken'd one that was sleeping in his dining room, saying, *I can scarce withhold my self from beating thee to death.* The voice was the voice of *Cuntius*. . The watchmen of the Town also affirmed, that they heard every night great stirs in *Cuntius* his House, the fallings and throwings of things about, and that they did see the gates stand wide open betimes in the mornings, though they were never so diligently shut o'er night ; that his Horses were very unquiet in the Stable, as if they kick'd, and bit one another ; besides unusual barkings and howlings of the Dogs all over the Town.   But these were but preludious suspicions to further evidence, which I will run over as briefly as I may.

A Maid-servant of one of the Citizens of *Pentsch* (while these Tragedies and Stirs were so frequent in the Town) heard, together with some others lying in their beds, the noise and tramplings of one riding about the House, who at last ran against the Walls with that violence, that the whole House shaked again, as if it would fall, and the windows were all fill'd with flashings of light.   The Master of the house being informed of it, went out of doors in the morning to see what the matter was ; and he beheld in the Snow the impressions of strange feet, such as were like neither Horses, nor Cows, nor Hogs, nor any Creature that he knew.

Another time, about eleven of the clock in the night, *Cuntius* appears to one of his Friends that was a witness to a Child of his, speaks unto him, and bids him be of good courage, for he came only to communicate unto him a matter of great importance. *I have left behind me*, said he, *my youngest Son* James, *to whom you are God-father.   Now there is at my eldest Son* Steven's, *a Citizen of* Jegerdorf, *a certain Chest, wherein*

I have put four hundred and fifteen Florens : This I tell you, that your God-son may not be defrauded of any of them, and it is your duty to look after it ; which if you neglect, wo be to you. Having said this, the *Spectre* departed, and went up into the upper rooms of the House, where he walked so stoutly that all rattled again, and the roof swagged with his heavy stampings. This *Cuntius* his Friend told to the Parson of the Parish a day or two after for a certain truth.

But there are also several other notorious passages of this *Cuntius*. As his often speaking to the Maid that lay with her Mistress, his Widow, to give him place, for it was his right ; and if she would not give it him, he would writh her neck behind her.

His galloping up and down like a wanton horse in the Court of his House. He being divers times seen to ride, not only in the streets, but along the vallies of the fields, and on the Mountains, with so strong a trot, that he made the very ground flash with fire under him.

His bruising of the body of a Child of a certain Smiths, and making his very bones so soft, that you might wrap the corps on heaps like a glove.

His miserably tugging all night with a *Jew* that had taken up his Inn in the Town, and tossing him up and down in the lodging where he lay.

His dreadful accosting of a Waggoner, an old acquaintance of his, while he was busie in the stable, vomiting out fire against him to terrify him, and biting of him so cruelly by the foot, that he made him lame.

What follows, as I above intimated, concerns the Relator himself, who was the Parson of the Parish, whom his Fury so squeez'd and press'd when he was asleep, that wakening he found himself utterly spent, and his strength quite gone, but could not imagine the reason. But while he lay musing with himself what the matter might be, this *Spectre* returns again to him, and holding him all over so fast, that he could not wag a finger, rowled him in his bed backwards and forwards a good many times together. The same happen'd also to his Wife another time, whom *Cuntius*, coming thro' the casement in the shape of a little Dwarf, and running to her bed-side, so wrung and pulled as if he would have torn her throat out, had not her two Daughters come in to help her.

He pressed the lips together of one of this *Theologer's* Sons so, that they could scarce get them asunder.

His House was so generally disturbed with this unruly Ghost, that the Servants were fain to keep together anights in one room, lying upon straw, and watching the approaches of this troublesome Fiend. But a Maid of the House, being more couragious than the rest, would needs one night go to bed, and forsake her company. Whereupon *Cuntius* finding her alone, presently assaults her, pulls away the bedding, and would have carried her away with him ; but she hardly escaping fled to the rest of the Family, where she espied him standing by the candle, and straightway after vanishing.

Another time he came into her Master's Chamber, making a noise like a Hog that eats grain, smacking and grunting very sonorously. They could not chase him away, by speaking to him ; but ever as they lighted a Candle, he would vanish.

On another Time about Evening, when this *Theologer* was sitting with his Wife and Children about him, exercising himself in Musick, according to his usual manner, a most grievous stink arose suddenly, which by degrees spread itself to every corner of the room. Here upon he commends himself and his family to God by Prayer. The smell nevertheless encreased, and became above all measure pestilently noisom, insomuch that he was forced to go up to his chamber. He and his Wife had not been in bed a quarter of an hour, but they find the same stink in the bed-chamber ; of which, while they are complaining one to another, out steps the Spectre from the Wall, and creeping to his bed-side, breathes upon him an exceeding cold breath, of so intolerable stinking and malignant a scent, as is beyond all imagination and expression. Here upon the *Theologer*, good soul, grew very ill, and was fain to keep his bed, his face, belly, and guts swelling as if he had been poysoned ; whence he was also troubled with a difficulty of breathing, and with a putrid inflammation of his eyes, so that he could not well use them of a long time after.

But taking leave of the sick Divine, if we should go back, and recount what we have omitted, it would exceed the number of what we have already recounted. As for example, The trembling and sweating of *Cuntius* his Gelding, from which he was not free night nor day : The burning blue of the Candles at the approaches of *Cuntius* his Ghost : His drinking up the milk in the milk-bowls, his flinging dung into them, or turning the milk into blood : His pulling up posts deep set in the ground, and so heavy, that two lusty Porters could not deal with them : his discoursing with several men he met concerning the affairs of the Waggoners : His strangling of old men : His holding fast the Cradles of Children, or taking them out of them : His frequent endeavouring to force women : His defiling the Water in the Font, and fouling the Cloth on the Altar on that side that did hang towards his grave with dirty bloody spots : His catching up Dogs in the streets, and knocking their brains against the ground : His sucking dry the Cows, and tying their tails like the tail of an Horse : His devouring of Poultry, and his flinging of Goats bound into the Racks : His tying of an Horse to an empty oat-tub in the Stable, to clatter up and down with it, and the hinder foot of another to his own head-stall : His looking out of the Window of a low Tower, and then suddenly changing himself into the form of a long staff : His chiding of a Matron for suffering her servant to wash dishes on a Thursday,[5] at what time he laid his hand upon her, and she said, it felt more cold than ice : His pelting one of the Women that washed his corps, so forcibly, that the print of the Clods he flung, were to be seen upon the wall : His attempting to ravish another, who excusing herself and saying, *My* Cuntius, *thou seest how old, wrinkled, and deformed I am, and how unfit for those kind of sports*, he suddenly set up a loud laughter, and vanished.

But we must insist upon these things ; only we will add one passage more that is not a little remarkable. His grave-stone was turned of one side, shelving, and there were several holes in the earth, about the bigness of mouse-holes, that went down to his very Coffin, which, however they were filled up with earth over night, yet they would be sure to be laid open the next morning.

It would be a tedious business to recite these things at large, and prosecute the Story in all its particular Circumstances. To conclude therefore, their calamity was such, from the frequent occursions of this restless fury, that there was none but either pitied them, or despis'd them ; none would lodge in their Town, Trading was decay'd, and the Citizens impoverished by the continual stirs and tumults of this unquiet Ghost.

And though the *Atheist* may perhaps laugh at them, as men undone by their own Melancholy and vain imaginations, or by the waggery of some ill neighbours; yet if he seriously consider what has been already related, there are many passages that are by no means to be resolved into any such Principles; but what I shall now declare, will make it altogether unlikely that any of them are.

To be short therefore, finding no rest, nor being able to excogitate any better remedy, they dig up *Cuntius* his body with several others buried both before and after him. But those both after and before were so putrify'd and rotten, their Sculls broken, and the Sutures of them gaping, that they were not to be known by their shape at all, having become in a manner but a rude mass of earth and dirt; but it was quite otherwise in *Cuntius*: His Skin was tender and florid, his Joynts not at all stiff, but limber and moveable, and a staff being put into his hand, he grasped it with His fingers very fast; his Eyes also of themselves would be one time open, and another time shut; they opened a vein in his Leg, and the blood sprang out as fresh as in the living; his Nose was entire and full, not sharp, as in those that are ghastly sick, or quite dead: and yet *Cuntius* his body had lien in the grave from *Feb.* 8 to *July* 20 which is almost half a year.

It was easily discernible where the fault lay. However, nothing was done rashly, but Judges were constituted, Sentence was pronounced upon *Cuntius* his Carcase, which (being animated thereto from success in the like case, some few years before in this very Province of *Silesia*, I suppose he means at *Breslaw*, where the Shoemakers body was burnt) they adjudged to the fire.

Wherefore there were Masons provided to make a hole in the wall near the Altar to get his body through, which being pulled at with a rope, it was so exceeding heavy, that the rope brake, and they could scarce stir him. But when they had pull'd him through, and gotten him on a Cart without, which *Cuntius* his Horse that had struck him (which was a lusty-bodied Jade) was to draw; yet it put him to it so, that he was ready to fall down ever and anon, and was quite out of breath with striving to draw so intolerable a load, who not with-standing could run away with two men in the same Cart presently after, their weight was so inconsiderable to his strength.

His body, when it was brought to the fire, proved as unwilling to be burnt, as before to be drawn ; so that the Executioner was fain with hooks to pull him out, and cut him into pieces to make him burn. Which, while he did, the blood was found so pure and spiritous, that it spurted into his face as he cut him ; but at last, not without the expence of two hundred and fifteen great billets, all was turned into ashes. Which they carefully sweeping up together, as in the foregoing Story, and casting them into the River, the *Spectre* never more appeared.

I must confess, I am so slow witted myself that I cannot so much as imagine, what the *Atheist* will excogitate for a subterfuge or hiding place, from so plain and evident Convictions."

In his *Historia naturalis curiosa regni Poloniae* published at Sandomir in 1721 Gabriel Rzazcynsci, a learned Jesuit, writes : " De cruentationibus cadauerum in specie agens, mira profert de mortuis in tumulis adhuc uoracibus et uicinis uiuentes in spectorum modum trucidantibus a Polonis speciali nomine *Upiers* et *Upierryea* appellatis. De quibus quae producit authentica documenta ulteriorem fortasse disquisitionem merentur."

The following document was guaranteed by Monsieur de Vassimont, a councillor of the Confederation of Bar in Podolia, who had been sent as an envoy to Moravia by his Royal Highness Leopold I, Duke of Lorraine, in order to conduct certain businesses on behalf of his brother, Prince Charles Joseph of Lorraine, Bishop of Olmutz and Osnabruck[6] and later Archbishop of Trèves (1698—1715). Monsieur de Vassimont was generally informed that in those districts it was no unusual thing to see men who had been dead for some long time suddenly appear in the midst of a general assembly, and that not infrequently they entered a room and took their place at table with friends or acquaintance, that they never uttered a word, but that some sign either with the head or the hand was given to one of those present and that this person almost certainly died not very many days later. These extraordinary phenomena were vouched for by many very respectable individuals, and amongst others by an aged rector who declared that he had actually witnessed more than one instance of this.

The bishops and the priests of that province officially consulted Rome with regard to such extraordinary occurences ;

but it appears they received no reply, because no doubt, all this was regarded as purely imaginary and as having no existence beyond the fancy of the common folk. They determined then to exhume the bodies of those who returned in this way and to cremate them, or at any rate entirely to destroy them in some other manner. And thus, at length, they were freed from the importunity of these phantoms who nowadays are far less frequently to be seen in this country than in former times. The rector, a learned and most honoured man, solemnly declared that what he related was entirely true.

It was, indeed, the report of these apparitions which gave Charles Ferdinand de Schertz the occasion to write his book *Magia posthuma*, which, as has been mentioned above, appeared at Olmutz in 1706, and which was dedicated to Prince Charles of Lorraine, Bishop of Olmutz and Osnabruck. Schertz relates that in a certain village a woman who had recently died without receiving the last Sacraments[7] was buried in the usual way in the cemetery. Four days after her decease the inhabitants of the village heard an extraordinary noise and a terrible storm arose, when they saw a ghost which appeared to some people in the form of a dog, to others in the shape of a gaunt and hideous man, and who was seen not only by one individual but by many, and who caused persons the greatest alarm and torment by assaulting them fiercely, by seizing their throats so that they were almost suffocated, by exhausting the strength from their whole frame so that they were reduced to the last degree of feebleness and everyone noted how pale, attenuated and ill they appeared.

The ghost even attacked animals, and cows were found half dead just as if they had been severely beaten. These poor beasts by their mournful lowing showed what pains they were suffering. Horses were observed overcome with fatigue, sweating and trembling, over-heated, breathless, covered with foam, as if they had just been roughly driven at full gallop along some long and difficult road. These troubles persisted for many months.

Schertz, who was an eminent lawyer, argues the facts from a legal point of view. He examines the circumstances with perfect impartiality, and he weighs the evidence in the nicest manner according to precedent and routine. Granting that these troubles, these noises, these disturbances actually emanate from the person who is suspected of being their cause he inquires whether her body should be burned, as is the usual procedure in the case of the bodies of other apparitions who return from the grave and inflict injuries upon the living. He cites several examples of similar happenings and particularly describes the evil consequences which ensued. There was for instance a herdsman belonging to the village of Blau near the town of Kodon in Bohemia who after his death appeared to several persons in the district, and he used to call these unfortunate wretches loudly by name. Whether it was from fright, or whether it was because this Vampire exhausted their vitality, those whom he had thus summoned expired, it was remarked, within the course of a few days, invariably less than a week. The peasants of Blau exhumed the body, and drove a large stake right through the heart so that it was pinned to the ground. In spite of this precaution that very night the body appeared again and in so awful a guise that he frightened several persons to death, whilst he attacked and actually suffocated a yet greater number. He jeered horribly at those who had thought to have put an end to this plague, and mockingly thanked them for having given him a fine stick to drive away the dogs. When morning had come the place was in a panic, and the village authorities caused the body once again to be disinterred. It was then handed over to the common executioner who threw it into a tumbril and conveyed it beyond the village to a waste piece of ground where it was burned. The corpse, bloated and swollen, yelled like a madman kicking and tearing as though it had been alive, and when they pierced it with sharpened piles of white thorn it howled horribly, writhing and champing its blub red lips with the long white teeth whilst streams of warm red blood spurted out in all directions. At last it was thrown on a blazing pyre, and when execution had been duly performed, and the body reduced to ashes, the apparitions and molestations at last ceased.

Schertz says that exactly the same procedure has been followed in a great many other districts, and that to his knowledge many villages had been annoyed in this way. In each case when they have exhumed the body the Vampire was discovered as if it were alive, with a fresh complexion. Several other writers of authority are quoted and these fully bear out what he relates concerning these spectres, who, he remarks, particularly infest the mountainous districts of Silesia and Moravia, particularly the Carpathian ranges. Not only do they appear at night but they are often seen during the day, and, what is very extraordinary, objects which have belonged to the dead persons are moved from one place to another and are conveyed from room to room without anybody who visibly touches them. According to Schertz, the only remedy is to disinter the body, cut off the head, and burn the corpse to ashes. But this, says he, must not be done without due authority, and such proceedings are to be carried out in a formal and official manner. An inquiry must be held ; witnesses are to be called and examined ; the evidence is not to be too readily accepted ; when the bodies in question have been exhumed they must be examined by medical men and theologians who may determine whether it is actually these persons who are molesting the living, and who may note the marks which undoubtedly evince vampirism. Should these conditions appear, then the bodies shall be officially handed over to the common executioner who will be instructed to burn them. It is said that cases are known when apparitions appear for some three or four days after the body has been burned. Should such an instance be authentic, and there is no reason to suppose otherwise, it must follow that this is not a Vampire but a ghost, and the spectre can neither draw upon nor nourish itself with the vitality of the living, although, indeed, it is quite true that ghosts themselves can be actually harmful and there are many cases upon record where spectres who are particularly malignant have actually attacked living persons and endeavoured to strangle them. So it must not be supposed that the evil powers of an apparition are only confined to frightening and alarm. It is particularly related that the clothes of a person who is a Vampire will often be moved from one place where they were hanging to another, as for example even though a suit of clothes may be locked up in a wardrobe, it has been found that these are mysteriously laid out upon a bed as if ready set for the person to change his attire. Schertz mentions that not many months before he wrote, there occurred at Olmutz certain disturbances that were very widely talked of and discussed. A house was troubled by an apparition which moved the furniture and pelted persons with stones and other missiles. But it would seem that here we have to deal with a poltergeist, a species of haunting very prevalent at the present day, and indeed, often investigated because it is so common. There are reported a very large number of examples of this especial haunting. One of the latest instances of these disturbances which took place at a house in Eland Road, Lavender Hill, London, S.W.11, during January of last year (1928) caused a tremendous sensation.[8]

The following incidents which happened about the year 1720 are placed beyond all manner of doubt both on account of the number and the position of the witnesses as also on account of the weight of the evidence which is sensible, circumstantial and complete. A soldier, who was billeted at the house of a farmer residing at Haidam, a village on the frontiers of Hungary, when one day he was at table with his host, the master of the house and the family, saw a stranger enter and take his place at the board among them. There seemed nothing extraordinary in this circumstance, but the goodman exhibited symptoms of unusual terror, as indeed did the rest of the company. Although he did not know what to think of it the soldier refrained from any comment, although it was impossible that he should not have remarked their confusion and fear. On the next morning the farmer was discovered dead in his bed, and then the reason for their perturbation could no longer be kept secret. They informed the soldier that the mysterious stranger was the farmer's old father, who had been dead and buried for more than ten years, and who had thus come and taken his place by the side of his son to forewarn him of his death, which indeed the terrible visitant had actually caused.

As might have been expected, the soldier recounted this extraordinary incident to his friends and companions and so it came to the ears of several officers by whom it was carried to the general. A consultation was held, and it was resolved that the Count de Cadreras, commander of a corps of the Alandetti Infantry, should institute a full inquiry into so extraordinary circumstances. Accordingly this gentleman with several other officers, an army surgeon and a notary, paid an official visit to Haidam. Here they took the sworn depositions of all the people belonging to the house, and these without exception gave it on oath that the mysterious stranger was the father of the late master of the house, and that all the soldier had said and reported was the exact truth.   These statements were unanimously corroborated by all the persons who lived in that district.   In consequence of this the officers decided that the body must be exhumed, and although ten years had passed it was found lying like a man who had just died, or even rather, like one who was in a heavy slumber, since when a vein was pierced the warm blood flowed freely as if that of a living person.   The Count de Cadreras gave orders that the head should be completely severed, and then the corpse was once more laid in his grave.   During their inquiry they also received information of many others who returned from the tomb, and among the rest of a man who had died more than thirty years before, who had come back no less than three times to his house at the hour of the evening's meal ; and that on each occasion he had suddenly sprung upon an individual whose neck he bit fiercely, sucking the blood, and then vanishing with indescribable celerity.   The first time he thus attacked his own brother, the second time one of his sons, and the third time one of the servants of the farm, so that all three expired instantly upon the spot.   When this had been attested upon oath the Commissioner ordered that this man also should be disinterred, and he was found exactly like the first, just as a person who was still alive, the blood gushing out slab and red when an incision was made in the flesh.   Orders were given that a great twopenny nail should be driven through the temples, and that afterwards the body should be laid again in the grave.

A third, who had been buried more than sixteen years, and who had caused the death of two of his sons by sucking their blood, was considered especially dangerous and forthwith cremated.   The Commissioner made his report to the highest army tribunal, and they were so struck by the narration that they required him personally to deliver it to the Emperor Charles VI, who was so concerned at these extraordinary facts that he ordered a number of eminent lawyers, officers of the highest rank, the most skilled surgeons and physicians, and his most learned theologians to visit the district and conduct a most searching inquiry into the causes of these unusual and terrible occurences.   The papers dealing with the case are still extant and the whole story was related in

1730 by the Count de Cadreras himself to a responsible official of the University of Fribourg who took down the details from the Count's own lips. It is hard to see how more reliable evidence is to be obtained of any happening or event.

The following history is given by several authorities and is also related in the *Lettres Juives*,[9] by the Marquis d' Argens, a well-known book the first edition of which was translated into English and published London, 1729 as *The Jewish Spy*, "being a philosophical, historical, and critical correspondence by letters which lately pass'd between certain Jews in Turkey, Italy, France, etc." In this work which through the supposed medium of a foreigner, whose views are unbiased by the ideas and associations to which the mind of a native is habituated, are presented remarks on the manners and customs of a nation, interspersed with accounts of any extraordinary happenings that may recently have attracted particular notice. Although the medium is imaginary it must not by any manner of means be supposed that these letters had not a very serious import and intention. This method was perhaps the safest and most popular way in which one might criticize existing institutions and correct prevalent abuses, and the various histories which the author presents are related as facts deserving grave attention and communicated to his readers because they contain something extraordinary which demands scientific investigation and the consideration of a philosopher. When the question of vampirism was so largely occupying the attention of the learned it was natural that in such a work as the *Lettres Juives* some history of this kind, well authenticated and officially sanctioned, should find a place. The following was attested by two officers of the tribunal of Belgrade and by an officer in command of the imperial army at Gradiska, all three of whom investigated the affair in the year 1725. At the beginning of September, 1728, in a village named Kisolova, which is about nine or ten miles from Gradiska, there died a farmer by name Peter Plogojowitz who still appeared hale and hearty being only sixty-two years of age. Three days after his death, at midnight, he appeared to enter his house and asked his son for food. When this was set before him it seemed as if he partook of it and then left the room. On the next day the son who had been exceedingly alarmed told his friends and neighbours what had happened. That night the father did not appear, but on the following night he was again seen and he again asked for food. This time the son refused it upon which the apparition regarded him with a threatening look and on the next day he was found to have suddenly expired. Within a very few hours five or six other persons fell ill in the village. Their symptoms were complete exhaustion and a faintness as though from excessive loss of blood. They complained that they had been visited by a fearful dream in which the dead Plogojowitz seemed to glide into the room, catch them by the throat biting hard and suck the blood out of the wound. In this way he killed nine persons in less than a week. In spite of all that the local apothecary could do the sick men expired within a few days. The chief magistrate of the district learning what had taken place from the parish priest at once committed the facts to writing and sent them to Gradiska where there happened to be staying the Commander of the Imperial forces. Taking with him two officers of great experience and ordering the common executioner to attend, he visited the village of Kisilova which was thus tormented. They opened the graves of all who had died since the first week in September, and when they came to that of the farmer they found him as though he were in a trance, gently breathing, his eyes wide open and glaring horribly, his complexion ruddy, the flesh plump and full. His hair and nails had grown, and when the scarfskin came off there appeared a new and healthy cuticle. His mouth was all slobbered and stained with fresh blood. Thence they at once concluded it was he who must be the Vampire thus molesting the district, and it was necessary at once to put a stop to his ravages in case he should infect the whole village. The executioner armed with a heavy mallet drove a sharp stake through his heart, during which the grave was deluged with the blood that gushed from the wound, his nose, ears, and every orifice of the body. A big pyre of logs and brushwood having been built, the body was placed thereon. It was dry weather and the wood when kindled soon burned brightly, the flames being fanned by a gentle breeze. In a very short time the body was reduced to ashes. No marks of vampirism being found upon the other bodies they were reburied with due precautions, garlic and whitethorn being placed in the coffins, and thenceforth the village was freed from any molestation.[10]

One of the best-attested, most detailed, and most famous histories of vampirism is concerned with the village of Meduegna near Belgrade, just at the time when the two dioceses of Belgrade and Smederevo were united by Benedict XIII, and Vincent Bagradin became the first holder of the double title. As will be later seen the document which gives full particulars of the following history was signed on 7 January, 1732, by three army surgeons and formally countersigned by a lieutenant-colonel and a sub-lieutenant. Of its authenticity and absolute fidelity no doubt at all can be entertained.

In the spring of 1727 there returned from service in the Levant to his native village Meduegna, a young man named Arnold Paole, who although he had seen military service but a few years had, according to his own accounts, met with many and varied adventures in that part of the world, a career which afforded him opportunity to save enough to purchase a good cottage and an acre or two of land in his native place, whence he was determined not to stir for the remainder of his days. It appeared a little remarkable to some that a man in the early prime of life, far from ill-looking, one who must have seen the rough as well as the smooth and companied with many a good fellow, should settle down so early in a quiet and out-of-the-way village. Yet his scrupulous honesty in all business transactions, his disciplined habits of work, his steady conduct, soon showed that the adventures with which he must have met in his travels had not, as is only too often the case with young soldiers, affected his probity and self-control. Nevertheless some noticed a certain uneasiness, a certain strangeness in his manner, which gave them food for suspicions, although they could not exactly tell whither these suspicions tended. It seemed as though he almost systematically avoided meeting Nina, the daughter of a rich farmer whose land ran along his own. And yet, as the gossips of the village said, what more equal match could there be ? He was young ; he had a decent property which in time would greatly improve ; he had health, he was obviously of industrious habits, and he himself had been heard to declare that he had formed no connexions and had no ties in other lands.

As time passed on Arnold could not always avoid the society of his neighbours, and no surprise was felt when it was announced that he had been formally betrothed to Nina. And yet, as she often told her friends, the maiden felt that there was a shadow between them. At last she resolved to tackle him on the subject and she boldly asked what trouble so continually oppressed him. After a while he consented to tell her, and having informed her that he was always haunted by the fear of an early death he related a strange adventure which had befallen him at Kostartsa near Granitsa whilst he was on active service. He said that in those parts of Greece the dead returned to torment the living. By some evil chance they had been stationed in a terribly haunted spot, and he had experienced the first visitation. Immediately he sought the unhallowed grave and executed summary vengeance upon the Vampire. He had then, in spite of the persuasion of his superiors, sent in his resignation from the army, and had literally fled to his native village. It was true that so far he experienced no ill effects, and he trusted that he might have been able to counteract the evil. It so happened that during the harvest-home Arnold fell from the top of a loaded hay-waggon and was picked up insensible from the ground. They carried him to bed but he had evidently received some serious injury for after lingering a short time he died. In a few days his body was laid to rest, as they thought, in the village church-yard. About a month later, however, reports began to be circulated that Arnold after night-fall had been seen wandering about the village, and several persons, whose names are entered upon the official report, complained that they were haunted by him, and that after he had appeared to them they felt in a state of extraordinary debility. But a short time went by when several of these persons died, and something like a panic began to spread through the neighbourhood. As the dark winter nights approached no man dared to venture outside his doors when once dusk had fallen, yet it was whispered that the spectre was able easily to penetrate closed windows and walls, that no locks or bars could keep him out if he wished to enter. Throughout the whole winter the wretched village seems to have lived in a state of frantic terror and dismay. The evil, as we may well imagine, was aggravated by the cold hungry nights of a snow-tossed December and January. At length some ten weeks, or rather more,[11] after his funeral it was resolved that the body of Arnold must be disinterred with a view of ascertaining whether he was indeed a vampire. The party consisted of two officers, military representatives from Belgrade, two army surgeons, *Unterfeldscherern*, a drummer boy who carried their cases of instruments, the authorities of the village, the old sexton and his assistants. Dr. Mayo thus reconstructs the scene. "It was early on a grey morning that the commission visited the quiet cemetery of Meduegna, which, surrounded with a wall of unhewn stone, lies sheltered by the mountains that, rising in undulating green slopes, irregularly planted with fruit trees, ends in an abrupt craggy ridge, feathered with underwood. The graves were, for the most part, neatly kept, with borders of box, or something like it, and flowers between ; and at the head of most a small wooden cross, painted black, bearing the name of the tenant. Here and there a stone had been raised. One of considerable heighth, a single narrow slab, ornamented with grotesque Gothic carvings, dominated over the rest. Near this lay the grave of Arnold Paole, towards which the party moved. The work of throwing out the earth was begun by the bent crooked old sexton, who lived in the Leichenhaus beyond the great crucifix. He seemed unconcerned enough ; " but, as might well be supposed the young drummer boy was gazing intently, fascinated by horror and suspense. Before very long the coffin was rather roughly dragged out of the ground, and the grave-digger's assistant soon knocked off the lid. It was seen that the corpse had moved to one side, the jaws gaped wide open and the blub lips were moist with new blood which had trickled in a thin stream from a corner of the mouth. All unafraid the old sexton caught the body and twisted it straight. "So," he cried, "You have not wiped your mouth since last night's work." Even the officers accustomed to the horrors of the battlefield and the surgeons accustomed to the horrors of the dissecting room shuddered at so hideous a spectacle. It is recorded that the drummer boy swooned upon the spot. Nerving themselves to their awful work they inspected the remains more closely, and it was soon apparent that there lay before them the thing they dreaded—the vampire. He looked indeed, as if he had not been dead a day. On handling the corpse the scarfskin came off, and below there were new skin and new nails. Accordingly they scattered garlic over the remains and drove a stake through the body, which it is said gave a piercing shriek as the warm blood spouted out in a great crimson jet.

When this dreadful operation had been performed they proceeded to exhume the bodies of four others who had died in consequence of Arnold's attacks. The records give no details of the state in which these were found. They simply say that whitethorn stakes were driven through them and that they were all five burned. The ashes of all were replaced in consecrated ground.

It might have been thought that these measures would have put an end to vampirism in the village, but such unhappily was not the case, which shows that the original vampire at Kostartsa must have been of an exceptionally malignant nature. About half-a-dozen years after the body of Arnold Paole had been cremated the infection seems to have broken out afresh and several persons died apparently through loss of blood, their bodies being in a terribly anæmic and attenuated condition. This time the officials did not hesitate immediately to cope with the danger, and they determined to make a complete examination of all the graves in the cemetery to which any suspicion attached. Accordingly several surgeons of eminence were summoned from Belgrade and a very thorough investigation took place which yielded the most extraordinary results. The medical reports from which the following cases of vampirism are quoted were officially signed on 7 January, 1732, at Meduegna by three distinguished army surgeons, Johannes Flickinger, Isaac Siedel, Johann Friedrich Baumgartner, and formally countersigned by the lieutenant-colonel and a sub-lieutenant then in residence at Belgrade.

The most remarkable examples were the following :

A woman by name Stana, twenty years of age, who had died three months before, after an illness which only lasted three day and which followed directly after her confinement. Upon her death bed she confessed that she had anointed herself with the blood of a vampire to liberate herself from his persecutions. Nevertheless, she, as well as her baby, had died. The body of the child, owing to a hasty and careless interment, had been half scraped up and devoured by wolves. The body of the woman, Stana, was untouched by decomposition. When it was opened the chest was found to be full of fresh blood, the viscera had all the appearance of soundest health. The skin and nails of both hands and feet were loose and came off, but underneath was a clean new skin and nails.

A woman of the name of Miliza, who had died after an illness lasting three months. The body had been buried nearly one hundred days before. In the chest was liquid blood, and the bowels were sound and entirely healthy. The corpse was declared by a heyduk who recognized it to look better and to be far plumper than during life. The body of a child eight years old, that had likewise been buried ninety days. It was in the Vampire condition.

The son of a heyduk named Milloc, a lad some sixteen years old. The body had been buried ninety days ; it was rosy and flabber, wholly in the Vampire condition.

One Joachim, a boy of seventeen, who was likewise the son of a heyduk. He had died after a short illness of three days, and had lain buried for eight weeks and four days. His complexion was fresh, and the body unmistakably in the Vampire condition.

A woman, named Ruscha. She had died after a sickness lasting ten days. She was buried six weeks before. New blood and warm was found in her chest and in fundo uentriculi.

A young girl ten years of age, who had died two months before. Her body was in the Vampire condition, and when pierced with a stake a great quantity of hot blood poured forth and swilled the grave.

The wife of a villager named Hadnuck, who had been buried seven weeks before ; and that of her babe, eight weeks old, who had lain interred only twenty-one days. It was remarked that these corpses although buried in the same ground and hard by the others were far gone in decomposition.

A serving-man, Rhade, who was twenty-three years old. He had ailed for some three months before his death, and the body which had been buried for five weeks was much tainted with corruption.

A woman and a child who had been buried five weeks, and whose bodies were entire, showing every trace of vampirism.

A heyduk named Stanko, a much-respected and important character in the village. He had died six weeks previously at the age of sixty. In the chest and abdomen there was found to be a quantity of rich new blood, and the whole body was in the Vampire condition.

Millock, a heyduk, twenty-five years old. The body which

bore every trace of vampirism had been in the earth six weeks.

Stanjoika, the wife of a heyduk, twenty years old. She died after a brief illness of three days and had been buried more than a fortnight before. Her face was full and florid ; the limbs supple and without any cadaverous coldness. There was a quantity of new blood in her chest and *in uentriculo cordis*. The viscera were sound and healthy. The skin appeared fresh and comely as in life.

It should be observed that this list by no means exhausts the cases of vampirism which were then collected, and particular details, moreover, have been most fully recorded in each instance, but to amplify the catalogue would involve much reiteration that might prove wearisome without adding anything material to the tale of a demonstration already conclusively established.

Erasmus Franciscus in his commentary upon Baron Valvasor's *Die Ehre des Herzogthums Krain*, Ljubljana, 1689, gives an interesting account of a Vampire in Carniola. There lived in the district[12] of Kranj, and not far from the city of that name, a certain peasant, a landowner, who was called Grando. During his life he had always been held a quiet industrious man of good repute, but after his death the neighbourhood was much plagued by the attacks of a vampire and there could be no doubt that this was Grando. Accordingly the ecclesiastical authorities gave directions that he should be disinterred. When they opened his grave, after he had been buried for many months, the body was found as though he slept. Not only was his complexion fresh and ruddy, but the features gently quivered as if the dead man smiled. He even parted his lips as if he would inhale fresh air. He opened his eyes wide, and those engaged began to recite litanies and prayers, whilst a priest holding aloft the Crucifix adjured the Vampire in these words : " Raise thine eyes and look upon Jesus Christ who hath redeemed us from the pains of hell by His most Holy Passion and His precious Death upon the Rood," whereupon an expression of extraordinary sadness came over the dead man's face and tears began to flow fast down his cheeks. Finally after a solemn commendation of his soul they struck his head from the body which moved just as if it had been alive.

It will not be impertinent to quote here a very interesting passage which occurs in *The Travels of three* English *Gentlemen*, written about 1734, and published in the *Harleian Miscellany*, vol. iv, 1745. The travellers have arrived at Laubach.

" We must not omit Observing here, that our Landlord seemed to pay some Regard to what Baron *Valvasor* has related of the *Vampyres*, said to infest some Parts of this Country. These *Vampyres* are supposed to be the Bodies of deceased Persons, animated by evil Spirits, which come out of the Graves, in the Night-time, suck the Blood of many of the Living, and thereby destroy them. Such a Notion will, probably, be looked upon as fabulous and exploded, by many People in *England* ; however, it is not only countenanced by Baron *Valvasor*, and many *Carnioleze* Noblemen, Gentlemen, &c. as we were informed, but likewise actually embraced by some Writers of good Authority. M. *Jo. Henr. Zopfius*, Director of the *Gymnasium* of *Essen*,[13] a Person of great Erudition, has published a Dissertation upon them, which is extremely learned and curious, from whence we shall beg Leave to transcribe the following Paragraph : " The *Vampyres*, which come out of the Graves in the Night-time, rush upon People sleeping in their Beds, suck out all their Blood, and destroy them. They attack Men, Women, and Children, sparing neither Age nor Sex. The People attacked by them complain of Suffocation, and a great Interception of Spirits ; after which, they soon expire. Some of them, being asked, at the Point of Death, what is the Matter with them, say they suffer in the Manner just related from People lately dead, or rather the Spectres of those People ; upon which, their Bodies, from the Description given of them, by the sick Person, being dug out of the Graves, appear in all Parts, as the Nostrils, Cheeks, Breast, Mouth, &c. turgid and full of Blood. Their Countenances are fresh and ruddy ; and their Nails, as well as Hair, very much grown. And, though they have been much longer dead than many other Bodies, which are perfectly putrified, not the least Mark of Corruption is visible upon them. Those who are destroyed by them, after their Death, become *Vampyres* ; so that, to prevent so spreading an Evil, it is found requisite to drive a Stake through the dead Body, from whence, on this Occasion, the Blood flows as if the Person was alive. Sometimes the Body is dug out of the Grave, and burnt to Ashes ; upon which, all Disturbances cease.

The *Hungarians* call these Spectres *Pamgri*, and the *Servians*
Vampyres ; but the Etymon, or Reason of these Names,
is not known." Vid. *Dissert. de* Vampyres Seɪviensibus *quam*
Suprem. Numin. Auspic. Præsid. M. Joan. Henr. Zopfio*Gymnas.*
Assind. *Direct. publice defend.* &c. Christ. Frid. Van Dalen
Emmericens, &c. P. 6, 7. DUISBURGI *ad* RHENUM, Typis
JOHANNIS SAS, Academiæ Typographi, Anno MDCCXXXIII.

These Spectres are reported to have infested several Districts
of *Servia*, and the Bannat of *Temeswaer*, in the Year 1725,
and for seven or eight Years afterwards, particularly those of
Mevadia, or *Meadia*, and *Parakin*, near the *Morava*. In
1732, we had a Relation of some of their Feats in the Neighbourhood of Cassovia ; and the publick Prints took Notice
of the Tragedies, they acted in the Bannat of *Temeswaer*, in
the Year 1738. Father *Gabriel Rzaczynski*, in his Natural
History of the Kingdom of *Poland*, and the great Duchy of
Lithuania, published at *Sendomir*, in 1721, affirms, that in
Russia, *Poland*, and the great Dutchy of *Lithuania*, dead
Bodies, actuated by infernal Spirits, sometimes enter People's
Houses in the Night, fall upon Men, Women, and Children,
and attempt to suffoate them ; and that of such Diabolical
Facts his Countrymen have several very authentic Relations.
The *Poles* call a Man's Body thus informed *Upier*, and that
of a woman *Upierzyca*, i.e. *a winged* or *feathered Creature* ;
which Name seems to be deduced from the surprising Lightness
and Activity of these incarnate Demons. If we remember
right, an Account of them also, from *Poland*, is to be met with,
in some of the News-Papers for 1693, perfectly agreeing with
those of the *Servian Vampyres* given us by M. *Zopfius*. In
Fine, the Notion of such pestiferous Beings has prevailed from
time immemorial over a great Part of *Hungary, Servia, Car-
niolo, Poland*, &c. as is [14] evinced by several Authors in Con-
junction with the aforesaid M. *Zopfius*. To which we shall
beg Leave to add, that the antient *Greeks* also seem to have been
firmly persuaded, that dead Bodies were sometimes acted by
evil Spirits, as appears from a Fragment of *Phlegon* [15]. Neither
is this Opinion, however it may be ridiculed by many People,
altogether without Foundation ; since the Supreme Being *may*
make wicked Spirits his Instruments of Punishment here, as
well as Plagues, Wars, Famines, &c. and, that he *actually has*
done so, is sufficiently apparent from [16] Scripture, to omit

what has been said on this Head by some of the most eminent profane Authors.

Before we take Leave of the City of *Laubach*, it will be proper to observe, that, though the Bulk of the People there speak the *Carniolian*, or *Sclavanian*, Tongue, and have some Customs peculiar to themselves, they agree in most Points with the other *Germans*. All the People of Fashion and Distinction speak *German* fluently and purely—*Laubach* was taken by *Ottocar*, King of *Bohemia*, in 1269; and attacked ineffectually by the *Turks* in 1472, and 1484. *Albert*, Archduke of *Austria*, likewise failed in his Attempt upon it, in 1441. The Streets are not very broad, nor the Houses grand; though, every Thing considered, it may be esteemed a fine City. Here we lay, for the first Time, betwixt two Feather-beds; which threw the Writer of this Account into so violent a Sweat, that he had scarce any Rest all Night, and found himself extremely faint the next Morning. Many of the *Germans*, however, like this Sort of Lodging; though it is very disagreeable, for the most Part, to Gentlemen of other Nations."

About the years 1730-32 occurred the case of Stephen Hubner of Treautenau, who after his death returned and not only attacked individuals but also killed cattle. From the official report it would seem that this vampire strangled them. This case was very shortly taken in hand and by order of the supreme court of the district the body was disinterred. Although actually five months had passed since the time of burial it was found with all the marks of vampirism. Being taken to the public gallows it was there decapitated by the common executioner. The remains were burned to ashes and scattered to the wind. For precautions sake the bodies of those near Hubner were exhumed and reverently cremated, and then once again interred in their original resting place.

Although these histories belong for the most part to the eighteenth century the belief in vampires among Slavonic peoples is yet as strong as ever. The Serbians still paint crosses with tar on the doors of their houses and barns to keep out the vampires,[17] just as in the old days among the Highlanders of Scotland it was believed that tar daubed on a door kept off witches. In many districts of Bosnia, when the women of a village go to pay a visit to a neighbour's house where a death has recently occurred they put a sprig of hawthorn

(*Weissdorn*) behind their head-cloth, and just after they have left the house they throw it away in the road. If the dead has turned into a vampire he will be so busily engaged in picking up the hawthorn that it will not be possible for him to track them to their own homes.

In various parts of Germany, especially in certain districts of West Prussia the Vampire tradition long prevailed, and even now instances of vampirism are occasionally, if rarely, found in the remoter thorps and burghs. No new features or extraordinary happenings are recorded, and it is but seldom that cases excited any very general attention. Among the most remarkable were those of a citizen of Egwanschiftz who in 1617 was attacked and long tormented by a vampire who at last slew the victim whereupon the bodies both of the vampire and the luckless prey were cremated in two several pyres at a deserted spot some distance from human habitation. Two hundred years later, in 1820, a rich landowner whose possession of extensive properties in the vicinity of Danzig made him a very prominent figure throughout the district was sorely beset by a vampire, and only delivered from these attacks by the prayers and mortifications of certain holy Cistercian monks who had been ejected from their house by the abominable decrees of the Prussian government of 28 April, 1810.

In his chronicle under the year 1343 Sebastian Moelers relates that during a terrible visitation of the Black Death cases of vampirism were numerous in the Tyrol, and the Benedictine abbey of Marienberg was much infested, one at least of the monks, Dom Steino von Netten, being commonly reputed to have been slain by a vampire. In 1348 the plague swept off every inmate of this famous cloister except Abbot Wyho, a priest, one lay brother, and Goswin who later became the eminent chronicler.

At Danzig in 1855 there was a fearful outbreak of cholera, and it was bruited throughout the whole province that the dead returned as Vampires to fetch the living. It is said that the fears of the people terribly increased the mortality.

From time immemorial in many parts of Europe the peasants at a season of especial distress, particularly when the cattle have been attacked by some wasting disease, are wont to resort to a ceremonial kindling of bonfires, the general name for which is need-fire.[18] The exact signification of this name is a little doubtful. Grimm would derive it from *need* " necessity " (German, noth), so that the term need-fire signifies a " forced fire." This is also the interpretation given by Lindenbrog.[19] (Eum ergo ignem *nodfeur* et *nodfyr*, quasi necessarium ignem uocant.) On the other hand C. L. Rochholz connects the word *need* with a verb *nieten* " to churn," in which case need-fire would mean a " churned fire."[20] The superstition of kindling need-fires comes down through the ages from Pagan times, and it was one of those heathen practices the continuance of which was again and again forbidden. Whilst King Pepin was ruling the Franks a synod which had been convened under S. Boniface in 750[21] prohibited the kindling " illos sacrilegos ignes, quos *niedfyr* uocant " as heathenish and profane. Nevertheless the tradition persisted and with other Pagan practices the knowledge of it was handed down by the covens and colleges of witches. In the year 1598 when a fatal epidemic was raging at Neustadt, near Marburg, a sorcerer by name John Kohler actually persuaded the burgomaster and leading citizens to assay this magic operation. All fires upon the hearths and elsewhere having been extinguished sparks were produced by friction and from these a pyre was kindled between the gates of the town and all the cattle driven through the smoke and flames. Throughout the town all fires were relit by means of brands which had been taken from the public bonfire. It is not surprising to learn that this piece of witchcraft had no good effect ; the pest raged as before ; and the only result appears to have been that grave suspicion attached itself to Kohler who in December 1605 was burned having been found guilty of midnight conjurations and necromancy.

Nevertheless in many parts of Germany until the middle of the nineteenth century, in Lower Saxony, in the Hartz Mountains, in Brunswick, in Silesia and Bohemia, the practice still prevailed. In 1682 it was forbidden by Gustavus Adolphus, Duke of Mecklenburg, but his law had no effect. The need-fire is said still to survive in the remoter parts of Switzerland, of Norway and Sweden ; and, although the fact is hardly recognized, in Yorkshire and in Northumberland on the occasion of rinderpest the practice of lighting need-fires continued well within living memory, and, it has been said, is not altogether unknown in the remoter districts even to-day.

There are many ways of preparing the need-fire, but it is essential that it should not be struck with flint and steel, nor, of course, must a match be used. The first sparks are to be made by prolonged friction, and it is usual to have ready tow, a piece of linen or some other inflammable substance which will immediately burst into a flame whence the brush wood or straw can be set ablaze. Unless every light in the village shall have been previously put out the fire will probably fail of its effect. Formerly in many parts it was kindled annually as a preventive, but in more recent times it was only resorted to in the case of an actual murrain.

However, in Russia (at least until lately), in Poland, in Serbia and among the Slavonic peoples generally, an epidemic among the cattle is generally ascribed to a vampire who is draining them of their vitality. Accordingly the reason for the need-fire takes a slightly different aspect. It is kindled with a very definite reason, to wit that the flames may keep off the vampire who cannot pass through them. One of the chief days, in Poland at any rate, upon which it was usual to kindle these fires, was the feast of S. Roch[22] who during his lifetime devoted himself both to persons and animals stricken by the plague, as is related in an old sequence which is found in the fifteenth century missels of Sarum, Utrecht, Autun, Toulouse and other cities.[23]

At post mortem sui patris
Et decessum suae matris,
Peregre diuertitur ;
Et ad domos infirmorum
Peste dira perpessorum
Festine ingreditur
Jesum Christum Deum clamat,
Signo crucis cunctos sanat
Sua prouidentia.
Ad quem uenit uir beatus,
Prorsus fuit hic sanatus
Diuina potentia.
    Ciuitates Italiæ,
Romæ, Longobardiæ,
Sanat suis precibus.
Hospitali Placentiæ
Percussus pestis silice,
Abiectus e mœnibus ;
    Languens dum in silua sitit

Fontem Deus sibi mittit
Præostensa nebula.
Paruus canis panes portat
A Gothardo, et reportat ;
Cane uiro regula.
  Sic uir sanctus confortatur
Dum Gothardo consolatur
In ualle miseriæ ;
Et per angelum sanatur
Qui a Deo mittebatur,
Raphael in nomine.[24]

In 1414 during the council of Constance when the plague broke out in that city the fathers of the council ordered public prayers and processions in honour of S. Roch, and immediately the pestilence ceased. Accordingly with S. Sebastian and S. Adrian he is generally invoked against the plague, and in Poland he is regarded as the saint who will protect against the ravages of vampires since they spread their infection as a poisonous pestilence.

That well-known occult investigator and authority the late Dr. Franz Hartmann has given us particulars of some cases of vampirism which actually came under his own observation. The following which were related in *Borderland*, vol. III 1895,[25] occurred in the neighbourhood of Vienna but a short time before they were published.

A young lady at G— had an admirer who asked her in marriage, but as he was a drunkard she refused and married another. Thereupon the lover shot himself, and soon after that event a vampire, assuming his form, visited her frequently. She could not see him but felt his presence in a way that could leave no room for doubt. The medical faculty did not know what to make of the case, they called it " hysterics," and tried in vain every remedy in the pharmacopœia, until she had at last the spirit exorcised by a man of strong faith. In this case there is an elemental making use of, and being aided by, the elementary of the suicide.

A very similar example, which has already been quoted at length (p. 115), was related by the Hon. Ralph Shirley in the *Occult Review*.[26]

Dr. Hartmann also gives the following typical instances of vampirism, and these may serve for many thus avoiding superfluous repetition. A miller at D— had a healthy servant-boy, who soon after entering his service began to fail. He acquired a ravenous appetite, but nevertheless grew daily more feeble and emaciated. Being interrogated, he at last confessed that a thing which he could not see, but which he could plainly feel, came to him every night about twelve o'clock and settled upon his chest, drawing all the life out of him, so that he became paralised for the time being, and neither could move nor cry out. Thereupon the miller agreed to share the bed with the boy, and made him promise that he should give a certain sign when the vampire arrived. This was done, and when the signal was made the miller putting out his hands grasped an invisible but very tangible substance that rested upon the boy's chest. He described it as apparently elliptical in shape, and to the touch feeling like gelatine, properties which suggest an ectoplasmic formation. The thing writhed and fiercely struggled to escape, but he gripped it firmly and threw it on the fire. After that the boy recovered, and there was an end of these visits. "Those who like myself," remarks Dr. Hartmann, "have, on innumerable occasions removed 'astral tumours,' and thereby cured the physical tumours will find the above neither 'incredible' nor 'unexplainable.' Moreover, the above accounts do not refer to events of the past but to persons still living in this country."

"A woman in this vicinity has a ghost, or as she calls it, a 'dual' with whom she lives on the most intimate terms as wife and husband. She converses with him and he makes her do the most irrational things. He has many whims, and she being a woman of means, gratifies them. If her dual wants to go and see Italy 'through her eyes,' she has to go to Italy and let him enjoy the sights. She does not care for balls and theatres ; but her dual wants to attend them, and so she has to go. She gives lessons to her dual and 'educates' him in the things of this world and commits no end of follies. At the same time her dual draws all the strength from her, and she has to vampirize every one she comes in contact with to make up for the loss."

Mrs. Violet Tweedale in her *Ghosts I have Seen*[27] gives a very curious account of a certain Prince Valori who was everywhere attended by a familiar or "satyr," invisible to many people, but often seen in his company by those who had psychic faculties. The familiar became attached to him on an occasion when he had had the incredible folly to attend a Sabbat in the Vosges. A Russian clairvoyante who knew all the circumstances informed Mrs. Tweedale that a certain ancestor of her own, the Bohemian noble de Laski, famous as having befriended Dr. Dee and Kelly, entertained a familiar called Buisson. As among the covens of witches two centuries since the familiars who wait upon modern adepts of black magic have various names, Minette, Verdelet, etc., Mrs. Tweedale tells us that "General Elliot, who commanded the forces in Scotland" and "was a very well-known society man about twenty-five years ago" had a familiar, Wononi, and used actually to speak aloud with him in the middle of a dinner-party. "To look at he was the very last man that one would associate with matters occult."

The erotic familiar is by no means unknown to-day. As in former times he is often required to assume the likeness of some person whom the witch lusts to enjoy. There is an allusion to this practice in Middleton's drama *The Witch*,[28] where when the young gallant visits the witch's abode Hecati cries on seeing him :

'Tis Almachildes—fresh blood stirs in me—
The man that I have lusted to enjoy :
I've had him thrice in incubus already.

It will readily be remembered that in *La-Bas*[29]—and Huysmans here is not writing fiction—Madame Chantelouve says to Durtal : " Enfin, tenez, je vous possède quand et comment il me plaît, de même qui j'ai longtemps possédé Byron, Baudclaire, Gérard de Nerval, ceux qui j'aime . . .

—Vous dites ?

—Je dis qui je n'ai qu' à les désirer, qu' à vous désirer vous, maintenant, avant de m'endormir . . .

—Et ?

—Et vous seriez inférieur à ma chimère, au Durtal que j'adore et dont les caresses rendent mes nuits folles.

—Il la regarda, stupéfié. Elle avait ses yeux dolents et troubles ; elle semblait même ne plus le voir et parler dans le vide. Il hésita, aperçut en un éclair de pensées, ces scènes de l'incubat dont Gévingey parlait . . ."

Sinistrari in his famous treatise *De Daemonialitate*[30] gives several instances which actually came under his own notice of incubi who attach themselves with vampirish pertinacity to certain individuals and who are only expelled and dismissed with great difficulty. He also relates the case of a woman who confessed to long and indecent intercourse with an erotic incubus who appeared to her under the form of a comely youth and exhausted her vitality.

Under the heading " A Modern Case of Vampirism " Dr. Hartmann relates the following, by which we see that the strong wish to injure another can be sufficiently concentrated to form a psychic tie between the person who is bitterly antagonistic and his enemy so that there can actually take place the absorption of vitality from the one to the other. " In the night of 31 December, 1888, Mr. and Mrs. Rose (the names in this story are pseudonyms, but the facts are true) went to bed as poor people and on the morning of 1 January, 1889, they woke up finding themselves rich. An uncle to whom they owed their poverty because he kept them from coming into the legal possession of their rightful property, had died during the night. There are some occurences of an occult character, connected with this event, which will be interesting to those who wish to find practical proofs and demonstrations in their investigations of the ' night side of nature.'

" Mr. Rose is a young, but very clever, professional man in this city, who being at the beginning of his career has, therefore, only an exceedingly limited number of clients. His young wife is one of the most amiable ladies whom it has been my good fortune to meet ; a spiritually minded woman and more of a poetess than an economist. She had been brought up under the most affluent circumstances, her father being very rich, and she was the only and therefore the pet child in her luxurious home. It would be too complicated a task to tell how it happened that the property which she inherited fell first into the hands of her uncle, a spiteful and avaricious man. Sufficient to say that this man, whom we will call Helleborus, had by his intrigues and law-suits managed to keep Mrs. Rose's property in his hands ; giving her and her husband no support whatever. More than once they were forced to borrow money from their friends, in order to keep themselves from starvation.

" As ' Uncle Helleborus ' was in the last stage of consumption, their only hope was that his death would soon put an end to his law-suits, and bring them into possession of what rightfully belonged to them.

" Uncle Helleborus, however, did not seem inclined to die. Year after year he kept on coughing and expectorating; but with all this he out-lived many who predicted his death. After making to Mr. and Mrs. Rose a proposal of a settlement, which would have left him in possession of nearly all the property and given to them only a pittance, he went to Meran, last autumn, to avoid the cold climate of Vienna.

" In their embarrassing circumstances, they were much inclined to accept the settlement; but they concluded to first consult about it a friend, an eminent lawyer; and this gentleman (whom we will call Mr. Tulip, as everybody in Vienna knows his real name) advised them to the contrary. This enraged Helleborus against Tulip; and starting into a blind rage, he swore that if he found an opportunity of killing Tulip, he would surely do so.

" Mr. Tulip was an extraordinary strong, well-built and healthy man; but at the beginning of December last, soon after Mr. Helleborus's departure for Meran, he suddenly failed in health. The doctors could not locate the disease, and he grew rapidly thinner and weaker, complaining of nothing but extreme lassitude, and feeling like a person who was daily bled. Finally, on 20 December, last, all Vienna was surprised to hear that Mr. Tulip had died. Post-mortem examination showing all the organs in a perfectly normal condition, the doctors found nothing better to register but death from *marasmus* (emaciation), as the cause of this extraordinary event. Strange to say, during the last days of the disease (if it can be so called), when his mind became flighty, he often imagined that a stranger was troubling him, and the description which he gave of that invisible personage fitted Mr. Helleborus with perfect accuracy.

" During Mr. Tulip's sickness, news came from Meran that Mr. Helleborus was rapidly gaining strength and recovering from his illness in a most miraculous manner; but there were some people who expressed grave doubts as to whether this seeming recovery would be lasting. On the day of Mr. Tulip's funeral, Mr. ——, a prominent member of the Theosophical Society, now in Austria, remarked to Mrs. Rose : ' You will see that now that Mr. Tulip is dead, his Vampire will die too.'

"On 1 January, 1889, Mr. Rose dreamed that he saw Uncle Helleborus looking perfectly healthy. He expressed his surprise about it, when a voice, as if coming from a long distance said: 'Uncle Helleborus is dead.' The voice sounded a second time, and this once far more powerfully, repeating the same sentence; and this time Mr. Rose awoke with the sound of that voice still ringing in his ears, and communicated to his wife the happy news that 'Uncle Helleborus was dead.' Two hours afterwards a telegram came from Meran, announcing the demise of Uncle Helleborus, which had occurred on that very night, and calling upon Mr. Rose to come and attend to the funeral. It was found that Mr. Helleborus had begun to grow rapidly worse from the day when Mr. Tulip died.

"The only rational explanation of such cases I have found in Paracelsus."

In *The Occult Review* for September, 1909, under the title "An Authenticated Vampire Story" was given the following history which was contributed by Dr. Hartmann.

On 10 June, 1909, there appeared in a prominent Vienna paper (*The Neues Wiener Journal*) a notice saying that the castle of B—— had been burned by the populace, because there was a great mortality among the peasant children, and it was generally believed that this was due to the invasion of a Vampire, supposed to be the last Count B——, who died and acquired that reputation. The castle was situated in a wild and desolate part of the Carpathian Mountains, and was formerly a fortification against the Turks. It was not inhabited, owing to its being believed to be in the possession of ghosts; only a wing of it was used as a dwelling for the caretaker and his wife.

Now it so happened that, when I read the above notice, I was sitting in a coffee-house at Vienna in company with an old friend of mine who is an experienced occultist and editor of a well-known journal, and who had spent several months in the neighbourhood of the castle. From him I obtained the following account, and it appears that the Vampire in question was probably not the old Count, but his beautiful daughter, the Countess Elga, whose photograph, taken from the original painting, I obtained. My friend said: "Two years ago I was living at Hermannstadt, and being engaged in engineering

a road through the hills, I often came within the vicinity of
the old castle, where I made the acquaintance of the old
castellan, or caretaker, and his wife, who occupied a part
of the wing of the house, almost separate from the main
body of the building. They were a quiet old couple and
rather reticent in giving information or expresing an opinion
in regard to the strange noises which were often heard at
night in the deserted halls, or of the apparitions which the
Wallachian peasants claimed to have seen when they loitered
in the surroundings after dark. All I could gather was that
the old Count was a widower and had a beautiful daughter,
who was one day killed by a fall from her horse, and that
soon after the old man died in some mysterious manner,
and the bodies were buried in a solitary graveyard belonging to
a neighbouring village. Not long after their death an unusual
mortality was noticed among the inhabitants of the village ;
several children and even some grown people died without any
apparent illness ; they merely wasted away ; and thus a
rumour was started that the old Count had become a Vampire
after his death. There is no doubt that he was not a saint, as
he was addicted to drinking, and some shocking tales were in
circulation about his conduct and that of his daughter ; but
whether there was any truth in them, I am not in a position
to say.

"Afterwards the property came into the possession of ——,
a distant relative of the family, who is a young man and
officer in a cavalry regiment at Vienna. It appears that the
heir enjoyed his life at the capital and did not trouble himself
much about the old castle in the wilderness ; he did not
even come to look at it, but gave his directions by letter to the
janitor, telling him merely to keep things in order and to
attend to repairs, if any were necessary. Thus the castellan
was actually master of the house, and offered its hospitality
to me and my friends.

"One evening I and my two assistants, Dr. E——, a young
lawyer, and Mr. W——, a literary man, went to inspect the
premises. First we went to the stables. There were no
horses as they had been sold ; but what attracted our special
attention was an old, queer-fashioned coach with gilded
ornaments and bearing the emblems of the family. We
then inspected the rooms, passing through some halls and

gloomy corridors, such as may be found in any old castle. There was nothing remarkable about the furniture; but in one of the halls there hung in a frame an oil-painting, a portrait, representing a lady with a large hat and wearing a fur coat. We were all involuntarily startled on beholding this picture—not so much on account of the beauty of the lady, but on account of the uncanny expression of her eyes; and Dr. E——, after looking at the picture for a short time, suddenly exclaimed : ' How strange. The picture closes its eyes and opens them again, and now it begins to smile.'

"Now Dr. E—— is a very sensitive person, and has more than once had some experience in spiritism, and we made up our minds to form a circle for the purpose of investigating this phenomenon. Accordingly, on the same evening we sat around a table in an adjoining room, forming a magnetic chain with our hands. Soon the table began to move and the name *Elga* was spelled. We asked who this Elga was, and the answer was rapped out : ' The lady whose picture you have seen.'

"' Is the lady living ? ' asked Mr. W——. This question was not answered; but instead it was rapped out : ' If W—— desires it, I will appear to him bodily to-night at two o'clock.' W—— consented, and now the table seemed to be endowed with life and manifested a great affection for W—— ; it rose on two legs and pressed against his breast, as if it intended to embrace him.

"We inquired of the castellan whom the picture represented ; but to our surprise he did not know. He said that it was the copy of a picture painted by the celebrated painter Hans Markart of Vienna, and had been brought by the old Count because its demoniacal look pleased him so much.

"We left the castle, and W—— retired to his room at an inn a half-hour's journey distant from that place. He was of a somewhat sceptical turn of mind, being neither a firm believer in ghosts and apparitions nor ready to deny their possibility. He was not afraid, but anxious to see what would come of his agreement, and for the purpose of keeping himself awake he sat down and began to write an article for a journal.

"Towards two o'clock he heard steps on the stairs and the door of the hall opened ; there was the rustling of a silk dress and the sound of the feet of a lady walking to and fro in the corridor.

"It may be imagined that he was somewhat startled ; but taking courage, he said to himself : ' If this is Elga let her come in.' Then the door of .the room opened and Elga entered. She was most elegantly dressed, and appeared still more youthful and seductive than the picture. There was a lounge on the other side of the table where W—— was writing, and there she silently posted herself. She did not speak, but her looks and gestures left no doubt in regard to her desires and intentions.

"Mr. W—— resisted the temptation and remained firm. It is not known whether he did so out of principle or timidity or fear. Be this as it may, he kept on writing, looking from time to time at his visitor and silently wishing that she would leave. At last, after half an hour, which seemed to him much longer the lady departed in the same manner in which she came.

"This adventure left W—— no peace, and we consequently arranged several sittings at the old castle, where a variety of uncanny phenomena took place. Thus, for instance, once the servant-girl was about to light a fire in the stove, when the door of the apartment opened and Elga stood there. The girl, frightened out of her wits, rushed from the room, tumbling down the stairs in terror with the lamp in her hand, which broke, and came very near to setting her clothes on fire. Lighted lamps and candles went out when brought near the picture, and many other ' manifestations ' took place which it would be tedious to describe ; but the following incident ought not to be omitted.

"Mr. W—— was at that time desirous of obtaining the position as co-editor of a certain journal, and a few days after the above-narrated adventure he received a letter in which a noble lady of high position offered him her patronage for that purpose. The writer requested him to come to a certain place the same evening, where he would meet a gentleman who would give him further particulars. He went, and was met by an unknown stranger, who told him that he was requested by the Countess Elga to invite Mr. W—— to a carriage drive, and that she would await him at midnight at a certain crossing of two roads, not far from the village. The stranger then suddenly disappeared.

"Now it seems that Mr. W—— had some misgivings about the meeting and drive, and he hired a policeman as detective to go at midnight to the appointed place, to see what would happen. The policeman went and reported next morning that he had seen nothing but the well-known, old-fashioned carriage from the castle, with two black horses, standing there as if waiting for somebody, and that as he had no occasion to interfere, he merely waited until the carriage moved on. When the castellan of the castle was asked, he swore that the carriage had not been out that night, and in fact it could not have been out, as there were no horses to draw it.

"But that is not all, for on the following day I met a friend who is a great sceptic and disbeliever in ghosts, and always used to laugh at such things. Now, however, he seemed to be very serious and said : ' Last night something very strange happened to me. At about one o'clock this morning I returned from a late visit, and as I happened to pass the graveyard of the village, I saw a carriage with gilded ornaments standing at the entrance. I wondered about this taking place at such an unusual hour, and being curious to see what would happen, I waited. Two elegantly dressed ladies issued from the carriage. One of these was very young and pretty, but threw at me a devilish and scornful look as they both passed by and entered the cemetery. There they were met by a well-dressed man, who saluted the ladies and spoke to the younger one, saying : " Why, Miss Elga ! Are you returned so soon ? " Such a queer feeling came over me that I abruptly left and hurried home.'

"This matter has not been explained ; but certain experiments which we subsequently made with the picture of Elga brought out some curious facts.

"To look at the picture for a certain time caused me to feel a very disagreeable sensation in the region of the solar plexus. I began to dislike the portrait and proposed to destroy it. We held a sitting in the adjoining room ; the table manifested a great aversion to my presence. It was rapped out that I should leave the circle, and that the picture must not be destroyed. I ordered a Bible to be brought in, and read the beginning of the first chapter of St. John, whereupon the above-mentioned Mr. E—— (the medium) and another man present claimed that they saw the picture distorting its face. I turned the frame and pricked the back of the picture with my penknife in different places, and Mr. E——, as well as the other man, felt all the pricks, although they had retired to the corridor.

"I made the sign of the pentagram over the picture, and again the two gentlemen claimed that the picture was horribly distorting its face.

"Soon afterwards we were called away and left that country. Of Elga I heard nothing more."

That a belief, and a very well founded belief in vampirism, still retains in Hungary, is evident from the following account which was reported in *The Daily Telegraph*, 15 February, 1912. "A Buda-Pest telegram to the *Messaggero* reports a terrible instance of superstition. A boy of fourteen died some days ago in a small village. A farmer, in whose employment the boy had been, thought that the ghost of the latter appeared to him every night. In order to put a stop to these supposed visitations, the farmer, accompanied by some friends, went to the cemetery one night, stuffed three pieces of garlic and three stones in the mouth, and thrust a stake through the corpse, fixing it to the ground. This was to deliver themselves from the evil spirit, as the credulous farmer and his friends stated when they were arrested."

Of Montenegro in his *Voyage Historique et Politique au Montenegro* M. le Colonel L. C. Vialla de Sommières writes as follows : " In no country is the belief in ghosts, in witches, and in evil spirits stronger than in Montenegro. Apparitions, dreams, omens ceaselessly haunt their brains, but nothing equals the terror inspired by *brucolaques*, that is to say the dead bodies of those who died excommunicate, and which are huddled into the earth without any burial rites or prayer. The very ground which has covered them is for ever accursed ; the spot is shunned and avoided by all, and if a thought of the place crosses a man's mind he believes that he is being pursued by avenging ghosts. In fine these men who court every danger and dare every peril think of nothing but of witches and of demons ; they are for ever discoursing of the terror with which evil spirits inspire them. It would require no mean authority on demonology with a facile pen to write the long narratives of all manner of devils which they never tire of relating and the myriad adventures of this sort that they love to tell."[31]

A little later the author gives a somewhat farcical adventure which happened to a man whom he himself had known, and who was alive as late as 1813. " A certain *Zanetto*, a droll sort of fellow, who was something given to drink, one day when he was rather more than half seas over happened to be caught in a heavy shower. Having stumbled home he threw himself on his bed fully dressed as he was, well-warmed with wine but chilled with the drenching rain. Suddenly he was seized by terrible convulsions ; about eleven o'clock he fell into a state of coma, he was icy cold, he did not even breathe ; at last he was surely dead . . . at eight o'clock the next morning they were going to bury him. In order to carry him from his house to the Church the *cortège* had to climb a very difficult path and to descend by one which was even worse. The irregularity of the ground, for the whole way was strewn with rocks and large stones, compelled the bearers from time to time to make sudden and abrupt movements. This continual shaking up recalled *Zanetto* to life. He began to stir himself briskly and to some effect ; he sat up, looked all around him and bawled out at the top of his voice : ' What the devil are you about you drunken rascals ? ' At these words the bearers flung down their burden and thunder-struck one and all fairly took to their heels. Those who were following the bier scattered helter skelter among the vineyards on either side uttering piercing cries as they ran ; those who went before looked back and terrified at the sight they rushed pell-mell as far as the neighbouring town where they spread the utmost alarm since some were dumb with terror, whilst others told the wildest tales, but all of them were shaking with fear. Only the priests remained in the funeral train, and they were wondering what might be the cause of this disorder, when they heard these words shouted out by the awakened *Zanetto :* ' You fiends, you borachios, I will make you pay for this ; you trapped me finely at home and have brought me all this way ; and you will carry me back to my house again ; if not in good earnest I will send the lot of you to the very place where you thought you were going to pack me off for good and all ; yes, and this time I'll drink everything up ; I won't leave you the value of a ha'penny.' But the priests with great gentleness and without any sort of hurry or impatience conveyed him back to his house. There they did all in their power to quiet the fellow and calm his temper, for he was raving away like a frenzied bedlamite. I have heard him tell the tale himself in merry mood."[32]

In *The Observer*, 2 September, 1923, there was an account of an apparition which appeared in Belgrade and haunted a house, No. 61, Bosanska Street, which runs from the old "Gates of the Town," near the railway station, into the well-known thoroughfare Balkanska Street. Bricks and stones seemed to have been thrown at the house until all the windows were broken and the family barracaded the apertures with boards, tables and chairs. The furniture was shifted violently from place to place, and often thrown down to be smashed to pieces. A procession of devout persons proceeded throughout the premises, entering every room and also proceeding round the exterior of the house chanting psalms and sprinkling holy water. It was stated that the troublesome apparition was a Vampire, although its activities certainly seemed to be those of a poltergeist. It is, of course, quite possible that a Vampire who wished to annoy and molest the inhabitants of a house might resort to poltergeist tricks which albeit generally merely mischievous and vexing, can prove, as records show, dangerous in no small degree.

It is true that Professor Barrett in a discussion of the poltergeist phenomena says: "The movement of objects is usually quite unlike that due to gravitational or other attraction. They slide about, rise in the air, move in eccentric paths, sometimes in a leisurely manner, often turn round in their career, and usually descend quietly without hurting the observers . . . Stones are frequently thrown, but no one is hurt."[33] Yet during the disturbances at Lenagh, Mountfield, Co. Tyrone, in 1864-65 the inmates of the house were so pelted with bricks that they had to fly the place, and an incredulous visitor whilst boasting of his superior unbelief was so sharply assaulted by a shower of stones which pelted his back that he rubbed off without any further ceremony. A girl also was struck by a hard clod of earth and knocked into a pail of water. In a more recent case, the Battersea poltergeist of Eland Road, Lavender Hill, London, S.W.11, whose doings caused so great a sensation in January, 1928, Miss Robinson who resided in the house related how "Lumps of coal, potatoes,

onions and other missiles have come hurtling through the
air both day and night breaking our back windows, and
threatening our welfare. . . . In the room in which
my brother sleeps a wardrobe collapsed with no apparent
reason. . . . A china bowl on a side table in my sister's
room splintered to pieces and crashed on to the ground."[34]
Indeed her father's health had broken down under the strain
and he had been obliged to remove elsewhere.

Although I would not without further inquiry assert that
all these phenomena and similar sporadic happenings which
might be collected from well nigh every county are in their
origin necessarily demoniacal, yet it certainly does appear
warrantable that in the majority of cases they can safely
be assigned to a Satanic source.[35] At the same time a quota
may be the effluence of volitional but eccentric forces in some
way directed by mysterious and seemingly invisible entities
who find an outlet for their manifestation through an unconscious medium, generally a young person of either sex.
In their details far too many of these curious cases nearly
resemble the violent disturbances, and even the physical
assaults upon the Saints, which are recorded in hagiography,
and which (we know) were the work of the devil, to be deemed
anything but suspect in the very highest degree. In the life
of Blessed Christina of Stommeln[36] it is told that on 21
December, 1267, when she was first visited by Peter of Dacia,
a Dominican of Gotland who was in Cologne as a pupil of
Blessed Albertus Magnus, the holy maiden was actually
thrown to the ground several times in succession and severely
wounded without it being apparent that anyone had touched
her. The evil spirits were wont to plague and vex her in the
most noisome ways very often drenching her with stinking
ordure and fæces that burned like fire. They flung stones
about the house, so that her father was seriously wounded
in the head and well nigh had his arm broken owing to a
blow. A jewess who visited Christina and who began to mock
at the ouphs and elfin rogues, as she dubbed them was so
pelted with brickbats that her body was bruised from head to
foot before she could escape into the street beyond the range
of the missiles.

Blessed Franco, a Carmelite,[37] was long vexed and perse-
cuted beyond measure by what might seem to be a series of

poltergeist molestations. Objects of which he had need would be suddenly snatched away and at length found hidden in a distant part of the cloister. When he was in the kitchen the pans, dishes, bowls and plates were frequently whisked out of sight and only discovered after a painful search. But when he commanded in a loud voice : " In the Name of Jesus of Nazareth, I bid thee, foul wretch, be gone," yells of hideous laughter were heard after which all was suddenly still and for a while there were no more disturbances.

A good Jesuit of Sassari in Sardinia, Father Sebastian del Campo, would frequently be annoyed by showers of stones cast by an unseen hand. As they struck him they caused a more than ordinary pain but no bruise nor livid marks appeared after the blows.

In her chamber the stigmatized Marie de Möerl, who died in 1868, was plagued in a very similar manner. Often she would be thrown out of her bed with insane violence ; at midnight in the midst of a freezing winter her blankets and coverlet would be filched away, whilst the most horrible racket aroused the whole household. The Bishop, however, enjoined exorcisms after which the diabolic persecution in this kind was stayed.

Perhaps the most famous and most rigidly documented case in more recent years is that of S. John Baptist Vianney, the Curé d'Ars.[38] The *grappin*, as the Saint had dubbed his demoniac persecutor " would seem to be hammering nails into the floor, cleaving wood, planing boards, or sawing, like a carpenter busy at work in the inside of the house ; or he would drum upon the table, the chimney-piece, the water-jug, or on whatever would make the greatest noise." In the winter of 1826 when the holy Curé was staying at the Presbytery of St. Trivier-sur-Moignans several of the priest who were also sleeping in the house somewhat disdainfully discussed these vexations to which the abbé Vianney was subjected and " agreed that all this infernal mysticism was nothing in the world but reverie, delusion, and hallucination." Some attributed the noises to squadrons of rats, for these animals no doubt kept high revels in the presbytery at Ars, since it was a forlorn and crazy building of a truly venerable antiquity. And so all went to bed to sleep their soundest. " But, behold ! at midnight they are awakened by a most

terrible commotion. The presbytery is turned upside down,
the doors slam, the windows rattle, the walls shake, and
fearful cracks seem to betoken that they are about to fall
prostrate."

Among the older authorities who deal with these manifestations the following may be profitably consulted : Pierre
Le Loyer, *Discours et histoires des spectres, visions, apparitions
des esprits, anges, demons, et ames se monstrans visibles aux
hommes*, first edition, Angers, 2 vols., 1586 ; Robert du Triez,
Les ruses, finesses et impostures des Esprits malins, Cambrai,
1563 ; and the third book, *De Terrificationibus Nocturnisque
Tumultibus* of the *De Spirituum apparitionę*, Cologne, 1594,
by Peter Thyraeus, S.J., sometime Professor of Theology at
Mainz.

To conclude this chapter I have judged it not impertinent
to give, with due cautels, a translation of the famous *Dissertatio De Masticatione Mortuorum* which was pronounced by
Phillip Rohr at the University of Leipzig, 16 August, 1679,
and was printed at that city in the same year. The book is
exceedingly scarce, and although it is not quite so fully considered as the longer works of Zopfius and Rohlius it is one of
the earliest and most typical of these treatises. There are, of
course, theological errors and these not a few, but I think my
notes will be a sufficient safeguard in this respect.

Philip Rohr in his day stood in fair repute for his scholarship
and he was also known as an occult investigator. His work
on the Kobolts who haunt mines is held in esteem. It may be
remarked, however, that the subject had previously been
treated by Georg Landmann, the famous metallurgist, in his
De Animantibus subterraneis, which with other of his treatises
was published at Bale, folio, 1657.

*Dissertatio Historico-Philosophica De Masticatione Mort-
uorum, Quam Dei & Superiorum indultu, in illustri Academ.
Lips. sistent Praeses M. Philippus Rohr Marckran-stadio-
Misnic. & Respondens Benjamin Frizschius, Musilavia-
Misnicus, Alumni Electorales. ad diem XVI. Augusti Ann.
M. DC. LXXIX. H. L. Q. C. Lipsiae, Typis Michaelis Vogtii.*

α and ω. Those who have written of the history of funeral
rites and of the mysteries of death have not neglected to place
on record that there have been found from time to time bodies
who appear to have devoured the grave clothes in which they

were wound, their cerements, and whilst doing so to have uttered a grunting noise like the sound of porkers chawing and rooting with their groyns. Now different writers have pronounced very different opinions upon this matter, and some learned men have ascribed this phenomenon to natural causes which are not clearly known to us ; whilst others have only been able to explain it by assuming that there are certain animals which glut their hunger for human flesh by feeding upon corpses, but what animals these may be they do not tell ; and others again have advanced yet other opinions. This phenomenon then seemed to us to be a fit subject which might be treated in a public and formal disputation, all the rules and regulations being duly observed, in order that we might arrive at the best explanation of this matter and to some extent at any rate elucidate it. Accordingly we determined and resolved after due study to set down the sum of our researches in the following pages, relying upon the kindly indulgence of our readers to make full allowances for the extreme obscurity of those points upon which it has not been possible to pronounce a definite opinion, and also taking our stand upon the authority of those Eminent Doctors and writers whose opinions, and often whose very words, we have quoted in resolving these hard matters. The subject would seem obviously to fall into two parts, of which the first may be reviewed historically ; whilst the second demands to be closely examined from a purely philosophical point of view (alterum philosophicam διάσκεψιν sibi uendicat).

PART I. AN HISTORICAL SURVEY.

I. *The Dead concerning whose ability of manducation we are now to treat, must not be understood to be those who having been raised to life by the Divine Power have once more partaken of food.*

According to the words of Scripture many who died were recalled to life. In the Bible, in the Old as well as in the New Testament, there are recorded several examples of this. *III Kings*, xvii, 22 (*A.V. I Kings*, xvii, 22) ; *IV Kings*, xiii, 21 (*A.V. II Kings*, xiii, 21) ; *S. Matthew*, ix, 18-26 ; *S. Luke*, vii, 11-17 ; *S. John*, xii, 1. Many examples also have been collected from Ecclesiastical History by Beierlingius in his

Theatrum Uerae Historiae Lit. R. post medium, 320, *sqq.*   Martin Delrio in the Second Book of his *Disquisitionum Magicarum Libri Sex*, quotes and exposes the falsity of many stories of resurrection from the dead which are told by Ethnic poets and writers.[39]

II. *We do not now understand by Dead those who have appeared to have expired, and who after burial by some lucky accident were able to come forth from their tombs, or who not yet having been committed to the grave have awakened, and afterwards have partaken of food.*

We first state the facts which have been quite clearly shown by Kornmannus in his work *De Miraculis Mortuorum,*[40] Part ii, c. 33, where he says : " The soul often remains united to the human body, but every movement or motion of the limbs is prevented and entirely restricted so that it is by no means easy to discover and to discern whether bodies of that kind are alive or dead."   And hence it has sometimes happened that those who have no technical knowledge of such things have taken to be dead, persons who in fact were not, and they have been at the charge and care of interring such bodies and committing them to the earth, whence, verily, these unfortunate wretches, in whom life seemed to be extinct would indeed inevitably have perished had not some lucky chance happened which gave them the power of struggling and rescuing themselves from so grave a danger.   Such death-like trances and comas are often called by the physicians "mute diseases," ἄφωνοι.   In this category Delrio includes (1) Those who are taken with an apoplexy, those who are planet-struck and palsied, and those who are rendered insensible and stupified through any great amazement or fear.   (2) Those whose brains are benumbed and stunned.   (3) Those who suffer from certain forms of hysteria ; women who experience strangulation of the womb and who fall into sore fits of the mother. (4) Those who are liable to collapse into a trance-like swoon, a disease with which John Duns Scotus was afflicted, and although he was yet living (as it afterwards appeared) he was buried being thought to be dead.   This circumstance is related by Kornmannus, *De Miraculis Mortuorum*, Part VI, c. lvi, where he quotes that elegant poem which was composed by Janus Vitalis[41] on the death of Scotus, in which appear these pleasing lines :

Quod nulli unquam hominum accidit, Uiator
Hic Scotus iaceo semel sepultus
Et bis mortuus, omnibus Sophistis
Argutus magis atque captiosus.

In chapter lix of the same work Kornmannus gives an example from the *Annals* of Joannes Zonaras[42] of a similar accident which befell the Emperor Zeno.[43] Several writers record extraordinary accidents in which fortune certainly was kind to those who were thought to be dead and committed to the grave, since by some lucky chance it has not seldom happened that they awakened and were rescued. Kornmannus chronicles such an account, which to use his own words was "in sober sooth marvellous and well-worthy to be remembered." In the Church of the Holy Apostles at Cologne[44] he noticed a votive picture, the subject of which we will relate as briefly as may be. In the year 1357 there died of the plague a certain wealthy lady belonging to that town whose name was Richemodis. Now on account of his great love for his wife her husband could not bear that her wedding ring should be withdrawn, and accordingly this was left upon her finger. Of such great value was the jewel that the sexton took especial note of it and coming with his servant that same night to the tomb he opened the monument whilst the servant went down into the vault and proceeded to draw the ring from the hand. No sooner had he touched the body than the woman sat up in her coffin. The two thieves leaving their lanthorn fled in an extremity of terror, but the lady thus provided with a light found her way back to her own home, where she was welcomed with the utmost joy by her husband and her mourning friends. Here we have an historical example of a person who is buried as dead and is rescued from the grave by some individual owing to great good fortune. Not widely dissimilar are the instances which Pliny relates in his *Historia Naturalis*, VII, where he tells of one Aviola,[45] a man of consular rank who actually came to life whilst he was on the funeral pyre, and he also relates the precisely similar case of Lucius Lamia. This latter is further recorded by Valerius Maximus, Book I, 8. With regard to these particular instances it is the opinion of Delrio that the warmth of the flames disperses the cold and syncoptic humours. Such accidents must certainly teach men not to bury the departed in any haste or without undue care.

In ancient Rome it was usual upon such occasions to wail loudly and indeed to make a great noise at the bedside of the deceased that they might ascertain whether the soul did not yet linger in the body, and accordingly those who were dead indeed and who assuredly could not return to life were called *conclamati*. [*Conclamare aliquem mortuum* is a religious term applied to the dead signifying to call repeatedly by name and to lament the departed seven, or according to some authorities, eight days, until the actual burial. See Servius upon Virgil, *Æneid*, vi, 218 ; and also the Scholiast upon Lucan, ii, 23]. In his *De Animæ Tranquillitate*, Seneca writes : "Toties in uicinia mea conclamatum est " which is to say, " How many funerals have taken place in this neighbourhood." Moreover, the Glossarists tell us that *conclamata corpora* signifies those who are dead and buried.[46]

III. *When we treat of the manducation of the dead we do not now understand by the dead those apparitions or wraiths which issue forth from the tomb by the aid of demons and evil spirits.*

It is certain that the devil cannot raise the dead to life. This is a dogma divinely revealed to us. It is also manifest from all the arguments and reasons of sound philosophy for such a thing is opposed to nature.

At the same time we do not deny that it has often happened and may very well be happening to-day that by the Divine permission the bodies of some who are dead issue from their graves owing to the agency of the devil and that these corpses perform various àctions, or rather seem to perform such actions, and consequently they may also partake of food. Instances of this can be seen in Kornmannus, *De Miraculis Mortuorum*, II, cs. x and xiii ; in Johan Georg Godelmann,[47] whose work has been translated by Georg Schwartz, Rector of the University of Marburg, as *von Zaubern Hexen und unholden*, I, iv, 47 ; and in Delrio *Disquisitionum Magicarum*, Liber II, qu. 29. sect. 1. post medium 308, sqq. When he has given various examples from Pagan history of dead men who were supposed to have been raised from the tomb Delrio adds not impertinently : " Of a truth many an illusion and deception can be wrought by the Devil with regard to these mysterious happenings. For sometimes he will steal away the bodies of those who are dead, and he will substitute other phantasmal forms, which move exactly as though they were human and alive. And it is not unknown that he will enter into and possess the bodies of the deceased. Nay, moreover, he will sometimes cause the very corpses to appear to live, and this is done by his power (permitted to him) when he energizes and possesses them : and just as a pilot will move a vessel so will he move them, and he will compel these dead bodies exactly to imitate the actions and gestures of living men."

IV. *It is not our intention to consider here those who seem to be dead, and who when they had been buried in some monument awoke and ate of their own impulsion and motion.*

An example of this is related by Kornmannus, *De Miraculis Mortuorum*, Part VI, c. lix. The reader must himself be the judge as to the exact truth of the event. It may also be found in the *Annales Ecclesiastici* of Baronius.[48] These writers say that Zeno having been struck down by an epileptic fit was thought to be dead, and as such was actually interred, but afterwards he came to life again in his monument when, tortured by hunger, he gnawed the brawn of his own arms and even bit the leather of his buskins.

V. *The theme then of our disputation will be that there are some who were actually dead and who were buried, but energized by an unusual and extraordinary power altogether external to themselves they have even within their tombs been known to eat and partake of food.*

There is an old and well-known saw which is quoted by many writers and recorded by Erasmus in his *Adagia*.[49] The burden thereof is this : Dead men do not bite ($\tau\epsilon\theta\nu\eta\kappa\sigma\tau\epsilon\varsigma$ $\sigma\dot{\upsilon}$ $\delta\acute{\alpha}\kappa\nu\sigma\upsilon\sigma\iota\nu$). This indeed is a truth that there is no disputing ; a dead man if he be passive cannot be compelled by any exterior force to perform such an extraordinary action as to eat. For eating is an action which is wholly confined to living beings, a certain operation whereby food, if it be solid, is absorbed, humected by the saliva of the mouth, and lightly fricated for the benefit of the strength of the muscles of the human body, so that it passes into the stomach and is there agreeably digested. *The object* of this act of eating is *Food* which may be defined as " a mixed body which by a certain natural change is formed into the substance of a living animal." This is a convenient definition which we have derived from various works of Aristotle, *The Physics* to wit, especially thè $\phi\upsilon\sigma\iota\kappa\dot{\eta}$ $\dot{\alpha}\kappa\rho\dot{o}\alpha\sigma\iota\varsigma$ and the $\pi\epsilon\rho\acute{\iota}$ $\gamma\epsilon\nu\acute{\epsilon}\sigma\epsilon\omega\varsigma$ $\kappa\alpha\grave{\iota}$ $\phi\theta\sigma\rho\hat{\alpha}\varsigma$. Whence it clearly follows that we are not using the word "manducation (or eating)" in its strict and specific sense but rather in its etymological sense. For it deprives the object of its peculiar and direct quality which is sustentation, that is to say the affording of nourishment, and it only comprises that action which is the function of the teeth, that is to say the mastication of any food taken into the mouth. For the sake of clarity it is preferable to use this term, manducation, in this restricted sense which we have set forth, since any manducation on the part of the dead must be merely analogous to the same act when it is performed by a living person, just in the same way as one may without any danger of falling into error or misleading others speak of the portrait of a man by the name of the man himself. And if anyone should desire to regard the two terms "manducation" and "eating" and any similar words as synonyms, by all means let him do so. For in the vernacular we make use of the words *metzschen*, *schmetzen*, and *netzschen*, which are onomatopoeic vocables, taken from the sound, and this noise (they say) is made by those who eat in their graves. Whence Heinrich Rothen in his *Tractatus de peste Sagerhusana* speaks of "schmetzende Todte." And this phrase is also used by Conrad Schlüsselburg who writes : "man höret und ersähret offtmahls in Sterbens-Läufften dass todte Leute—in dem Grabe ein Schmetzen getrieben nicht anders als eine Sau wenn sie isset." Kornmannus, also, in his *De Miraculis Mortuorum*, Part II, c. 64, remarks : "It is known by instances which are proven that certain dead people in the graves have devoured and even swallowed their linceuls and cerements."

VI. *Chronicles and historical monuments show us that the dead of both sect have been heard and even have been seen to swallow food or some object.*

Although both the corpses of men and of women are known to have grunted, gibbered, and squeaked,[50] yet examples show us that it is more often the bodies of the weaker sex who have thus uttered curious voices. This is manifest from actual experience. The reason for it will be given below. It appears that most authors who treated with these matters have not troubled to specify whether the dead person was a man or a woman, and hence it has often been generally taken that they were men. Those authors and historians who have either accidentally or intentionally neglected to afford these details are surely much to be blamed. For in a difficult matter such as this omissions may tend to obscure the truth.

VII. *Examples of happenings of this kind may be recorded in a definite order chronologically and in sequence.*

In order that we may not appear to be treating of mere empty nothings, as has been the fault of some who have proposed a certain subject of discussion and then departed from it as widely as may be, it is well to set forth certain examples of the dead who were known to eat in their tombs, and from such instances the truth of these relations may stand out all the more plainly. It will be sufficient to mention the year and the place where such strange happenings occurred and to put them on record here. Further references may be made to the original authors from whom we have extracted these relations, which in the first place are generally affirmed by assistants and eye-witnesses of the whole circumstances. In the year of our Lord 1345 at Levin, a town of Bohemia, the body of a woman ate in her grave (Georg. Philipp. Harsdorffer in his *Theatrum Tragicorum Exemplorum*, which account is taken from the one hundred and fifteenth chapter of the *Chronicon Bohemiae* of Hegenezius). The same thing happened in the days of Martin Luther, when there was also seen the body of a woman who had gnawn her own flesh (Luther's *Colloquia*, xxiv). The same thing happened in the year 1552 in a village which is near Freiburg (Muller in his *Annales Freiburgenses*, p. 254). The same in the year 1553 at Luben in Silesia (Conrad Schlüsselburg, *Gründlicher Erklarung des XCI Pf. Cons. XII*, Part iii). The same happened in 1565 at Sangerhausen. (This example also is from Schlüsselburg.) The same happened in the year 1579 in the neighbourhood of Weismarien. (This is from the same author.) Adam Rother in his treatise on the plague says that when this scourge was raging in Marburg many bodies both in the town itself and in country places round about were heard to utter strange voices. This happened in the year 1581. When the plague was decimating Schisselbein the people noticed that the same thing took place in certain graveyards. This is related by Ignatius Hanielus in his *Tractatus de peste in Schisselbein*. At the beginning of this present century in the year 1603, in the village of Nienstade, which is not far from Hamburg, a body was heard to be uttering from the grave a hoarse sound like the heavy grunting of swine. A full account will be found in the work of Schlüsselburg. The eminent Harsdorffer, whom we have quoted above, mentions a similar occurrence, when the body of a man not only devoured and swallowed his own linen shroud but also half-devoured the corpse of a woman in a neighbouring grave. But our author does not give the year. This happened at Egwanschitz, a town of Moravia. Only seven years ago, in 1672, there was an exactly similar case in a certain village which lies at a distance of three miles from this very town, and it was observed by an intimate friend of mine, one who is worthy of the utmost confidence. The body of a man, whose name although known to me, I prefer not to mention, having been most rashly exhumed by the villagers was found to have eaten his own limbs. I may add that references to a larger number of books and a more intensive study of history would afford many more examples. But enough has been said conclusively to prove the truth of our thesis, namely that the dead have actually been known to perform the act of manducation.

PART II. SOME PHILOSOPHICAL CONSIDERATIONS.

I. *So far we have discussed those points which relate to the historical survey of our thesis ; we will now consider the reasons for and the causes of the object of our thesis, and these we divide into the false and the true*

II. *The manducation of the dead is erroneously ascribed to some hidden faculty.*

There are certain authors who, believing some idle superstition or the other, try to discover that the cause of this manducation originates in the corpse itself, and since they are unable to explain it so it pleases them to call it a " hidden cause." Of their number must be reckoned Kornmannus since he says : " Undoubtedly there is a hidden cause for this manducation " (Part VI, c. 64). Now in order that we may meet these fairly on their own ground it will be well very briefly to consider what in Physics are these " hidden causes," and hence it will soon be seen whether this effect can proceed from such a cause. There are indeed certain hidden qualities which are undiscovered and unknown natural forces owing to the action of which natural things are subjective or objective, and the reason for their action cannot be clearly demonstrated. All authors are agreed that the origin of such forces must be external or internal. Those who hold that there are external forces consider these to be the planets and the heaven under whose influence natural things are impelled to certain actions yet the exact reason for such actions remains inexplicable. Contrariwise other authors—in my opinion very rightly— altogether reject this theory of external influences and they rather concentrate their attention upon the body, or the soul, or the object which is combined of both, and they seek in it itself the cause of natural action. It were impertinent for us here to discuss at length the various opinions that have been given, and yet we think that it will certainly be useful to make some distinction. Let it suffice to say then that these hidden influences in all cases sometimes originate from bodies or from the soul or from the substance partaking of both in an instrumental and secondary manner; but from the very essence in a primary and efficacious manner. And this distinction may be clearly shown. The point then that we have made will be of use in refuting the opinions of those who think that the manducation of the dead may be ascribed to some hidden cause. For assuredly no one would say that this happened owing to the influence of heaven and of the planets which are universal causes and which if they indeed did produce such an effect would produce it (1) Far more frequently; (2) In the case of all the dead, or at least in a very great many more instances; (3) Both at periods of pestilence as well as when the land was free from any visitation of the plague. For it is not at all agreed why at the time of pestilence alone the stars should exercise this influence upon the deceased, and at other times such should not be the case. In a word it is mere folly to refer universal causes to particular effects. Moreover, nobody who was of sound mind would refer this manducation to the effect of the soul, since when the soul has left the body it is detained in its appointed place. Again we imagine that everybody must agree that when the soul is departed the mere carcass can do nothing of itself. And so none of these qualities and conditions have any influence at all since if the essential principle is lacking (and it is lacking in the case of a corpse) they are powerless. And if there be no causation there follow no effect.

III. *To maintain that they are devoured by Azazel is an idle and inept fiction, a legend which is somewhat' foolishly fathered upon the Jewish Rabbis.*

We have already shown that to suppose such manducation can be subjective is altogether erroneous. And now we encounter another opinion which is demonstrably false although this relates to an objective cause, namely to Azazel. Two propositions are maintained : (1) That these corpses are devoured by Azazel.   (2) That this is the opinion of the Rabbis. Among those who support the first belief although they do not (it is true) emphasize and push it to its logical conclusion are Kornmannus, *De Miraculis Mortuorum*, Part VII, c. 64 ; Paulus Schalichius in his treatise *De Demonio Infernali*, 48 ; and Pistorius in his *Daemonomania*, where he speaks of being devoured by Azazel. These authors appear to take Azazel to be a serpent, and some say that the Jewish Rabbis main-tain this identification, and so these bodies become the food of a serpent. This is indeed to trifle. Yet they assert the Jews prove this from the text in *Genesis*, III, 14 : "And the Lord God said to the serpent :. Because thou hast done this thing, thou art cursed among all cattle, and beasts of the earth : Upon thy breast shalt thou go, and earth shalt thou eat all the days of thy life." Also Isaias says, LXV, 25 : "And dust shall be the serpent's food." One can scarcely forebear from laughing at such a gloss. Both the passages refer to the reptile, the serpent which is an animal, who is never called Azazel but נחש, which is the ordinary name for a serpent or snake when the animal is spoken of in the Bible. Moreover, it is obvious to anybody who reads the context in both passages of Holy Scripture that the references are to earth and the dust of the ground, not to any corpse. A fine exegesis of the Scripture this and well worthy of those Jewish Rabbins among whose sifting and shifting of Holy Writ such twists and acro-batic turns of sense may not infrequently be found. And at the same time it were well that our commentators should be quite sure that this opinion was ever held by the Rabbinists. We are led to doubt this on several grounds. And the first reason is because the Rabbis do not explain Azazel as a serpent but as a spirit, an evil spirit, to wit a demon.   Johann Buxtorf[52] tells us : " Azazel is the name of an angel who together with his comrade Samchasai, fell from heaven " *Lexicon Talmudicum,*

col. 1593. Claudius Frischmuthius definitely tells us that
"the names of the four principal demons among the Jews
were Sammael, Asasel, Asael, and Muchazael." The same
authority has collected a vast deal of cognate matter from
the writings of the Rabbis, and he treats very amply of Azazel
in his tractate *De Hirco Emissario*, I, *sqq.*, where he quotes an
author who may also be profitably consulted on this point,
Johann Benedict Carpzov,[53] who in his *Disputatio de Gigantibus*,
iv, has brought together a great many of these Jewish legends
concerning Azazel, collected from Rabbinical writings, but it
is never said anywhere that this spirit was metamorphosed
into a serpent or appeared under that form. Those who wish
to inquire further may profitably consult Meyer's *Philosophia
Sacra*, Part II, pp. 231-37 ; and Bang's *Coelum Oriens*. Moreover, and this is another reason for being highly suspicious of
any such interpretation, the Jewish commentators when
dealing with the texts which have been quoted from *Genesis*
and *Isaias* have no mention of the word Azazel, but they
keep the term נחש ; and they assuredly know nothing about
these corpses which are chawed and devoured by Azazel in
the form of a serpent, since this term they use merely means
the earth or the ground. This being the case then, the question
may arise whence is it that certain scholars have derived this
extraordinary legend which they attribute to the Rabbis ?
It has come from the various traditions which are recorded
by the Jewish Talmudists concerning the Angel of Death, and
which have been something exaggerated in common parlance
and creed. Johann Buxtorf in his *Synagoga Iudaica*, c. xxxvi,
relying upon the authority of Elias Grammaticus in his *Lexicon*
(*sub uerbo* "Tischbi ") writes : "The Rabbis believe that
after one of the Hebrew race dies and has been buried the
Angel of Death cometh and taketh his station by the grave,
and at the same instant of time the man's soul returns to his
body, and the body is vitalized once more, whilst this Angel
of Death having an iron chain, which is in part icy cold, and
in part red hot, smites this body or corpse with the said chain,
and at the first blow all the limbs of this body are rent asunder
and fall apart, but at the second blow all the bones are scattered
afar, and then at the third and last blow of the chain the whole
body falls into dust and ashes." This then is what the Jews
believe about the Angel of Death, but he certainly was not

an Angel who devoured and ate corpses. On the other hand the old Pagans indeed supposed that there was such a being and he is actually mentioned by Pausanias in his Tenth Book when speaking of the Phocians he says : "Among the Gods of the underworld they place a certain Eurynomus, whose rites are celebrated at Delphi, and they say that this evil spirit devours and crams the flesh of corpses so that anon nothing is left but their bare bleaching bones." A little later this dark genius is described : "In complexion he is something between black and very swarthy, the colour of a fat blue-bottle such as those who fly-blow fresh meat ; he shows white gleaming teeth ;[54] his skin is bewrinkled like that of a vulture." It is true that there was among the Jews some story of a mouse which as soon as a body was buried began to gnaw and bite it most cruelly so that the dead man cried aloud and shrilled bitterly. Let him who lists believe such a tale. Several writers have mentioned this legend, see Geier, *Tractatus de luctu Hebraeorum*, V, 17. It may not be altogether imperti-nent to remark that the Mohammedans have just as many idle stories of serpents and snakes as the Jews, and there is some legend of a dragon who has ninety-nine necks each furnished with seven heads and when an unbeliever is buried each one of these heads bites him as a punishment for his sins. Edward Pocock[55] in his *Miscellanies*, and Garmer in his *De Miraculis Mortuorum*, III, 3, assure us that the Turk actually believes this foolery. It is this sort of silly fable, no doubt, which has given rise to the absurd fiction related by some writers, namely that a snake may be born from the spine of a dead man. For this see Kornmannus, *op. cit.* VI, 30. It were idle to pursue the matter further. And indeed all these tales and many like to them are the emptiest nursery lore, and as has been said by that most eminent theologian John Conrad[56] Dannhuerus they are "mere poppied nonsense and idlest dreams, which may be left to the inhabitants of those cities whose light is darkness, whose truth is a lie, who surround themselves with ignorance as with a wall." As for Eurynomus, Pausanias even expunges him from any catalogue of the gods of the underworld. "This deity is not mentioned in the *Odyssey*, nor does his name occur in the *Minyas* nor do I find him in that poem which is entitled *Reditus*, and these are the poems which tell us more details than any other sagas have about the underworld and about their black secrets and their gods, yet the name Eurynomus does not occur in any one of them as an infernal power."[57]

IV. *It is sheer folly to ascribe this manducation to birds (strigibus) who suck blood, or to hyaenas, since these animals are entirely unknown in our country.*

This fact is so clear that it hardly needs any lengthy argument or disquisition. As for the *Striges*, for whom see Delrio *Disquisitiones Magicae*, I and III *passim*, if indeed there are any birds which may be so designed, they are said very gently to suck the blood of living people especially children.[58] But what has this to do with dead bodies ? And how does this explain the extraordinary noise and gruntings as of manducation made by corpses ? With regard to the hyaena, this animal is entirely unknown amongst us, and we should be doing it a wrong if we were to say that it could possibly come to this country and rove through our cemeteries. Even supposing that some of these animals were to prowl about amongst graveyards undiscovered by anybody, even in this remote and impossible case, I say, how could we ascribe this manducation to them ? It is true that in their own land they may feed upon bodies, whole and entire, which they have scraped up out of graves, just as the fierce bears in Muscovy, whose habits have been fully described by various travellers, will eat corpses. We may even quote S. John Chrysostom who in his *Thirteenth Homily on S. Mark* says : "The hyaena is never seen in the day time, but always in the night ; it is never seen in the light, but always in the darkness. It has so fierce a nature that it will plough up from their graves the bodies of the dead and then devour them. Wherefore if it so happen that one who has passed away is buried carelessly in no depth of earth the hyaena at night will dig up the body and carry it off and devour it. For wherever there is a cemetery, wherever there is a burying place, there is the hyaena's den."

V. *Now that we have examined and proved all these causes of the manducation of dead bodies, and shown them to be erroneous, we are obliged to conclude that the demon is the cause of this manducation.*

We are indeed bound to attribute this operation to the evil spirit, for logically we must do so since we cannot escape from that postulate, accepted by all theologians and scholars, that if we find some action or circumstance which is beyond the natural powers of man and there does not appear any reasonable or fitting cause why it should be directly ascribed to Almighty God or to the ministry of good Angels, then must it necessarily be the work of the demon. With regard to this manducation which is the subject of our inquiry : (1) It has already been shown that it cannot proceed from the body, since a corpse is deprived of that essential quality, and so is unable to perform any action whatsoever. (2) It were absurd to ascribe it to any animal of any kind whatsoever. (3) The purity and goodness of the holy Angels must entirely forbid us from even venturing to suppose that they would lend themselves to these foul horrors. What have these blessed and angelic spirits to do with charnel-houses, with the filth of rotting corpses ? They inhabit heaven, they do not frequent vaults and coffined crypts. Truly they guard the bones of the righteous, but they do not make use of them to work uncouth marvels and strange miracles. Therefore it can but be the evil spirit who is the cause of this horrible and monstrous manducation. For, like some bat or obscene bird of night he takes his pleasure in graves and foul sepulchres, as is told in Holy Scripture, S. *Mark*, V, 2-5[59] ; S. *Matthew*, VIII, 28.[60]

Psellus[61] also in his treatise *De Natura Daemonum*, when he describes the six kinds of demons informs us that the fifth rank or category consists of those who live underground and in the very bowels of the earth, " and these abide in caves and caverns and in most remote gullies among the loneliest mountains." Caspar Schott[62] is of the same opinion in his *Physica Curiosa*. S. John Chrysostom in his *Homilies on S. Matthew*,[63] cap. x, says that it was not merely commonly believed among folk generally but that it was held as certain by scholars and all learned men that evil spirits and demons dwell in graveyards lurking about the tombs and here they incessantly wander to and fro finding no rest.[64] The famous Jesuit exegete, Sanchez of Alcala[65], tells us the same in the sixty-fifth chapter of his Commentary on the prophet Jeremias.

VI. *At this point if our examination is to be continued without any ambiguity arising it will be necessary that we should distinguish and divide the active cause of this manducation into two terms, namely, the principal cause and the instrumental cause.*

VII. *The principal cause is the Devil himself who actually causes and brings about this manducation of the dead.*

There can be no doubt at all as to his desire and his will to produce such an effect, for he is indeed the craftiest of enemies (μυριοτεχνίτης hostis), a foe who is ever seeking every occasion and opportunity to hurt and harm poor wretched mortals. After death hatred no longer rages in the heart of a man, but it is always raging in the temper of the demon whose sole pleasure and delight it is to injure and destroy the human race at any time and in any way he may be able to do so. He betrayed his inveterate malice indeed in his contention with the Archangel S. Michael over the body of Moses, *S. Jude*, 9.[66] Many of the other lying wonders which he effects show us that he is quite well able to produce this extraordinary manducation. We do not allow that he has that power over the soul when it is separated by death from the body, which is attributed to him by Delrio—far too unguardedly as we conceive (*Disquisitiones Magicae*, q. 25); but that he has a considerable power over the human body, in so far as God permits, we would not venture to deny.[67] "If God will, the demon is able to distress us during our lives, to torment us with horrible dreams and disturb our repose, to deform and distort our limbs, nay, to afflict us with sickness and disease." This is the opinion of S. Cyprian of Carthage in his treatise *Quod Idola dii non sint*,[68] and these words are quoted by Binderus in his treatise *De Causa Pestis*. The Devil, to cite Delrio's exact phrase, is able " to perform the most marvellous things with regard to dead bodies, and to bring to pass such extraordinary happenings that it would seem as if the very corpses were alive again and informed by intellect and soul. He can, for example, cause blood to flow from the wounds of a dead man in the presence of his murderer[69]; he can also cause dead bodies to remain whole and entire without corruption, yet this can happen naturally either through the art of the embalmer, or from the peculiar nature of the place where the deceased are buried[70], and sometimes even from the kind of death ; and this incorruption is often effected by the mysterious power of the demon, so that to answer his purpose for a long while at all events the remains shall not be cremated." It is indeed quite impossible to give any account of all the extraordinary happenings which the power of the demon can bring to pass in connexion with dead bodies. Nor can there be any doubt at all that he can produce manducation, and this he causes to be accompanied by a horrible grunting noise.

VIII. *It is highly probable that in connexion with this horrid business those lieutenants of the evil spirit, Witches, co-operate, and we need not doubt that they are often a secondary or instrumental cause, their master being the principal and determining cause.*

The devil is indeed the principal in all this business, but there can be no doubt that he often avails himself of the agency of witches for these operations, and we shall be the more easily assured of this when we consider what other extraordinary wonders these wretches are able to perform owing to the power of that old serpent. Not impertinently does Delrio tell us that " witches are able to perform many extraordinary things with the help of the demon, and this is by the permission of God." *Disquisitiones Magicae*, II, qu. 7.[71]   The same author also in his following chapters has collected a large number of facts of this kind, and he quotes both from old and established authorities as well as from distinguished writers of more recent date. For example, he quotes from Suidas the instance of Julian the Chaldaean[72] who had extraordinary powers which allowed him to put an end to epidemics and the plague. But as Conrad Schlüsselburg, to whom we have referred before, tells us, it is very generally believed that the plague may be induced by this manducation of the dead, and since this is the case it is very certain that witches will busy themselves to induce this manducation. We may remember what Tibullus has written of a certain witch in his second Elegy (Liber I) :

> Haec cantu finditque solum, manesque sepulcris
> Elicit, et tepido deuorat ossa rogo.

And Ovid in his *Heroides*, the Epistle of Hypsipyle to Jason, writes :

> Per tumulos errat passis discincta capillis,
> Certaque de tepidis colligit ossa rogis.[73]

If they secretly snatched away bones from the funeral pyres, they will not spare the flesh of dead bodies in the grave. More particularly because as Godelmann[74] tells us they make great use of corpses in preparing their deadliest poisons, *De Magis, Ueneficis et lamiis tractatus,* I, c. 8.[75] Paulus Grilllandus,[76] who is quoted by Delrio writes : " It is certain that witches sacrilegiously exhume the dead." Lucan in his *Pharsalia*, VI, has described a witch of this kind :

> Ast ubi seruantur saxis, quibus intimus humor
> Ducitur, et tracta durescunt tabe medullæ
> Corpora : tunc omnes auide desaeuit in artus
> Immergitque manus oculis, gaudetque gelatos
> Effodisse orbes . . .

Delrio, who was one of the most learned of writers on these subjects, has collected from various authors a large amount of matter dealing with this point, for which one may see his *Disquisitiones Magicae*, III, Part i, qu. 3.[77] One may also consult the *Tractatus de Impietate Sagarum* of Theodore Thummius ; *quaestio v.*[78]. Since so many eminent authors assure us that necromancers and witches use the members torn from dead bodies in their charms, we are bound to suppose that they often bring about this loathly manducation for reasons of their own. It should be borne in mind that we have not been able to quote more than a few notable authorities, selecting these writers from a vast library.

IX. *The instrumental cause of this manducation must logically be these human corpses.*

It is plain that naturally the demon is unable to perform any corporeal action, because he has no body of his own proper to himself. Wherefore if he wishes to produce any such action he abuses our human nature by energizing with activity some body that is purely passive, or else he effects this by falsely vitalizing with movements certain bodies of dead men as if they were themselves of themselves endowed with motion, so that they may stimulate such effects as in the natural order of things would proceed from a body animated by the soul. In his treatise *De Causa Pestis* Binderus tells us that the Devil is able to employ natural objects and natural causes to produce the effects he desires. Accordingly the Devil cannot bring about the act of manducation unless he employ some other suitable body to whom this act is natural, as his instrument or agent, and therefore because this act is natural to a living body that most foul enemy of the human race enters those dead bodies and by these he fulfils his desire, although being dead of themselves they must remain passive and without movement unless they are moved and energized by some superior cause. Yet it seems that certain writers are doubtful whether he can be said to perform the act of manducation by means of a corpse. For example, Conrad Schlüsselburg writes : " es ist gewiss dass diss Schmetzen nicht geschehe von den Cörperm der Todten in Grabe." To this I reply : Technically this may be true, that is, if the act of manducation is considered as being a separate and definite operation, but none the less it is effected by the demon, as Garmann precisely states in his well-known treatise,[80] where he declares that the Devil may in a grave make curious noises, he may knock, he may lap like some thirsty animal, he may chaw, grunt and groan. But yet the demon cannot perform these actions unless he use the body as an instrument for this manducation. In the same way legend says that Pope Sylvester II, who on account of his great learning in common fable was reputed to be an adept in occultism,[81] kept certain bones in a shrine or an ark and thence upon occasion was heard to arise a murmuring and certain noise. The story is told by Schlüsselburg who says he had it from Cardinal Lodovico Simonetta.[82] However this may be, there can be no doubt that witches can exercise their power over dead bodies and raise them up so that they appear to be alive both by their walk and their gestures, examples of which may be found in many authors who have written upon these subjects. This is further confirmed by the αὐτοψία of certain authors who describe that corpses have devoured their rotting flesh and with their teeth torn to tatters the cerements and shroud.[83] Wherefore it may very fairly be said that these dead bodies do perform the act of manducation, although they do not do this of their own initiative but by some foreign power, which is to say that they are merely the instruments that cause this operation. But if some person objects that I am allowing too much power to the demon by saying that he has influence over these bodies which, as all other things, are in the keeping of Almighty God, then will I thus make reply, (1) The power of the devil is straitly restricted, yea, and limited by Divine Providence ; it is kept well within bounds and he is only permitted to exercise it for the just trial and the proving of good men. (2) We do not allow the demon, by arguing that he has this restricted power over dead bodies, any greater power than the Holy Scriptures allow him, for it is written that he is able most grievously to possess living men,[84] and he on occasion may afflict even the holiest with terrible diseases.[85] And it has been said in a Commentary upon the Epistle of S. Paul to the Galatians that if it be heaven's will we are all of us so far as our bodies and mere temporal things in the power of the demon εἰς τὴν ἀπώλειαν, (fitted for destruction).[86]

X. *The object or the matter of this manducation may be considered as being of a double kind.*

These corpses swallow and craunch the cerements and the linen napkins which wrap their jaws, as was noted in the instance which occurred in the year 1345, and which Harsdorffer records: " Als man sie ausgegraben hat sie den Schleier damit Ihr das Haupt ist verbunden gewesen halb hinein dessen gehabt welcher ihr blutig aus dem Halfe gezogen worden." And again : " Der Hencker zog Ihm au sdem Maul einen langen grossen Schleier Welchen er seinem Weibe von dem Haupte himweg gefressen hatte." Other corpses feed on their own flesh and greedily raven their very entrails, as happened in the case of the carcass whose grave was examined in the time of Martin Luther, whereof Schlüsselburg writes : " Also lesen wir dass an Herr M. Georg Röhrern gen Wittenberg ein Pastor von einem Dorffe geschrieben wie in seiner Gemeine ein Weib gestorben die fresse sich nun selbst im Grabe." And a little later he adds : " man hats also befunden wenn man das Grab eröffnet dass solche Weiber die Lippen und Schleier oder das Tuch am Halfe gefressen." Kornmannus, *De Miraculis Mortuorum*, also has an example of this kind, a dead woman who chawed her own flesh. This he quotes from Hohndorff who mentions the instance in his *Theatrum Historiae*.

XI. *The form of manducation is the ordinary and natural proceeding, to wit the reception of some edible into the mouth, the mastication of such edible which is triturated with the teeth, and the swallowing of such cribbled edible into the oesophagus ; which manducation is accompanied by a sound exactly resembling the noise of porkers grunting over their food.*

Concerning this noise we shall speak later. Here we have to consider three formal operations, for the swallowing of the food into the oesophagus may, if we are not over nice in terms, be for our purpose accounted the end of manducation, and since the fullest and best explanation consists in giving examples and we have already mentioned many instances in the course of our thesis it is hardly necessary here to go over the same ground again.[87]

XII. *There are yet certain details of this manducation which must be considered, and especially these two, the extraordinary noise which accompanies this manducation, and the time at which such manducation occurs.*

It will be well before we sum up our concluding arguments to give a little attention to these two circumstances, the causes of which will be explained in the logical developments of our thesis.

XIII. *The grunting noise made by these dead bodies as of porkers eating proceeds from the Devil, who is the sole cause of this manducation.*

Not only do corpses eat but they also make an extraordinary grunting noise. As it is beyond a doubt that this manducation is caused by the demon, so also is it certain that he is the cause of the noise. It has been asked if this noise proceeds from the grave itself being made by the instrumental means of the incorrupt organs of the corpse or whether it may not be caused by the devil outside the tomb altogether in the surrounding atmosphere, so that it thus strikes upon the hearing of those who become cognizant of it. Assuredly the devil can produce this noise as from the corpse, and he effects this in the same way as he has spoken through many bodies, for we have the over-whelming testimony of antiquity that the demon utters sounds by means of many objects and instruments, such as through oracles, caves, oak trees, and even statues.[88] Yea, he hath even spoken from skulls and from the rotting lips of dead men, as Delrio informs us, *Disquisitiones Magicae*, II, *qu.* 25, sect. 3. He is far more able then to utter a voice from a body which is but newly interred. Nor does the weight of earth which fills in the grave heaped heavy on the coffin in any way prevent the sound issuing forth from the tomb, for as nature sometimes will make noise in the caverns and hollow places which are in the interior of the earth, and these noises are very plainly heard by men who dwell upon the face of the earth (to say nothing of those terrible rumbling and bellowings which volcanic fires produce in the very bowels of the earth) so it is certain that the devil can produce a strange noise down in graves, which after all are not dug very deep, and this noise issuing forth is heard by men. Yet in our opinion, which we are ready to submit to the better judgement of our superiors, it were quite reasonable to suppose that the devil often mocks and cheats men's senses by making some strange noise in the air hard by the grave so that to the human ear the sound seems to proceed from the earth. That the devil delights to mislead and bemuse our senses is plainly stated by Gisbert Voet[89] in his *Disputationes Selectae*, part I, " De Operatione Daemonum," and these are his words : " The devil can cheat and deceive a man's five senses and the organs of sense in more ways than one. For example the evil spirit can mock the ears by imaginary noises, etc." In his *Tractatus Theologicus de Sagarum impietate* Theodore Thummius expresses himself of the same opinion. " The devil," writes this learned divine, " will often persuade a man that he hears or it may be feels something when the sound or the object in truth is nothing save glamour which has been most cunningly interposed by the evil spirit." It were no difficult matter to treat at length of the wiles and deceits of the infernal old serpent, which is the devil and Satan, but we must now leave this argument, breaking off as it were even in the midst.

XIV. *Corpses in their graves chew with this horrible grunting noise chiefly during a great plague. At other times, when no pestilence rageth, this loathly manducation is seldom observed.*

This is amply proved by the examples we have cited, all of which save the first and the last our authorities tell us took place during some mortal visitation of a great sickness. Conrad Schlüsselburg writes : " man höret und ersähret offt in Sterbenstäufften." For this point see Dunt *Decisio Casuum Conscientiae*, XXIII, *qu.* 19, the text where he quotes Pruknerus *Mortuorum Quaestio Illustrium*. Both these authors say that corpses only eat in the time of plague. Nevertheless we must not deny that this manducation also takes place on other occasions when the land is free from the pest, although instances are rare. Yet the cases we gave as our first and our last examples seem to prove that corpses eat in their graves at a time when no pestilence is raging, and this is amply proven by the histories Harsdorffer relates in his *Theatrum Exemplorum Tragicorum*.

XV. *The reasons why Satan impels corpses to eat in their graves are two in number ; a Theological reason, and a Physical reason.*

We must not idly suppose that our infernal enemy does not conceive that by this manducation of the dead he may harm men, for he ever has his reasons for what he does. We have divided these into two categories ; the Theological reasons and the Physical reasons, and older authors have treated of the matter. Schlüsselburg in his glosses upon *Psalm XC* (*A.V.* XCI), *Qui habitat in adiutorio Altissimi*, gives a list of six such reasons, whereof some affect the dead, others the living. By this manducation the devil strives to bring the deceased into ill repute so that people will begin to believe that he led a vile and wicked life. " Es kan wohl an frommen Leuten geschchen." And that eminent theologian not impertinently emphasizes that this is the very reason why we find the devil most frequently employs the corpses of women to practise this loathly manducation. He is ever at war with the weaker sex, because of a Woman is born the Man Who is stronger than himself, and hence he will leave no stone unturned to injure a woman's good fame in whatsoever way and by whatsoever means he possibly can hurt and harm her. The remaining causes concern the living. The demon produces this manducation partly that he may awaken doubts in the hearts of men who will weakly begin to question the Divine Providence Who watcheth over the living and into Whose care the dead are entrusted. (The next point is brought out and argued with the utmost skill by Schlüsselburg). He produces this operation partly that he may persuade men wholly to forget and disregard the sins of their past lives, and so to lap them in a false and foolish security. For this beast who is an insatiable glutton of souls would persuade them that these corpses are paying the penalty for their iniquities and in the consideration of the transgressions of others they will forget to repent of their own sins which are daily provoking God to anger. Again he works this wonder partly to give the living occasion to indulge in uncharitable and malicious thoughts of the dead ; partly also to stir up strife and quarrels among the living, and this he most cunningly and adroitly achieves when some people declare that if any extraordinary manducation is heard the corpses must be exhumed, whilst the relatives and friends of the dead, taking such a suggestion very hardly, most strongly oppose any scheme of disinterment. Hence arise numberless quarrels, oaths, blasphemies, and much false swearing not unmixed with violence.

These then are the Theological Causes. In his *Tractatus de Miraculis Mortuorum*, I, 3, Johann Christopher Frederick Garmannus numbers two Physical Causes. The first is that the living may be horribly alarmed and struck with panic by this monstrous manducation. The second is, that if it be necessary to exhume the body, therefrom may proceed infection and pestilence. Either of these two things is a very ready means to spread the black plague. Schlüsselburg observes : " Wenn man eines todten Menschen Grab der an der Pestilenz gestorben wiederum erössnet kan dadurch leichtlich die Lufft vergifftet und andere Leute mit der Pest angesteck et wergen." And this opinion is amply borne out by facts. We may instance what happened in the year 1603 at Neinstade, a village near Hamburg, when (as has been mentioned above) a corpse was exhumed by the peasants of the district, and the head severed from the carcass. The rotting members with their offal stench so polluted and infected the whole air for a league and more that a shepherd who dwelt not very far from the graveyard in question died together with his wife and his two daughters. It is very certain, too, that fright and terror do much to increase the ravages of any epidemic plague. This is particularly noted by the celebrated Athanasius Kircher[90] in his *Scrutinium physico-medicum contagiosae luis, quae pestis dicitur.*[91]

XVI. *It remains to consider the various remedies which are generally employed in the case of these extraordinary happenings, and it must be inquired whether these remedies are efficacious, or nugatory and of no avail.*

We shall not, I think, be shooting our arrows idly and at random (ἄσκοπα τοξεύειν)[92] if now we say something about those remedies which are wont to be employed upon the occasion of such extraordinary and terrible happenings. In some cases a wise precaution has attempted to counteract these operations of evil spirits by certain amulets and charms, and in some cases it would seem that reliance upon these periapts is merely superstitious. Since, therefore, obviously they are not all of the same value we will divide them into two

general classes, the true and the false. Among the false we
may at once include that old custom of the Jews which is
described by Schickhardus in his works upon Hebrew rites
and ceremonies. For there he mentions that the Jews clasp
the hands of the dead so that in their disposing they fancifully
form the name of Almighty God שדי. And this, the learned
Buxtorf observes in his *De Synagoga Iudaeorum*, xxv, inspires
Satan with the greatest fear and he dare not so much as
approach the body. This practice is also mentioned by the
eminent Dilherrus in his *Disputationes Academicae*, tom. I,
(p. 510), where speaking of this custom of the Jews he says that
sometimes they draw a long thread from the garments of the
deceased and this they twist about his fingers so that it seems
to represent the sacred letters שדי. Some may think this
efficacious, but for my part I cannot agree with them. I can
scarce believe that the letters שדי in some way impressed
upon the hands of the deceased would drive away the evil
spirit. Assuredly if they were impressed upon the hands of
a living man the demon would not any the less spare to tempt
him, to endeavour to lead him astray, and to weary him with
wicked suggestions. For the same reason I should not perhaps
put such faith in the consecration of cemeteries,[93] [*loquitur
Haereticus*] which is treated at great length by Durandus[94]
and by Angelus Clavassius, who are quoted in the work of
Kornmannus to which we have already referred. Delrio
tells us[95] that the demon has indeed a certain power over the
bodies of the dead, and he may indeed take their form and
appear in this shape ; and his power is especially great over
those which are buried in unconsecrated ground.

A practice that is not uncommon in certain districts is to
place a morsel of new earth upon the lips of the dead, and in
this they would seem to be following an old custom of the
Jews which Geier in his *Tratatus de luctu Hebraeorum*, V,
commenting upon the book *Minhagim* records : "Man soll
sehen dass Ihm (dem Toden) nichts von den תכריכין (Ster-
bekleidern oder Lemwandten Gezeug) ins Maul kommt es ist
fonst סכנה Gefahr." Some deeming this not altogether
sufficient before they close the lips of the dead place a stone
and a coin in the cold mouth, so that in his grave he may bite
on these and refrain from gnawing further. That this custom
still persists in very many parts of Saxony we learn on the

authority of Gabriel Rollenhagen, from the fourth book of whose *Mirabilis Peregrinatio* Kornmannus has very ample quotations. Garmannus in the *De Miraculis Mortuorum* emphasizes the fact that this is merely an ethnic custom. He says : "Those who do this are merely following a Pagan practice, for as is well-known the Pagans used to put a little coin (δανακὴν) in the mouths of their dead which was the fee for the boatman Charon, to pay him his dole so that he might ferry them over the river Styx." These, however, may be deemed but the remedies which prevail among peasants and the ignorant.

And it has sometimes happened that more drastic treatment has been sought. For bodies have actually been exhumed, their heads lopped off, and stakes driven through the heart pinning them to the earth. Instances of this kind are recorded as having taken place in the years 1345, 1603, and even more frequently. But such a proceeding is wrong from every point of view. It is both morally wrong, and physically wrong, and wrong from the legal standpoint. It is morally wrong for it is a sin against God since we are forbidden to consult the dead, and it is a species of necromancy when the dead are exhumed. It is also a sin against one's neighbour, for the reputation of the dead person must be most gravely injured by the horribly degrading circumstances of such an exhumation, the hacking off of the head and the driving a stake through the heart. Moreover it not infrequently happens that by the noisome stench of such a rotting carcass the whole atmosphere is infected and the poison of the plague spread far and wide. The devil, no doubt, rejoices at this and it is in sooth one of the ends at which he aims. Wherefore our divines when they have been consulted on the matter by those who happen to be sore vexed with these intolerable evils have with one consent made reply that nobody must violate a graveyard nor must they disturb those bodies who are sleeping there. Yet certain arguments have, it is true, been advanced to the contrary, and these are set forth at length, not without considerable skill by several writers amongst whom are Schlüsselburg, from whom we have so amply quoted ; by Martin Behaim[98] ; who however has but briefly mentioned the matter in passing ; and by Andreas Wilkius who in his twenty-sixth Oration has dealt with the subject at some length.

The laws of all countries have always regarded exhumation as a most serious offence, nor do they allow it even in cases of this kind, and any act of the sort is strictly forbidden under the severest penalties. A very large number of statutes dealing with this point have been collected from the various codes and capitularies by Kornmannus, and these are of sufficient importance to deserve careful study. It will not be impertinent here to quote the words of Caspar Sanctius in his Commentary upon the second chapter of *Amos* where he speaks of the crime of exhuming the dead. "Hence it is very plain that to exhume the dead is one of the gravest of sins, for it is indeed an insult to their poor ashes. It is to engage them in an unjust quarrel, it is to deprive them of that decent respect which good men give those who have departed, it is indeed, if I may speak in metaphors, to slay them yet once again and to cause them to suffer the pains of death anew. It is a crime from which nature shrinks and which is so detested by Heaven that if any enemy so heinously offend verily they will not go unpunished. To use such cruelty towards the dead and to dishonour them by savagery of this kind is in the opinion of all wise and good men to give way to the passions and rage of mere beasts of prey. Even to speak ill of the dead, or to say aught that may injure those who have gone before is rightly esteemed improper in the highest degree, nay, a bitter wrong, and persons who malign the departed are to be compared to wild animals, who ravening with hunger scratch up with fierce paws corpses from their graves to glut their bellies with horrid meat. Truly these who scandalize the dead and who expose before the eyes of all men those faults which are hidden by the kindly earth are to be compared to these mad wolves. Far greater then is their offence who disinter the bones of the dead and burn them, and, certes, such terrible deeds are worthy of the severest punishment."[99]

Theodore Thummius in his tractate that we have already quoted and Johann Conrad Dammhauers most excellently sum up for us the true remedies by which we may oppose these devices of Satan, by which indeed, we may defend ourselves against all these ghostly deceits of the devil as also against the power of his sworn servants and bondslaves, sorcerers and witches. The first of these remedies is to have a lively trust and firm faith in Our Blessed Lord Who hath crushed the serpent's head, and withal to nourish in our hearts a purpose of amendment and a hatred of sin. The second is the Word of God, that sharp sword which the Holy Apostles have put into our hands, relying upon which weapon under the protection of God we may utterly foil and frustrate the open attacks and the dark ambushes of Satan. The third protection is Prayer, the scourge of evil spirits, a sure safeguard against the wiles of the demon. The fourth protection is the help of the Holy Angels who by God's command are ever at our side to keep us safe, so that we may have no fear " of the arrow that flieth in the day, of the business that walketh about in the dark: of invasion, or of the noonday devil " (*Psalm*, Xff, 6). All these remedies are treated of at greater length in the works of our eminent Theologians. In a thesis which is discussed by the Chair of Philosophy we need do no more than name them thus briefly with reverent recommendation.

[It will be well here to add other and truly important aids and remedies which Rohr omits. One can only speak of these very briefly, but it were not seemly that they should be passed over in silence. In the first place there is no stronger defence against the secret snares and open onslaughts of the demon than the Most Holy Sacrament of the Altar. Frequent, yea daily, attendance at Mass; devout Communions; visits to the adorable Prisoner of the Tabernacle; fervent worship of the Sacrament; all these disarm and crush the devil. Again, the most powerful safeguard against demoniacal outrages lies in the protection of the Immaculate Mother of God, Who in Her complete and perfect sinlessness has so signally triumphed over the enemy of mankind. The invocation of Her most Holy Name puts devils to flight, and he who trusts in Her shall never fail. Wherefore pious practices in Her honour should be multiplied, the Rosary continually recited, and the coldness of devotion to Mary fanned to a flame. Most efficacious are Holy Relics, which should be often exposed with lights and all due ceremonies for meet veneration, which may even be devoutly carried on the person and honoured with great reverence. Sacramentals; the sprinkling of Holy Water; Paschal Wax; and other approved matters possess a particular power of their own to drive away evil spirits whose baleful operations so seriously affect the physical activities and good estate of man. Such pious practices as the carrying upon one's person the first fourteen verses of the Gospel according to S. John, engraved or written out in a fair hand are not to be neglected. Holy Medals, as the Medal of S. Benedict, should be worn. Mortifications may be practised, especially the discipline and the wearing of a cilice. Private devotion and the counsel of a director, skilled in mystic theology, will suggest many more precautions and protections against the incursion of evil.

Should a grave seem at all suspect, not perhaps of vampirism, but as being a focus of exceptional phenomena, a requiem or even trentals will be sung or said for the deceased. If ultimate measures have to be taken these, of course, will be directed according to the canon by ecclesiastical authority].

Rohr concludes his dissertation with the following aspirations : " Let us therefore most humbly pray to Almighty God that He would avert from this province and especially from this home and nursery of all liberal arts and sciences every ill, and that He may be pleased to shield us from the innumerable crafts of Satan ! From the snares of the devil and from all pestilence, Good Lord deliver us ! "

NOTES.   CHAPTER III.

[1] *Revue Britannique*, Août, 1869, pp. 341-369.

[2] 1614-1687.

[3] *An Antidote against Atheism*, Book III, c. viii.

[4] *op. cit.*, Book III, c. ix.

[5] There seems to have prevailed in this district a local superstition concerning household work done on a Thursday which was deemed unlucky. The same belief was found in parts of France. " Les Bretonnes ne veulent point coudre les Jeudis et les Samedis parce que le travail ces jours-là ferait pleurer la Vierge." De la Charbouelais Chesnel, *Dictionnaire des Superstitions, Erreurs, Préjuges et Traditions populaires.*—2 tom. 4to, 1855.

[6] This diocese is directly subject to the Holy See.

[7] In Ireland formerly persons who died without the Sacraments were not buried in consecrated ground. *Uita Sancti Mochoemog*, xviii. Special cemetries for unbaptized children may be found in all parts of Ireland to-day.

[8] Mr. Arthur Machen has an article in *The Referee*, 22 January, 1928, p.12. Cf. in the same number " The Racketing Spirit." For Poltergeist hauntings see my *Geography of Witchcraft*, 1927, pp. 184, 271-280 and 282-6.

[9] Edition of 1738 ; Lettre cxxxvii.

[10] An account is given in Georg Conrad Hurst's *Zauber-Bibliothek*, 1821, vol. I, pp. 253-55. Other details are found in contemporary journals. Gabriel Rzazeynsci, S.J. in his *Historia naturalis curiosa regni Poloniae*, published at Sandomir in 1721 relates several other cases of a similar nature.

[11] One account says twenty or thirty days after the decease of Arnold, and Dr. Mayo who follows this in his description of the disinterment speaks

of " a gray morning in early August."—*Popular Superstitions*, Second edition, 1851, p. 25.

¹² Carniola (Krain) is divided into eleven districts, consisting of 359 communes.

¹³ *Essen* is an Imperial City in the *Dutchy of Bergue*, that enjoys many Privileges granted it by the Emperor Charles V, in 1523. Here is a noble and rich Nunnery, founded by St. Alfrid, Bishop of Hildersheim, about the year 877 ; to which at present belongs the greatest part of the town, together with several large Manours in the Neighbourhood. The Revenues were at first settled for the Maintenance of fifty-two Nuns and twenty Canons ; but these Numbers have since been retrenched. Some Time since, scarce any Girls were admitted into the Nunnery, but the Daughters of Barons, and other superior Nobility. These Ladies are at Liberty to marry, when they please. Here is also a fine Gymnasium for the liberal Education of Youth.

¹⁴ Many Authors might here be produced, but we shall content ourselves with the two following : *P. Gengell*, S. I. in Evers. Atheism and *P. Gabr. Rzaczynski*, in Hist. Nat. curios. Regn. Polon. magn. Ducat, Lituan. annexarumque Provinciar. in Tract. 20 divis. P. 365, Sandomiriæ, 1721.

¹⁵ *Phlegon, Trallian*, de Reb. admirabil. Cap. 1.

¹⁶ See *Calmet's* Dissertation upon good and bad Angels, prefixed to his Comment. on *St. Luke* ; as also his Biblical Dictionary, at the Words *Angels, Demon, Devil, Diabolus, Satan*, &c. Many Texts might be produced on this Occasion ; but the following will be sufficient to prove what is here advanced. Psalm lxxviii. v. 49. *Job*, Chap. i ; *Matth.*, Chap. xii. v. 22-32 ; *Mark*, Chap. iii. v. 22-31 ; *Luke*, Chap. xi. v. 14-31 ; Chap. xiii. v. 16 ; *Acts*, Chap. xix., v. 13-17.

¹⁷ F. S. Krauss, " Vampyre im südslavischen Volksglauben." *Globus*, lxi (1892), p. 326.

¹⁸ See the detailed study, *The Need-fire*, by Sir James Frazer, *The Golden Bough : Balder the Beautiful*, vol. I, 1923, pp. 269-300.

¹⁹ Glossary on the *Capitularies, apud* J. Grimm, *Deutsche Mythologie*, Fourth edition, Berlin, 1875-78, I, p. 502.

²² *Deutsche Glaube und Brauch*, Berlin, 1867, II, pp. 149, *sqq.*

²¹ S. Boniface was appointed Archbishop of Mainz and Primate of Germany by Pope S. Zachary on 1 May, 748 (747).

²² His feast formerly celebrated on 16 August has, owing to this day being now fixed for the Solemnity of S. Joachim, being generally transferred to 17 August. It is kept by the Franciscan family as a *duplex maius*. Wadding tells us that in 1485 the Relics of S. Roch were conveyed to Venice and enshrined in San Rocco. The church of San Rocco was rebuilt in 1725. The Scuola di San Rocco is especially famous.

²³ Ahun ; Montpellier ; Naples : Nice ; Parma ; Venice ; etc.

²⁴ S. Raphael (" God has healed ") is the " Angelus medicus." He was the Archangel who " descended at certain times into the pond " called Probatica, " and the water was moved. And he that went down first into the pond after the motion of the water was made whole of whatsoever infirmity he lay under," as is related by S. John, v, 1-9. The Feast of S. Raphael is observed 24 October, and this Scripture is read as the Gospel of the Mass.

¹⁵ *Borderland*. A Quarterly Review and Index, ed. by W. T. Stead. 1894-1896.

²⁶ Vol. XI, No. 5, November, 1924, pp. 258-59.

²⁷ Second edition, London, 1920, pp. 47-52.

²⁸ Probably *circa* 1610-12. First printed in 1778 from a MS. now in the Bodleian.

²⁹ Chapter X.

³⁰ Translated by the Rev. Montague Summers. *Demoniality*. Fortune Press, London, 1927.

³¹ Nulle part la croyance au revenans, aux sorciers, aux malins esprits n'est plus invétérée qu'au Montenegro. Les fantômes, les rêves, les prestiges poursuivent sans cesse leur imagination ; mais rien n'égale la terreur que leur inspirent les *brucolaques*, c'est-a-dire les cadavres des individus frappés

d'excommunication, jetés au hasard sans sepulture. Le sol qui les a recu est une terre maudite à jamais ; ils s'en éloignent à une grande distance ; et si le lieu se présente à leur souvenir, ils se croient poursuivis par *revenans*. Enfin, ces hommes qui affrontent tous les périls, ne rêvent que sorciers et esprits malins ; tous leurs discours peignent le terreur dont ils sont atteints ; il faudrait être un habile démonographe pour faire la longue histoire de tous les diables dont ils s'entretiennent, et de toutes les aventeurs qu'ils en racontent.

[32] L. C. Vialla de Sommicres, *op. cit.*, vol I, pp. 282-83. Un nommé *Zanetto*, homme tout à fait original, mais adonné à la boisson, fut saisi par une averse, un soir qu'il s'était plus particulièrement enviré. En rentrant chez lui, il se jette sur son lit avec ses vêtemens ; chaud de vin, mais froid de la pluie, il éprouve d'horribles convulsions ; vers les onze heures, il reste sans mouvement, sans chaleur, sans respiration ; enfin il est dans l'état de mort. . . . à huit heures du matin, on va l'inhumer. Pour le porter de sa maison à l'église, il fallait monter un chemin difficile et descendre par un plus difficile encore. L'inégalité du sol, partout coupé de rocs et de grosses pierres, forçait les porteurs à des mouvemens violens. Ces fréquentes secousses rappellent *Zanetto* à la vie. Il s'agite brusquement, se lève, regarde autour de lui, et crie en forcené : " Que diable faites-vous, ivrognes ? " A ces mots, les porteurs le jettent à terre, et s'enfuient comme frappés de la foudre. Ceux qui suivaient le cercueil se précipitent dans les vignes en poussant de grands cris ; ceux qui précèdent, se retournent, et terrifiés à ce spectacle, courent pêle-mêle dans la ville voisine où ils portent la consternation, les uns par leur silence, les autres par l'incertitude de leur narration ; tous sont glacés d'effroi. Les prêtres seuls étaient restés sur le chemin, ignorant encore la véritable cause de ce désordre, lorsqu'ils entendent cette apostrophe du ressuscité Zanetto : " Démons vivans, vous me le paierez ; vous m'avez pris à la maison, vous m'y rapporterez ; autrement je vous jette tout de bon où vous pensiez me laisser pour toujours ; oh ! pour cette fois, je boirai tout ; je ne vous laisserai pas un sol." Les prêtres le portèrent effectivement chez lui avec humilité et sans aucune sorte d'impatience ; ils firent tous leurs efforts pour calmer cet homme qui était furieux. Il faut entendre raconter cet événement par lui-même.

[33] *Proceedings of the Society for Psychical Research*, vol. XXV, p. 378.

[34] *The Morning Post*, 24 January, 1928.

[35] It is significant that during the poltergeist disturbances in the house of Dr. Phelps, a Presbyterian Minister of Stratford, Connecticut, in 1850, when Dr. Phelps was one day writing in his study and had turned his back for a minute he found inscribed upon the sheet before him, the ink which formed the large uncouth letters being still wet : "Very nice paper and very nice ink for the devil."

[36] 1242-1312. Although the general veneration of the Church has not been officially granted to Christina the anniversary of her death, 6 November, is observed at Jülich where a monument to her exists.

[37] His feast is celebrated in the Order on 11 December.

[38] *Le Curé d'Ars*, par l'Abbé Alfred Monnin. 2 vols, Paris, 1861. For convenience sake I quote the salient passages from the English abridgement *Life of the Blessed Curé d'Ars*, "with a Preface by Henry Edward Manning, Cardinal Archbishop of Westminster," n.d. The life of S. John Baptist Vianney by the Abbé Trocher may also be consulted. English translation by Dom Ernest Graf, O.S.B., London, 1927. There are, of course, very many biographies and studies of the Saint.

[39] The Biblical examples quoted from the Old Testament are the raising by Elias of the son of the widow of Sarephta ; the dead man who came to life when his body was put into the sepulchre of Eliseus and had touched the bones of the prophet ; from the New Testament the daughter of Jairus, the son of the widow of Naim, and Lazarus of Bethania.

Martin Anton Delrio, S.J., was born at Antwerp, 17 May, 1551 ; and died at Louvain 19 October, 1608. He was the author of many theological treatises of importance, but the work by which he is best known is his *Disquisitiones Magicæ* which was first published at Louvain in 1599, and has run into more than ten editions. A French translation by André Duchesne appeared at Paris, 1611.

[40] H. Kornmann : *De miraculis mortuorum, opus nouum et admirandum in X partes distributum, in quo mirabilia Dei miracula et exempla mortuorum et U. et N. Test. collecta habentur.* Frankfort, 8vo, 1610.

[41] Among the later Latin poets Janus Vitalis is eminent for the elegance of his lines and the epigrammatic turn which so pleasingly informs his graceful verses.

[42] Joannes Zonaras, the celebrated Byzantine historian and theologian lived in the twelfth century under the Emperors Alexius I Comnenus and Calo-Joannes. Besides his theological works there is still extant his *Annales* (Χρονικόν), in eighteen books, from the creation of the world to the death of Alexis in 1118. It is compiled from various Greek authors, whose very words Zonaras frequently retains, and is of considerable value. Editions by Du Cange, Paris, 1686, folio ; and by Dindorf, Leipzig, 1875.

[43] The Emperor Zeno ruled from 474-491, but he was obliged to defend his authority against repeated insurrections. Upon his death in 491 his widow, Ariadne, the daughter of Leo the Great, decided the succession by bestowing her hand on Anastasius Silentiarius.

[44] The Church of the Holy Apostles is one of the most note worthy in Cologne. Standing in the north-west angle of the Neumarket, this edifice is of the late Romanesque period. It has double transepts, a dome, and a square western tower. The Church occupies the place of an older building. It was originally erected in the year 1036 as a flat-roofed basilica, but the aisles were vaulted about 100 years later ; the nave and choir being also vaulted about 1200. The brilliant mosaics which now cover the dome, the choir and the transept were commenced in 1895, and are the work of Kleinertz and Stumnel.

Baedeker, *The Rhine*, has the following note : " The two horses' heads affixed to the upper story of a house on the north side of the Neumarket at the corner of the Richmond-Strasse are connected by tradition with the miraculous awakening of Richmondis, wife of Knight Mengis von Aducht from a trance. Her husband declared he would sooner believe his horses could ascend to the loft of his house than that his wife should return from the tomb. Scarcely had he spoken the words, however when the heads of his horses were seen looking from the upper windows." It has been suggested that the heads were possibly part of the armourial bearings of Nicasius von Haquenay who built the house.

[45] Aviola could not be rescued and was burnt alive. Pliny writes : " Auiola consularis in rogo reuixit : et quoniam subueniri non potuerat praeualente flamma, uiuus crematus est. Similis causa in Lucio Lamia praetorio uiro traditur." He adds a further example. " Nam Caium Aelium Tuberonem praetura functum a rogo relatum, Messala Rufus, et plerique tradunt." *Historia Naturalis*, VII, liii, 52 (Ed. Brotier, Paris, 1779, tom II, p. 143).

[46] Lucan, *Pharsalia*, II, 21-26, has :

> Errauit sine uoce dolor, sie funere primo
> Attonitæ tacuire domus, cum corpora nondum
> Conclamata iacent, nec mater crine soluto
> Exigit ad sæuos famulorum brachia planctus :
> Sed cum membra premit fugiente rigentia uita,
> Uultusque examines, oculosque in morte iacentes . .

[47] Johann Georg Godelmann was an important writer upon witchcraft. His *De magis, ueneficis et lamiis tractatus*, was reprinted several times, and is re-issued as late at 1676 and 1691. Rohr refers to the German translation *Bericht von Zauberern, Hexen und Unholden. A. d. Lat. von Geo. Nigrinus.* 4to, 1592.

[48] The *Annales Ecclesiastici* of the Venerable Cesare Baronio (1538-1607) have been truly said to mark an important epoch in the writing of history, and, after Eusebius, to the author has been applied the name " the Father of Ecclesiastical History."

⁴⁹ The *Adagia*, a collection of Greek and Latin proverbs first appeared in 1500. In 1508 was published a greatly enlarged edition.

⁵⁰ The word used by Rohr is *glocitare*. Festus gives : " Glocire et glocidare gallinarum proprium est, cum ouis incubituræ sunt." Upon this Dacier has the following note : " Lege : *glocire et glocitare*. Glocire a κλώζειν uox a sono efficta. Columel. lib. 7, cap. 5. *Ut oua quam recentissima supponantur glocientibus*. Gloss. gluttit, κροκκᾷ ἡ ὄρνις, glocit auis. leg. *glocit*. Hanc uocem Uascones retinent qui dicunt *cloucir*, et ipsam auem glocientem *clouque* ut Hispani *clueca*." *Festus* . . . notis *et emendationibus illustrauit Andreas Dacerus* . . . *Amstelodami* . *ı*. . MDCC., p. 163.

⁵¹ On the Day of Atonement amid the mystic rites of that most solemn time two buck-goats were chosen to stand before the Lord. Lots were cast ; one of the animals was to be offered in sacrifice, the other the emissary-goat (the scape-goat) was to be sent forth into the wilderness bearing all the sins of the people. Full details of the ritual of the feast of expiation are given in *Leviticus xvi*. The one goat is offered to the Lord for sin ; " But that whose lot was to be the emissary goat, he shall present alive before the Lord, that he may pour out prayers upon him, and let him go into the wilderness." " Duos hircos stare faciet coram Domino in ostio tabernaculi testimonii : Mittensque super utrumque sortem, unam Domino, et alteram capro emissario : Cuius exient sors Domino, offeret illum pro peccato : Cuius autem in caprum emissarium statuet eum uiuum coram Domino, ut fundet prices super eo, et emittat eum in solitudinem." (7-10). " After he hath cleansed the sanctuary, and the tabernacle, and the altar, then let him offer the living goat : And putting both hands upon his head, let him confess all the iniquities of the children of Israel, and all their offences and sins : and praying that they may light upon his head, he shall turn him out by a man ready for it into the desert. And when the goat hath carried all their iniquities into an uninhabited land, and shall be let go into the desert, Aaron shall return into the tabernacle of the testimony." " Postquam emundauerit Sanctuarium, et tabernaculum, et altare, tune offerat hircum uiuentom : Et posita utraque manu super caput eius, confiteatur omnes iniquitates filiorum Israel, et universa delicta atque peccata eorum : quæ imprecans capiti eius, emittet illum per hominem paratum in desertum. Cumque portauerit hircus omnes iniquitates eorum in terram solitariam, et dimissus fuerit in deserto, Reuertetur Aaron in tabernaculum testimonii." The Vulgate *caper emissarius* (emissary goat ; *A.V.*, Scapegoat) represents an obscure Hebrew word עֲזָאזֵל *Azazel*, which is to be found nowhere else in the Bible and the meaning of which has been variously interpreted. It is clear that such explanations as is found in both Mishna and Gemara taking it to be the name of a place where the man who led the goat away (*homo paratus*) used to throw it over a precipice so that it could not come back since such a return would bode evil are nugatory and inept. (See Rabbi David Joel's *Der Aberglaube und die Stellung des Judensthums zu demselben*. Part I (p. 63), Breslau, 1881). Azazel is, in point of fact the name of a demon, and this spirit is actually mentioned in the *Book of Henoch*, which it must be remembered is quoted by S. Jude in his Epistle (verses 14, 15, from *Henoch*, c. I, verses 9 and 4, Ethiopic). Moreover *The Book of Henoch* was highly esteemed by the Fathers, whilst Clement of Alexandria, Tertullian, Origen, and S. Augustine himself suppose the work may contain some genuine writings of the antediluvian patriarch.

In later Jewish literature Azazel is a demon, and it may be that the symbolism of the ceremony on the day of Atonement showed that the sins of the people were sent back to the source whence they derived their origin.

Azazel was the familiar of the heresiarch Marcus, founder of the Marcosians, a sect of Valentinian Gnostics. In their conventicles prophecy was habitually practiced, as well as the abominations of women playing the preacher and the priest. This was entirely due to demoniacal influences. It has been well said that the practices inculcated by Marcus exhibit his system as the most worthless of any that passed under the name of knowledge or religion in the early centuries.

[52] Johann Buxtorf was born at Camen in Westphalia in 1564 and died in 1629. After a course of study at various universities he became Professor of Hebrew at Bâle where his attainments were very highly esteemed. He published many works both in German and in Latin, and several of the MSS. which he left were edited by his son who succeeded to his father's chair. This son also was followed by his eldest child Johann Jacob Buxtorf, who died in 1704, leaving his chair to a nephew, Johann Buxtorf who died in 1732, so we have the remarkable circumstance that the chair of Hebrew at Bâle was for more than a century and a half held by members of the same family.

[53] Professor Johann Benedict Carpzod was Dean of the theological faculty at Leipzig in the later years of the seventeenth century. His writings, of no small influence in his day among those of a particular school of thought are now generally superseded. He is chiefly remembered owing to his determined opposition to the Pietist movement which he was largely instrumental in suppressing at Leipzig during his tenure of power.

[54] It will be borne in mind that the sharp white teeth are considered a distinguishing mark of the Vampire. Leone Allacci definitely emphasizes as distinguishing features " os hians, dentes candidi."

[55] This learned Orientalist was born at Oxford, 8 November, 1604. In 1629 he was appointed Chaplain to the English factory at Aleppo, but after about six years he returned to Oxford and filled the chair of Arabic which had recently been founded by Archbishop Laud. In 1648 he became Professor of Hebrew at Oxford. Under the Parliament he was continually harried and annoyed, but naturally these persecutions ceased with the Restoration. After a long life of intense scholarly industry he died at Oxford 12 September, 1691, being in his eighty-seventh year.

[56] Professor of Theology at Strasburg during the middle years of the seventeenth century, Johann Conrad Mannhauer enjoyed a considerable reputation in his day. In controversy he was completely defeated by the two Bishops, the celebrated brothers, Adrian and Peter von Walenburch. Of his works which are now little remembered perhaps the most important were *Dissertatio de custodia Angelica*, Strasburg, 1641 ; *Scheid-und Absag-Brieff, einem ungenannten Priester aus Cöllen aus sein Antworts-Schreiben, über das zu Strassburg vom Teuffel besessene adeliche Jungfräulein gegeben*, Strassburg, 1654 ; and *Scheid-und Absagbrief uber das zu Strassburg vom Tuefel besessene Fräulein*, Strassburg, 1667.

[57] Sir James Frazer in his translation of Pausanias (1898), vol. V, p. 375, has the following note upon the passage in question : Book X, c. 28. " *Eurynomus*. This demon appears to be mentioned by no other ancient writer. Prof. C. Robert regards him as a personification of death, pointing out that his name, which signifies 'wide-ruling,' would on this hypothesis be appropriate (*Die Nekyia des Polygnot*, p. 61 ; *Die Marathonschlacht in der Poikile*, pp. 117-119). Mr. A. Dieterich prefers to consider him as a personification of the grave in which the dead are laid and which, as it were, consumes their bodies, leaving only the bones (*Nekyia*, p. 47 *sq.*)

Of the lost Greek epics the *Minyas* was anonymous, the *Reditus* or *Nostoi* (*The Returns*) in five books, was attributed to Hagias of Troezen. In the abstract by Proclus fo the *Reditus* there is no mention of a descent into hell. See *Epicorum Graecorum fragmenta*, ed. Kinkel, p. 52 *sqq.* Hence D. B. Monro conjectured (*Journal of Hellenic Studies*, 4 (1873), p. 319) that the editor or editors who abbreviated what Proclus calls the " Epic Cycle " omitted this episode since a similar description had been given in the *Odyssey*, xi.

[58] As has been remarked in an earlier chapter this is a well-known action of the vampire-bat. De Lancre, *Tableau de l'Inconstance des mauvais Anges* (Paris, 1612, pp. 302-303) says : " Les stryges, les Lamies, les loups-garous qui en sont les bourreaux, sont couchez en son estat. Les loix Saliques font mention de la Strie que les latins appellent *Strix*, qui mange les hommes, *Si Stria hominem comederit, octo millia denariorum qui faciunt solidos* 200 *culpabilis iudicetur*. Ce nom (comme aucūs disent) estant venu à *Lestrigonibus* anciens antropophages dãs Homere, ou comme d'autres estiment de

l'oyseau appelle *Strix*, en nostre langue Fresaye, duquel les sorcieres prenent la forme.

> *Carpere dicuntur lactantia corpora rostris,*
> *Et plenum poto sanguine guttur habent."*

An anonymous *Tractatus de dæmonibus* (MS. *c.* 1415) has : "Interdum eciam maligni spiritus uisi sunt in domibus, ubi paruuli nutriuntur, qui apud uulgum dicuntur striges et lamie, et uisi sunt paruulos traxisse de cunabulis et ipsos lauasse et assasse, et apparuerunt sub specie uetularum."

[59] Et exeunti ei de naui, statim occurrit de monumentis homo in spiritu immundo, Qui domicilium habebat in monumentis, et neque catenis iam quisquam poterat eum ligare : Quoniam saepe compedibus et catenis uinctus, dirupisset catenas, et compedes comminuisset, et nemo poterat eum domare.   Et semper die ac nocte in monumentis, et in montibus erat, clamans, et concidens se lapidibus.   (And as he went out of the ship, immediately there met him out of the monuments a man with an unclean spirit, Who had his dwelling in the tombs, and no man now could bind him, not even with chains.   For having been often bound with fetters and chains, he had burst the chains, and broken the fetters in pieces, and no one could tame him. And he was always day and night in the monuments and in the mountains, crying and cutting himself with stones).

[60] Et cum uenisset trans fretum in regionem Gerasenorum, occurrerunt ei duo habentes dæmonia, de monumentis exeuntes sæui nimis, ita ut nemo posset transire per uiam illam.   (And when he was come on the other side of the water, into the country of the Gerasens, there met him two that were possessed with devils, coming out of the sepulchres, exceeding fierce, so that none could pass by that way.)

[61] Michael Psellus the famous Byzantine statesman, scholar, and writer was born in 1018, apparently at Constantinople, and he died probably in 1078. At any rate his history which forms a continuation to the chronicle of Leo Diaconus concludes in 1077.   His literary work covers an immense field, and this together with the elegances of his style give him a distinguished place among the writers of his day.

[62] This celebrated German physicist was born at Konigshofen, 5 February, 1608, and he died at Augsburg in 1666 on 12 or 22 May.   He entered the Society of Jesus on 20 October, 1627, and after an absence of many years in Italy and Sicily he returned to Augsburg where he spent the rest of his life as a teacher of science and in literary work.   He was the author of a vast number of books on mathematics, physics and magic,   These contain much curious information and formerly were very widely read.   One may consult a study by St. Leger, *Notice des ouvrages de G. Schott*, Paris, 1765.

[63] These homilies, which are ninety in number, and which are generally considered the most important of the Commentaries of S. John Chrysostom were written about the year 390.

[64] Among all Oriental nations the favourite resorts of demons are damp places, unhealthy and deserted spots, latrines, ovens, ruined houses, rivers, whence in the East sickness often arises.   Thus among the Jews demons were actually designated according to the diseases which they originated. Knut L. Tallquist in his "Die assyrische Beschwörungserie Maqlu, etc." (*Acta Societatis Scientiarum Fennicæ*, Tomus xx, 1895) says that among the Assyrians demons were named after the diseases due to them.   He further adds that so close was the connexion that the names of demons and the corresponding diseases came to be identical.

[65] Died 1628.

[66] Cum Michael Archangelus cum diabolo disputans altercaretur de Moysi corpore, non est ausus iudicium inferre blasphemiæ : sed dixit : Imperet tibi Dominus. (When Michael the Archangel, disputing with the Devil, contended about the body of Moses, he durst not bring against him the judgement of railing speech, but said : The Lord command thee).   This contention which is nowhere else mentioned in holy writ, was originally known by revelation, and transmitted by tradition.   It is thought the occasion of it was, that the

Devil would have had the body buried in such a place and manner, as to be worshipped by the Jews with divine honour.

[67] The most striking example of this is the Patriarch Job. In his *Dæmonologie*, Edinburgh, 1597, King James I (of England) says that there are, generally speaking, three kind of folks who may be plagued and even hurt in their bodies by witches." "The wicked for their horrible sinnes, to punish them in the like measure : The godlie that are sleeping in anie great sinnes or infirmities and weaknesse in faith, to waken them up the faster by such an vncouth forme : and even some of the best, that their patience may bee tryed before the world, as Jobs was."

[68] This treatise is printed in all editions as S. Cyprian's, and we have the overwhelming authority of S. Jerome and S. Augustine to that effect. Certainly it is largely made up out of Tertullian and Minucius Felix, but it is accepted as genuine by Bardenhewer, Monceaux, and Benson; Haussleiter attributes it to Novatian, whilst it is rejected by von Soden, Watson, and Harnack. De Labriolle writes : "L'authenticité du *Quod idola dii non sint* n'est pas absolument certaine. Cependant saint Jérôme et saint Augustin l'attribuaient à Cyprien, et un tel témoignage ne saurait être écarté à la légère. Ce médiocre opuscule, emprunté presque tout entier, non seulement pour les idées, mais même, parfois, pour l'expression, a Tertullien et à Minucius Felix, se devise en trois parties : critique de la mythologie, au point de vue éuhémériste (I-VII) ; attributs de Dieu, parmi lesquels l'unité est placée au permier plan (VIII-IX) ; esquisse d'une Christologie (X-XV). C'est sans doute un travail tout voisin de la conversion de Cyprien, qui n'a cru pouvoir mieux faire, zélé comme un néophyte, que de résumer les idées qu'il rencontrait dans les plus notoires apologies de l'époque."

[69] Bacon in his *Sylva* says : "It is an usual observation that if the body of one murdered be brought before the murderer, the wounds will bleed afresh. Some do affirm that the dead hath opened his eyes." But so far from this blood flowing from the wounds of a murdered man in the presence of his assassin being attributed to any demoniacal influence, it is generally supposed to be a sign appointed by heaven. King James in his *Dæmonologie* writes : "As in a secret murder, if the dead carcase be at any time thereafter handled by the murtherer, it will gush out of blood, as if the blood were crying to the heaven for revenge of the murtherer, God having appointed that secret supernatural sign for trial of that secret unnatural crime."

[70] As is well-known there are many places where this phenomenon occurs as for example the Capuchin cemeteries of Palermo and Malta. Even more striking perhaps, is the Church of S. Michan at Dublin. "As is well-known the preservative qualities of the vaults under S. Michan's Church are most remarkable, and decay in the bodies committed to them is strangely arrested . . . the antiseptic qualities are believed to be largely attributable to the extreme dryness of the vaults and to the great freedom of their atmosphere from dust particles." H. F. Berry, *The Registers of the Church of S. Michan*, Dublin, 1907, Preface, p. vi.

[71] The First Part of the *Malleus Maleficarum* treats "Of the three Necessary Concomitants of Witchcraft, which are the Devil, a Witch, and the Permission of Almighty God." In "To the Reader," prefixed to *Dæmonologie*, King James says : "*But one thing I will pray thee to obserue in all these places, where I reason upon the deuils power, which is the different ends and scopes, that God as the first cause, and the Devill as his instrument and second cause shootes at in all these actions of the Deuil (as God's hang-man :)*"

[72] Chaldaeus is used as equivalent to a wizard, a soothsayer. See *The Geography of Witchcraft*, by Montague Summers, pp. 13-15.

[73] Heinsius notes on this passage : "Et rogis non omnia magi ossa colligant, sed praesertim articulos ad ueneficia."

[74] Johann Georg Godelmann, an eminent jurist of Mecklenburg, is the author of two works of great merit which are much quoted by the demonologists, *Disputatio de Magis*, Frankfort, 1584 ; and *De Magis tractatus*, Frankfort, 1591. This latter was twice reprinted in 1601, in 1676, and again in 1691.

[75] Rohr quotes from the German translation *Von Zaeuberern, Hexen vnd Vnholden. Warhafftiger vnd Wohlbegründter Bericht, wie dieselbigen zuerkennen vnd zustraffen. Deutsch von G. Nigrinus.* Frankfort, 1606.

[76] His most authoritative work is the *De Haereticis et sortilegiis, omnifariam coïtu eorumque poenis,* which appeared at Bologna, c. 1525. Grilland who was born at Florence was "diocesis Aretinæ (Arezzo) criminalium causarum auditor seu p.d. Andreæ du Iacobatiis, sanctissimi domini nostri Papæ almaeque Urbis uicarii generalis." Negri *Scrittori Fiorentini,* Florence, 1722. Andreas Jacobazzi, a canon of S. Peter's, was named Vicar of Rome in 1519, but not consecrated Bishop of Lucera until the following year. During the brief interval of a few months the *pontificalia* or ceremonial rights were committed to Vincentius, Bishop of Ottochaz-Zengg.

[77] This reference is rather to Book III, Part I, Question iv, Section 2, where Delrio quotes at length from Lucan, *Pharsalia,* VI.

[78] The *Tractatus Theologicus de Sagarum impietate, nocendi imbellicitate et poenæ grauitate* of Theodore Thummius, a distinguished member of the School of Divinity at the University of Tübingen, was published at Tübingen in 1666. A second editon followed in 1667.

[79] For a full consideration of these abominable practices one may consult the learned Francesco-Maria Guazzo, whose *Compendium Maleficarum* was published at Milan in 1608,; second edition, 1626. III, 2, we have : "Sagæ utuntur Cadaucribus Humanis ad necem Hominum."

[80] Johann Christian Frederick Garmann, *De Miraculis Mortuorum libri,* III. A later edition, Lipsiæ, 4to, 1709, was edited by Immanuel Henry Garmann.

[81] Pope Sylvester II (Gerbert) was born in the district of Aurillac, Auvergne, France about 940-50 and died at Rome 12th May, 1003. During his youth he studied much in Spain, at Barcelona, Cordova and Seville. His great genius soon led to his advancement and when Gregory V died on 18th February, 999, he was elected to the Chair of S. Peter. He showed himself an exemplary and energetic pontiff ; owing to his vast learning the common people regarded him with great awe and many idle legends grew up about his name. Collin de Plancy in his *Dictionnaire Infernal* (sixième édition, 1863, p. 643) says : "Il faisait sa principale étude après les sciences sacrées, des sciences mathématiques : les lignes et triangles dont on le voyait occupé parurent a des yeux ignorants une espèce de grimoire et contribuèrent à le faire passer pour un nécromancien. . . . D'autres ajoutent qu'autrefois son tombeau prédisait la mort des papes par un bruit des os en dedans, et par une grande sueur et humidité de la pierre au dehors. On voit, par tous ces contes ridicules, que autrefois comme de nos jours, l'Église et ses plus illustres pontifes one été en butte aux plus sottes calomnies."

[82] Cardinal Lodovico Simonetta, one of the most celebrated theologians of his day, was Bishop of Lodi, and presided at the Council of Trent.

[83] The following example is related in the *Malleus Maleficarum,* Part I, Question 15. "A town once was rendered almost destitute by the death of its citizens ; and there was a rumour that a certain buried woman was gradually eating the shroud in which she had been buried, and that the plague could not cease until she had eaten the whole shroud and absorbed it into her stomach. A council was held, and the Podesta with the Governor of the city dug up the grave, and found half the shroud absorbed through the mouth and throat into the stomach, and consumed. In horror at this sight the Podesta drew his sword and cut off her head and threw it out of the grave, and at once the plague ceased. Now the sins of that old woman were, by divine permission, visited upon the innocent on account of the dissimulation of what had happened before. For when an Inquisition was held it was found that during a long time of her life she had been a Sorceress and Enchantress."

[84] There are very many instances of this in the Gospels. One may note S. Matthew xii, 22 : "Then was offered to him one possessed of a devil, blind and dumb : and he healed him, so that he spoke and saw." Also S. Matthew ix, 32, 33 : "Behold, they brought him a dumb man, possessed with a devil, and after the devil was cast out the dumb man spoke." Also

S. Mark ix, 14-28, where the youth is possessed of a dumb spirit, "who wheresoever he taketh him dasheth him, and he foameth, and gnasheth with the teeth, and pineth away." The patient had been thus afflicted "from his infancy, and often times hath he cast him into the fire and into water to destroy him." See further, my *History of Witchcraft*, Chapter VI, "Diabolic Possession."

[85] As in the case of holy Job.

[86] *Romans* ix, 22-23: "What if God, willing to show his wrath, and to make his power known, endured with much patience vessels of wrath, fitted for destruction, that he might show the riches of his glory on the vessels of mercy, which he hath prepared unto glory?"

[87] *Non opus sit crambem bis coctam apponere.* The phrase "crambe bis cocta" is from the *Adagia* of Erasmus. Upon Juvenal's line *Occidit miseros crambe repetita magistros* (VII, 154) see Politian's *Miscellanea*, xxxiii: "Crambe quæ sit apud Iuuenalem, superque ea Graecum prouerbium." (Δὶς κράμβη θάνατος).

[88] Rohr refers to such oracles that of Apollo at Delphi and the sanctuary of the oaks whence Jupiter spoke at Dodona. Originally on the spot afterwards occupied by the most sacred shrine (*adytum*) of the Delphic oracle there gaped a dark chasm in the ground, and Aeschylus (*Eumenides, Isqq*) speaks of Earth as the goddess who first gave oracles at Delphi. Since the prophetic influence came forth from this fissure "it was natural terra herself should have been regarded as the power that answered the worshippers. Thus, there were also deep caves sacred to Demeter who gave oracles from them, and in ancient Prussia there were oracular trees, mighty oaks, inhabited by the gods, whence they delivered audible answers to inquirers. See M. C. Hartknoch, *Alt und neues Preussen*, Leipzig, 1684, p. 120. Livy mentions as a portent statues which have spoken. It is now considered that the ancient oracles were the operation of demons.

[89] Gisbert Voet, a well-known Dutch divine was born at Heuste, 3rd March, 1589, and was educated at Leyden. In 1619 he was a prominent figure at the synod of Dort. In 1634, he was appointed to a chair of theology at Utrecht, and in this office he continued until his death in 1676. He was among the most copious of the divines of his age and party, and his writings, which are almost all of a violently polemical character, have little, if any value.

[90] Athanasius Kircher, S. J., who was so celebrated for the versatility of his knowledge, and particularly distinguished in the natural sciences, was born 2nd May, 1601, and died at Rome, 28th November, 1680.

[91] Romae, 1658.

[92] The phrase occurs in Lucian's dialogue, *Toxaris siue Amicitia*.

[93] The practice of blessing Christian graves and cemeteries is extremely ancient and may easily be traced back to the time of S. Gregory of Tours, who died in 593.

Rohr's opinion here is very faulty, and his theology extremely unsound.

[94] William Duranti (Durandus) was one of the most important mediæval liturgical writers. He was born about 1237 and died at Rome, 1st November, 1296. His most famous work is the *Rationale diuinorum officiorum* of which the first edition by Fust and Schoeffer was issued at Mainz, 1459. It was frequently reprinted and the last complete edition is Naples, 1839. Book I treats of the Church, altar, pictures, bells, and churchyard.

[95] *Disquisitiones Magicæ*, II, 5.

[96] δανάκη is strictly a Persian coin something more than an obol. The word was soon particularly used to denote the coin buried with a corpse as Charon's fee. See Julius Pollux, *Onomasticon*, ix, 82.

[97] In very many districts of Greece and in parts of Asia Minor at the present day the practice still prevails of placing in the mouth (or more rarely upon the heart) of the deceased a small coin, which in the neighbourhood of Smyrna is actually known as τὸ περατίκι, the boatman's fare. Not many years ago this coin was actually laid in the mouth of the dead for Charon, but now even where the custom prevails this traditional meaning

has been forgotten.   Mr. Lawson in his *Modern Greek Folklore* gives it as his opinion that the classical interpretation of the custom was merely " an ætiological explanation of a custom whose significance even in an early age had already become obscured by lapse of time." He further says that the explanation he could obtain of the use of the coin was " it is useful because of the aerial ones," εἶναι καλὸ γιὰ τἀερικά.   It seems uncertain whether it was the fare to be paid to the " aerial ones " who would assist the soul on its journey, or whether it was a charm against the assaults of such beings. But it is plain that in Saxony the latter was intended.   Probably this was also the case in Greece, as in many parts a symbol of definitely Christian character has taken the place of the coin.   This is often a piece of pottery on which is cut the sign of the cross with the legend I.X.NI.KA.   The object used in Naxos is a wax cross although this still bears the old name ναῦλον "fare." It is even not unknown that between the lips of the dead is placed a particle from the consecrated Host.   In Chios and Rhodes it is definitely asserted that this precaution is employed to prevent a demon entering the dead body and re-animating it.   Mr. Lawson has some very valuable details which may be found in his work that has just been mentioned, Chapter II, pp. 108-114 with the various references.

[98] The famous German cartographer and navigator who was born at Nuremburg in 1459, and died at the German hospice of S. Bartholomew in Lisbon, 29th July, 1507.

[99] This, of course, is spoken of unauthorized exhumations, not of such disinterments as are ordered and sanctioned by ecclesiastical authority should some demoniacal phenomenon be suspected.

CHAPTER IV

MODERN GREECE

IN no country has the Vampire tradition more strongly prevailed and more persistently maintained its hold upon the people than in modern Greece. To the confirmation and perpetuation of this and cognate beliefs, a large number of factors have lent their varying influences, and not the least remarkable of these has been the quota furnished by the popular superstition of antiquity, legends and practices which were even in Pagan days more or less covertly accepted and employed and which after the advent of Christianity although driven to the most obscure and the most ignorant hiding places, obstinately survived and helped to mould and modify the religion of the Greek peasant when once the Great Schism had allowed these weeds and tares of antiquity an opportunity of verdure and efflorescence.

It seems undeniable that the modern Greek superstition of the Vampire owes much to Slavonic influences. Indeed, the actual word vrykolakas is due to Slavonic etymology, and it is identical with a word that is found in all the Slavonic groups of languages. It is true that various attempts have been made by Greek scholars to deny this foreign original, but a very laudible patriotism seems to have lead them astray, and even such plausible arguments as those of Koraes must be rejected. This writer deftly selecting a local form βορβόλακας sought to identify it with a supposed ancient form μορμόλυξ connected with μορμώ a hobgoblin or bugaboo.[1] But that eminent authority Mr. J. C. Lawson tells us that among the Greeks the Slavonic[2] word which we have borrowed in the form "vampire" is almost, if not altogether unknown. "In parts of Macedonia indeed where the Greek population lives in constant touch with Slavonic peoples, a form βάμπυρας or βόμπυρας has been adopted and is used as a synonym of vrykolakas in its ordinary Greek sense; but in Greece proper and in the Greek islands the word 'vampire' is, so far as

I can discover, absolutely non-existent, and it is *vrykolakas* which ordinarily denotes the resuscitated corpse."[3]

With regard to the Macedonian term, Mr. Abbott in his *Macedonian Folk-lore*,[4] speaking of the Vampire says : " The name given to this hideous monster in Macedonia is, generally speaking, the same as that by which it is known in some parts of Greece proper ; but its form is slightly modified in various districts. Thus at Melenik (North-East) it is called Vrykolakas (ὁ βρυκόλακας or τὸ βουρκολάκι), or Vampyras (ὁ βάμπυρας) ; whereas at Kataphygi (South-West) it appears as Vroukolakas, or Vompiras, the latter form being also used as a term of abuse. The name has been variously derived by philologists, some holding that it comes from the ancient Greek μορμολυκεῖον, a hobgoblin. This is the view of some modern Greek scholars, followed by Hahn. Others, like Bernhard Schmidt,[5] more plausibly assign to it a Slavonic origin."

It must be borne in mind that in the actual usage of all Slavonic languages save one, the vrykolakas is the exact equivalent of the English werewolf, and it seems certain that the Greeks originally borrowed the name in this sense, whence it passed by an easy transition to the meaning " vampire," since there is a general belief among Slavonic peoples that a man who has been a werewolf in his life will be a vampire after death.

Bernhard Schmidt, indeed, after having carefully distinguished between the werewolf and the vampire, unhesitatingly states that " The modern Greek vrykolakas answers only to the latter."[6] This, however, is demonstrably incorrect, and there is overwhelming evidence that in Greece to-day the word *vrykolokas* does locally and occasionally bear its original meaning. Hanush records that he was plainly told by a Greek of Mytilene that there were two species of *vrykolakes*, the one kind being men already dead, and the other individuals who were yet alive but who were subject to mysterious trances or somnambulism and were seen abroad at night particularly when the moon was at its full.[7] Again in his *Les Slaves de Turquie*[8] Cyprien Robert describes the *vrykolakes* of Thessaly and Epirus thus : " These are living men mastered by a kind of somnambulism, who seized by a thirst for blood go forth at night from their shepherd's-huts, and scour the country biting and tearing all that they meet both man and beast."

It is curious that Schmidt who knew of these two passages does not appear to appreciate their significance as he very cursorily dismisses them with an inadequate footnote.[9]

However, even if these witnesses were not enough, Mr. Lawson tells us that " on the borders of Aetolia and Acarnania, in the neighbourhood of Agrinion, I myself ascertained that the word vrykolakas was occasionally applied to living persons in the sense of werewolf, although there as elsewhere it more commonly denotes a resuscitated corpse." In many parts of Greece it is believed that certain children are exceedingly liable to a form of lycanthropy, and this is conspicuously the case in the districts Mr. Lawson specifies. Of his own observation he informs us that if in a family one or more children die without any very evident cause, the mother will often regard the smallest or weakliest of the survivors—more especially if there be one at all deranged or deformed—as most certainly the cause of the brothers' or sisters' death, and the unfortunate suspect is at once accounted a *vrykolakas*. With the object of detering it from its fatal and blood-thirsty ways, the helpless infant is visited with abuse and ill-treatment amounting to cruelty for " Εἶσαι βροκόλακας καὶ φάγες τὸν ἀδερφό σου," "you are a *vrykolakas* and have devoured your brother."

Had the tradition of dead men remaining in certain cases and issuing from their graves to torment and even slay the living been first derived by the Greeks from the Slavs it follows that they must certainly have borrowed the word by which the Slavs designated these malignant individuals. But since, as a matter of fact, the Greeks did not adopt the Slavonic name vampire, it is clear that there must have been already some word in use among them to express that idea, and therefore there was already rife some superstition which was but elaborated and, it may be, emphasized by Slavonic influence. Indeed there was not only one term but a large number of native Greek words, such for example as τυμπανιαῖος[10], which was well-known to Leone Allacci; σαρκωμένος[11]; ἀναικαθούμενος[12]; καταχανᾶς[13]; and many more, all of which still survive among the Greek islands although they have practically died out and are obsolete on the mainland.

This is exactly what we might expect, for naturally it was the mainland which was generally pervaded by Slavonic influences owing to continual immigration, whilst the islands Crete, Cyprus, Chios, Cythera and the rest stood outside the area of such innovations.   In the course of time, however, although they retained their own local phraseology, in the course of their relations with the mainland they must have become familiar with the new Slavonic word which was gradually being adopted, and without dropping their peculiar nomenclature they added the general term to their individual vocabulary.   This is well summed up by Mr. Lawson who says : " These insular names for the *vrykolakas* may there-fore be regarded as survivals from a free pre-Slavonic, and, though they are now merely dialectic, it is reasonable to suppose that one or more of them formerly held a place in the language of mainlanders and islanders alike.   In the tenth century no doubt " *vrykolakas* meant a ' werewolf,' and a ' vampire ' was denoted by τυμπανιαῖος or some other Greek word, nowadays *vrykolakas* almost always means a ' vampire ' and τυμπανιαῖος is well-nigh obsolete."[14]

The teaching of the Orthodox Church also had great influence in its effect upon the modern tradition of the Vampire in Greece.   It has already been shown at some length that the incorruptibility of the body of any person bound by a curse, were that curse parental or ecclesiastical, was established as a definite doctrine, and the offender who passed away under the ban of excommunication was doomed to remain whole and undissolved after death until the body was set free by an official and equipollent absolution being pronounced over it and the sentence of excommunication thus revoked. This state of being "unloosed" after death was exactly expressed by the term τυμπανιαῖος and Christophorus Angelus in his Ἐγχειρίδιον περὶ τῆς καταστάσεως τῶν σήμερον εὑρισκομένων Ἑλλήνων[15], cap. xxv, tells us that the word is used in this signification by an ancient Greek historian, Cassianus.[16] "Unloosed" was, indeed, understood in two senses.   It conveyed that the person had not been absolved, and it also signified that his dead body had not been dissolved.[17]

Very ample accounts of the tradition of the Vampire in Greece and of the various methods which were practised by the Greeks in order to secure themselves against and rid themselves of these demoniacal pests are to be found in many excellent writers of the seventeenth century. To-day the Vampire still ravages the villages, and the tale of his exploits may often be heard from the peasants, but as may be readily supposed in modern times cases of vampirism are much less common than they were two hundred, or even fifty years ago, and it is comparatively rarely that a stranger may witness the traditional ceremonies by which a district rids itself of a vampire, concluding the cremation of the body. This is not to say that the practice is in any way discontinued or out of date, but such an operation constitutes a breach of the law and therefore must necessarily be conducted under conditions of strictest secrecy. Yet as we shall see later instances of vampirism occur even to-day, and Mr. Lawson writing in 1910 states : " Even now a year seldom passes in which some village of Greece does not disembarrass itself of a *vrykolakas* by the traditional means, cremation."[18]

In his extremely interesting and well-written work *Travels in Crete*, published in 1837, Robert Pashley, who was a Fellow of Trinity College, Cambridge, has the following account of the Vampire tradition as he personally investigated it. " The Vampire, or Katakhanas, as he is called in Crete, is denominated Vurvúlakas, or Vrukólakas, in the islands of the Archipelago, where the belief is generally prevalent, that if a man has committed a great crime, or dies excommunicated[19] by a priest or bishop, the earth will not receive him when he dies, and he therefore rambles about all night, spending only the daytime in his tomb. Many believe that, even in the day time, it is only once a week, on the Saturday, that he is allowed to occupy his burial-place. When it is discovered that such a Vurvúlakas is about, the people go, on a Saturday, and open his tomb, where they always find his body just as it was buried, and entirely undecomposed. The priest by whom they are accompanied reads certain parts of the ritual, supposed to be of peculiar efficacy for putting a stop to every restless Vampire's wanderings, and sometimes this course suffices to restore the neighbourhood to peace and quiet. But cases happen in which the priest is not a sufficiently powerful exorcist thus easily to stop the nocturnal rambles and misdeeds of the undying one, who, like Shakespeare's ghost, is doomed to walk the night, as a punishment for the foul crimes done in the days of nature. Whenever, then, this ordinary religious ceremony, to which recourse is first had, is found inefficacious, the people of the neighbourhood go to the tomb on a Saturday, take out the body, and consume it with fire ; an operation which nothing but extreme necessity would ever make Greeks consent to perform, on account of their religious horror of burning a body on which the holy oil has been poured by the priest when performing the last rite of his religion over the dying man.

Even the rough Hydhraeans[20], whose seafaring life and intercourse with other countries, might have been supposed likely to have diminished the prevalence of such notions among them, are generally believers in these Vurvúlaki. As in Sfakía, so also at Hýdhra,

> Both well attested, and as well believ'd,
> Heard solemn, goes the *Vampire*-story round ;
> Till superstitious horrour creeps o'er all.

"Many Hydhraeans have assured me there used to be a great number of Vampires in Hydhra, and that their present freedom from them is to be attributed solely to the exertions of their bishop, who has laid them all in Santoréne, where, on the desert isle, they now exist in great numbers, and wander about, rolling stones down the slopes towards the sea, ' as may be heard by any one who passes near, in a kaik, during the night.'

"The Sfakians also generally believe that the ravages committed by these night-wanderers, used, in former times to be far more frequent than they are at the present day ; and that they are becoming comparatively rare, solely in consequence of the increased zeal and skill possessed by the members of the sacerdotal order."[21]

Even to-day the island of Santorini, the most southerly of the Cyclades,[22] is notorious for its vampires, and I myself, when I visited it in 1906-1907 heard many a gruesome legend of vampire events which were said to have taken place there quite recently. The author of *Murray's Handbook for Travellers in Greece*[23] speaking of Santorini says : " The antiseptic nature of the soil, and the frequent discovery of undecayed bodies, have given rise to many wild superstitions among the peasantry of the island. It is supposed to be the favourite abode of the

Vrukolakos, a species of Ghoul or Vampire, which, according to a belief once popular in Greece, has the power of resuscitating the dead from their graves and sending them forth to banquet on the living." As we say "to carry coals to Newcastle "[24] so in Greece at the present day they talk of "sending vampires to Santorini" and Professor N. P. Polites of Athens University in his Παραδόσεις τοῦ ἑλληνικοῦ λαοῦ, published in 1904, says that the inhabitants of this island enjoy so vast a reputation as experts in effectively dealing with vampires and putting an end to them that there are two instances of quite recent date one of which occurred in the island of Mycomos and the other at Sphakia in Crete both of which concluded with the dispatch of the body of the local vampire to Santorini to be cremated and finally disposed of there.[25] As we shall see a little later in full detail Father François Richard, a Jesuit priest who belonged to the house of the Society on this island in his work *Relation de ce qui s'est passé de plus remarquable a Sant-Erini Isle de l'Archipel, depuis l'etablissement des Peres de la compagnie de Jesus en icelle*, published at Paris, 1657, has given very ample details of the vampires which haunted the island.

The earliest, and in many ways the most important of the seventeenth century writers on Greek customs and traditions is the famous and erudite Leone Allacci, to whom reference has already more than once been made. Allacci in his treatise *De quorundam Graecorum Opinationibus*[26] deals with very many Greek traditions, and in particular gives detailed attention to the vampire.[27] Since his authority has several times been quoted in foregoing chapters to illustrate notable characteristics of the vrykolakas in lieu of transcribing his pages *in extenso* a few excerpts may profitably be made even at the risk of the recapitulation of a few minor points. Discussing various superstitions, which he is inclined to allow might possibly be tolerated for awhile, he proceeds to treat of the "Burculacas ; whom some call the Bulcolaccas, and others the Buthrolacas ; than whom no plague more terrible or more harmful to man can well be thought of or conceived. This name is given him from vile filth. For βοῦρκα means bad black mud, not any kind of mud but feculent muck that is slimy and oozing with excrementitious sewerage so that it exhales a most noisome stench. Λάκκος is a ditch or a cloaca in which foulness of this kind collects and reeks amain. The vampire is the body of a man of most evil and wicked life—very often of one who has been excommunicated by his Bishop. Now such bodies unlike those of other dead men do not when they have been buried suffer decomposition and fall to dust, but having, as it seems, a skin of extreme toughness they are puffed and swell out and are much inflated throughout every limb so that the joints and tendons can scarce be crooked or bent, but the skin is taut like the parchment of a drum, and when struck returns the same sound; wherefore the *vrykolakas* has been given the name τυμπανιαῖος (drum-like). Into such a body, so horrible in its deformity, the devil enters and possessing it brings terrible misfortunes upon wretched and hapless mortals. For very often, inhabiting this body, he comes forth from the grave, and going abroad through villages and other places where men dwell, more especially at night, he makes his way to whatsoever house he will, and knocking upon the door he calls aloud by name in a hoarse stentor voice one of those who dwells within. If such a one answers he is lost; for assuredly he dies on the following day. But if he does not answer he is safe. Wherefore in this island of Chios[28] all the inhabitants, if during the night they are called by anybody, never make reply the first time. For, if a man be called a second time it is not the *vrykolakas* who is summoning him but somebody else. They say that this monster is so destructive to men that sometimes he actually appears in the full daylight, even at noon, and that not only within houses, but in the fields and on the high roads and in the enclosures of hedged vineyards, and he does not spare to advance in a threatening manner upon the passers-by or any who happen to be going that way, and so horrible is his mere appearance and look that he slays men without a word or without even touching them. If the men who see him have the courage to speak, the monster vanishes from sight; but, none the less, he who has addressed the vampire dies. Accordingly if at any time an unwonted mortality occurs and persons begin to die when there is no epidemic of sickness to account for it, the citizens shrewdly suspecting what the cause may be, proceed to open the graves of those who have been recently interred. And before long they find a body whole and entire of some person who has been dead, it may be a short time ago

or it may be a long while since. This then is taken out of the
grave and whilst prayers are being recited by the priests it
is thrown on to a blazing pyre. Very often before the devout
prayers and litanies are finished the joints and ligatures of the
corpse fall apart and then the remains are burned to ashes.
Some think that it is the devil who by glamour assumes the
appearance of a dead man and in this shape he slays those
persons whom he is minded to destroy. This belief is by no
means new or of recent growth in Greece ; in olden days and
in modern times alike, holy and religious men who are accustomed to hear the confessions of their flock and to act as
spiritual directors have constantly tried to root it out of the
mind of the people."[29]

A little later Allacci adds : " The Greeks when they see
bodies of this kind, which after death are discovered to be
whole and entire in their graves, are persuaded that such are
the remains of those who have been excommunicated, and that
after absolution has been pronounced these will fall to dust."[30]

A page or two later he speaks of " that fond and foolish
opinion which so entirely prevails among the Greeks with
regard to the bodies of those who have been excommunicated.
For they think that these do not crumble to dust, and if ever a
body is found incorrupt it is held to be most certainly that of
a man who has died excommunicate. They then exhume it
and they proceed with many prayers and litanies formally
to pronounce absolution, most exactly following in such a
rite the Nomocanon, cap. lxxxii. And when this ceremony
has been performed they assert and maintain that the body
suddenly falls to dust. I can only say that myself I never
saw anything of the kind in Greece. None the less I must
confess that I often heard the Metropolitan of Imbros,[31]
Athanasius, a most pious and prudent man, and one who would
utterly have disdained to lie or exaggerate the truth, relate
the following story. When he was sojourning at a college
which stands just outside the city adjoining the church of
S. George at Thasos,[32] he was most earnestly entreated by the
citizens that he would solemnly recite the appointed formula
of absolution from all kinds of excommunication over a number
of bodies which were to be seen there whole and entire. Won
by their prayers he did as he was desired, and lo, before he had
finished pronouncing the words of absolution the corpses all

crumbled away to dust.   The same prelate told me of a certain
Constantine Rezepio, who had been converted to Christianity
from Mohammedanism, but who on account of his wicked and
impious life for he continued in every crime and enormity, was
excommunicated.   He was buried, however, in the Greek
church of SS. Pietro e Paolo[33] at Naples, and for many years
his body remained incorrupt, but when at length the Metropolitan Athanasius with two other Metropolitans, Athanasius of
Cyprus and Chrysanthus of Leondari, pronounced a solemn
absolution over this and several other bodies that were buried
in the church it forthwith fell to dust.   And what is more
surprising still is the following history which took place whilst
Raphael was Patriarch, and which is attested by that prelate.
A certain Bishop who had pronounced excommunication
against a man was afterwards so sorely deluded of Satan that
he apostatized.   But when the man died, although he was a
good Christian, his body remained whole and entire.   As soon
as the Patriarch was informed of this he sent for the new Turk,
the bishop who had pronounced the ban, and requested him
to give absolution.   At first he curtly refused, saying that he
was entirely averse to any such rite, that the Turks had nothing
to do with the Christian religion, and so let Christians absolve
a Christian.   However, when they pleaded hard with him and
redoubled their entreaties he gave way, and he recited the words
of absolution over the body of the excommunicated person.
What follows is vouched for by the evidence of an eye-witness.
At the conclusion of the absolution the foggy and horribly
swollen corpse subsided and then the remains fell to dust.
The Turk stood amazed and afraid.   Without any delay he
betook himself to the chief magistrate of the district and he
related the facts exactly as they had occurred, proclaiming
aloud to all that the Christian religion was true, that holy
religion which he—miserable sinner—had abandoned, but to
which he returned, abjuring the law of the prophet.   He was
immediately warned by the Turks to bethink himself more
cautiously lest he should be delivered to the tormentors.   But
he was constant in affirming that he would die a Christian.
Little then remains to be told.   They condemned him as
obstinate and contumacious.   As he was led forth to the place
of execution he proclaimed aloud the verity of the Christian
faith and he was straightway put to death in exquisite tortures."

In his treatise *The Life and Customs of the Greeks To-day*, c. xxv, Christophorus Angelus relates several histories concerning those who have been excommunicated. Nor must I omit the instance which he gives from the historian Cassian. " Cassian is an old Greek historian and he writes in his chronicle that in a certain place there was once held a particular synod of a hundred bishops, and all of these assented to a certain orthodox decree. But one of them stood out against the rest. And then for his pertinacity they excommunicated him, and he died whilst he was yet under the ban. And his body remained bound, like iron, for a hundred years. And after a hundred years there was again held a certain synod of a hundred bishops in the same place. And when these bishops said one to another, surely that bishop who was excommunicated sinned against the church, and the church cut him off under a ban. But now we are the church and we will surely absolve him, for it is human to err. And they absolved him, and immediately after the absolution the body which had been bound for a hundred years fell to dust."[34]

A very striking history in which the Mohammedans are impressed with the verities of Christianity owing to the power of the Church in excommunication and the results of the ecclesiastical ban is related by Emanuel Malaxus.[35] A Sultan, who was searching into the evidences of Christianity, was informed by the Orthodox priests that one proof of the power of the Church lay in the fact that the bodies of those who had been excommunicated remained entire until the formula of absolution had been pronounced over them. The potentate, accordingly, desired to witness some instance of this. He bade them seek out a person who had been buried unshriven and who might be properly absolved. Recourse was had to the Patriarch, who instituted inquiries, and these brought to his knowledge the fact that a priest's widow had been excommunicated by one of his predecessors, the Patriarch Gennadius. (This is no doubt Gennadius II, an important figure in Byzantine history. He was the first Patriarch of Constantinople under the Turk, and was regarded with favour by Mohammed II, the Conqueror. Gennadius ruled as Patriarch from 1454-1456, in which year he resigned.[36] He died at the monastery of S. John Baptist at Seres in Macedonia, 1468.)[37]

It appeared that the woman in question had been rebuked

by the Patriarch for her whoredoms, whereupon she retaliated, publicly asserting that having failed to seduce her he resorted to this charge in revenge.   Gennadius replied to the calumny by making open supplication one Sunday in the presence of all the clergy and people, praying that if her words were true she might be forgiven all her sins and might hereafter enter into happiness, her body dissolving according to the usual wont ; but if, on the other hand, her accusations were slander and malice, then under the divine favour he exercised his patriarchal power of separating her from the communion of the Orthodox to suffer unpardoned, her body remaining whole and entire.   Forty days afterwards the woman died of dysentry her body was buried and later was found to be incorrupt.

At the wish of the Sultan this woman was accordingly exhumed from the grave.   The corpse was entire, without corruption, although the skin appeared of a dark hue as if mummified and stretched taut like the bracing of a drum. Having been examined it was removed, and placed in a new coffin which was tied round with cords and hermetically sealed by the impression of the Imperial signet.   Thus it was kept for a time until the Patriarch was ready to pronounce the absolution.   This was read amid circumstances of great solemnity, and from within could be heard the crackling of the bones as the corpse broke up and the joints were loosed asunder, but the coffin was not opened for a few days.   When it was produced the seals and cords were found to be intact, but none the less upon the lid being lifted it was seen that the body had dissolved and decomposed, having at length obtained pardon and peace.   The Sultan was so impressed by this miracle that he exclaimed aloud : " Yea, verily, the Christian religion is true beyond all manner of doubt."

Leone Allacci does not question the fact of non-decomposition, indeed, he refers to several authorities who confirm him in this opinion.   Among others he cites Crusius who tells in his *Turco-Graecia*[38] of the body of a Greek which was found in this condition by the Turks, and since the man had been dead for two years the corpse was burned by them.   Allacci even states that whilst he was a school-boy at Chios he was himself the eye-witness of a similar occurrence.   For some reason a tomb was opened at the Church of S. Antony, and " on the top of the bones of the other man there was found lying a body perfectly whole. It was of stature abnormally tall ; clothes there were none for they had perished owing to damp or time ; the skin was stretched tight, hard, and livid, and so flabber and foggy that the body had no plane members but bombasted like a fat boracho filled to the brim. The face was covered with crisp dark hair, but the head was parti-bald, and little hair appeared on the limbs which were smooth ; so swollen was the trunk that the arms had been forced out on either side ; the hands were open, the eyelids drooped, the mouth gaped wide with sharp gleaming teeth." The writer does not relate in what way they disposed of this corpse.

The narrative of Father François Richard, a Jesuit priest of the island of Santorini in his *Relation de l'Isle de Sant-erini,*[39] Paris, 1657, is very valuable, for his integrity and good faith are above suspicion, and since the book is exceedingly scarce I have translated Chapter XV of this important work. It bears the rubric : " *Des faux resuscitez, que les Grecs appellent* βρουκολάκας."[40]

Of a truth very rightly does Saint Paul speak of the "devices" of the Devil, not merely because the demon is full of craft, but because he is for ever essaying his deceits and his wiles. (That we be not overreached by Satan. For we are not ignorant of his devices. II *Corinthians*, ii, 11.) It is a matter of common knowledge throughout the whole of France that in his cunning the evil spirit works through the means of sorcerers and witches during the whole of their wicked lives : but in this country we are not without experience of the extraordinary effects which he produces by means of the dead bodies of those whom he possesses entirely and wholly. This is indeed an amazing marvel. He energizes these dead bodies, he preserves them for a long time without corruption, he is seen under their appearance and with the face of the deceased, sometimes he goes to and fro about the streets, and at other times he wanders in the fields and open country ; he makes his way into houses, and thus he fills some with the utmost horror whilst in their sore afright some have been struck dumb. Others have even been slain. Not a few have been assaulted and attacked ; even more have been very seriously injured and alarmed. A terrible fear chills every heart. We need not be surprised then that when one of these monsters, who seems to have risen from the dead, although in truth such is not actually the case, appears in any place, all who dwell in that neighbourhood at dusk assemble in one house or in some one dwelling in order that they may pass the night a little more securely in the confidence of companionship.

When I first heard these reports I believed that they concerned those apparitions which are not altogether unknown in France, that they were indeed the souls of the dead, who came back in order to ask for pious help so that they might the sooner be delivered from the pains of Purgatory. But, upon reflection I asked myself whether it was possible that these apparitions should be those of the Holy Souls ? For it is quite certain that many of these who are seen and who are noted to have strong and vigorous bodies are those who have led lives of criminal wickedness. It may be argued that Purgatory is not for those who do not believe in it, and the souls who come from Purgatory never commit such excesses as are wrought by these apparitions, such hideous assaults, such destruction of property, nay murder itself and every kind of outrage and violence.

We must conclude then that these are not the Holy Souls ; but they are in truth demons who animate these bodies and by their power are able to preserve them in their entirety, in the same way as a devil named Baltazo animated the dead body of a criminal who was hanged on the plain of Arlon. This happened owing to the spells and command of a sorcerer, and the whole account may be found in the history of the woman who was possessed at Laon. [The woman's name was Nicole Obry, and she was exorcized in the Cathedral at Laon, 1566. There are several contemporary pamphlets which give detailed accounts of the affair. The present allusion is probably to the *Histoire du Diable de Laon*, 1566. There is a more extensive work by Jehan Boulaese, *Le manuel de l'admirable victoire du corps du Dieu sur l'esprit maling Beelzebub, obtenue à Laon* 1566, Paris, 1575. An important work by the Abbe J. Roger is *Histoire de Nicole de Vervins, d'après des historiens contemporains et temoins oculaires, ou le Triomphe du Saint-Sacrement sur le Démon à Laon en* 1566, Paris, 1853.]

The following facts entirely persuade me that these cases are instances of a particular kind of demoniacal possession. When the Greeks are molested and disturbed by these monsters,

their priests, having applied to the Bishop for formal permission
assemble on a Saturday, since they believe that on no other
day will they find in the grave the body which serves as a
retreat and a covert for the demon. They then recite certain
prayers, after which they exhume the body of the person who
is suspected of having become a *vrykolakas*. And when they
find it whole, fresh and gorged with new blood, they take it
for certain that it was serving as an instrument of the Devil.
Therefore they conjure the foul spirit with many holy exorcisms to leave this body, and they do not cease to continue
their prayers and ceremonies until the Devil has departed,
and as he departs the body begins rapidly to decompose,
little by little to lose its colour and plumpness, and finally it
is left a ghastly and stinking mass of corrupted matter. It
was only a few years ago in this very city that there was a
remarkable instance of this in the case of a maiden named
Caliste, the daughter of a Greek priest. The body of this
maid being found whole and entire was exorcized by a Greek
priest, who was believed to be orthodox, and in the presence
of all the assistants it began to deflate and decay, suddenly
falling to putrefaction and emitting so fetid and noisome a
stench that nobody could remain in the Church. So they
buried the thing immediately, after which the girl never again
appeared.

It sometimes happens that the exorcism of the Greek priests
may fail of effect, and this is either to be attributed to their
lack of faith, or to the fact that they have to deal with a very
powerful and obstinate demon who will not be driven from the
body that he has possessed. And then they burn the bodies
to ashes, as is generally done in France with those who have
been convicted of being witches, and who have been condemned by the law for this terrible crime   A short time
before my arrival at Stampalia[41] (Astypalæa) five bodies had
been cremated on this account, and of these three were the
carcasses of married men, the fourth that of a Greek monk,
and the fifth a young girl. The same thing has been not
infrequently known in the island of Nio (Ios),[42] where a woman
who was confessing to me declared that fifty days after he had
been buried she had seen the body of her husband, whole and
entire, although they had carefully changed his place of interment, and they had performed over him all the usual ceremonies

to lay the disturbed spirit. But as they realized that he was beginning again to vex and torment people, so that he actually killed some four or five individuals, they exhumed the body for the second time, when they publicly burned it to ashes. Only two years before and for the same reason they cremated two other bodies in the island of Siphanto, and rarely does a year pass in which people do not speak with terror of these seeming resuscitations from the dead.

An incident which was very widely talked of in the island of Santorini and caused the greatest astonishment was the extraordinary friendliness that one of these *vrykolakes* showed to his wife who was still alive. By name Alexander, in his lifetime he had been a cobbler and he had lived in the little village of Pyrgos. After his death he appeared to his wife just as if he were still living. He even used to come and work in his house, for he mended his children's shoes; he went to draw water from the reservoir; and he was very often seen in the neighbouring coombs and dingles where he was wont to cut down wood for the use of his family. But after this had been going on for some time the villagers and those who lived round about became thoroughly frightened, so they exhumed his body which was cremated, and with the smoke of the flames the power of the demon also dissipated and was dispersed. These facts go to show us that the history which is recounted by Phlegon, who was a freedman of the Emperor Hadrian is true in every particular. This author tells us that a young girl named Philinnion, of Thessaly, after she had been buried some months appeared to one Machates a Macedonian, and cohabited some while with him, until the pair of them were discovered, when the Devil abandoned this body to whom he had given the power of movement and she was buried for the second time just as if she had only died a day or two before.[43]

I have been assured by one who was most trustworthy and whose word must be believed that in the island of Amorgos[44] these dead persons who are supposed to have returned to life sometimes prove so bold that not only do they wander abroad at night time but even in the full light of day they may be seen, sometimes as many as five and six together in the fields and open country, where they appear to be feeding upon green beans. And when I heard this I confessed that I could heartily wish that some of our fine atheists in France, who in order to appear mighty brave fellows boast that they believe in nothing, would take the trouble to visit this land in order that they might believe, not their ears, but their very eyes, and that they might see as plain as daylight how grossly they deceive themselves when they try to persuade themselves that if a man dies all is at an end. Yet another proof of the truth of what I say follows.

The Abbot of the famous Monastery of Amorgos[45] related this history to me. A certain merchant named Patino of the island of Patmos, having gone to Natolia in order to purchase certain commodities, unluckily for him instead of doing good business as he had hoped, died away from home. His wife no sooner learned the sad news than she sent a vessel expressly to bring his body back to his native place in order that he might be laid to rest with the usual rites that accompany a Christian burial. The body then was put in a large coffin and carried aboard the vessel. Now it happened that by some accident one of the sailors seated himself upon the coffin, when he felt that the body was moving within. Immediately he told what had happened to his companions and they determined that they would open the coffin in order that they might see the corpse. To their amaze they found the body intact and incorrupt just as if Patino were still alive. It is not difficult to imagine what an access of terror seized them, and how bitterly they regretted that they had ever undertaken such a charge. Nevertheless since they were obliged to carry out their duty by handing the coffin over to the widow they forced themselves to nail it up fast again. But no sooner had they arrived in port than they delivered their consignment yet without saying a word of what had taken place. The lady immediately gave direction that her husband should be buried in the Church with all solemn rites and accustomed ceremony. But in a very short space of time the dead man plainly betrayed that he was a vampire. At night he forced his way into various houses, yelling, howling and dealing blows right and left, so that in a few days more than fifteen persons, some of sheer fright, others as the result of his violence, took their deaths and the whole district was in a state of panic. The Priests and the Monks in the vicinity did all in their power to put an end to so terrible a state of affairs, but in vain. Their litanies and their exorcisms seemed of no avail, whence they concluded that this body must be carried back to the place from which it had been conveyed. Actually this was not done, for the sailors who were ordered to see to the business unshipped the corpse on the first desert island, and instead of digging a grave they burned it there upon a mighty pyre. After the body had been reduced to ashes both the panic and the molestations came to an end. It was evident that the power of the demon had been dissipated, since the dead man never again appeared.

This Abbot would have persuaded me that this possession by demons was a certain proof of the truth of the orthodox faith; because as he used to say, it has never been known that any Turk[46] or Catholic after his death became a *vrykolakas*. To this I replied: "We must rather conclude the contrary. Surely these possessions by demons are far more striking proof of the bad estate of the Greeks, of damnation rather than of salvation." Now although he said that no Turk and no Catholic ever became a *vrykolakas* after his death, such is far from being the case, for the History of the Arabs shows us the contrary, and one has only to read the twenty-third Chapter of this History to learn how frequently vampires appear in the vast Arabian deserts. Nay, without going any further, we may very well bear in mind what actually took place in Santorini itself, where a certain cleric in minor orders became a Mohammedan, and took the name of Mamouti. Owing to his abominable life and horrible crimes, at the common request of all the people, this apostate wretch was hanged on the sail of a mill. Now notwithstanding the fact that he had turned Turk, he incessantly plagued the living after his death, and these vexations continued until they had cremated his body. It is true that within the memory of man and so far as our knowledge extends no native of France who ever died within the fold and in the belief of the Holy Catholic Church, has become a *vrykolakas*, nor has anyone after his death appeared to be possessed by a demon after this manner which is not uncommon among the Greeks. Wherefore most humbly thank we the Divine Goodness. Some attribute this grace to the efficacy of the holy oils with which the body is anointed; others to the virtue of our holy water; and some again to the sanctity of our cemeteries. However this may be, or no, I leave to be pronounced by those who are able to judge of the truth of like matters.

Yet I would add that one of the principal inhabitants of this island, a Greek, who was in a mortal apprehension lest he might appear in this terrible fashion after his death, wished to be buried in our Church, being fully persuaded that the presence of the Blessed Sacrament and the sanctity of the place would protect his body from any attack on the part of the demons. Wherefore in the year 1652 when he had fallen seriously ill he expressed by a codicil to his testamentary dispositions the order that he should be buried in our Church. But it pleased Almighty God to restore him to perfect health, after he had made a general confession to Father François Rossiers, and addressed his vows to S. Joseph, following the advice which we had given him. I pray God that he may die, when his hour comes, in a state of grace, in order that he may be indeed safe and secure from any snare or molestation on the part of the demon.

The fear that he might return was suggested to this good and worthy man by the fact that one of his relations, Iannetis Anapliotis, came back after his death and frequented the streets, creating a universal panic. This Iannetis was accounted the most notorious and wealthiest usurer in all Santorini, and happily about a year before his death the Divine Goodness was pleased graciously to touch his heart, so that he was inspired to make a general confession to one of our Fathers, who gave him the best advice that he could for the safety of his soul. Iannetís also made restitution wherever it was possible to do so and gave away much money in charity. Moreover, some time before he fell ill he strictly charged his confessor to let it be generally known that if any person felt that he had exacted excessive interest from them, or that he had unjustly seized upon their goods, such were most earnestly requested to inform him of the circumstances inasmuch as he was both willing and anxious to make amends. Moreover, he left a particular charge to his widow that if after his death any person came forward with a just claim she was to satisfy it. Yet how happy is the man who does not lay upon another's shoulders the burden of securing his own safety ! After the death of her husband the widow distributed much in charity in those quarters which pleased her rather than discharging the obligations her husband had laid upon her. And so it came to pass that she was applied to by some poor folk who felt that they had been hardly treated and robbed, and it happened that one day she refused to meet a just claim which was presented. That very night Iannetis who had been dead for more than six weeks, by the permission of God, began to rush up and down the streets and most particularly to molest the houses of all his relatives and kin, especially concentrating his forces, as it seemed, upon the dwelling of his wife. As he was a man of the highest position, at first they shrank from openly publishing his name. Very early in the mornings, before cock crow, he used to arouse the Greek priests telling them that it was high time they betook themselves to Church to sing Matins ; he also suddenly threw off the coverlets from people who were lying fast asleep, and violently shook the beds whereon persons were slumbering. He plagued the district with a hundred other vexations, such as turning the taps of wine barrels which were stored in his own cellars and in the vaults of others so that all the good wine ran out and was lost. They actually endured a full month of these molestations before they ventured to publish his name. On one occasion a poor woman who during the day was gathering herbs was so alarmed by his fearful looks when he leaped out upon her that she lost the power of speech for three whole days ; and another woman whose bed he shook with the utmost violence fell into premature labour so that she miscarried from fear. After this they were obliged to make his name known and they bade the widow take such steps as she could to check these riots.

The Chancellor of the Island, who happened to be the brother-in-law of the deceased, came to consult me in order that he might inquire what in my opinion were the best measures to adopt to ensure the repose of the dead. I told him that the dead man would never enjoy peace until his widow satisfied the just claims of those who felt that they had been wronged in the past. This pill, however, was too bitter for the good lady to swallow, and so she had recourse to other remedies, and these she sought from those who were not able to afford them. The Greek priests to whom she addressed herself supposed that it was merely a question of a dead man who was just the same as any other *vrykolakas*, and accordingly on the following

Saturday they very privately betook themselves to the grave
whence they exhumed the body in order to exorcize it. They
remarked none the less that it was quite different from others
of the vampire kind. In spite of all their exorcisms the dead
man continued to molest and to plague the people with the
same horrid insistence as before, and matters proceeded at
such a rate that at last the widow was obliged to follow my
advice, and eventually she satisfied those who were asking for
restitution to be made them. When she had done this in order
to make matters doubly sure she caused the body of her husband
to be exhumed again, and to be exorcized anew. I now had
the curiosity to examine it, and with this object in view I went
together with our Brother Charles Louger to the Church where
they were engaged in the ceremonies of exorcism. The corpse
was stretched out upon the floor of the Church and covered
over with foul linen of a poor quality. A Greek priest willingly
raised the pall in order that I might see it fully exposed ; but
by an unhappy accident in drawing back this old cerement he
overturned their μοργαρίη,[47] that is to say the box or pyx of
wood in which they reserve the Holy Eucharist for Communion,
and this ciboire they had put upon this dead man without
any sign of respect or lights. I was indeed horribly chagrined
at this piteous disorder, and after having caused them to collect
the sacred particles, and after having had the box with its Holy
Contents reverently put back in its proper place, I carefully
examined the body which was still shrouded in its robes of
tiffany just as it had been put in the tomb. The head was all
black and desiccated, and both eyes and nose had fallen quite
away, so it seems probable that the man's sconce had decomposed in his grave, and it had no doubt been more affected by
the damp than the hands which were whole and shrivelled of
the colour of parchment. The entrails also had entirely suffered
putrefaction. After having made a careful survey I remarked
to the Superior who was directing the ceremony that I could
see nothing extraordinary in the condition of the corpse, and
that certainly it did not appear to me to resemble that of a
vrykolakas. He hardly attempted to deny this, but another
priest who was standing by replied that if but the heart were
whole and entire that sufficed to afford the devil lodgement.
I could have wished that they would have shown me that it was
true that the heart of this dead man was untouched and entire

as they affirmed, but they would not permit any further examination. Accordingly we withdrew, whilst they continued their exorcisms until evening, and then hacking the body to pieces with great strokes of mighty axes they had brought, they buried the remains in a new grave.

It is true that this dead man for the future never molested anybody, but I believe that the restitution which was made proved far more efficacious than the prayers and the exorcisms of these Greek priests who did not know what to think about it at all or how to explain it. The Reverend Mother Prioress of the Convent of Dominican Nuns was equally perturbed for she complained to one of our Fathers of the terrible alarm which this dead man spread throughout her cloister. This Father told her that if the *vrykolakas* appeared to her she was to spit in his face, and then she would see what he would say. And this she did. For that very night he suddenly appeared just when she was beginning to fall off to sleep, and seizing her rosary which was hanging at the head of her bed he rolled it to and fro along the floor of the room. Fully waking up at the noise with the utmost courage and spirit she carried out the advice that had been given. "So," she cried to the apparition, "you have come then, accursed wretch, in order to vex us and torment us if you can," and so saying with contempt she spat in his face. Whereupon he immediately replied, "Aha! this is the advice of your Doctor!" This good Religious, in order to help herself pluck up a stout courage as well as to assist the Holy Souls began to invoke Our Blessed Lady and the Saints, whose Litanies she recited aloud, and all this while it seemed that the apparition seated itself upon a little chest, and uttering deep groans with piteous sighs it wailed and lamented until she had finished her prayers. Then suddenly snatching at the shoes of the Prioress it carried them off and flung them in the drinking-water cistern. On the following day she gave an account of all these happenings to her Director who encouraged her zealously to persist in her prayers on behalf of this poor soul since he seemed to be at any rate in the way of salvation. Our good Father informed her, moreover, that on the same evening he offered up to God for the repose of this soul all the merits which he had acquired during the most holy season of Advent, and when night came no sooner had he retired to rest than he felt two ice cold hands which were suddenly placed on

the pit of his stomach and awakened him. Without fear he
seized one of these and would have recited an exorcism. But
perhaps for some reason or another his zeal was not acceptable
to Heaven. The only thought that crossed his mind was that
the spirit had come to thank him for the little offering which
he had made in order to effect its deliverance. In giving to
the Holy Souls one becomes their debtor. For one gains as
much in giving to them, as one loses if one refuses them any
alms or an act of charity. It is my belief that as this poor soul
did not resemble those of whom we spoke above, the real
vrykolakas, in his material form, that is to say in his body, so
did he differ widely from them as regards his spiritual advantages
and merits.

I know full well that these histories of false resuscitations
will engage the attention of a great many and it may be excite
their curiosity to look for something more than I have told.
Wherefore I would add that in Greek cemeteries there are to be
found dead bodies of another kind, and these after fifteen and
sixteen years—and sometimes even twenty and thirty years—
are discovered blown up and inflated like balloons, and when
they are thrown on the ground or rolled along they sound like
hollow drums, whence they are commonly called ντουπί
(drum).[48] Certes I cannot undertake here to enter into a
discussion of how this happens or why it happens, only I will
record the general belief among the Greeks that this is a sure
sign that those whose bodies are discovered inflated and blown
up taut are men who died in a state of excommunication ; and
in truth Greek Priests and Bishops when they launch the ban
of excommunication against a person always add this anathema,
καὶ μετὰ τὸν θάνατον ἄλυτος καὶ ἀπαράλυτος, "and after thy
death thy body shall remain incorrupt and entire." Now with
regard to this point the common folk who often see these bodies
which remain whole and indissoluble, dread the excommunication which is pronounced by a simple parish priest just as much
as though it were some Metropolitan or Patriarch who was
launching the ban. However, you may guess that magic or
some spell must be at work here, as is known to happen when
there has been an extraordinary continence of urine as we noted
in the preceding chapter, and indeed this is to be shrewdly
suspected. Nevertheless the Greeks hold a very different
opinion. With regard to these bodies, in an old MS. which

formerly belonged to the Church of Sancta Sophia[49] at Thessalonica (Salonica) I found the following :

Ὁποῖος ἔχει ἐντολὴν ἢ κατάραν, κρατοῦσι μόνον τὰ ἔμπροσθεν
τοῦ σώματός του.
Ἐκεῖνος ὁποῦ ἔχει ἀνάθεμα φαίνεται κιτρινὸς καὶ ζαρωμένα τὰ
δακτύλιά του.
Ἐκεῖνος ὁποῦ φαίνεται ἄσπρος, εἶναι ἀφωρισμένος παρὰ τῶν
θείων νόμων.
Ἐκεῖνος ὁποῦ φαίνεται μαῦρος, εἶναι ἀφωρισμένος ὑπὸ ἀρχιερέως.

" Whosoever has left unfulfilled a command of his parents or who
 lies under their curse,
When he is dead has only the front portions of his body incorrupt.
' He who is under the ban of an anathema looks yellow and his
 fingers are all bewrinkled.
' He who looks livid and ghastly white has been excommunicated
 by divine laws.
' He who looks black has been excommunicated by a Bishop."

Since the power of excommunication and its dread results
of incorruption and vampirism were so keenly insisted upon by
the Orthodox it will not be impertinent here to quote Chapter
XIV of Paul Ricaut's *The Present State of the Greek and Armenian
Churches. Anno Christi.* 1678.[50] The rubric runs : " *Of the
treatment the* Greeks *use towards their dead, and the Opinion they
have of Purgatory, or the middle state of Souls.*" " The *Greeks*
in the time of sickness and mournings for the dead retain not
only Ceremonies by us accounted superstitious, but also
savouring somewhat of ancient *Gentilism.* If the head ache,
or be ill-affected, the Priest binds it with the Vail of the
Sacramental Chalice, and administers to the sick a draught of
consecrated Water, in which is *Basil,* or *Dittamon,* or some other
odoriferous Herb, blessed with the touch of a Crucifix, or the
Picture of our Lady, and administered as a spiritual Medicine,
as well operative for the benefit of the Soul, as conducing to the
health of the Body. But in case the indisposition increase, the
holy Oyl, or extream Unction is applied, called ἀπομυρισμὸν,
mixed with some of that Water which was consecrated at the
Sacrament of the Communion ; and some Prayers, proper for
that occasion, are rehearsed, together with such Chapters and
Verses out of the new Testament which relate to the resurrection of the dead. It is likewise usual amongst them, as in the
Roman Church, to make Vows upon recovery; and on the Altar

to tender the form of a Leg, Arm, or Eyes of some other Member ill-affected in Silver or Gold, in rememberance and gratitude for the late mercy of Almighty God. But when the party dyes, the lamentations which they make are most barbarous. For after his eyes are shut, his Corps are clothed in its best Apparel, and, being stretched on the Floor with a Taper at the head, and another at the feet, then begins the Scene of sorrow': the Wife, the Children, and the rest of the Family and Friends entring with their Hair dishevelled, their Garments loose and torn pulling their Locks, and beating their Breasts, and scratching their Faces with their Nails

. . . *Fœdantes unguibus ora.*""

make such deep sighs and sad cryes, as might justly incur the reprehension of the Apostle, who gave them that reasonable Counsel of, *Mourn not like those without hope*, 1 *Thes.* 4, *v.* 13. The Body thus dressed up with a Crucifix on the Breast, attended by the Priests, and Deacons, is carried to burial, and the Prayers solemnized with Incense, that God would receive his Soul into the Region of the blessed ; the Wife follows her departed Husband, with such passion to perform the last office of kindness, as if she intended with violence of her shreeks to force out her own Soul, and to bear company with the Corps of her Husband in his Cave of darkness : And where passion is not found so vigorous and violent in its representation of sorrow, by reason of the gentle and more even temper of some Wives ; there want not Women, who are perfect Tragedians, that are hired to follow the Corps of the dead, and to act in behalf of the Relations, all the distracted postures and motions of real grief and confused sorrow. The Corps being placed in the Church, and the Office for the dead being ended, the Friends which accompany it first kiss the Crucifix on the Breast, and then the Mouth, and Forehead of the deceased, and afterwards every one eats a piece of Bread, and drinks a glass of Wine in the Church, wishing rest to the Soul departed, and consolation to the afflicted Relations ; which done, they attend them home, and so end the Ceremonies of Burial.

"At the end of eight days after the Burial, the friends of the deceased make their charitable Visits to condole with, and comfort, the nearer Relations, and accompany them to the Church, to joyn with them in the Prayers offered for the quiet and rest of the departed Soul ; at which time the men eat and drink again in the Church, whilst the Women renew their barbarous lamentations with shreeks and cryes, and with all other evidences of distraction and sorrow ; but such as can pay others to act this part of passion, force not themselves with that violence, but send them to lament and mourn over the Sepulcher for the space of eight days ; the third day after, which they call τὰ τρίμερα, on which Prayers are said for the Soul departed : In like manner at the end of nine days, and at the end of six months, and at the end of the conclusion of the year, Prayers and Masses are said for the repose of the Soul, which being ended, those then present are entertained with boiled Wheat, and Rice, Wine, and dryed fruits, and this is called τὰ πέρνα, which is a custom esteemed by the *Greeks* of great Antiquity, which they more devoutly solemnize on the *Fryday* before their entrance into the *Lent* of *Advent, Good-Fryday,* and the *Fryday* before the Feast of *Pentecost,* which are special days observed for Commemoration of the dead, as well such as dyed of violent, as of natural deaths.

"Now as to the Opinion which the *Greek* Church holds concerning the condition of Souls departed this life, there is some diversity, being a matter not clearly determined by Councils. Howsoever the *Anatolian* Confession, which is generally accepted and approved by the *Greek* Divines, doth clearly and expressly maintain this Doctrine, That the Souls, so soon as they are cleared and loosed from the Fetters of the Body, go either to Heaven or to Hell ; the first hath the name of Paradise, *Abraham's* Bosom, the Kingdom of Heaven, where the Saints sit and intercede for those who are on Earth, in honour of whom are daily sung Hymns of praise and glory.

"Such as go to Hell, called the Grave, the eternal Fire, the Bottomless Pit, and the like, are of two sorts. The first are such who dye in the state of Divine anger, on whom are immediately imposed Chains, and Fetters, which can never be taken off, nor loosed to all Eternity. The second are such who enter or who are introduced into the Mansions of Hell, without those Bonds, Fetters, Pains and Torments, which for ever enslave and afflict the damned ; but departing this life with dispositions of Justice, Repentance, and a new life, with the advantagious assistances of Confession and Absolution of the Priest, though the work of Grace be not thoroughly perfected in them, nor their resolution of godliness proceeded to action, have yet their resolutions, dispositions, and beginnings of Piety made acceptable, and brought to maturity and esteem in the sight of God, not by any works performed in the next World, according to that of the Psalmist, *who shall praise thee in the Grave, or shall the dead give thanks unto thee in the Pit ?*[52] but by the Offertories, Oblations, and Almes, and Prayers of the Church, made in behalf of the dead by the living on Earth ; and this is the meaning of those Prayers. *Tu autem Domine repone animam ejus in loco lucenti, in loco quietis consolationis, ex quo longe est omnis mœstitia, dolor & suspirium, condonans ei omne peccatum. Do thou Lord repose his Soul in the Mansions of light, of quietness and consolation, from whence are banished all sadness, grief, and sighs.* But this place (it seems) they account no different *Limbo* from Hell, and is no Purgatory, whose flames purge and cleanse, or whose torments afflict the Soul, or make the least satisfaction for sin, according to the sentence of the second Council of *Constantinople*,[53] which condemned the Opinion of *Origen* herein : for the soul then becomes uncapable either by its sufferings or repentance to obtain pardon in its own behalf.

"But whatsoever is to be done in this matter, is to be performed by the Soul united with the Body in this life ; afterwards, the Bridegroom being entered, the Gate is shut, and no path or way is left to repentance, only the Prayers of the Saints on Earth, their Almes-deeds, and Offertories of frequent Sacrifices without Blood, with the intercession of the Blessed Martyrs and Church triumphant, open the doors of Paradise to languishing and wishing Souls : but this is not done, until the Judgment of the last day, in which *interim* the *Greek* Church holds, That neither the Sentence of the four Patriarchs, nor the Decrees of the Universal Synod, nor all the Bishops of the whole World assembled, are able by their Authority, Bolles or Indulgences, to prescribe a time for release of one Soul from the confines of Hell ; only the Mercies of God, who vouchsafes to be moved by the Prayers of the Church, can sign this release and delivery at what time he shall think fit : And that as the Blessed receive not their repletions of Glory in Heaven until after the day of Judgment, so neither shall the Damned their fullness of Torment in everlasting flames : By which it appears, that the Tenents of the *Greek* Church are in this point :

"First, that the Repository of longing Souls is not locally

different from Hell it self : Secondly, that they endure no other
punishment than only the sense of deprivation from God and
Heaven, and are not purged by Fire and Flames : And thirdly,
that no Indulgences nor Pardons of all the Patriarchs, or of the
Universal Bishop, can by their Authority remit one moment
of detention to the imprisoned Souls, farther than as they are
Members of the Church Militant, by whose Prayers and good
works only those Souls find ease and benefit ; and this is the
true and certain meaning of the *Greek* Church in this point,
against which and their Tenent about the Pontificial Authority,
the *Romanists* make their greatest exception."

A yet more famous traveller than Ricaut, the celebrated
French botanist Joseph Pitton de Tournefort[54] in 1700-2
visited the Orient passing through Greece and in his account of
this journey, *Relations d'un Voyage du Levant*, 2 vols., Paris,
1717, which has long since become a classic,[55] he has left us a
most interesting account of the cremation of a vampire's body
at which he himself was present,[56] the keenest of observers.
Having spoken of various Greek funeral customs, particularly
the μνημόσυνα or "memorial-feasts," the food proper to which
is known as κόλλυβα, a boiled grain resembling furmety,
Tournefort continues : "We witnessed an entirely different
and very tragic scene in this same island, Myconos,[57] in connexion with one of those dead men[58] who, as they confidently
believe, return after they have been buried. The man, whose
story we are going to relate, was a peasant of Myconos, in
disposition naturally churlish and very quarrelsome, and this
is a detail which is worth noting, for it often occurs in similar
instances. This man, then, was murdered in some lonely
country place, and nobody knew how, or by whom. Two days
after he had been buried in a small chapel or oratory in the
town it began to be noised abroad that he had been seen at
nights walking about with great hasty strides, that he went
into houses, and tumbled about all the furniture, that he
extinguished candles and lamps, that he suddenly fast gripped
hold of people behind and wrought a thousand other mischiefs
and very knaveries. At first people something laughed at the
tale, but when the graver and more respectable citizens began
to complain of these assaults the affair became truly serious.
The Greek priests candidly acknowledged the fact of these
disturbances, and perhaps, they had their own reasons for so

doing. A number of masses were duly said, but in spite of it
all, hob the peasant continued to drive his old trade and
scarcely showed himself at all inclined to mend his ways for all
that they could do. The leading citizens of the district, a
number of priests and monks met together to discuss the
business several times, and in accordance with some ancient
ritual of which I do not know the purport, they decided that
they must wait for a clear nine days after the burial.

" On the next day, that is the tenth, a solemn mass was sung
in the chapel where the body lay in order to expel the demon
who, as they believed, had taken possession of it. The body
was exhumed after the mass, and presently everything was
ready to tear out the heart, according to custom. The town
flesher, an old and clumsy-fisted fellow, began by ripping open
the belly instead of the breast : he groped a good while among
the entrails without finding what he sought, and then at last
somebody informed him that he must dissever the diaphragm.
So the heart was finally extracted amid the wonder and applause
of all who were present. But the carrion by now stank so
foully that they were obliged to burn a large quantity of
frankincense, when the hot fume commingled with the bad
gases that were escaping from this putrid corpse but served to
augment and extend the fetor which seemed to mount to the
brains of those who were intent upon the loathly spectacle.
Their heated imaginations reeled, and the rank horror of the
thing inflamed their minds with wildest fantasies. Some even
commenced to cry aloud that a thick cloud of smoke was being
spewed out by the dead body, and in sober sooth amid the
frenzy we did not dare to assert that this was merely the thick
fume pouring from the thuribles. Throughout the whole
chapel, then, and in the square which lies before it, one heard
nothing but cries of *Vroucolacas*, for this is the name that is
given to these persons who return in this evil wise. The
bawling and noise spread throughout all the neighbouring
streets and this name was shouted so loudly that it seemed to
cleave the very vault of the chapel itself. Many of the
bystanders asserted that the blood of this poor wretch was a
rich vermil red in hue ; whilst the flesher swore that the body
was still quite warm as in life. Thereupon all mightily blamed
the dead man for not being really dead, or rather for allowing
his body to be re-animated by the devil, for this is the true

idea that they have of a *Vroucolacas*. As I have said, this name re-echoed on every side in a most extraordinary manner. Large numbers of people went up and down through the crowd asserting that they could clearly see that the body was still supple with pliant unstiffened limbs when they bore it from the fields to the church to bury it, and that obviously he was a most malignant *Vroucolacas*. One could hear nothing but that word being repeated over and over again.

"I am very certain that if we had not ourselves been actually present these folk would have maintained that there was no stench of corruption, to such an extent were the poor people terrified and amazed and obsessed with the idea that dead men are able to return. As for ourselves, we had carefully taken up a position quite near the body in order that we might exactly observe what took place, and we were retching and well nigh overcome by the stench of the rotting corpse. When we were asked what we thought about this dead man, we replied that we certainly believed he was indeed dead, but as we wished to soothe or at least not to inflame their diseased imaginations we tried to convince them that there was nothing at all extraordinary in what had taken place, that it was hardly surprising the flesher should have felt a degree of warmth, as he fumbled with his hands amid the decomposing viscera ; that it was quite usual for mephitic gases to escape from a dead body just as they issue from an old midden when the heap is stirred or moved ; as for this bright red blood which still stained the flesher's hands and arms 'twas but foul-smelling clots of filth and gore !

"But in spite of all our arguments and all our reasoning a little later on they burned the dead man's heart on the sea-shore, and yet in spite of this cremation he was even more aggressive, and caused more dire vexation and confusion than before. It was commonly reported that every night he beat folk sorely ; he broke down doors and even the roofs of houses ; he clattered at and burst in windows ; he tore jerkins and dresses to rags ; he emptied all the jugs and bottles. 'Twas the most thirsty devil ! I believe that he did not spare anyone except the consul in whose house we lodged. Howbeit I have never seen anything more pitiful and more sad than the state of this island. All the people were scared out of their wits, and the wisest and best among them were just as terrorized as the

rest. It was an epidemical disorder of the brain, as dangerous
as a mania or as sheer lunacy. Whole families left their houses
and from the furthest suburbs of the town brought little
tent-beds and pallets into the public square, in order to pass
the night in the open. Each moment somebody was complaining of some fresh vexation or assault ; when night fell nothing
was to be heard but cries and groans ; the better sort of people
withdrew into the country.

"At such a crisis and in the midst of so great confusion and
mortal alarm, we resolved to hold our peace, making no
comment and proffering no opinion. It is certain that for any
criticism not only should we have been considered shallow and
ignorant fools, but more, we should have been regarded as
godless atheists. It was entirely out of our power to counteract
the effects of an old and common tradition. Those who shrewdly
suspected that we had grave doubts with regard to the true
explanation of what had occurred used to visit us with the
obvious intention of rebuking our unbelief, and they made it
their business to prove that there actually were *Vroucolacas* by
the evidence of various authorities whom they quoted from
The Shield of the Faith (ταργα τῆς Ρωμαικῆς πίστεως), a work
by Father Richard, a Jesuit missionary.[59] "He was a Latin,
a Roman of Rome," they insisted, "and consequently you
most surely ought to believe him." We did not attempt to
deny the logic of their argument, and so every morning they
kept coming to us with their tale, an exact relation of some
fresh assault which this night-bird had committed, some new
plague or vexation ; they even accused him of the most
hideous and abominable crimes.

"Those inhabitants who had the public good sincerely at heart
believed that a mistake had been made in one of the essential
points of the ceremony, for in their opinion the Mass should
not have been celebrated until they had extracted the heart
from the corse of this vile wretch ; they were quite certain
that if this precaution had only been taken the devil must
inevitably have been caught and that he could not have
re-entered the dead body, instead of which, since the officiants
had begun by celebrating the Mass first of all, the devil,
according to their idea, had found ample opportunity to escape
and then when the liturgy was over there was nothing to hinder
him from returning at will.

"The sole result of all these discussions was that they found themselves exactly in the same difficulty as they were at the beginning. Night and morning the village council met ; they deliberated at great length. Solemn processions paraded the streets for three days and three nights ; all the priests most rigidly fasted ; they continually went from house to house each carrying his aspergillun in his hand, sprinkling holy water and washing the doors with it ; they even poured a quantity into the mouth of the miserable *Vroucolacas.*

"For our part, we kept impressing upon the Magistrates of the town ('Επιτρόποι) that in such circumstances it was their duty as pious Christian folk to appoint a special watch all night long in order to see what took place in the streets ; and owing to this precaution at last they caught a number of beggars and other vagabonds who most certainly had been responsible for a good deal of the disorder and pother. This is not to say that they had originated it, or that they were even mainly to blame for the turmoil and disturbances. Yet they had some small part in the panic, and apparently these ruffians were released from prison a great deal too soon, for two days afterwards in order to make up for the hard fare which had been their lot whilst they were in jail, they once more began to empty the jars of wine of those who were foolish enough to leave their houses empty and unguarded all night long without any sort of protection. Nevertheless the inhabitants placed their faith in prayers and religious observances.

" One day as they were chanting certain litanies, after they had pierced with a large number of naked swords the grave of the dead body, which they used to exhume three or four times a day merely to satisfy any idle curiosity, an Albanian who happened just then to be visiting Myconos took upon himself to say in a tone of the most absolute authority that in a case like this it was to the last degree ridiculous to make use of the swords of Christians. ' Can you not see, poor blind buzzards that you are, that the handles of these swords, being made like a cross, prevents the devil from issuing out of the body ? Why do you not rather employ Ottoman scimetars ? ' The advice of this learned man had no effect at all ; the *Vroucolacas* was incorrigible, and all the inhabitants were thrown into the utmost consternation. They were at their wits end to know what Saint to invoke, when suddenly, just as if some cue had been given, they began to proclaim aloud throughout the whole town that the situation was intolerable ; that the only way left was to burn the *Vroucolacas* whole and entire ; and after that was done let the devil possess the body if he could ; that it was better to adopt these extremest measures than to have the island entirely deserted. For, indeed, already some important families had begun to pack their goods and chattels with the intention of definitely withdrawing to Syra or to Tenos.[60] The Magistrates therefore gave orders that the *Vroucolacas* should be conveyed to the point of the island of S. George,[61] where they had prepared a great pyre with pitch and tar, lest that the wood, bone-dry as it was, should not burn fast enough of itself. What remained of the carcass was then thrown into the flames and utterly consumed in a very few minutes. This took place on 1 January, 1701. We saw the blaze as we were sailing back from Demos, and it might justly be called a festal bonfire, since after this there were no more complaints about the *Vroucolacas*. The people laughingly said to each other that the devil had been finely caught this time, and there were even composed a number of street songs and popular ballads mocking him and turning him into ridicule.

"Throughout the whole Archipelago there is no Orthodox Greek who does not firmly believe that the devil is able to re-energize and re-vitalize dead bodies. The inhabitants of the island of Santorini in particular, have the utmost dread of this kind of werewolf (ces sortes de loups-garous). The people of Myconos after their present fears had been dissipated expressed the utmost apprehension of the consequences which might follow such proceedings should the matter come to the knowledge of the Turkish authorities or to the ears of the Bishop of Tenos. Indeed, not a single priest would consent to go to S. George when they burned the body. The clergy were afraid that the Bishop might fine them a round sum of money for having suffered a body to be disinterred and cremated without his express sanction. As for the Turks, it is quite certain that, if they caught wind of it, the next time they visited the island they would make the whole community pay dearly for the blood of this poor wretch who had become the dread and the abomination of the whole countryside."

This relation is extremely valuable and although the sceptical undertone which runs throughout the whole is much to be deplored, we are none the less grateful for so vivid and authoritative an account. One may well be shocked at the horror of the scene, at the barbarous treatment of the dead body, but it must be steadily borne in mind that the people had to cope with a most malignant and terrible foe and in order to destroy him they were obliged to employ rough and terrible methods.

We have pointed out a little above the reason why the Greeks so painfully shrink from burning a corpse save in the last extremity. To the Orthodox it is little less than sacrilege to consume with fire " a body on which the holy oil has been poured by the priest when performing the last rite of his religion over the dying man."

The custom of burning the bodies of the dead dates back to very early times. The Pre-Canaanites practised it until the introduction among them of inhumation, which was brought with the civilization of the Semetic peoples about 2500 B.C. There is, actually, among the Jewish nation no trace of incineration, except in the extraordinary circumstances of war and pestilence. It is well-known with what solemn ceremonies so advanced a people as the Egyptians surrounded the embalming of their dead. The Persians, indeed, regarded any attempt at cremation as a capital crime, and special regulations were followed in the purification of fire so desecrated. Even among the Greeks and the Romans the practice was by no means so general as is often supposed, and certainly it never entirely superseded what Cicero tells us was the older rite among the Roman people. It is significant that the Gens Cornelia, which was one of the noblest and most cultured houses, did not permit the burning of their dead. The only exception seems to have been Sulla, and this occasioned much comment and remark. In the *De Legibus*, II, xxii, we have: " At mihi quidem antiquissimum sepulturæ genus id fuisse uidetur, quo apud Xenophontem Cyrus utitur : redditur enim terræ corpus, et ita locatum ac situm, quasi operimento matris obducitur : eodemque ritu in eo sepulcro, quod procul ad Fontis aras, regem nostrum Numam conditum accepimus ; gentemque Corneliam usque ad memoriam nostram hac sepultura scimus esse usam. C. Marii sitas reliquias apud Anienem, dissipari iussit Sulla uictor, acerbiore odio incitatus, quam si tam sapiens fuisset, quam fuit uehemens.

" Quod haud scio an timens suo corpori posse accidere,

primus e patriciis Corneliis igni uoluit cremari : declarat enim Ennius de Africano, *Hic est ille situs*."

The early Christians did not burn their dead, but during the persecutions the Pagans, in order to destroy faith in the resurrection of the body and believing that they could render this impossible, often committed the bodies of Martyrs to the flames. The whole matter has been well summed up by Minucius Felix in his dialogue *Octauius*,[62] which Renan not unjustly termed " la perle de la littérature apologétique,"[63] and the words of the renowned Latin advocate[64] are as true for us to-day as they were in the third century. Refuting the assertion that cremation made the resurrection of the body an impossibility, Minucius says : " Nec, ut creditis, ullum damnum sepulturæ timemus sed ueterem et meliorem consuetudinem humandi frequentamus." (" Nor do we in the slightest degree fear, as you imagine, any harm at all from the manner of sepulture, but we adhere to the old, and better custom.")

On 27 July, 1892, the Archbishop of Freiburg, amongst other questions asked the Roman Congregation whether it was lawful to co-operate in the cremation of bodies by command or counsel, or to take part as doctor, official, or labourer working in the crematorium. It was answered that formal co-operation involving the assent of the will is never allowed, either by command or counsel. On the other hand, material co-operation, the mere aiding in the physical act, may be tolerated under certain conditions ; if the cremation be not regarded as a distinctive mark of a Masonic sect ; if there be nothing in the ceremony which of itself, directly or of intent, expresses denial of Catholic doctrine and approbation of a sect ; if it is clear that the officials and others have been not assigned or invited to take part in contempt and prejudice of the Catholic Faith. It will be evident that the above restrictions are very generous, and so co-operators are left in good faith, but they may always be warned not to purpose nor intend any active co-operation in the cremation.[65]

It may definitely be stated then that there is in the practice of cremation nothing directly opposed to any dogma of the Church. In certain exceptional circumstances it may be permitted, and such instances are not so rare that in the experience of many priests they have applied to the Bishop for sanction in a particular instance. Myself I have had to submit a case where cremation seemed advisable for episcopal authorization. And yet the legislation which forbids cremation rests on strong grounds; for in the majority of cases to-day cremation is undoubtedly combined with circumstances that make it a public profession of materialism and irreligion. Continental Freemasonry first obtained official recognition of this practice from various governments, and the Church has from the beginning naturally opposed a practice urged and used chiefly by notorious enemies of the Christian Faith. It should perhaps be added that in England the objections to cremation are not so clearly understood by the generality. Tournefort remarks upon the apprehension which was felt by the inhabitants of Myconos lest the Turkish authorities should hear of the cremation of the vampire, but this was not on account of any repugnance which the Mohammedans felt with regard to the burning of a body, for they entertained no religious scruples of this kind. The only fear the islanders had in this case was that their oppressors would seize the opportunity as a pretext for extortion and impost. There are, indeed, upon record cases in which the Turks discovering a body which has the appearance of a vrykolakas have burned it according to the traditional manner.[66] Some modern authorities, indeed, state that Turks themselves are far more likely to become vrykolakas than Christians, and Schmidt writes: "Sehr begreiflich ist endlich die wohl alles Orten in Griechenland vom volke gehegte Ansicht, zu desen Verbreitung wiederum dic Priester das thrige mögen beigetragen halen dass dic der orthodoxen Kiche nicht Angehöreden, zumal die Türken und deren Glaubensgenossen vice leichter und häufiger dem Vampyrismus verfallen als die Griechen"[67]. By the Orthodox Church it is considered that those who die unbaptized or apostate are especially liable to return as vampires after death. The Mohammedan, of course, is not baptized. It is generally believed that baptism will prevent children from becoming werewolves, and consequently from becoming vrykolakas. As for the apostate he is *ipso facto* excommunicate, even if no formal ban be pronounced against him.

With regard to the fact that the clergy refrained from being present when the body of the vampire was burned on the point of the Island of S. George and their anxiety that the matter should not reach their superior, the Bishop of Tenos, a very pertinent passage may be quoted from William Martin Leake who in his *Travels in Northern Greece*, published in 1835, when speaking of Epirus, writes of the belief in the vampire as follows:

" It would be difficult now to meet with an example of the most barbarous of all those superstitions, that of the Vrukolaka. The name being Illyric, seems to acquit the Greeks of the invention, which was probably introduced into the country by the barbarians of Slavonic race. Tournefort's description is admitted to be correct. The Devil is supposed to enter the Vrukolaka, who, rising from his grave, torments first his nearest relations, and then others, causing their death or loss of health. The remedy is to dig up the body, and if after it has been exorcized by the priest, the demon still persists in annoying the living, to cut the body into small pieces, or if that be not sufficient, to burn it. The metropolitan Bishop of Larissa lately informed me, that when metropolitan of Grevena, he once received advice of a papas having disinterred two bodies, and thrown them into the *Haliacmon*, on pretence of their being Vrukolakas. Upon being summoned before the bishop, the priest confessed the fact, and asserted in justification, that a report prevailed of a large animal having been seen to issue, accompanied with flames, out of the grave in which the two bodies had been buried. The bishop began by obliging the priest to pay him 250 piastres (his holiness did not add that he made over the money to the poor). He then sent for scissors to cut off the priest's beard, but was satisfied with frightening him. By then publishing throughout the diocese, that any similar offence would be punished with double the fine and certain loss of station, the bishop effectually quieted all the vampires of his episcopal province."[68]

The passage is certainly interesting and relevant, but we must be careful to correct it in one important particular. So far from a belief in the *vrykolakas* being on the wane in modern Greece it still universally prevails, and it is curious that Leake should have fallen into the very gross error of supposing that this tradition was in any way obsolescent. There is hardly a traveller who does not contradict him flatly on this point. Both Pashley and Tozer, to mention no other names, are emphatic that the superstition is still flourishing, and if, owing to the natural caution of the Greek peasant, it does not exhibit itself quite so prominently to-day, it none the less persists undiminished, although kept rather more in the background than of former years. In my own experience I have met it as most marked and enduring in modern Greece, both on the mainland and more particularly among the isles. That eminent scholar Mr. Lawson bears ample witness to the Greek tradition and the Greek practice. Moreover, in the preface to his *Modern Greek Folklore*[69] he speaks with great shrewdness of the difficulty of acquiring intimate information concerning these phenomena. How truly does he remark that "the peasant who honestly believes the superstitions and scrupulously observes the customs of which he may happen to speak is silenced at once by the sight of a note-book."

In any consideration of the modern Greek *vrykolakas* one is continually met by the fact of the immense importance which is attached to the dissolution of the body. The Greek funeral banquets and memorial feasts, those " gifts to the dead " which play so prominent a part in the life of Greek people have already been described, and when we bear in mind the paramount consequence assumed by dissolution, it might appear at first sight that their treatment of the departed involves two contradictory motives, namely the desire to sustain a certain existence by providing for the bodily wants of the departed, and also an intense longing for the annihilation of the body. It is impossible that two such diametrically opposed and mutually exclusive ideas should co-exist, and the one satisfactory conclusion is that dissolution so far from implying annihilation implies the reunion of body and soul.

If then as soon as dissolution is complete body and soul are united there can be no obligation on the part of a man's relatives to provide him with food and gifts.

We may now inquire when complete dissolution is generally supposed to have been effected, and the crucial period is reckoned by the common folk as forty days. A nenia which keened in the isle of Zakynthos (Zante) unmistakably tells us this in somewhat Websterian strain[70] :

κaὶ μέσ' 'στο σαραντοήμερο ἀρμοὺς ἀρμοὺς χωρίζουν,
πέφτουνε τὰ ξανθὰ μαλλιά, βγαίνουν τὰ μαύρα μάτια,
καὶ χώρια πάει τὸ κορμὶ καὶ χώρια τὸ κεφάλι.

("And within the forty days, the dead are separated asunder joint from joint, their glossy bright hair falls away, their dark liquid eyes fall out, and asunder are severed trunk and head.")

Moreover, the fortieth day after a death is universally observed throughout Greece as the occasion upon which the relatives of the deceased make a memorial dinner to which are bidden friends and neighbours. In Crete, if a dead man is suspected of becoming a *vrykolakas* the people are ever anxious to deal with him before the period of forty days is passed, since if natural dissolution has not then taken place, he will surely become, as it were, a confirmed vampire.

Here, however, the authority of the Church stepped in and considerably modified popular belief. The period required for dissolution according to ecclesiastical canon is three years, and consequently, although the idea of forty days still popularly prevails, the Church has impressed her rule upon the people and in obedience to ecclesiastical influence the gifts of food made at the tomb continue for no less a space than three years, at the end of which period exhumation takes place. I quote the following passage from Mr. Lawson, as it not only very clearly illustrates the various points under consideration but has the authority of his own personal observation. " Nowadays, on the contrary, the presents of food to the dead are generally continued up to the third anniversary, when exhumation takes place. Then, if the evidence of men's eyes assures them that dissolution has been fully effected—that the body is gone and only the white bones remain—there is no further thought or provision for the dead ; but in the rare cases in which the disintegration of the corpse is not yet complete, the relatives are not freed from their obligations. I witnessed a remarkable case of this kind at Leonidi on the east coast of Laconia. Two graves had just been opened when I arrived, and the utmost anxiety prevailed because in both cases there was only partial decomposition—in one case so little that the general outline of the features could be made out—and it was feared that one or both of the dead persons had become *vrykolakas*. The remains, when I saw them had been removed to the chapel attached to the burial-ground. Meanwhile the question was debated as to what should be done with them. Dissolution must be effected both in the interests of the dead themselves and in those of the whole community. Extraordinary measures were required. The best measure—I am reporting what I actually heard—the best measure next to prayer (which had been tried without effect) was to burn the remains, and the bolder spirits of the village counselled this plan ; but this would have been a breach of law and order, and the authorities of the place would have none of it.   The priest proposed re-interment ; but here the relatives objected.   They had had trouble enough and expense enough ; they had kept ' the unsleeping lamp ' burning at the grave, and had provided all the memorial feasts ; they would not consent to re-inter the body and to be at the same charge for an indefinite time, without knowing when the corpse might be properly ' loosed ' and their tendance of it over.   They would find some way of dissolving it, and that speedily.

And so indeed they did ; and I, for a short time, was a spectator of the scene.   On the floor of the chapel there were two large baskets containing the remains ; there were men seated beside them busy with knives ; and there were women kneeling at wash-tubs and scouring the bones that were handed to them with soap and soda.   The work continued for two days. At the end of that time the bones were shown white and clean. All else had disappeared—and probably been burnt in secret, but the secret was kept close.   It was therefore claimed and allowed that dissolution was complete.

The attitude adopted by the relatives on this occasion makes it perfectly clear that all the care expended on the dead is obligatory up to the time of dissolution, but no longer.   So long as the fleshy substance remains in this world, provision of food must be made for it; when it has disappeared and only the bones are left, the departed cease to be dependent upon their surviving relatives, and no further anxiety is felt for their welfare."[71]

It may be remarked that a skeleton and human bones are treated by the Greeks in a way which would appear to us brutal and impious. In the case of canonized Saints, indeed, the bones will be preserved as hallowed relics, but under ordinary conditions, once the body has dissolved the bones are merely thrown into a fosse or pit, adjoining the churchyard indeed, but actually outside the sacred precincts.   These receptacles which are quite common throughout Greece are certainly called by the Church " cemeteries," κοιμητήρια, as technically opposed to νεκροταφειὸν, the place of preliminary interment.[72]   But these cemeteries are treated with no respect. The churchyard itself demands devotion and awe, but the common dyke where the bones are thrown is utterly neglected and disesteemed. When we consider the extraordinary care of the Greeks for their dead, their elaborate funeral liturgy, their dirges and threnody, it must inevitably be realized that this attitude, seemingly so callous, is no mere brutal thoughtlessness or wanton disregard. There exists a very sound explanation, and the reason is that when the body has dissolved and is again re-united with the soul in a state where it is both individual and active, the mere bleached atomy, the empty framework, is useless and less than useless, a thing that has served its purpose and now is of no account at all.

Although, as we have seen, cremation was never favourably regarded by Christianity, and the Church uncompromisingly condemned it because of its intimate association with heathen rites ; yet it is worth noting that the Orthodox, whilst undoubtedly preferring inhumation, did not adopt quite the same strict attitude as the Catholic Church, and under certain conditions they were willing that some indulgence should be possible. The boon which the people were most anxious to secure for their dead was that of dissolution, and there can be no question that although terrene burial might be known to fail in bringing about this result, it was inevitably and, we may say, immediately secured by cremation ; whilst although in the case of inhumation the relatives, if they had any doubts might be left in some suspense were a body burned they themselves could be eye-witnesses that it was verily and rapidly consumed. The Slavonic method employed to dispose of a vampire was to drive at one blow a stake of aspen or of whitethorn through the heart. The Greeks knew a yet securer way. Some tradition of the ancient manner of incinerating the dead in old Hellas lingered, although not in actual practise. When more modern descendants were faced by a terrible and threatening danger they remembered the antique practice which by ensuring the immediate and complete dissolution of the body, would at once put an end to all connexion between the living and the deceased, who after cremation would no longer be able to return and molest them. Nor does it appear that in these extreme cases their remedy encountered any serious ecclesiastical opposition. The people argued that since the Christian rite had proved to a certain extent ineffectual, for the vampire returned from his grave, it was surely permissible to employ other and more drastic measures, even if such might be tainted with heathenism. In the case of an epidemic or a plague it was allowable to burn the bodies lest the pestilence should be spread. Assuredly it was equally allowable to burn the body of a monster who would sparge the infection of vampirism. And this argument was tacitly conceded. Indeed, the priests in the remoter villages and loné country districts would, no doubt, be as anxious as the people to rid themselves of the *vyrkolakas*, and almost any means would be considered legitimate and approved. When cases came to the ears of a Bishop, they met with some pretty severe censure, especially in later days. But it was quite within the power of a Bishop to give leave for the body of a vampire to be exhumed and burned. Just as now, if exceptional circumstances demand it, a Bishop may permit cremation. The Greeks judged that those of the dead who returned and who suffered from incorruptibility must be helped, and the one certain way in which dissolution which secured them rest and repose could most certainly be effected was cremation. Not a measure to be adopted lightly, but nevertheless a measure which, if inevitable, was an act of charity both to the living and to the dead.

Of the travellers in Greece, from the seventeenth century when their voyages were first recorded in detail, down to the present day, there are few, if any, who have not spoken of the *vrykolakas* or vampire. The important evidence of Father François Richard and of Tournefort has already been recorded. Paul Lucas, whose *Voyage au Levant* was published at the Hague in 1705, thus writes his observations in the island of Corfu. " Des personnes qui paroissent avoir le bon sens parlent d'un fait assez singulier qui arrive souvent en ce pays, aussi bien que dans l'Isle Santeriny ; des gens morts, disent-ils, reviennent, se sont voir en plein jour, & vont meme chex eux, ce qui cause de grandes frayeurs à ceux qui les voyent. C'est ce qui fait que quand il en paroit quelqu'un, on va promptement au cimetière deterrer le cadavre, on le coupe par morceaux, & ensuite on le brule par Sentence des Gouverneurs & Magistrats. Cela fait ces morts pretendus ne reviennent plus. Monsieur Angelo Edmé, Provediteur & Gouverneur de l'Isle, m'assura lui-meme avoir donné une pareille Sentence, ou il se trouvoit plus de cinquante personnes raisonnables qui assuroient le fait."[78] (" Several persons who seemed to be thoroughly sensible relate an extraordinary fact which often happens in this place, as also in the island of Santorini. According to what they say dead men return and appear in open day, even going into the various houses and terribly alarming those who set eyes on them. In consequence of this, whenever any one of these apparitions is seen the authorities proceed at once to the cemetery to exhume the corpse, it is cut up into tiny gobbets, and finally it is burned by the official sentence of the Governors and Magistrates. Once this is done these dead men or semi-dead men never return again. Monsieur Angelo Edmé, Warden and Governor of the Island, assured me that he himself had actually pronounced sentence in a case of this kind, where more than fifty responsible and entirely trustworthy individuals were found unanimously to testify to the facts.")

It will not be out of place here to quote a most interesting passage from the *Viaggio in Dalmazia* of the Abate Giovanni Battista Alberto Fortis.[74] This portion of the book is addressed to a member of a noble Venetian house, Morisini. The Abbate writes : " *Of the Superstition of the Morlacchi.* The Morlacks, whether they happen to be of the Roman, or of the Greek church, have very singular ideas about religion ; and the ignorance of their teachers daily augments this monstrous evil. They are firmly perswaded of the reality of witches, fairies, enchantments, nocturnal apparitions and sortileges, as if they had seen a thousand examples of them. Nor do they make the least doubt about the existence of Vampires ; and attribute to them, as in Transilvania, the sucking the blood of infants. Therefore when a man dies suspected of becoming a vampire, or *Vukodlak*, as they call it, they cut his hams, and prick his whole body with pins ; pretending, that after this operation he cannot walk about. There are even instances of Morlacchi who, imagining that they may possibly thirst for children's blood after death, intreat their heirs, and sometimes oblige them, to treat them as vampires when they die.

" The boldest Haiduc would fly trembling from the appar- ition of a spectre, ghost, phantom, or such like goblins as the heated imagination of credulous and prepossessed people never fail to see. Nor are they ashamed, when ridiculed for this terror, but answer, much in the words of Pindar : ' fear that proceeds from spirits, causes even the sons of the Gods to fly.'[75] The women, as may be naturally supposed, are a

hundred times more timorous and visionary than the men ;
and some of them, by frequently hearing themselves called
witches, actually believe they are so. The old witches are
acquainted with many spells ; and one of the most common
is to transfer the milk of other people's cows to their own. But
they can perform more curious feats than this ; and I
know a young man, who had his heart taken out by two
witches while he was fast asleep, in order to be roasted and
eat by them. The poor man did not perceive his loss, as may
easily be imagined, till he awoke ; but then he began to complain of feeling the place of his heart void ; a begging friar,
who lay in the same place but was not asleep, beheld the whole
anatomical operation of the witches, but could not hinder
them because they had charmed him.[76] The charm, however,
lost its force when the young man without the heart awoke,
and both wanted to chastise the witches ; but they, rubbing
themselves with a certain ointment, flew away. The friar
went to the hearth, took the heart, then well broiled, and gave
it to the young man to eat ; which he had no sooner done, than
he was perfectly cured, as may reasonably be supposed. The
good father told this story, and will tell it often, swearing to
the truth of it ; and the people dare not suspect that wine had
made him see one thing or another, and that the two women,
one of whom was not old, had flown away for quite another
reason than for being witches. The enchantresses are called
Gestize ; and that the remedy may be at hand, there are others
called *Babornize*, equally well skilled in undoing the spells ;
and to doubt to these two opposite powers, would be worse
than infidelity."

Rather more than half-a-century after the good abate Pashley
tells the following story in his *Travels in Crete* (1837):[77] "Once
on a time the village of Kalikráti, in the district of Sfakiá,
was haunted by a Katakhanás, and people did not know what
man he was or from what part. This Katakhanás destroyed
both children and many full grown men ; and desolated both
that village and many others. They had buried him at the
church of Saint George at Kalikráti, and in those times he was
a man of note, and they had built an arch over his grave.
Now a certain shepherd, his mutual Sýnteknos,[78] was tending
his sheep and goats near the church, and, on being caught by
a shower, he went to the sepulchre, that he might be shaded

from the rain. Afterwards he determined to sleep, and to pass the night there, and, after taking off his arms, he placed them by the stone which served him as his pillow, crosswise. And people might say, that it is on this account[79] that the Katakhanás was not permitted to leave his tomb. During the night, then, as he wished to go out again, that he might destroy men, he said to the shepherd : ' Gossip, get up hence, for I have some business that requires me to come out.' The shepherd answered him not, either the first time, or the second, or the third ; for thus he knew that the man had become a Katakhanás, and that it was he who had done all those evil deeds. On this account he said to him, on the fourth time of his speaking, ' I shall not get up hence, gossip, for I fear that you are no better than you should be, and may do me some mischief : but, if I must get up, swear to me by your winding-sheet, that you will not hurt me, and on this I will get up.' And he did not pronounce the proposed words,[80] but said other things : nevertheless, when the shepherd did not suffer him to get up, he swore to him as he wished. On this he got up and taking his arms removed them away from the monument and the Katakhanás came forth and after greeting the shepherd said to him ' Gossip, you must not go away, but sit down here ; for I have some business which I must go after ; but I shall return within the hour, for I have something to say to you.' So the shepherd waited for him.

"And the Katakhanás went a distance of about ten miles, where there was a couple recently married, and he destroyed them. On his return, his gossip saw that he was carrying some liver, his hands being moistened with blood : and, as he carried it, he blew into it, just as the butcher does, to increase the size of the liver. And he showed his gossip that it was cooked, as if it had been done on the fire. After this he said, ' Let us sit down, gossip, that we may eat.' And the shepherd pretended to eat it, but only swallowed dry bread, and kept dropping the liver into his bosom. Therefore, when the hour for their separation arrived, the Katakhanás said to the shepherd, ' Gossip, this which you have seen, you must not mention, for, if you do, my twenty nails will be fixed in your children and yourself.' Yet the shepherd lost no time, but gave information to priests, and others, and they went to the tomb, and there they found the Katakhanás, just as he had been buried. And all the people became satisfied that it was he who had done all the evil deeds. On this account they collected a great deal of wood, and they cast him on it, and burnt him. His gossip was not present, but, when the Katakhanás was already half consumed, he too came forward in order that he might enjoy the ceremony. And the Katakhanás cast, as it were, a single spot of blood, and it fell on his foot, which wasted away, as if it had been roasted on a fire. On this account they sifted even the ashes, and found the little finger-nail of the Katakhanás unburnt, and burnt it too."

"I have heard," continues our author, "other Katakhanádhes spoken of at Anopolis as having made terrible ravages: Καὶ προτήτερος ἄῤῥος ἕνας—καὶ ὅσους κὰν ἀποθάνασι τῇ ἔπερνα, καὶ ἐγυρίσασι (ἄῤῥοι Καταχανάδες) κὰι ἐπηράσασι ποῤῥοὺς ἀνθρώπους."

Pashley further remarks: "We also find traces of a principal similar to that in which the modern superstition had its rise, in Plato: he speaks, in the Phaedo, of certain obscure phantasms belonging to impure souls, which had been unable wholly to free themselves from their fleshy prison-house, and which haunted tombs.[81] Plato, however, assigns no such blood-sucking propensities to these phantasms, as are attributed to the modern Vampire.

"It is impossible to leave the subject without regretting our loss of the works of Damascius, among which there was one book 'respecting. the souls which appear after death.' His writings seem, by the admission of the Patriarch Photius, to have possessed considerable literary merit, and would doubtless have made a great addition to the demonology of the ancients."[82]

A few pages later Mr. Pashley relates the following history: "My hostess here, at Anopolis, was once traversing the mountains, accompanied by one of her daughters, and, when about three miles from the village of Muri, they heard sounds as of voices singing ('Ωσαν τραγὸνδι), but it was impossible to distinguish what were the words uttered ("Ομως δὲν ἐκαθαρίσθη τὶ εἶπεν). The demon, for such she supposed the unseen object of her alarm to be, then began to throw stones, which fell both before and behind them. Although she saw him not, yet she immediately pronounced aloud some holy text, which are a never failing charm against any common demon (Δαίμονας).

When she found that the evil spirit continued to sing, and to cast stones at them, she knew that it must be a Katakhanás ; and, therefore, crossing herself, and calling on the Holy Mother of God, she immediately repeated : ' In the beginning was the Word, and the Word was with God, and the Word was God.' (Ἐν αρχῇ ἦν ὁ ῥόγος, καὶ ὁ ῥόγος ἦν πρὸς τοῦ θεόν, καὶ θεὸς ἦν ὁ ῥόγος.). This sentence she pronounced twice, but it was all in vain : the Katakhanás kept rolling down the stones as before. (Ἐρρήκετεε τζῂ πέτραις.) She next repeated a part of the Greek ritual, which produced no better effect. (She said it from the ἦχος of the Panaghia, and began thus : Ἄγγελος πρωτοστάτης οὐρανου, etc.) The Katakhanás continued to persecute and terrify her. At length, on seeing two women, as she approached the village, she summoned courage enough to address him in a bolder strain, and, on her doing so, he ceased to molest her. (Her words were : Ἔξελθέ, διάβολέ, ἀπὸ μᾶς, διατὶ θὰ σοῦ βάρρω τὸ ῥαβδί μου εἰς τὸ κώλο σου : as soon as she said this, ἔγενε ἄθαντος.) "

We here have a vampire of the less malignant kind who indulges in many of the tricks of the poltergeist. It should be remarked also that he is appearing during the day, he is the *deamonium meridianum* ' the noon-day devil of the Psalmist.'[83] Mr. James Theodore Bent in a paper read before the Anthropological Institute, 24 November, 1885, *On Insular Greek Custom*,[84] mentioned the vampire and some cognate traditions.

" In this village [in Naxos] they actually retain a trace of the old ' obolos for Charon,' the freight money. It is only in the name ναῦλον, ' freight money,' which they give to the little wax cross, with I X N Ἰησοῦς Χριστὸς νικᾶ, ' Jesus Christ conquers,' engraved thereon, which is put on the closed lips of the deceased. Thus has Christianity adapted to itself the pagan ritual. In Byzantine times, long after the introduction of Christianity, coins of the Eastern Empire have been found in tombs, placed on the skulls.

" Scattered amongst the islands are various customs connected with burial which carry us back into the past. At Seriphos each landowner is buried in a tomb on his own field, built like a little shrine. I never saw this custom in any other island, except Corsica, and it reminded one of the days when an Athenian left in his will instructions that he should be buried in his own land.

" In one village of Karpathos they bury their dead in tombs attached to the churches and belonging to various families. In these the body of a defunct member is deposited without any earth, and then allowed to decay, so that a noisome odour is generally the result in hot weather ; into the cement at the top of this tomb they insert plates. I asked the reason of this, and none whatsoever could be given ; it is evidently a survival of the old feast for the dead, which was laid out in the tombs. It was a curious coincidence that in some ancient tombs which I opened not far from this very village I found the plates thus set out with bones of fishes and traces of other food on them which had been there for over two thousand years.

" Many of the ceremonies concerning burial are of ancient origin ; there are the κόλλυβα, that is to say, boiled wheat, adorned with sugar plums, honey, sesame, basil, etc., which are presented to the dead. Sometimes they call these μακάρια, or blessed cakes, out of euphony no doubt ; these κόλλυβα are put on the tombs on stated days after the decease with additional lamentations, and remind one forcibly of the ancient feasts for the dead which are likewise offered on stated days, and the idea of offering boiled wheat is but a survival of that embodied in the story of Demeter and her daughter, and expressed in Christian language by ' sown in corruption and raised in incorruption.'

" Then again the vampire dread is widely extant still in the isles of Greece, the belief that a wicked man cannot rest after death ; they say that if the flesh is not decayed off the bones at the expiration of a year, when they are removed from the tomb to a charnel house, the spirit of the deceased wanders about, and ' feeds on his own,' as the expression goes, that is to say, he sucks the blood of his relatives, and thereby derives force for his ghostly wanderings. This reminds one of Homer's story that the shades of Hades believed that by filling themselves with blood they could return to life, and consequently eagerly lapped up the blood of slaughtered sheep."

Sir Rennell Rodd in his extremely interesting studies *The Customs and Lore of Modern Greece* (David Stott, London, 1892), deals with the vampire at some length, and it will not be impertinent to quote what he has so excellently expressed. " Another mysterious evil spirit of antiquity, the *Gillo*, whose

origin may be traced to the island of Lesbos, is frequently
alluded to by mediæval writers. More universal to-day is the
dread of the *Strigla* (στρίγλαις), the *Strix* of the Romans. In
modern Italy the *Strega*, like the Greek *Strigla*, is looked upon
as a witch-woman, who has the power of changing her form,
and flying by night in the shape of a crow, sucking human
blood, with breath of deadly poison ; distinct, however, from
the vampire, which is generally held to be a material resuscita-
tion of a dead person, while the Strigla is a living being who
has assumed a birdlike form. This view of the Strix is
curiously illustrated by a law of Charlemagne's[85] for the
province of Saxony, which decrees the penalty of capital
punishment on any ' who led away by the devil to believe,
after the manner of pagans, that a certain man or woman be a
Strix, and feed upon human beings, should therefore burn
such, or distribute their flesh to be eaten, or eat thereof himself.' Such it appears was the barbarous antidote, as it
formerly was in Russia and Poland against the vampire, where
blood of the body from which it was supposed to emanate was
eaten in a paste of meal.

" The modern Strix appears more rarely in a masculine form
(στρίγλος), and the name is applied as an epithet of hatred or
contempt to old men as well as to aged crones who have an
uncanny reputation. In this application it is about equivalent
to our witch.

" The genuine vampire is the Vourkólakas, of whom a
number of stories are still current, though Colonel Leake more
than fifty years ago expressed the opinion that it would be
difficult in Greece to find anyone who still believed in such a
barbarous superstition. The Albanians call it Wurwolakas,
and the name has a number of slightly varying forms in
different parts of Greece. The word itself is undoubtedly of
Slavonic origin, being found in Bohemia, Dalmatia, Montenegro, Servia, and Bulgaria ; while it appears as Vilkolak
among the Poles, with the signification rather of weirwolf than
vampire. The superstition itself is, however, of extreme
antiquity, and the name only was introduced by the Sclavonic
immigrants, for we find the vampire in Crete and Rhodes
where the Sclaves never penetrated, under the name of
Katakhanas (καταχανὰς), the ' destroyer,' in Tenos as the
Anakathoumenos (Ανακαθόυμενος), the ' snatcher,'[86] and

again in Cyprus as the Sarkomenos (Σαρκομένος), a name implying either that the dead body from which the vampire issues has retained its flesh, or that it must be gorged with flesh."

It will not escape notice how Leake remarks that the tradition of the vampire may be thought to be dying out is flatly contradicted by all authorities. Sir Rennell Rodd proceeds to trace the history of the vampire in classical sources, in the *Iliad* (xxiii. 181, etc.) ; the *Odyssey* (ix, 48, etc.) ; and more particularly in Pausanias. From the latter he quotes the well-known instance of the " demon " of Temesa and the story " how the land of Orchomenus was afflicted by a spectre, which sat upon a stone, and that when the oracle was consulted, its answer was that the men of Orchomenos should search for and bury the remains of Actaeon ; make a brazen image of the spectre, and fasten it to the stone." " Finally, the Mormo, the Empusa, and the Lamia possessed the blood-sucking reputation of the vampire in the popular superstitions of antiquity."

Sir Rennell Rodd resumes : " And here it may be mentioned that the Vourkolakas is not invariably the blood-sucking vampire in recent tradition, but that the name is sometimes extended to include mere spectres of the departed who return to earth, and that in this sense, at any rate, the superstition is by no means so extinct as Colonel Leake appears to have believed. In the memoirs of N. Nicholas Dragoumis[87] there is an interesting account of its effect on the population of Naxos, where early in the thirties a cholera epidemic had carried off a great number of victims. The rumour was circulated that the Naxian dead in the other world were so numerous that they had overpowered Charos [the lord of the dead],[88] and were coming back again to earth to take possession of their own. The fear of these Vourkolakas, as they call them, was so great that the inhabitants rushed to their houses at sunset, barred doors and windows, and piled furniture against them ; but often in vain, for the spectres entered through the key-holes and scared the living for many an anxious day."

It will be remembered that in a preceeding chapter I have mentioned the fear of vampires which thrilled Danzig during the terrible cholera visitation of 1855. Many persons finding themselves languid and ill with anxiety, although they had not actually been infected by the disease, declared that they had been attacked by malignant vampires, that the dead returned to fetch them, and no inconsiderable numbers incontinently expired of their own panics and affrightments with no sign of the prevailing sickness.

"The Vourkolakas," continues Sir Rennell Rodd, "is, however, generally ravenous." The Vourkolakas who returns as a mere spectre, however alarming such an appearance may be, is not, of course, the true vampire. In the account given by M. Nicholas Dragoumis of the occurrences at Naxos emphasis is laid upon the ghastly and horrible looks of these apparitions. They seem thin and fearfully emaciated, in a starving condition as it were. Food is their most urgent demand, and often they will rob eggs, even poultry and cattle. This craving for nourishment is a link, which may not be purely accidental although it has infiltrated through many a devious source, with the Assyrian vampire who ravens to satisfy the pangs of hunger. When they are bent upon human prey it is with their nearest relatives that the monsters begin. If men are at home they will be the first to be attacked, perhaps as being the stronger and more vigorous, and they generally die from these assaults. If the male folk are abroad in the fields, the vampires ravish the women, and curiously enough the objects of their lust are held to survive, nay, even to bear children to their loathly paramours.[89]

In Greece one still hears that the island of Hydra[90] was "once upon a time" infested by vampires, but a zealous primate by his prayers and exorcisms banished them all to Therasia in the Santorini group, and here they walk up and down all night long, since they are unable to cross the salt water to seek their prey. He who is daring enough to venture too near the shore may hear their piercing shrieks and unearthly yells, cries which always herald a coming storm or even some more terrible disturbance of nature.

A Cretan informed Sir Rennell Rodd that those at whose baptism some portion of the ceremony had been left incomplete will certainly become vampires ; and in Cephalonia marriage with a Koumbáros[91] is said to have the same effect. Having given at length from Pashley the story of the Katakhanas, which has been narrated a little above, Sir Rennell Rodd adds : "Pashley's experience, of course, dates back a good many years, but I was myself told a story in Crete of a man well known to my informant, who had the power of foretelling when people were going to die. From time to time this man would fall ill in a mysterious manner, and his invariable explanation was that the dead whose doom he had foretold were returning as Katakhanades to torment him in various manners, though it would seem rather as ghosts of the common sort than as vampires, and in this explanation he appeared to be perfectly sincere."

In his very particular study of the folk-lore of the isle of Kythnos[92] M. Henry Hauttecoeur tells us that the islanders hold many diseases, particularly consumption, to be a result of the attacks of vampires. "Pour la phtisie pulmonaire il y a longtemps que les Kythniotes en on trouve le microbe. De même qu'à Andros il s'imaginent que ce sont de mauvais ésprits, qu'ils appellent Erynies, qui dévorent les parties vitales des poumons, et, lorsque le malade vient à mourir, on prend toutes les precautions necessaires pour chasser ces nouveaux anthropophages. Personne ne peut entrer dans la chambre du mort, avant que l'on ait fait un trou dans le plafond au-dessus du lit du défunt. Les Erynies s'évaporent par cette issue et la maison est deliverée de tout danger."[93]

According to M. Hauttecoeur the people of Kythnos believe that should a body rapidly fall to dust the deceased must be a veritable saint, and it is generally supposed that the evil apparitions which haunt the island are none other than the souls of those wretched beings whose bodies remain in a mummified condition. "And yet some say there are no ghosts at all nowadays because they boast that they have found a fine way to prevent any ghost from appearing. What is a ghost, indeed, but simply the devil who takes possession of a corpse, making his entry through the dead man's mouth. Very well, then, in order to prevent any such public misfortune there is only one thing to be done, and that is to place in the mouth of a dead person, as soon as he has breathed his last sigh, a little cross made out of wax. The devil would never dare to pass over the cross. And so there are no more ghosts who are able to appear. Yet in spite of this panacea apparitions are still seen on the island of Kythnos, not as many perhaps as there used to be in the good old days, but yet there are some ghosts left. Andilaveris, for instance, everybody on the island knew all about him, . . . he was the most vexatious.

Without the slightest consideration for the high esteem in which his family and his relations were so deservedly held, he unmercifully plagued the whole village. At night he came out of his grave and he used to walk up and down every street in Messaria.[94] Sometimes he would even make his way into a house, he would sit down at table, he would eat like a hungry giant and drink like a fish, and then when he had gorged his fill of wine and swallowed all the dainties he pleased, he used to amuse himself by smashing the plates and the glasses, by clattering the pots and the pans, howling horribly all the while like a mad werewolf.

"The whole place was in a state of frenzied panic; directly dusk fell the people one and all shut themselves up in their houses behind locked doors and nobody dared to set foot abroad. The women whose husbands were away used to go and sleep at the homes of their parents. Never was there known such a vicious devil as this Andilaveris. He used to laugh at everybody, and defied the very Saints in Heaven. On certain days he would take it in his head to climb up on to the roof of the Church, and from that height he would drench those who passed underneath with floods of urine, staling away like the Manneken-Pis himself.[95] Before long it was found necessary to adopt those drastic remedies which are generally employed to destroy the vampirish apparitions that are wont to wander abroad at night. Andilaveris was not content then to remain quietly in his grave. Very well, in a little while he would find out to his cost exactly what they were going to do to him. A Friday was chosen[96] as being the only day of the week when the *Broukolakes*, these apparitions, remain in their graves. The village priest, the sexton, and a number of other persons went to the cemetery and opened his tomb. They took the body which was fast asleep, comatose as a snake replete with food, and they bundled it into an old sack which they had brought along with them, putting their horrid burden on the back of a sturdy mule. The little procession took its way to the sea-side hamlet of Bryocastro. Immediately all went on board a barque which was awaiting them, and they conveyed their fardel to the tiny islet of Daskaleio. There the priest buried the body in a remote and lonely spot, but this was not done without much difficulty. Andilaveris, who no doubt guessed what was happening to him, awoke from his weekly slumber, and attacked the good priest with vollies of mud and ordure.   But in the end they came back home with the satisfaction of knowing that they had freed their town from the visitations of this foul spectre, for never can a *vrykolakas* cross the sea.   It is written[97] that only ' the spirit of God moved over the waters.' "[98]

In the vast collections of folk-lore made by Professor Polites there occur no inconsiderable number of contemporary histories of vampires in Greece to-day.   It is true, as remarked a little before, that for obvious reasons the old practice of burning bodies has been perforce discontinued, and recourse is had, not altogether willingly, to other expedients.   It must always be borne in mind that exhumation after three years' burial is an established rite of the Greek Church.   In Scyros, for example, a body found incorrupt is to-day carried round to forty churches in turn, and then once more replaced in its grave.   In parts of Crete, in Kynthos, and in several of the islands it is the custom to convey the corpse to a tomb on some completely deserted and uninhabited islet.[99]   But these measures obviously do not commend themselves to the people.   In 1890 a paragraph appeared in the Athenian Press relating that the body of a vampire had just been burned in a deme of the island of Andros, and if one may trust word of mouth this is by no means the last example of such an occurrence.   A Greek scholar who has written a series of monographs upon the Cyclades, gives as his opinion : " The ignorant peasant of Andros believes to this day that the corpse can rise again and do him hurt ; and is not this belief in *vrykolakes* general throughout Greece ? "[100]   In Kynthos the names of several persons, including a woman, who became *vrykolakes* are still remembered with terror, and it is suspected that their bodies were disposed of in the traditional manner.[101]   When Mr. Lawson visited Scyros in 1900 he heard of several fairly recent cases of vampirism,[102] and I myself when staying in the island a few years later was told of more than one vampire whose ravages had only just been checked, if indeed, they had really ceased, which many doubted.   Of course, I am unable to say whether these examples were several histories or the same instances.

Mr. James Theodore Bent, who visited Andros about 1884, tells us that only a few months before he came to that island the grave of a suspected *vrykolakas* was opened by a priest, the body exhumed, cut into smallest gobbets, and cremated.[103]

In January, 1895, at Mandoudi[104] in Euboea, a woman was supposed to have become a vampire and to be the cause of many deaths throughout the district. The peasants resolved to disinter the body and burn it, which there is reason to believe was effected.[105] In this neighbourhood I myself heard oral traditions of vampires at the hamlets of S. Anna, and at Kokkinimilia, a tiny thorp beyond which is reached by a mule path passing through some magnificent forest scenery. Mr. Lawson writes : " In 1899, when I was in Santorini, I was told that two or three years previously the inhabitants of Therasia had burnt a *Vrykolakas*, and when I visited that island the incident was not denied, but the responsibility for it was laid upon the people of Santorini."[106] Professor Polites records a similar case of burning a vampire at Gourzoumisa near Patras.[107] That similar cremations take place in Greek villages at the present time, though under conditions of secrecy which is year by year more strictly observed, cannot reasonably be doubted.

Mr. Lawson has translated[108] the following passage from a history of the district of Sphakiá in Crete, written by the hegumenos of a monastery there and published in 1888 :

" It is popularly believed that most of the dead, those who have lived bad lives or who have been excommunicated by some priest (or, worse still, by seven priests together, τὸ ἑπταπάπαδον) become *vrykolakes* ; that is to say, after the separation of the soul from the body there enters into the latter an evil spirit, which takes the place of the soul and assumes the shape of the dead man and so is transformed into a *vrykolakas* or man demon.

" In this guise it keeps the body as its dwelling-place and preserves it from corruption, and it runs swift as lightning wherever it lists, and causes men great alarms at night and strikes all with panic. And the trouble is that it does not remain solitary, but makes everyone, who dies while it is about, like to itself, so that in a short space of time it gets together a large and dangerous train of followers. The common practice of the *vrykolakes* is to seat themselves upon those who are asleep and by their enormous weight to cause an agonizing sense of oppression. There is great danger that the sufferer in such cases may expire, and himself too be turned into a *vrykolakas*, if there be not someone at hand who perceives his torment and fires off a gun, thereby putting the blood-thirsty monster to flight ; for fortunately it is afraid of the report of fire-arms and retreats without effecting its purpose. Not a few such scenes we have witnessed with our own eyes.

" This monster, as time goes on, becomes more and more audacious and blood-thirsty, so that it is able completely to devastate whole villages. On this account all possible haste is made to annihilate the first which appears before it enter upon its second period of forty days.[109] because by that time it becomes a merciless and invincible dealer of death. To this end the villagers call in priests who profess to know how to annihilate the monster—for a consideration. These impostors proceed after service to the tomb, and if the monster be not found there—for it goes to and fro molesting men—they summon it in authoritative tones to enter its dwelling-place ; and, as soon as it is come, it is imprisoned there by virtue of some prayer and subsequently breaks up. With its disruption all those who have been turned into *vrykolakes* by it, wherever they may be, suffer the same lot as their leader.

" This absurd superstition is rife and vigorous throughout Crete and especially in the mountainous and secluded parts of the island."

To talk of " absurd superstition " is well enough, and undoubtedly many of the details here given are exaggerated both in the telling and in the imaginations of the country folk, but for all this the Vampire tradition has a very genuine substratum, and something more than a substratum, of truth. Mr. Lawson has well said : " The ' educated ' Greek, whose pose is to despise the traditions of the common-folk, will discourse upon them no less tediously than inaccurately for the sake of having his vapourings put on record,"[110] and I have no doubt this good hegumenos of Crete shone as vastly modern, scientific, and superior in his own conceit.

The Vampire is a malignant thing, and although the following poem is entitled *The Vrykolakas* it is not a true Vampire who is the subject. Nevertheless it may be given here, since it is considered one of the finest of all the Romaic ballads. It exists in many versions, of which the one selected by Passow in his *Carmina Popularia*[111] runs :

" A mother had nine gallant sons, and one beloved daughter,
One only daughter, dearly prized, the darling of her bosom ;
For twelve long years she suffered not the sun to rest upon her,

But washed her at the fall of night, and combed her locks ere
    daybreak ;
And while the stars were still on high ranged them in dainty
    tresses.
Now, when there came an embassy from a far distant country,
And sought to lead her as a bride into the land of strangers,
Eight of her brothers were averse, but Constantine approved it :
' Nay send her, mother mine,' he said, ' into the land of
    strangers ;
To the far country I frequent, where I am wont to travel ;
So I shall gain a resting-place, a comfortable mansion.'
' Prudent you are, my son,' she said, ' but your advice is evil.
What if fell sickness visit me, or gloomy death approach me,
Or joy or sorrow be my lot, who then shall fetch her for me ? '
He sware to her by God on high and by the holy martyrs,
That if dark death should visit her, or sickness fall upon her,
Or joy or sorrow be her lot, he would go forth to fetch her.
And so she sent her Arete into the land of strangers.
But when there came a season fraught with pestilential sickness,
And they were struck with fell disease, and the nine brothers
    perished,
Then, like a bulrush in the plain, the mother sat deserted.
At all their tombs she beat her breast and raised her lamenta-
    tion ;
But when she came to Constantine's she lifted up the grave-
    stone,
And ' Rise,' she cried, ' my Constantine ; I need my darling
    daughter.
Didst thou not swear by God on high, and by the holy martyrs,
When joy or grief became my lot, that thou wouldst go to fetch
    her ? '

Lo ! from his tomb—there, where he lay,—her invocation
    raised him.
He rode upon the stormy cloud, the stars bedecked his bridle ;
His escort was the shining moon ; and thus he went to fetch her.
Before his flight the mountains rose, and disappeared behind
    him.
Till he beheld her where she combed her tresses in the moon-
    light.
Then from afar he called to her, and from afar he hailed her :
' Come with me ; come, my Arete ! our mother calleth for thee.'
' Alas ! ' she answered, ' brother dear, at such an hour as this is !
Say is thy summons one of joy ? shall I put on my jewels ?
Or, if 'tis gloomy, tell me so, and I'll not change my garments.'
' Come with me ; come, my Arete ! wait not to change thy
    garments ! '

Then as they passed along the road, accomplishing their journey,
The birds began to sing aloud, and this was what they uttered :

' O strange ! a spirit of the dead leading a lovely lady ! '

' O listen, Constantine,' she said, ' to what the birds are singing :

' " O strange ! a spirit of the dead leading a lovely lady ! " '

' Regard them not, the silly birds ; regard them not, my sister.'

So they passed on ; but, as they passed, again the birds were
    singing,

' O wondrous pitiable sight ! O mystery of sadness,

To see the spirits of the dead walking beside the living ! '

' O listen, listen, brother dear, to what the birds are singing :

' " Behold the spirits of the dead walking beside the living ! " '

' Regard them not, poor birds,' he said ; ' regard them not my
    sister.'

' Alas ! I fear thee, brother mine ! thy garments smell of
    incense ! '

' 'Tis naught,' he said ; ' on yestereve we worshipped at the
    altar,

And there the priest, in passing by, fumed me with clouds of
    incense.'

And once again, as they passed on, yet other birds were singing,

' Almighty God ! thine hand it is this miracle that worketh,

To send a spirit of the dead to lead this lovely lady.'

She heard the voices as they spake, and her heart sank within
    her.

' O listen, listen, Constantine, to what the birds are singing !

Say, where are now thy golden hair, and flowing fair
    moustaches ? '

' A wasting sickness fell on me, near to the grave it brought me ;

'Twas then I lost my golden hair and flowing fair moustaches.'

They came ; and lo ! the door was closed, the bolt was drawn
    before it,

And the barred windows, one and all, with spiders' webs were
    tangled,

' Open,' he cried, ' my mother dear ! behold I bring thy
    daughter ! '

' If thou beest Charon, come not here ; I have no other children.

My Arete, unhappy one ! lodges far off with strangers ! '

' Open, my mother ! tarry not ; 'tis Constantine that speaketh !

Did I not swear by God on high, and by the holy martyrs,

When grief or joy became thy lot, that I would go to fetch her ? '

She rose ; and as she reached the door the mother's soul
    departed ! "

NOTES. CHAPTER IV

[1] Bernhard Schmidt entirely rejects such a derivation ; *Das Volksleben der Neugriechen und das Hellenische Alterthum*, p. 158.

[2] Mr. Lawson notes " Whether this word is originally Slavonic appears to be uncertain but it is at any rate found in all Slavonic languages and is proved by the forms which it has assumed to have been in use there for fully a thousand years."—*Modern Greek Folklore*, p. 378, n.3.

[3] Lawson, *op. cit.*, p. 378.

[4] Abbott, p. 217.

[5] *Das Volksleben der Neugriechen*, p. 159.

[6] Schmidt, *op. cit.*, p. 159.

[7] W. Mannhardt, *Zeitschrift für deutsche Mythologie und Sittenkunde*, IV, 195. (1859).

[8] I, p. 69. Paris, 1844.

[9] *Op. cit.*, p. 159, n.2.

[10] " Drum-like," since the body is inflated like a balloon and the skin stretched taut like parchment. The word yet survives in the island of Kynthos (Thermia).

[11] Because the body has " put on flesh," being puffed out and flabber. This term is, if not peculiar to, at least general in Cyprus, where the word *vrykolakas* continues in some cases at any rate to have its original significa-tion " werewolf." For σαρκωμένος see Schmidt (*op. cit.*, p. 160) who refers to a periodical Φιλίστωρ, III, p. 359 ; and also Professor Polites, Παραδόσεις τοῦ ἑλληνικοῦ λαοῦ, I, p. 574.

[12] One who " sits up " in his grave. In many legends when a *vrykolakas* is exhumed he is found to be sitting upright in his grave. See Polites, *op. cit.*, I, p. 590.

[13] Koräes, 'Ατακα, II, p. 114, who is followed by Schmidt, would interpret this as " the destroyer," but Lawson with more probability suggests " the gaper " or " the one whose mouth yawns wide " since a gaping mouth and gleaming teeth are eminently characteristic of Vampires. In Allacci's phrase *os hians, dentes candidi*.

[14] Lawson, *op. cit.*, p. 384. As has been noted above to-day the word is only use in Kynthos.

[15] Cambridge, 1619.

[16] " Ελλην παλαιὸς ἱστορικός," who has not been certainly identified.

[17] Christophorus Angelus relates the story of a bishop who was excom-municated by an episcopal council and whose body endured " bound, like iron, for a hundred years " until another council of bishops at the same place absolved him when the body immediately fell to dust.

[18] Lawson, *op. cit.*, pp. 374-75.

[19] Τίνεται ἀφορισμένος ἀπὸ τὴν πίστιν του. Several forms of excom-munication, in which the offender is condemned to remain μετὰ θάνατου ἄλυτος αἰωνίως ὡς αἱ πέτραι καὶ τὰ σίδηρα are given by Christophorus Angelus, Ricaut, and Goar. (*On the Greek Euchology*, p. 688) all cited by J. M. Heineccius *De absolutione Mortuorum excommunicatorum seu tympani-corum in Ecclesia Græca* (Helmstad, 1709), pp. 10-13. The ministers of religion, who claimed the power of thus preventing a body from returning to dust, naturally held, that when *they* absolve the dead offender, it ought at once to become decomposed. It is said that this used always to be the case. A remarkable instance of the exercise of this power is quoted (of which Mohammed the Second is said to have been a witness), by Crusius, *Turco-Græcia*, ii, pp. 27-28. Goar, *Eucholog. Graec.*, p. 689. Allatius, l.c. Bzovius, in the year 1481, n. 19 and other authors cited in J. M. Heineccius, *De absolutione*, &c., p. 16.

[20] Οἱ 'Υδραῖα, who are commonly called Hydhriotes by European writers : I have adopted the name by which they are known to all who speak Greek.

[21] Vol. II, pp. 200-202.

[22] Santorini (Thera) is situated about 60 miles north of Crete and rather more than 12 miles south of Ios. The circumference of the island is some 30 miles. It owes its present name of Santorini to the patron Saint Irene who was martyred here in 304. " Cette Sainte étoit de Thessalonique, et y fut martyrisée le premier jour d'Avril en 304 sous le neuviéme consulat de Diocletien, et le huitiéme de Maximien Hercule : l'église latine en celebre la fête le même jour à Santorin, c'est le 5 May, ou il y a encore neuf ou dix chapelles dediées à Sainte Irene " (Tournefort).

[23] Seventh edition, 1900, pp. 924-25.

[24] The phrase " as common as coals from Newcastle," occurs in Heywood's drama, *If You Know Not Me You Know Nobodie, or, The Troubles of Queen Elizabeth*, Part II, 4to, 1606. John Graunt in the Dedication to his *Observations upon the Bills of Mortality*, London, 4to, 1661, has " to carry coals to Newcastle."

[25] Παραδόσεις, I, pp. 573 and 593. " In Mitylene the bones of those who will not lie quiet in their graves are transported to a small adjacent island, where they are re-interred. This is an effectual bar to all future vagaries, for the Vampire cannot cross salt-water." H. F. Tozer, *Researches in the Highlands of Turkey*, vol. II, p. 90.

[26] Cologne, 1645.

[27] Particularly pp. 142-158.

[28] Allacci was born on Chios in 1586 and his observations were chiefly made on, as his information is generally derived from, his native island.

[29] Allacci, *op. cit.*, p. 142. " Et haec ferenda uidentur, si unum excipias Burculacam ; alii Bulcolaccam uocant ; quo sane in genus humanum nihil potest excogitari immanius aut perniciosius. Nomen est inditum a foeditate. βοῦρκα limus est, non quilibet, sed qui jam putrescenti aqua maceratus, pessimam exhalat Mephitim, ut ita dicam. Λάκκος fossa, seu cauea, in qua similis limus fouetur. Est porro pessimi hominis, et facinorosi, saepeque etiam ab Antistite suo excommunicati cadauer, quod, non ut reliqua de mortuorum corpora defossa dissoluuntur atque in puluerem abeunt, sed quasi ex firmissima pelle constaret, per omnes sui partes intumescit, atque distenditur, ut uix flecti aliqua sui parte possit ; sed cutis, tanquam tympanum, extensa, eundem, ac tympanum, si pulsatur, sonum edit ; quare et τυμπανιαῖος dicitur. Corpus, sic deformatum, Daemon ingreditur, et miseris mortalibus infortunium parit. Saepe enim sub eo cadauere e sepulchro egressus, et per urbem et alia loca habitata circumiens, et noctu potissimum, ad quam sibi libuerit aedem, confertur, pulsatisque foribus, aliquem ex accolis aedis uoce sonora compellat. Si non responderit, saluus est. Hinc in ea insula ciues omnes, si noctu ab aliquo compellantur, nunquam prima uice respondent : nam, si secundo compellatus fuerit, iam, qui quaerit, Burcolacca non est, sed alius. Eamque pestem adeo exitiosam mortalibus esse dicunt, ut interdiu etiam, et meridie ipso, non intra aedes tantum, sed in agris, et uiis mediis, et sepibus uinearum, praetereuntes aggrediatur, et aspectu solo ac uisu conficiat, non uerbis tantummodo et contactu enecet. Homines ipsi, qui uiderunt, si alloquantur, spectrum disparet ; qui locutus est, moritur. Quare ciues, cum uident homines, nulla grassante infirmitate, in tanta copia emori ; suspicati quod est, sepulchra, in quibus recens defunctus sepultus est, aperiunt ; aliquando statim, aliquando etiam tardius, cadauer nondum corruptum, inflatumque, comperiunt ; quod e sepulchro extractum, precibusque effusis a sacerdotibus, in rogum ardentem coniiciunt ; et nondum completa supplicatione, cadaueris iuncturae sensim dissoluuntur, et reliqua exusta in cineres conuertuntur. Alii Daemonem esse, qui figuram de mortui hominis induerit, opinantur, sub eaque homines, quos ipse uult, conficere. Hanc opinationem ex populi animis euellere conati sunt, non ueteres modo (neque enim nupera est, aut hodie nata in Graecia, haec opinio,) sed etiam recentiores pii homines, qui Christianis a confessionibus sunt."

[30] *Idem.*, p. 149. " Graeci, cum similia uident corpora, quae post obitum in coemeteriis indissoluta comperiuntur, et tympani more extensa cute tumescunt, excommunicatorum esse corpora fatentur, eaque post absolution-emstatim dissolui."

[31] Imbros lies hard by the Dardanelles.

[32] Reading *Thasi* in place of *Ihasi*.

[33] The Greek liturgy is still used in this church which is embellished with frescoes by Correnzio.

[34] *Idem.*, p. 151. " Et stultissima ista de excommunicatorum cadaueribus indissolutis opinatio apud eam nationem adeo inualuit, ut iam nemo sit, si uspiam tale quid comperiatur, qui dubitet, cadauer illud esse excommunicati ; quod extrahunt, et uariis deprecationibus ac dicendi formulis absoluunt ; ordinemque, in tali absolutione seruandum, idem Nomocanon, cap. LXXXII, exactissime prosequitur, quibus exsolutis, asseuerantur dicunt, cadauer subito in cineres conuerti. Ipse nihil tale uspiam in Græcia uidi. Audiui tamen sæpius ab Athanasio, Imbri Metropolita, homine frugi, et qui rem factam mendacio non contaminasset, cum Ihasi moraretur in regione Theologi extra urbem in ecclesia sancti Georgii, exoratum a ciuibus, ut super cadauera, quæ ibidem pleraque consipiciebantur indissoluta, excommunicationis absolutionem recitaret, morem gessisse, neque dum finita absolutione cadauera ea omnia in puluerem abiisse. Referebat idem, Constantini cuiusdam cognomento Rezepii, qui ex Turca Christo nomina dederat, quod uitam uiueret omnibus flagitiis inquinatam, excommunicati, corpus tumulatum fuisse in ecclesia sanctorum Petri et Pauli nationis Græc-, orum Neapoli, et per plures annos indissolutum mansisse ; ab eodem postea, et aliis Metropolitis duobus, Athanasio Cypri, et Chrysantho Lacedæmonio, benedictione subactum, ut alia mortuorum cadauera, puluerem factum. Et quod admirabilius est, dum Raphael in Patriarchatu præsideret, eodem asserente, qui alium excommunicauerat, postea, compulsu Dæmonis, Christum eiurat, excommunicati licet Christiana demortui cadauer mansit indissolutum. De eo certior factus Patriarcha, accersitum Turcam, qui excommunicauerat, monet, ut absolutionem inpertiatur. Primum ille renuere, factum detestari ; nihil esse Turcis cum Christiana religione commune, dicere ; quare Christiani Christianum absoluerent : cum uero pertinacius exoraretur, obedit, et absolutionem super excommunicatum recitat ; oculatum se testem fatetur, qui perhibet ; prope finem absolutionis, cadaueris tumor cessat ; et in cineres omnia conuertuntur. Rei nouitate Turca attonitus, ad magistratum ocius aduolat, rem uti facta est narrat, edicit omnibus ueram religionem Christianem, quam ipse per summum nefas deseruerat ; eam se denuo amplecti, Mahumetanam detesatri. Monetur a Turcis, ut sapiat, ne tormentis se objiciat. Ille, se Christianum uelle mori, contendit. Quid plura ? pertinacem condemnant : ducitur ad supplicium, et Christianam religionem prædicans, morti, summo supplicio mactatus, deditur.

Plura de his excommunicatis narrat Christophorus Angelus, de uita et moribus recentiorum Græcorum, cap. XXV. Non præteribo uero, quod ille ex Cassiano Historico recitat. Ὁ δὲ νοῦς οὗτος ἔχει. Οὗτος ὁ Κασσιανὸς ἐστιν Ἕλλην παλαιὸς ἱστορικός, καὶ γράφει ἐν ταῖς ἱστορίαις αὐτοῦ, ὅτι ἐγένετο ποτὲ μερικὴ σύνοδος ἔν τινι τόπῳ ἑκατὸν ἐπισκόπων, καὶ πάντες ὀρθῶς ἔλεγον, εἰς δὲ ἐξ αὐτῶν ἐναντιοῦτο πᾶσι. Τότε ἐκεῖνοι ἀναθεμάτισαν ἐκεῖνον, καὶ οὕτω τέθνηκεν ἀφωρισμένος. καὶ ἔμεινε τὸ σῶμα ἐκείνου ἑκατὸν ἔτη δεδεμένον, ὡς σίδηρον. μετὰ δὲ ἑκατὸν ἔτη ἐγένετο πάλιν σύνοδος μερικὴ ἐκεῖσε ἑκατὸν ἐπισκόπων. Τότε ἐκεῖνοι οἱ ἐπίσκοποι εἶπον ἀλλήλοις, ὃ ἀναθεματισμένος ἐπίσκοπος ἐκεῖνος ἥμαρτεν εἰς τὴν ἐκκλησίαν, καὶ ἀφώρισεν ἐκεῖνον ἡ ἐκκλησία. Τὸ λοιπόν καὶ ἡμεῖς ἐκκλησία ἐσμέν, καὶ συγχωρήσωμεν ἐκεῖνον, ἐπειδὴ ἀνθρωπινόν ἐστι τὸ ἁμαρτάνειν καὶ συνεχώρησαν ἐκεῖνον, καὶ αὐτίκα μετὰ τὴν προσευχὴν ἐστράφη εἰς κόνιν ὁ ἑκατὸν ἐτῶν ἄλυτος.

[35] This history I know from the *Turco-Grecia* of Crusius (Basle, 1584) who relates it twice in slightly varying versions. According to Georgius Fehlavius, p. 539 of his edition of Christophorus Angelus *De statu hodiernorum Græcorum*, Lipsiæ, 1676, Emanuel Malaxus wrote a *Historia Patriarcharum Constantinopolitanorum* whence Crusius has derived much material.

[36] The reason seems obscure. See Michalescu, *Die Bekenntnisse und die wichtigsten Glaubenszeugnisse du griech.-orient. Kirche.*, Leipzig, 1904. Gedeon in his πατριαρχικοὶ Πίνακες, Constantinople, 1890, gives the date of resignation as 1459.

[37] Papageorgiu, *Byzantinische Zeitschrift*, III, 315.

[38] Allacci refers to Book viii, but I have been unable to trace the account in Crusius, and I note that Mr. Lawson also says " I cannot find the passage."

[39] *Relation de ce qui s'est passé de plus remarquable a Sant-Erini Isle de l'Archipel, depuis l'établissement des Peses de la compagnie de Jesus en icelle*, Paris, MDCLVII.

[40] Chap. XV, pp. 208-226.

[41] Cf. Ovid, *De Arte Amandi*, II, 82 :

Cinctaque piscosis Astypalæa uadis.

Astypalaea insula est Sporadum una, unam habens ciuitatem.

[42] Ios is remarkable for its large number of Chapels, which are said to amount to nearly 400. These were mostly founded by private individuals. This beautiful little island once a fief of the Venetian house Pisani was captured by the Turk as early as 1537. The town, Ios, occupies part of a small hill rising from the harbour. It was fabled that Homer is buried on these shores.

[43] Father Richard was no doubt quoting from memory, for as will be remarked there are several inaccuracies in his account of Phlegon's relation. He calls Philinnion a Thessalian maiden and Machates is from Macedonia. It is not likely that he had a more complete text than now exists for he speaks of the girl being buried a second time whereas the body was burned.

[44] A pleasant little island of which the chief town is Khora, Χώρα. This lies nearly three miles inland from the port of Katapola, κατὰ τὴν πόλιν, or Vathy (Baθύs), *Deep Bay*.

[45] " At the mouth of a cavern, in the face of the E. cliffs, about three miles N.E. of the town, is a celebrated convent founded by the Emperor Alexios Comnenos and dedicated to 'Η παναγια ἡ Χωζοβιώτισσα. The situation is exceedingly romantic, and the place well deserves a visit, even apart from the image of the Virgin supernaturally conveyed from Cyprus, and other curiosities which are treasured up by the Monks. The Church of S. George is built over a prophetic stream much consulted by sailors." Murray, *Greece* (1900).

[46] It is now generally believed that Turks are more subject to become *vrykolakes* than Christians. Cf. Bernhardt Schmidt, *Das Volksleben der Neugriechen*, p. 162.

[47] Among the Orthodox the consecrated Bread is moistened with the species of Wine and reserved as a kind of paste.

[48] Lawson has the following note : " Evidently a local form of τουμπί (=τόμπανον, cf. Du Cange, *Med. et. infra*. *Græc.*, S.U. τυμπανίτης), with metathesis of the nasal. Cf. the word τυμπανιαῖος."

[49] The Church of Santa Sophia, now a Mosque, stands in the high street (*Uia Egnatia*) of Thessalonica. " The Church of the Divine Wisdom at Salonica is said to have been built 100 years before its namesake at Constantinople. It suffered irreparable injury in the fire of 1891, which destroyed the roofs of the galleries, ruined the Turkish portico, and calcined the columns and capitals in the S. aisle of the nave. The leads are now being stripped off the dome, the damp is getting in, and patches of the beautiful mosaic work are peeling off and falling down. At the same time was burnt the old Cathedral of Salonica, whose ruins adjoin the Mosque.

The Church is built of brick and stone combined, but is lined internally with plaster. The fine porch is supported with eight columns of *verde antico*. The plan is the same as that of St. Sophia at Constantinople, but the proportions one-third smaller—externally 47 yds. by 38. The diameter of the central dome is 11 yds. On its ceiling is a find mosaic of the Ascension : on the E. side the Virgin ; on either side of her an angel, and figures of Apostles divided from each other by trees. The upper part of the figure of our Lord is defaced by a Turkish inscription, and obliterated with white-wash. Below the angels is a Greek inscription in four lines from Acts i, 11 (' Ye men of Galilee, etc.')."

[50] London, 1679.

[51] *Aeneid*, IV, 673 : Unguibus ora soror foedans, et pectora pugnis. . .

[52] *Psalm*, lxxxvii, 12 : Numquid narrabit aliquis in sepulcro misericordiam tuam, et ucritatem tuam in perditione ?

[53] The Second Council of Constantinople, the Fifth General Council, was held at Constantinople, 5 May—2 June, 553 having been convened by the Emperor Justinian. It has been called the last phase of the conflict inaugurated in 543 by the edict of Justinian against Origenism.

[54] Born at Aix in Provence, 5 June, 1656 ; died at Paris, 28 December, 1708.

[55] It was translated into English, 1741, and into German, 1776.

[56] Tournefort, *op. cit.*, vol. I, pp. 131-136.

[57] " Myconos is a rocky island, 36 miles in circumference, and producing only a little corn and wine. Many of its inhabitants, however, are large shipowners, and most of the male population are engaged in a sea-faring life. The town lies on a bay at the West side of the island, occupying an ancient site. In antiquity there was a second town at *Porto Panormo* on the North shore. . . . The town abounds in small churches and chapels, many of which have been erected as thank-offerings for escapes from shipwreck." Murray, *Handbook to Greece*. Seventh Edition, 1900, pp. 904-905.

[58] Tournefort here has the following marginal note : " Vroucolacas. βρουκόλακος καὶ βροὐκόλακας καὶ βουρκολάκας. βρουκόλακας, spectre composé d'un corps mort et d'un démon. *Il y en a qui croyent que βρουκόλακος signific une* charogne. βροὐκος & βουρκος, *c'est* ce limon si puant *qui croupit au fond des vieux fossez, car Λάκκος signifie* un fossé." This is evidently from Allacci.

[59] To whom and his important work ample reference has been made above.

[60] Syra is the principal island of the Cyclades. It once had a considerable trade, but of recent years general depression has well-nigh paralysed all commercial dealings at this port. There are extensive tanneries and a large engineering establishment. The island is ten miles in length by five miles in breadth.

Tenos is the ancient Ophioussa, the Isle of Serpents. In circumference it is sixty miles. The Greek Cathedral of Our Lady of Good Tidings (Evangelistria) is built almost entirely of white marble, and the interior is rich in gold and silver. The festivals of the Annunciation and the Assumption are celebrated with especial solemnity.

[61] Τεοργιονῆσι, the Island of S. George lies at the point of the bay on which stands the town Myconos with its harbour. It is on the right hand as one enters the bay.

[62] The exact date of the *Octavius* is not known, but Minucius Felix *floruit circa*, 160-300.

[63] *Mare-Aurèle*, p. 389.

[64] S. Jerome, *De Uiris illustribus*, lviii, records : " Minucius Felix, Romæ insignis causidicus, scripsit dialogum Christiani et ethnici disputantis, qui *Octauius* inscribitur."

[65] *Acta S. Scdis*, XXV, 63 ; *Collectanea S.C.P.F.* nn. 1608, 1609.

[66] Crusius, *Turco-Græcia*, viii, as cited by Leoni Allacci. But see note 38 *supra*.

[67] Bernhardt Schmidt, *Das Volksleben der Neugriechen und das Hellenische Alterthum*, p. 162.

[68] Leake's *Travels in Northern Greece*, vol. IV, chapter xxxviii, pp. 216-17.

[69] Preface ; pp. viii and ix.

[70] Bernhardt Schmidt, *Lieder, Märchen, Sagen, etc.* Folk-song, no. 33.

[71] Lawson ; *op. cit.*, pp. 540-41.

[72] The two terms, however, are often interchanged ; and indeed confused.

[73] pp. 209 and 210.

[74] Born 1740 ; died 1803. This eminent naturalist chiefly acquired celebrity owing to his scientific travels in Dalmatia of which he has obliged the world with so charming an account. I quote from the English version, *Travels into Dalmatia*. London. Printed for J. Robson, Bookseller, New Bond Street. MDCCLXXVIII.

[75] Pindar : The Nemean Odes, IX, 27 (which in the other reckoning=
63-65) :

$$\begin{array}{c}
\dot{\epsilon}\nu \ \gamma\dot{\alpha}\rho \\
\delta\alpha\iota\mu\text{ο}\nu\text{ί}\text{ο}\iota\sigma\iota \ \phi\text{ό}\beta\text{ο}\iota\varsigma \ \phi\epsilon\acute{\nu}- \\
\gamma\text{ο}\nu\tau\iota \ \kappa\alpha\grave{\iota} \ \pi\alpha\hat{\iota}\delta\epsilon\varsigma \ \theta\epsilon\hat{\omega}\nu.
\end{array}$$

[76] The episode of Aristomenes and Socrates 'will be remembered in the
Metamorphoses of Apuleius, I, v-xix.
[77] Vol. II, pp. 197-200.
[78] This term denotes the relation of a person to his godchild's father.
The one is the spiritual, the other the natural father of the same child ;
hence they are called Σύντεκνοι.
[79] Not because of the arms but because they had been laid in the form
of the Cross.
[80] The only oath which binds a Vampire : μὰ τὸ ἀναβόλιμοῦ : By my
winding-sheet.
[81] *Phædo*, 81. Περὶ τὰ μνήματά τε καὶ τοὺς τάφους κυλινδουμένη, περὶ ἅ δὴ καὶ
ὤφθη ἄττα ψυχῶν σκοτοειδῆ φάσματα, οἷα παρέχονται αἱ τοιαῦται ψυχαὶ εἴδωλα, αἱ μή
καθαρῶς ἀπολυθεῖσαι, ἀλλὰ τοῦ ὁρατοῦ μετέχουσαι. The same notion was prevalent
among the Jews : See Lightfoot on S. John, xi, 39. Elsner, Obs. Sacr.,
p. 47 (compare S. Matthew, viii, 28 ; S. Mark, v, 1 ; S. Luke, viii, 26)
(Pashley).
[82] On Damascius and his writings, see Photius, Biblioth. cod. 130. We
might perhaps have found more details respecting the prototype of the
modern Katakhanás in the work, Περὶ τῶν μετὰ Θάνατον ἐπιφαινομένων
ψυχῶν παραδόξων διηγημάτων κεφάλαια ξγʹ. (Pashley). Damascius the Syrian,
of Damascus, whence he derived his name, was the last of the renowned
teachers of the Neo-Platonic philosophy at Athens. He was born about
A.D. 480. When Justinian closed the heathen schools of philosophy at
Athens in 529, Damascius emigrated to King Chosroës of Persia. He afterwards returned to the West, since in a treaty Chosroës had stipulated that
the heathen adherents of the Platonic philosophy should be tolerated by
the Byzantine emperor. The only work of Damascius which has been printed
is entitled *Doubts and Solutions of the first Principles*, edited by Kopp,
Frankfort, 1828.
[83] *Psalm xci.*
[84] Printed in *The Journal of the Anthropological Institute*, vol. XV (1886),
pp. 391-401.
[85] *Capitularia pro partibus Saxoniæ*, I, 6.
[86] Rather, " he who sits up " in his grave. For these names see Notes 11,
12, 13, *ante*.
[87] Ν. Δραγούμης. Ἱστορικαὶ Ἀναμνήσεις, vol. I, p. 117.
[88] Charos to-day is not merely the ferryman of the Styx. Charos is
Death. He is the god of the lower world. See Lawson, *Modern Greek
Folklore*, pp. 98-117.
[89] Ἔνας καταχανᾶς ἐγύρισε εἰς τὴν Ἀνώπολιν, καὶ ἐπλάκωνε τῇ ἀνθρώπους, καὶ
ἔγαστρωσε καὶ μίαν γυναῖκα. Ὁ ἄνδρας τῇ εἶχε λείπει καὶ ἐπηγεν ἔνας Καταχανᾶς,
καὶ αὕτη θάρρωντας ὅπως ἔιναι ὁ ἄνδρας τῇ—καὶ, τὸ πουρνό δὲν ἠμπόρει καὶ ἦλθε καὶ
ὁ ἄνδρας τῇ, καὶ λέγει τῇ, "τί ἔχεις ;" καὶ ἡ γυναῖκα λέγει, "ἐγὼ δὲν ἦλθα." Καὶ
πάλιν ἡ γυναῖκα εἶπε, "ἔδα ὡσὰ δὲν ἦλθες ἐσύ, ἤτονι ὁ καταχανᾶς," ὑστειρνὰ τὸν
ἐξεχώσασι, καὶ ἐξορκίσανι τόνι καὶ ἐπεμψαν τὸν εἰς τὴν Σαντορίνην.
[90] This island measures about 11 miles by 3. The position is very beautiful
and Finlay well says : " Seen from the sea, the little town presents a noble
aspect, forming an amphitheatre of white houses, rising one above the other
round a small creek. The houses cling like swallows' nests to the sides
of a barren mountain, which towers far above them, and whose summit
is crowned by a monastery of S. Elias. The streets are narrow, crooked,
unpaved lanes, but the smallest dwellings are built of stone, and near the sea
some large and solidly constructed houses give the place an imposing aspect."
From 1730, when an Albanian colony from the Morea established itself in
Hydra, until 1821, this island formed a perfectly independant small republic
governed by a council of its own primates. It was only under considerable

pressure that Hydra joined in the struggle for liberty at the beginning of the nineteenth century.

⁹¹ This name is reciprocally given by godchildren to godfathers, and godfathers to godchildren, and covers all members of the family between whom such a tie exists. This artificial relationship acts as a bar on inter-marriage. At weddings also an influential friend or relation is named Koumbáros to the bride, and among the poorer people he provides a part at any rate of the wedding entertainment, and is bound to care for the wife and children should they be left destitute.

⁹² Henry Hautteweur, *Le Folklore de l'Ile de Kythnos*, Brussels, 1898.

⁹³ Hautteweur, *op. cit.*, p. 28.

⁹⁴ The modern capital of Kythnos situated inland about four miles from the Port of S. Irene.

⁹⁵ The famous statue (a fountain) at Brussels. The legend says that he was a little boy who having saucily urinated upon the skirts of an old woman endowed with magic powers was by her condemned to pass water for ever. He possesses eight (or more) suits and may often be seen dressed out in gala costume. He even boasts of a valet and in the nineteenth century an old lady bequeathed him a legacy of 1,000 florins.

⁹⁶ Unless Kythnos differs in this particular from the rest of Greece, and indeed from all other countries, which would be very extraordinary, there is a slight error here. Not Friday, but Saturday is the day when all Vampires are bound fast in their graves and unable to issue thence. Accordingly, as has been noted, it is on a Saturday that they are exhumed for cremation.

⁹⁷ *Genesis*, I, 2.

⁹⁸ *Le Folklore de Kythnos*, pp. 34-36.

⁹⁹ Ἀντών. Βάλληνδας, Κυθνιακά, p. 125.

¹⁰⁰ Ἀντ. Μηλιαρακης, Ὑπομνήματα περιγραφικὰ τῶν Κυκλαδῶν νήσων—Ἀνδρος, Κεως, p. 56.

¹⁰¹ Βάλληνδας, Κυθνιακά, p. 125.

¹⁰² Lawson, *Modern Greek Folklore*, p. 374.

¹⁰³ *The Cyclades*, London, 1885, p. 299.

¹⁰⁴ I am bound to endorse Murray's description of Mandoudi as a " wretched village," but Kymasi, two miles away, is a pretty little harbour, though actually much exposed to east winds.

¹⁰⁵ Πολίτης, Παραδόσεις, I, p. 577.

¹⁰⁶ Lawson, *op. cit.*, p. 374.

¹⁰⁷ Πολίτης, Παραδόσεις, I, p. 578.

¹⁰⁸ *Modern Greek Folklore*, pp. 372-3.

¹⁰⁹ " διπλοσαραντίση. I have given what I take to be the meaning of a popular word otherwise unknown to me." Lawson.

¹¹⁰ *Op. cit.*, Preface, p. viii.

¹¹¹ No. 517.

CHAPTER V

Russia, Roumania and Bulgaria

IT is no matter for surprise that in so sad and sick a country as Russia the tradition of the vampire should assume, if it be possible, an even intenser darkness. We find, indeed, a note of something deformed, as it were, something curiously diseased and unclean, a rank wealth of grotesque and fetid details which but serve to intensify the loathliness and horror.

There are still to be observed in Russia very distinct traces of survival from the old rites with which the ancient Slavonians, whilst yet Pagans, celebrated the obsequies of their dead. Concerning these we are fortunate enough to possess a considerable amount of detailed information. Important references to various customs that prevailed at Slavonic funerals may be found in such early writers as the Emperor Maurice[1], who in his *Strategica* comments upon the fact that the wives of Slavonian warriors refused to survive their lords. Theophylactus Simocatta, the Byzantine historian, who died 629 A.D.[2] relates that the Roman general Priscus invaded the Slavonic territory, and captured Mousokios, "the king of the Barbarians," who was lewdly intoxicated with wine after the celebrations with which he had honoured the funeral of one of his brothers. This gives evidence of the savage revelry that took place during these ancient burials, and the passage was incorporated by Theophanes Isaurus[3] in his *Chronicon*, which comes down to the year 811, and hence it has been copied by Anastasius the Librarian about 886. In the eighth century S. Boniface who was martyred 5 June, 755 (754), remarked that among the Slavonic Winedi, or Wends, the bonds of matrimony were considered to be so strong that it was usual for wives to kill themselves upon the death of their husbands, a custom to which reference will again be made a little later. During the first half of the tenth century those acute and observant Arabian travellers, Ibn Dosta, Masudi, and Ibn Fozlan, gave very striking accounts of Slavonic burials, drawing particular attention to the extraordinary nature of the sacrifices which were then offered. This material was largely drawn upon by Leo Diaconus, a Byzantine historian of the tenth century, whose chronicle[4] includes the period from the Cretan expedition of Nicephorus Phocas, in the reign of the Emperor Romanus II, A.D. 959, to the death of Joannes I Zimisces, 975. Dithmar (Thietmar), Bishop of Merseburg,[5] in his famous *Chronicon Thietmari* which comprises in eight books the reigns of the Saxon Emperors Henry I (the Fowler), the three Ottos, and S. Henry II, gives much valuable information regarding the contemporary history and civilization of the Slavonic tribes east of the river Elbe. In his encyclicals S. Otto, Bishop of Bamburg, (*circa* 1060,-30 June, 1139), reproves many Pagan customs which were beginning again to assert themselves, and amongst others he particularly forbids obscure burials in lonely woods and fields which were afterwards regarded as haunted, if not accursed spots. The "Herodotus of Bohemia," Cosmas of Prague, whose *Chronica Bohemorum* commences with the earliest times and brings the narrative down to 1125, affords very copious information upon this very subject, and his work is particularly valuable since as a historian Cosmas is truthful and conscientious, distinguishing between what is certain and what is based on tradition, and generally indicating his sources of information.[6] Rather more than four centuries later, a Latin poem by Klonowicz, *Roxolania*, Cracow, 1584, contains a vivid picture of Ruthenian obsequies in the sixteenth century. Even better known is the account given by Meletius (or Menetius) in a letter dated 1551, *De Sacrificiis et ydolatria ueterum Borussorum*, which was largely reproduced by Lasicius in his study *De Diis Samogitarum*. A summary of all that is valuable and pertinent in these authors will be found in the erudite if somewhat old-fashioned treatise by Kotlyarevsky, *O Pogrebal'nuikh Obuichayakh Yazuicheskikh Slavyan* (*On the Funeral Customs of the Heathen Slavonians*), Moscow, 1868.

Many scholars have debated the question whether the Old Slavonians buried their dead or burned them in funeral pyres. Some writers have maintained the first, and others as stoutly asserted the second. Again, it has been supposed that those Slavonians who led a nomadic life cremated their dead, but when they settled down in hamlets and villages the custom of inhumation was adopted. It has been suggested that among

these Pagans there were two religious sects or parties each of
which disposed of the dead in its own particular way. Not a
few writers, moreover, have thought that the wealthy Slavonians were burned, whilst the poor were merely interred.
Further it has been held that the Slavonians whilst they were
yet Heathen used to incinerate the dead, but that upon their
conversion they abandoned this practice. Kotlyarevsky after
a general review of the many arguments reaches the conclusion
that there was in fact no fixed rule, that some Slavonians
buried the dead, and that others first cremated the bodies and
then acting in accordance with an old family tradition interred
the ashes. It has been pointed out that during excavations
it is by no means unusual to find traces of both customs in the
one tomb ; for near the remains of a corpse which has been
interred without cremation lie the ashes of a body that has
been calcined.

It may be noted that no ancient word for " cemetery "
occurs in any Slavonic dialect, and general burying-grounds
do not seem to have been known, for research has shown that
almost always the tombs stand singly or in family groups.
Sometimes hills, and especially caves in hills, were chosen for
the graves of the departed. The tribes who lived around the
shores of the Baltic especially favoured lonely fields and the
depths of the forest. In common with many another savage
race when a corpse was burned or buried various objects
suffered the same fate. Warriors had passed before, and so
their favourite chargers were generally slain ; their armour,
dress, ornaments, and even household utensils, were destroyed
to serve them beyond the grave. But the most important of
the companions of the dead were the human beings who
either killed themselves or were put to death upon the occasion
of a chieftain's funeral. The Arabian traveller Ibn Dosta,
to whom reference has already been made, tells us that in
some cases it was customary for the dead man's wife to hang
herself in order that her body might be cremated with that of
her lord ; in other districts she was expected to allow herself
to be buried alive with him.[7] To this practice there are
constant allusions in the songs and customs of the people,
and this explains the so-called " marriages " between the
living and the dead. Among such songs are those Moravian
laments in which the dead are described as rising from their

graves, and carrying off their wives or the betrothed. In one *Builina* or metrical romance the dead Potok is buried together with his living wife. Writing in 1872 Ralston[8] says : " Marriage and death were often brought into strange fellowship by at least some of the Old Slavonians. Strongly impressed with the idea that those whom the nuptial bond had united in this world were destined to live together also in the world to come they so sincerely pitied the lot of the unmarried dead, that, before committing their bodies to the grave they were in the habit of finding them partners for eternity. The fact that, among some Slavonian peoples, if a man died a bachelor a wife was allotted to him after his death, rests on the authority of several witnesses, and in a modified form the practice has been retained in some places up to the present day. In Little-Russia, for instance, a dead maiden is dressed in nuptial attire, and friends come to her funeral as to a wedding, and a similar custom is observed on the death of a lad. In Podolia, also, a young girl's funeral is conducted after the fashion of a wedding, a youth being chosen as the bridegroom who attends her to the grave, with the nuptial kerchief twined around his arm. From that time her family consider him their relative, and the rest of the community look upon him as a widower. In some parts of Servia when a lad dies, a girl dressed as a bride follows him to the tomb, carrying two crowns ; one of these is thrown to the corpse, and the other she keeps at least for a time.

Ibn Fozlan[9] relates that certain " Russian " merchants with whom he became acquainted in Bulgaria loudly blamed their Arabian friend as belonging to a race who buried their dead to rot and be consumed of worms, in which case it was impossible to tell what might not befall the deceased, whereas they themselves at once cremated their dead, and so without delay the departed passed on to Paradise. It seems uncertain who were these " Russians," and Rasmussen the translator of the narrative into Danish roundly denies that they were Scandinavians, but most authorities are agreed that they must have been Varangian traders.

It may be noticed that the heathen Slavonians set up upon the mound which covers a grave a little hut or tent in which the soul might find rest and shelter when it came to revisit the body where it once inhabited, and hither also the relatives of the dead resorted when they desired to mourn over his remains. Half a century ago traces of this custom still persisted in Russia. In spite of the strictest ecclesiastical prohibition the White-Russians were wont to build over graves a kind of log-house. In some districts these were known as a *Golubets*, a term more properly applied to the roofed cross which is generally erected in God's acre. As may well be imagined, it was popularly supposed that these little lodgements, banned by the Church, were most fearfully haunted and were often the lurking places of werewolves and Vampires.

The Pagan Slavonians also encouraged the practice of burying in one tomb as many generations of a family as possible, and the more tenants there were in a grave the more their respect for it increased, since it was protected by so many " Fathers," whose abiding place it had become. It would appear that some remnant of this custom prevails in Bulgaria to-day, where, it is said, that if no relative dies within the space of three years the family tomb is opened, and any stranger who happens to pass away in the vicinity is buried in it, which no doubt is due to the old superstition that the grave required a victim.

Even to-day there persist practices which are obviously derived from this idea, and the connexion between the dead and the living must be broken for fear that the deceased may else return to claim some of those who are left. Thus in parts of Russia the bed upon which a dying person has lain, or at least the mattress must be destroyed. In England to-day the same custom is not wholly extinct, for in certain counties it is held to be unlucky for any person belonging to the family, any relative, or any one of the household to sleep in the bed where a person has died, and accordingly this piece of furniture is disposed of as soon as possible. The ill omen is not held to affect any person save those who have been in some way intimate with the deceased or who have lived in the same house. In Russia, the cottage whence there has just set forth a funeral, or at any rate the principal room, is strewed with corn. In England, in some houses the chamber in which a person has died is kept locked for seven days after the burial. The reason for this has entirely disappeared, but the original idea seems to be to prevent the spirit returning to the room. I have heard that the door is secured lest the ghost should issue from the room, and this seems to point to an old belief that after a period of seven days the power of an apparition wanes and fades.

There existed a former custom among the Bohemians that when returning from a funeral none of the party must look back, and it was considered lucky that they should throw sticks and stones over their shoulders behind them. This was obviously to keep off the dead man and prevent him from following in their track. An even more elaborate precaution was that of the mourners putting on masks and behaving in a strange and extraordinary manner as they came back from the churchyard.[10] They intended, in fact, to disguise themselves so that the dead man would fail to recognize them, and therefore could not follow them home. In most countries it is considered terribly untoward if a corpse is carried out of the house head foremost, as then he will see the door and assuredly find his way back again. This reason is definitely assigned for the practice in parts of the world so far distant from one another as various provinces of Germany and among the Indians of Chile.[11] Not many years ago it was still the custom in the north of England to carry a body to the graveyard by an unusual and roundabout way, and although the reason for this is entirely forgotten it was undoubtedly in order that the deceased should not discover the way to revisit the house. It is more than probable that the old practice of burying at night which to name but a few countries was practised in ancient Rome, in Scotland, in Germany, in Hawai and among the Mandingos, was originally intended to conceal from the deceased the path to the tomb.[12] It was also thought that the ghost could not penetrate through fire, and therefore the South Slavonians on their return from a funeral are met by an old woman who carries a brazier containing live coals. In some parts they take the glowing embers from the hearth and with a pair of tongs cast these backward over their shoulders. In Ruthenia this custom has so entirely lost all signification that they do no more than gaze steadfastly at the house stove and touch it with their hands. In other districts the idea prevailed that the spirit cannot cross a stream, and the Lusatian Wends are most scrupulous to pour out water in front of the house when they have returned from a burial. No doubt some belief in a lustral purification is not altogether unconcerned with this, and the necessity for some symbolism of cleansing is part'cularly marked among the Serbians. With them neither the spade that dug the grave nor the cart that carried the coffin may be brought into the farmyard. Even the horses which drew the bier must be turned loose into the pastures, and thus for a space of three days every instrument and accessory of burial must needs be left without, otherwise they might bring death into the house.

It is obvious from the above details, and very many more might be added, that throughout Russia, as in the other countries we have mentioned, there is a very marked dread of the return of the deceased. The power of the dead to inflict injury upon the living is not merely confined to any ghostly affrightment, but strikes something deeper. The dead may come back in their own bodies as malignant monsters eager to carry off the living to the shadowy realm where they have gone before. Hence all these elaborate ceremonials and semi-heathen rites to prevent such a visitation. This terror of the departed is a gloomy and terrible thing, and it stands out in sad contrast to the gentle thoughts of the Departed, the prayers and Requiems that solace the Holy Souls as the Catholic Church so sweetly teaches and enjoins.

The figure of the Vampire logically evolved from such dark superstitions. Although his pronouncement is in fact far from correct, it is easy to see why Hertz wrote : " The belief in vampires is the specific Slavonian form of the universal belief in spectres (*Gespenster*)." Concerning the Russian Vampire W. R. S. Ralston remarks[13] :

" The districts of the Russian Empire in which a belief in vampires mostly prevails are White Russia and the Ukraine. But the ghastly blood-sucker, the *Upir*, whose name has become naturalized in so many alien lands under forms resembling our ' Vampire,' disturbs the peasant-mind in many other parts of Russia, though not perhaps with the same intense fear which it spreads among the inhabitants of the above-named districts, or of some other Slavonic lands. The numerous traditions which have gathered around the original idea vary to some extent according to their locality, but they are never radically inconsistent.

" Some of the details are curious. The Little-Russians hold that if a vampire's hands have grown numb from remaining long crossed in the grave, he makes use of his teeth, which are like steel. When he has gnawed his way with these through all obstacles, he first destroys the babes he finds in a house, and then the older inmates. If fine salt be scattered on the floor of a room, the vampire's footsteps may be traced to his grave, in which he will be found resting with rosy cheek and gory mouth.

"The Kashoubes say that when a *Vieszcy*, as they call the Vampire, wakes from his sleep within the grave, he begins to gnaw his hands and feet ; and as he gnaws, one after another, first his relations, then his other neighbours, sicken and die. When he has finished his own store of flesh, he rises at midnight and destroys cattle, or climbs a belfry and sounds the bell. All who hear the ill-omened tones will soon die. But generally he sucks the blood of sleepers. Those on whom he has operated will be found next morning dead, with a very small wound on the left side of the breast, exactly over the heart. The Lusatian Wends hold that when a corpse chews its shroud or sucks its own breast, all its kin will soon follow it to the grave. The Wallachians say that a *murony*—a sort of cross between a werewolf and a vampire, connected by name with our nightmare—can take the form of a dog, a cat, or a toad, and also of any blood-sucking insect. When he is exhumed, he is found to have long nails of recent growth on his hands and feet, and blood is streaming from his eyes, ears, nose and mouth."

Ralston tells us that he has drawn his information concerning Russian Vampires for the most part from a study by the eminent authority Alexander Afanasief, *Poeticheskiya Vozzryeniya Slavyan na Prirodu* (*Poetic Views of the Slavonians about Nature*)[14], which was published in three volumes, Moscow, 1865-1869, and accordingly the best illustration of popular Russian tradition will be given by a consideration of those stories which Ralston has translated.

The following tale[15] is reported to have been heard in the Tambof Government :—

A peasant was driving past a grave-yard, after it had grown dark. After him came running a stranger, dressed in a red shirt and a new jacket, who cried,

"Stop ! take me as your companion."

"Pray take a seat."

They enter a village, drive up to this and that house. Though the gates are wide open, yet the stranger says, "Shut tight ! "

for on those gates crosses have been branded. They drive on to the very last house ; the gates are barred, and from them hangs a padlock weighing a score of pounds ; but there is no cross there, and the gates open of their own accord.

They go into the house ; there on the bench lie two sleepers— an old man and a lad. The stranger takes a pail, places it near the youth, and strikes him on the back ; immediately the back opens, and forth flows rosy blood. The stranger fills the pail full, and drinks it dry. Then he fills another pail with blood from the old man, slakes his brutal thirst, and says to the peasant :

"It begins to grow light ! let us go back to my dwelling."

In a twinkling they found themselves at the grave-yard. The vampire would have clasped the peasant in its arms, but luckily for him the cocks began to crow, and the corpse disappeared. The next morning, when folks came and looked, the old man and the lad were both dead.

The four very striking stories I now give are also from Afanasief, and Ralston's versions in *Russian Folk-Tales* have been used.

THE COFFIN-LID[16]. A moujik was driving along one night with a load of pots. His horse grew tired, and all of a sudden it came to a stand-still alongside of a graveyard. The moujik unharnessed his horse and set it free to graze ; meanwhile he laid himself down on one of the graves. But somehow he didn't go to sleep.

He remained lying there some time. Suddenly the grave began to open beneath him : he felt the movement and sprang to his feet. The grave opened, and out of it came a corpse— wrapped in a white shroud, and holding a coffin-lid—came out and ran to the church, laid the coffin-lid at the door, and then set off for the village.

The moujik was a daring fellow. He picked up the coffin-lid and remained standing beside his cart, waiting to see what would happen. After a short delay the dead man came back, and was going to snatch up his coffin-lid—but it was not to be seen. Then the corpse began to track it out, traced it up to the moujik, and said :

"Give me my lid : if you don't, I'll tear you to bits ! "

"And my hatchet, how about that ? " answers the moujik. "Why, it's I who'll be chopping you into small pieces ! "

"Do give it back to me, good man!" begs the corpse.

"I'll give it when you tell me where you've been and what you've done."

"Well, I've been in the village, and there I've killed a couple of youngsters."

"Well then, now tell me how they can be brought back to life."

The corpse reluctantly made answer:

"Cut off the left skirt of my shroud, and take it with you. When you come into the house where the youngsters were killed, pour some live coals into a pot and put the piece of the shroud in with them, and then lock the door. The lads will be revived by the smoke immediately."

The moujik cut off the left skirt of the shroud, and gave up the coffin-lid. The corpse went to its grave—the grave opened. But just as the dead man was descending into it, all of a sudden the cocks began to crow, and he hadn't time to get properly covered over. One end of the coffin-lid remained sticking out of the ground.

The moujik saw all this and made a note of it. The day began to dawn; he harnessed his horse and drove into the village. In one of the houses he heard cries and wailing. In he went—there lay two dead lads.

"Don't cry," says he, "I can bring them to life!"

"Do bring them to life, kinsman," say their relatives. "We'll give you half of all we possess."

The moujik did everything as the corpse had instructed him, and the lads came back to life. Their relatives were delighted, but they immediately seized the moujik and bound him with cords, saying:

"No, no, trickster! We'll hand you over to the authorities. Since you knew how to bring them back to life, maybe it was you who killed them!"

"What are you thinking about, true believers! Have the fear of God before your eyes!" cried the moujik.

Then he told them everything that had happened to him during the night. Well, they spread the news through the village; the whole population assembled and swarmed into the graveyard. They found out the grave from which the dead man had come out, they tore it open, and they drove an aspen stake right into the heart of the corpse, so that it might no more rise up and slay. But they rewarded the moujik richly, and sent him away home with great honour.

THE TWO CORPSES[17]. A Soldier had obtained leave to go home on furlough—to pray to the holy images, and to bow down before his parents. And as he was going his way, at a time when the sun had long set, and all was dark around, it chanced that he had to pass by a graveyard. Just then he heard that some one was running after him, and crying:

"Stop! you can't escape!"

He looked back and there was a corpse running and gnashing its teeth. The Soldier sprang on one side with all his might to get away from it, caught sight of a little chapel, and bolted straight into it.

There wasn't a soul in the chapel, but stretched out on a table there lay another corpse, with tapers burning in front of it. The Soldier hid himself in a corner, and remained there hardly knowing whether he was alive or dead, but waiting to see what would happen. Presently up ran the first corpse— the one that had chased the Soldier—and dashed into the chapel. Thereupon the one that was lying on the table jumped up, and cried to it:

"What hast thou come here for?"

"I've chased a soldier in here, so I'm going to eat him."

"Come now, brother! he's run into my house. I shall eat him myself."

"No, I shall!"

"No, I shall!"

And they set to work fighting; the dust flew like anything. They'd have gone on fighting ever so much longer, only the cocks began to crow.[18] Then both the corpses fell lifeless to the ground, and the Soldier went on his way homeward in peace, saying:

"Glory be to Thee, O Lord! I am saved from the wizards!"

THE DOG AND THE CORPSE. A moujik went out in pursuit of game one day, and took a favourite dog with him. He walked and walked through the woods and bogs, but got nothing for his pains. At last the darkness of night surprised him. At an uncanny hour he passed by a graveyard, and there, at a place where two roads met, he saw standing a corpse in a white shroud. The moujik was horrified, and knew not which way to go—whether to keep on or to turn back.

"Well, whatever happens, I'll go on," he thought ; and on he went, his dog running at his heels. When the corpse perceived him, it came to meet him ; not touching the earth with its feet, but keeping about a foot above it—the shroud fluttering after it. When it had come up with the sportsman, it made a rush at him ; but the dog seized hold of it by its bare calves, and began a tussle with it. When the moujik saw his dog and the corpse grappling with each other, he was delighted that things had turned out so well for himself, and he set off running home with all his might. The dog kept up the struggle until cock-crow, when the corpse fell motionless to the ground. Then the dog ran off in pursuit of its master, caught him up just as he reached home, and rushed at him, furiously trying to bite and to rend him. So savage was it, and so persistent, that it was as much as the people of the house could do to beat it off.

"Whatever has come over the dog ?" asked the moujik's old mother. "Why should it hate its master so ?"

The moujik told her all that had happened.

"A bad piece of work, my son!" said the old woman. "The dog was disgusted at your not helping it. There it was fighting with the corpse—and you deserted it, and thought only of saving yourself ! Now it will owe you a grudge for ever so long."

Next morning, while the family were going about the farm-yard, the dog was perfectly quiet. But the moment its master made his appearance, it began to growl like anything.

They fastened it to a chain ; for a whole year they kept it chained up. But in spite of that, it never forgot how its master had offended it. One day it got loose, flew straight at him, and began trying to throttle him.

So they had to kill it.

THE SOLDIER AND THE VAMPIRE. A certain soldier was allowed to go home on furlough. Well, he walked and walked, and after a time he began to draw near to his native village. Not far off from that village lived a miller in his mill. In old times the Soldier had been very intimate with him ; why shouldn't he go and see his friend ? He went. The Miller received him cordially, and at once brought out liquor ; and the two began drinking and chattering about their ways and doings. All this took place towards nightfall, and the Soldier stopped so long at the Miller's that it grew quite dark.

When he proposed to start for his village, his host exclaimed :
" Spend the night here, trooper ! It's very late now, and perhaps you might run into mischief."

" How so ? "

" God is punishing us ! A terrible warlock has died among us, and by night he rises from his grave, wanders through the village, and does such things as bring fear upon the very boldest ! How could even you help being afraid of him ? "

" Not a bit of it ! A soldier is a man who belongs to the crown, and ' crown property cannot be drowned in water nor burnt in fire.' I'll be off : I'm tremendously anxious to see my people as soon as possible."

Off he set. His road lay in front of a graveyard. On one of the graves he saw a great fire blazing. " What's that ? " thinks he. " Let's have a look." When he drew near, he saw that the Warlock was sitting by the fire, sewing boots.

" Hail, brother ! " calls out the Soldier.

The Warlock looked up and said :

" What have you come here for ? "

" Why, I wanted to see what you're doing."

The Warlock threw his work aside and invited the Soldier to a wedding.

" Come along, brother," says he, " let's enjoy ourselves. There's a wedding going on in the village."

" Come along ! " says the Soldier.

They came to where the wedding was ; there they were given drink, and treated with the utmost hospitality. The Warlock drank and drank, revelled and revelled, and then grew angry. He chased all the guests and relatives out of the house, threw the wedded pair into a slumber, took out two phials and an awl, pierced the hands of the bride and bridegroom with the awl, and began drawing off their blood. Having done this, he said to the Soldier :

" Now let's be off ! "

Well, they went off. On the way the Soldier said :

" Tell me ; why did you draw off their blood in those phials ? "

" Why, in order that the bride and bridegroom might die. To-morrow morning no one will be able to wake them. I alone know how to bring them back to life."

" How's that managed ? "

"The bride and bridegroom must have cuts made in their heels, and some of their own blood must then be poured back into those wounds. I've got the bridegroom's blood stowed away in my right-hand pocket, and the bride's in my left."

The Soldier listened to this without letting a single word escape him. Then the Warlock began boasting again.

"Whatever I wish," says he, "that I can do!"

"I suppose it's quite impossible to get the better of you?" says the Soldier.

"Why impossible? If anyone were to make a pyre of aspen boughs, a hundred loads of them, and were to burn me on that pyre, then he'd be able to get the better of me. Only he'd have to look out sharp in burning me; for snakes and worms and different kinds of reptiles would creep out of my inside, and crows and magpies and jackdaws would come flying up. All these must be caught and flung on the pyre. If so much as a single maggot were to escape, then there'd be no help for it; in that maggot I should slip away!"

The Soldier listened to all this and did not forget it. He and the Warlock talked and talked, and at last they arrived at the grave.

"Well, brother," said the Warlock, "now I'll tear you to pieces. Otherwise you'd be telling all this."

"What are you talking about? Don't you deceive yourself; I serve God and the Emperor."

The Warlock gnashed his teeth, howled aloud, and sprang at the Soldier—who drew his sword and began laying about him with sweeping blows. They struggled and struggled; the Soldier was all but at the end of his strength. "Ah!" thinks he, "I'm a lost man—and all for nothing!" Suddenly the cocks began to crow. The Warlock fell lifeless to the ground.

The Soldier took the phials of the blood out of the Warlock's pockets, and went on to the house of his own people. When he had got there, and had exchanged greetings with his relatives, they said:

"Did you see any disturbance, Soldier?"

"No, I saw none."

"There now! Why we've a terrible piece of work going on in the village. A Warlock has taken to haunting it!"

After talking a while, they lay down to sleep. Next morning the Soldier awoke, and began asking:

"I'm told you've got a wedding going on somewhere here?"

"There was a wedding in the house of a rich moujik," replied his relatives, "but the bride and bridegroom have died this very night—what from, nobody knows."

"Where does this moujik live?"

They showed him the house. Thither he went without speaking a word. When he got there, he found the whole family in tears.

"What are you mourning about?" says he.

"Such and such is the state of things, Soldier," say they.

"I can bring your young people to life again. What will you give me if I do?"

"Take what you like, even were it half of what we've got!"

The Soldier did as the Warlock had instructed him, and brought the young people back to life. Instead of weeping there began to be happiness and rejoicing ; the Soldier was hospitably treated and well rewarded. Then—left about face ! off he marched to the Starosta, and told him to call the peasants together and to get ready a hundred loads of aspen wood. Well, they took the wood into the graveyard, dragged the Warlock out of his grave, placed him on the pyre, and set it alight—the people all standing round in a circle with brooms, shovels and fire-irons. The pyre became wrapped in flames, the Warlock began to burn. His corpse burst, and out of it crept snakes, worms and all sorts of reptiles, and up came flying crows, magpies, and jackdaws. The peasants knocked them down and flung them into the fire, not allowing so much as a single maggot to creep away ! And so the Warlock was thoroughly consumed, and the Soldier collected his ashes and strewed them to the winds. From that time forth there was peace in the village.

The Soldier received the thanks of the whole community. He stayed at home some time, enjoying himself thoroughly. Then he went back to the Tsar's service with money in his pocket. When he had served his time, he retired from the army, and began to live at his ease.

"The stories of this class," Ralston tells us, "are very numerous, all of them based on the same belief—that in certain cases the dead, in a material shape, leave their graves in order to destroy and prey upon the living. The belief

is not peculiar to the Slavonians, but it is one of the characteristic features of their spiritual creed."[19]

Passing from folk-tales, which none the less contain more
than a grain or two of truth, we enter the realms of fact. In
that famous work *Isis Unveiled* by Madame Blavatsky the
following account is given of a Russian vampire, and t is
stated that the details were told by an eye-witness of these
terrible happenings. "About the beginning of the present
century, there occurred in Russia, one of the most frightful
cases of Vampirism on record. The governor of the Province
Tch—— was a man of about sixty years, of a malicious,
tyrannical, cruel, and jealous disposition. Clothed with
despotic authority, he exercised it without stint, as his brutal
instincts prompted. He fell in love with the pretty daughter
of a subordinate official. Although the girl was betrothed
to a young man whom she loved, the tyrant forced her father
to consent to his having her marry him ; and the poor victim,
despite her despair, became his wife. His jealous disposition
exhibited itself. He beat her, confined her to her room for
weeks together, and prevented her seeing anyone except in
his presence. He finally fell sick and died. Finding his end
approaching, he made her swear never to marry again ; and
with fearful oaths threatened that, in case she did, he would
return from his grave and kill her. He was buried in the
cemetery across the river, and the young widow experienced
no further annoyance, until, nature getting the better of her
fears, she listened to the importunities of her former lover,
and they were again betrothed.

On the night of the customary betrothal-feast, when all
had returned, the old mansion was aroused by shrieks proceeding
from her room. The doors were burst open and the unhappy
woman was found lying on her bed in a swoon. At the same
time a carriage was heard rumbling out of the courtyard.
Her body was found to be black and blue in places, as from the
effect of pinches, and from a slight puncture on her neck drops
of blood were oozing. Upon recovering she stated that her
deceased husband had suddenly entered her room, appearing
exactly as in life, with the exception of a dreadful pallor ;
that he had upbraided her for her inconstancy, and then
beaten and pinched her most cruelly. Her story was disbelieved ; but the next morning the guard stationed at the

other end of the bridge which spans the river, reported that, just before midnight, a black coach and six had driven furiously past them, towards the town, without answering their challenge.

The new governor, who disbelieved the story of the apparition, took nevertheless the precaution of doubling the guards across the bridge. The same thing happened, however, night after night; the soldiers declaring that the toll-bar at their station near the bridge would rise of itself, and the spectral equipage sweep by them despite their efforts to stop it. At the same time every night the coach would rumble into the courtyard of the house; the watchers, including the widow's family, and the servants, would be thrown into a heavy sleep, and every morning the young victim would be found bruised, bleeding and swooning as before. The town was thrown into consternation. The physicians had no explanation to offer; priests came to pass the night in prayer, but as midnight approached, all would be seized with the terrible lethargy. Finally, the archbishop of the province came, and performed the ceremony of exorcism in person, but the following morning the governor's widow was found worse than ever. She was now brought to death's door.

The governor was now driven to take the severest measures to stop the ever-increasing panic in the town. He stationed fifty Cossacks along the bridge, with orders to stop the spectre-carriage at all hazards. Promptly at the usual hour, it was heard and seen approaching from the direction of the cemetery. The officer of the guard, and a priest bearing a crucifix, planted themselves in front of the toll-bar, and together shouted: " In the name of God and the Czar, who goes there ? " Out of the coach window was thrust a well-remembered head, and a familiar voice responded: " The Privy Councillor of State and Governor C—— ! " At the same moment, the officer, the priest, and the soldiers were flung aside as by an electric shock, and the ghostly equippage passed by them, before they could recover breath.

The archbishop then resolved as a last expedient to resort to the time-honoured plan of exhuming the body, and pinning it to the earth with an oaken stake driven through its heart. This was done with great religious ceremony in the presence of the whole populace. The story is that the body was found gorged with blood, and with red cheeks and lips. At the instant that the first blow was struck upon the stake, a groan issued from the corpse, and a jet of blood spurted high in the air. The archbishop pronounced the usual exorcism, the body was re-interred, and from that time no more was heard of the Vampire."

Here we see that a strong individuality, cruelty and devilish hate are energized by the jealousy of lust—not love—and are perpetuated in this horrid manner even beyond the grave.

The following instance of vampirism was related to me by a friend who himself had it from Captain Pokrovsky in 1905. Captain Pokrovsky, a Russian-Lithuanian Guards officer, had been for a time relegated to his estates in Lithuania on account of some political indiscretion, but a little later he was allowed to spend a week or two with his uncle. His cousin, this nobleman's daughter, one morning invited him to go round with her while she was visiting her peasants. One man was pointed out to them as having mysteriously begun to fail in health and fade away since he had married his second wife. "He seems to shrivel from day to day, yet he is a rich farmer and eats meats ravenously at his meals." The man's sister, who lived with him, said, "Since he has re-married he cries out in the night." Captain Pokrovsky, who saw the man, described him as being pale and listless, not at all what a peasant of that stamp ought to appear, and accordingly he asked his cousin what actually was the matter with the fellow. The girl answered: "I do not know, but the villagers all declare that a vampire is getting at him." The Captain was so interested in the case that he sent for a doctor who came from a considerable distance. The doctor after a careful examination reported that the man, whilst not anæmic in a medical sense, seemed to have lost a great deal of blood, but no wound could be found serious enough to account for such a drain. There was, however, a small puncture in the neck with inflamed edges, yet no swelling as might have been expected in the case of the bite of an insect. Tonics were promptly prescribed, and strengthening food was given to the invalid.

In due course Pokrovsky went back to his own home, but some time afterwards he inquired of his cousin concerning the anæmic peasant. She replied that in spite of the meat juice and red wine she had given him, the man had died, and that the wound in his neck at the time of death was far larger than when

Pokrovsky had seen it. Further, the village was so entirely, convinced that the man had been vampirized, that his wife, although she had frequently eaten heartily of food in public, had been seen to cross herself devoutly, and was a frequent attendant at Mass, immediately found it advisable, nay necessary, to leave the district. It should be remembered that as this took place in Lithuania, the peasants were probably not Slavs or Orthodox, but Lithuanians and Latins. Pokrovsky suggested that the woman may have played vampire subconsciously, whilst asleep ; or that it may have been a case of vampiric possession. Either of these is possible, and it seems certain that one must be the correct explanation. Which of the two could only have been determined by an investigator upon the spot, an eye-witness. We have here then an indubitable history of vampirism, an instance of very recent date.

In the following narrative of an Armenian vampire, which is related by Baron August von Haxthausen in his *Transcaucasia*, London, Chapman and Hall, 1854[20] (pp. 190-191), we return to folk-lore and legend. The travellers were approaching Mt. Ararat and he writes : " Ararat is more than half covered with eternal snow, and now under the bright morning sun it was lighted up with various colours—crimson, orange, and violet . . .   on our right rose the glaciers of Allagas, and at two miles from Erivan commenced the mountains of Ultmish Altotem, stretching to a distance of forty or fifty versts. They are said to have 366 valleys, respecting which Peter related the following Armenian legend. There once dwelt in a cavern in this country a vampyre, called Dakhanavar, who could not endure any one to penetrate into these mountains or count their valleys. Every one who attempted this, had in the night his blood sucked by the monster, from the soles of his feet, until he died. The vampyre was however at last outwitted by two cunning fellows : they began to count the valleys, and when night came on they lay down to sleep, taking care to place themselves with the feet of the one under the head of the other. In the night the monster came, felt as usual, and found a head : then he felt at the other end, and found a head there also. 'Well,' cried he, 'I have gone through the whole 366 valleys of these mountains, and have sucked the blood of people without end, but never yet did I find any one with two heads and no feet !' So saying he ran away, and was never more seen in that country ; but ever after the people have known that the mountain has 366 valleys.''

In Roumania the vampire tradition extends back far into the centuries, and there is perhaps no supernatural belief which is so strongly prevalent both in city and market-town as in the villages and remoter country districts. Moreover the tradition is amplified and complicated by local legends and peculiarly romantic ideas of rustic fancy, which often proves poetical enough and not without a certain macabre beauty, but often exhibits itself as materially gross and saturnine. It is hardly too much to say that in Roumania we find gathered together around the Vampire almost all the beliefs and superstitions that prevail throughout the whole of Eastern Europe. Although, as will be noted later, a certain species of vampire may tend to merge into a mere mythical imagination (the *vârcolac*), and again although he may be at times identified with the witch who in her turn is frequently no more than the *baba* or wise woman of some hamlet, yet when he preserves his own horrid qualities he is a being much dreaded and feared throughout the whole country even at the present day.

The old folk tale says : " There was once a time when vampires were as common as blades of grass, or berries in a pail, and they never kept still, but wandered round at night among the people."[21] Although nowadays the appearance of a vampire may be regarded as exceptional, none the less it is a very distinct and a very terrible possibility, and against such visitations it is well to be on one's guard, and should any such suspicion arise wise heads will not neglect every remedy and precaution.

In Roumania also there is a belief which, however vaguely expressed when put into words, is very definite and clear in the peasant mind to the effect that after death the soul is not finally separated from the body and cannot enter Paradise until full forty days have passed. Accordingly if there be any presumption that the deceased is or may become a vampire this interval is one of great anxiety and distress. In actual practice bodies are religiously exhumed three years after death, if it be a child ; four or five years if it be a young person ;

and seven years in the case of those who are elderly or full
grown. Should the body not have fallen to putrefaction then
it is assuredly a vampire. If the bones however are white
and dry the soul has passed to its eternal reward. The atomy
is ceremonially washed in wine and water, it is wrapped in a
fair linen shroud, a requiem is sung, and it is devoutly re-
interred.

As in all other countries, so in Roumania, the suicide, the
witch, he who has trafficked in goetry and dark spells or led a
life of cruelty and wickedness, each one of these will certainly
become a vampire after death. Should a hapless child die
before it is baptized, it will become a vampire when seven
years have passed, and the spot where it is buried is unhallowed
ground. Men who seek material gain by perjury, who bear
false witness to the hurt of others, will become vampires six
months after death. When there are seven children of the
same sex the seventh will have a little tail and must become
a vampire. This is a remarkably curious idea and would seem
to be in complete contradiction to the general belief that a
seventh child is the child of luck. In Devonshire and in
Scotland,[22] for example, a seventh son and even a seventh
daughter were both credited with natural gifts of healing, and
their aid was often sought by sufferers. Occult powers and
the faculty of a close communion with the spiritual world are
generally attributed to a seventh son, or—more rarely—to
a seventh child of either sex. It is remarkable that this idea
should appear in a somewhat degraded and inverted form,
so to speak, among the Roumanians. It is perhaps remotely
connected with the primitive thought that offerings to the
dead must always be seven in number or a multiple of seven
survivals of which custom may yet be remotely traced.[23]

A man born with a caul becomes a vampire in less than the
fortieth day after he has been interred. This again is in
contradiction to the belief in other countries. Cotgrave remarks
that to be born with a caul is a sign of good luck : " Il est né
coiffé. Born rich, honorable, fortunate ; born with his
mother's kerchief about his head." The Italians name a caul
" la camicia della Madonna," and in his *Usi e Pregiudizi della
Romagna* (p. 25) Michele Placucci tells us : " Credono invul-
nerabile il detto uomo della camicia, ma solo però riguardo
al piombo, e perciò in caso di rissa il competitore sostituisce

alle palle di piombo altre di cera, o d'argento, oppure mitraglia e così credono eludere la virtù portata dalla ripetuta camicia." The same idea is recorded by the author of *Superstitions Anciennes et Modernes* (Amsterdam, 1736, ii) : " Non seulement, dit on encore, l'enfant qui est né coiffé est heureux ; il a même le privilege d'être invulnerable, pourvu qu'il la porte toute sa vie sur soi et encore mieux c'est s'il la mange." William Henderson in his *Notes on the Folk-lore of the Northern Counties of England and the Borders*, London, 1866, says : " On the borders persons born with cauls are supposed to possess special powers of healing, but with this restriction— that the virtue is held to be so much abstracted from their own vital energy, and if much drawn upon they pine away and die of exhaustion," an idea which very definitely partakes of an exercise of vampirism, the *né coiffé* being the subject whose vitality may be sucked and drained by others. The caul was regarded as a lucky charm, and in the Malvern *Advertiser*, March, 1872, a child's caul was advertised for sale. There are many literary references to this old belief. Thus in *Oberon's Palace, Hesperides*, 444, Herrick writes of Queen Mab's bed :

> For either sheet was spread the caul
> That doth the infant's face enthral,
> When it is born (by some enstyl'd
> The lucky omen of the child).

In Act V of the comedy, *Elvira ; or, The Worst not always true*, by George Digby, Earl of Bristol, produced at Lincoln's Inn Fields in 1663 ; 4to, 1667 ; Zancho cries :

> Were we not born with cauls upon our heads ?
> Think'st thou, Chichon, to come off twice arow
> Thus rarely from such dangerous adventures ?

It is said that sometimes in Roumania a man who knows that he was born with a caul will when he dies leave instructions to his family to treat his body as that of a vampire and so avert any future danger.

If a vampire cast his cold grey eyes upon a pregnant woman, especially if she be past her sixth month, and the spell be not undone by the blessing of the Church, the child she carries will become a vampire. If a pregnant woman does not take salt she is big with vampire.

A notable mark of vampirism is if a man does not eat garlic, for this plant has great virtue and is hateful to the vampire. Should a cat jump over a dead body, or a man step over it, or even the shadow of a living man fall upon it, the deceased will become a vampire. In many districts of Roumania it is thought that persons are doomed to become vampires and that they cannot escape their destiny. Whilst they lie asleep their soul comes out of their mouth like a little fly. If the body were to be turned round so that the head reposed where the feet had lain the soul would not be able to find its way back and the man dies.

That the soul of a sleeper wanders away from his body and often actually visits the places and performs the acts of which he may dream is a belief which has been held the whole world over. In the account of a trial for witchcraft at Mühlbach in the year 1746 it appeared that a woman had engaged two men to work in her vineyard. About noon all took the usual repose from the heat of the day. After an hour had passed the labourers got up and tried to wake the woman so that they might duly proceed to work. However, she was stretched out motionless and stark with her mouth wide open. Towards eventide when the sun was setting they returned but she still lay inert, scarce seeming to breathe, as though she were dead. Just then a large fly buzzed past and this was caught by one of the men who put it in his leather pouch. They then again endeavoured to wake the woman but without success. Afterwards they released the fly which flew straight into the woman's mouth and she instantly awoke. Upon seeing this the men could no further doubt that she was indeed a witch.[24]

The Serbians hold that the soul of a sleeping witch leaves her body in the form of a butterfly. If during its absence her body be turned round and her head placed in another position the butterfly soul will not be able to find its way back to the mouth, and the witch will die.[25] A precisely similar belief prevails among the Esthonians,[26] and in Livonia it is common knowledge that when the soul of a werewolf is abroad on his particular business his body lies dead as stock or stone. If during this time the body were moved to another place, or even if the position were accidentally shifted, the soul could not find its way back, but must perforce remain in the body of a wolf until death.[27] This is a particularly striking tradition when we bear in mind the intimate connexion that prevails between the werewolf and the vampire. There is a story of Languedoc which tells how a woman who was suspected of being a witch one day fell asleep in the hot summer sun among the reapers in the field. Scenting a fine opportunity to prove their suspicions the reapers carried her whilst she slumbered to another part of the field, and exactly upon the spot where she had first lain they set a large empty kilderkin. When her soul returned it entered the vessel which it adroitly rolled along at great speed until the moving pitcher actually came into contact with her body, of which it immediately once more took possession.[28]

Amongst some races it is not even necessary to alter the position of a sleeper's body for the soul to be thwarted in its return. The Coreans are convinced that during sleep "the soul goes out of the body, and if a piece of paper is put over the face of the sleeper he will assuredly die, for his soul cannot find its way back into him again."[29] The Malays declare that if a person's face be daubed or blackened while he sleeps the soul which has gone forth will not recognize its home and the man will sleep on until his face be washed.[30] In Bombay indeed it was considered nothing less than murder to disguise or in any way paint the face of a sleeper, for if the aspect of the countenance be changed the soul upon its return cannot recognise its body and the individual must shortly expire.[31]

In Transylvania a child should never be allowed to sleep with its mouth open lest the soul might slip out in the shape of a mouse and the child never waken again.[32] So in Brunswick, the country folk say that the soul issues from a sleeper's mouth as a white mouse or a little bird and that to catch the mysterious animal or bird would kill the sleeping person.[33] This theme occurs innumerable times in saga and legend. In an East Indian story the soul comes forth as a cricket[34]; in a Scotch story it is a humble bee[35]; and in Germany again it is a white mouse[36] or a red mouse[37].

In Roumania the vampire is generally of two kinds and Mrs. Agnes Murgoçi differentiates the "dead-vampire type" from the "live-vampire type."[38] The "dead-vampire" is the re-animated corpse, energized by the return of the soul. The corpse possessed by some demon seems unknown, or at any rate of the rarest, for Mrs. Murgoçi says: "I have found so far no instance in which the dead corpse is supposed to be reanimated by a devil and not by its own soul." "People destined to become vampires after death may be able in life to send out their souls, and even their bodies, to wander at cross-roads with reanimated corpses. This type may be called the live-vampire type. It merges into the ordinary witch or wizard, who can meet other witches or wizards either in the body or as a spirit."[39]

A third type of vampire, the *vârcolac*, is entirely mythical, being thought to be an extraordinary creature which eats the sun and moon and thus causes eclipses. A prominent authority I. Otescu in his *Credintele Țaranului Român despre Cer și Stele (Beliefs of the Roumanian peasant concerning the Sky and the Stars)*[40] gives the following account of the *vârcolaci*. " *Vârcolaci* are supposed to be different from any beings on the earth. They cause eclipses of the moon, and even of the sun, by mounting up to heaven and eating the moon or sun. Some think that they are animals smaller than dogs. Others that they are dogs, two in number. . . . They have different origins ; some say that they are the souls of unbaptized children, or of children of unmarried parents, cursed by God and turned into *vârcolaci*. . . . Others again say that *vârcolaci* originate from the air of heaven, when women spin at night, especially at midnight, without a candle, particularly if they cast spells with the thread they spin. Hence it is never good to spin by moonlight, for vampires and *vârcolaci* get up to the sky by the thread and eat the sun and moon. They fasten themselves to the thread, and the thread makes itself into a road for them. As long as the thread does not break the *vârcolaci* have power, and can go where ever they wish. They attack the heavenly bodies, they bite the moon, so that she appears covered with blood, or till none of her is left. But if the thread is broken their power is broken and they go to another part of the sky . . . ."

G. F. Ciaușanu, in his *Superstițiile poporului Român* reports that "in Vâlcea there are said to be beings who are called *vârcolaci*, because their spirit is *vârcolaci*. They are recognized by their pale faces and dry skin, and by the deep sleep into which they fall when they go to the moon to eat it. But they eat it only during an eclipse, and when the disc of the moon is red or copper-coloured. The redness is the blood of the moon, escaping from the mouths of the *vârcolaci* and spreading over the moon.

"When the spirit of the *vârcolaci* wants to eat the moon, the man to whom the spirit belongs begins to nod, falls into a deep sleep as if he had not slept for weeks, and remains as if dead. If he is roused or moved sleep becomes eternal, for, when the spirit returns from its journey, it cannot find the mouth out of which it came, and so cannot go in again.

. . . .

"Some say that God orders the *vârcolaci* to eat the moon so that men may repent and turn from evil."

With reference to the various Roumanian terms for a vampire, Mrs. Murgoçi writes as follows : "As regards the names used for vampires, dead and alive, *strigoi* (fem. *strigoica*) is the most common Roumanian term, and *moroii* is perhaps the next most usual. *Moroii* is less often used alone than *strigoi*. Usually we have *strigoi* and *moroii* consorting together but the *moroii* are subject to the *strigoi*. We find also *strigoi*, *moroii* and *vârcolaci*, and *strigoi* and *pricolici* used as if all were birds of the same feather. A Transilvanian term is *gişcoi*. *Vârcolaci* (*svârcolaci*) and *pricolici* are sometimes dead vampires, and sometimes animals which eat the moon. *Oper* is the Ruthenian word for dead vampire. In Bukovina, *vidme* is used for a witch ; it covers much the same ground as *strigoi* (used for a live vampire), but it is never used for a dead vampire."

The "live-vampires" are said to meet the "dead-vampires" on certain nights in old and forlorn cemeteries, in deserted houses, in the haunted depths of the forest and in other ill-boding places, where from the deceased who are the more powerful they learn the runes of black magic. In some country districts it is supposed that the "live-vampires" form covens, and at the head of each company is a master or a mistress as the case may be, the men following their officer, and the women together with their moderatrix. This arrangement exactly resembles that of the historical witch society, and it is plain that the "live-vampire" and the witch in rustic credence are identical. We are not surprised to learn that in the Mihalcea district it is supposed that chiefly women are vampires. They possess a certain control which enables them to extract the "power" of animals and objects for their own use. Thus they are able in some mysterious way to absorb or collect the vitality of fowls and bees, for example, and to concentrate this upon their own farm-yards and hives, so that their hens will become plump and lay abundantly ; their hives be exceedingly rich in honeycomb, whilst the poultry of the neighbours sickens and dies, and the aparies of the village contain no store of golden sweetness. It is told that one woman baked bread which was so light and good in the eating that half the country-side came to buy her loaves, and before long her pockets were well filled. The other wives in the village could not get their dough to rise, do what they would. Their bread seemed always mouldy and stale. Now this happened because the bakeress was a vampire, and knew how to obtain the essential goodness of bread from all the other ovens.

Some of these vampires can control the rain, and to them secret resort is constantly made by the farmers. They can also gather the " power " of beauty, which they sell for money, and here in fact we have the regular love-charms. These female vampires are generally of a dry burning skin and a notably florid complexion. The men are bald and distinguished by peculiarly piercing eyes. It is supposed that they can assume the shapes of various animals, and they particularly favour the form of a cat. When a vampire washes rain will soon fall, and it is said that in the olden days during a drought the great landowners and nobles would cause all the peasants of their estates to bathe in the river hoping that there might be a vampire among them. This influence over the weather conditions is generally considered to be the peculiar quality of "live-vampires," but at Zărneşti a series of extraordinarily heavy floods was supposed to be caused by a girl who had been recently buried and who was generally reputed to be a vampire.

The remedies effectually to dispose of a dead man who has become a vampire are much the same as in all other lands. It is strongly advised that precautions of this kind should be taken at burial, or as soon after as possible. A suicide must be put in running water. It may be remembered that running water dissolves all charms, and a witch cannot cross a stream. Water in itself is a holy element and as such has had its place in all religions, nor is the poet's conception of " waters at their priest-like task " without a very real truth. In Vâlcea it is usual to thrust a long needle into the heart of the vampire, but the general method is that which is common throughout the whole of Eastern Europe, at one blow to drive a stake through the navel or the heart. Again small pebbles and grains of incense may be placed in the mouth, ears, nose and navel, and in the quicks of the nails, so that the vampire may have something to gnaw at when he wakes. Millet should be scattered over him, for he will delay until he has counted and eaten every grain. Garlic may also be stuffed in the mouth. The body should be arranged face downwards, and a correspondent of the *Times* in June, 1874, writes that burying with the face downwards is resorted to in Maine, U.S.A., as a means of stopping consumption from running through a household. If reburial is necessary the corpse should be turned head to foot. Long garlands of wild roses should be wreathed round the coffin, which further may be confined with stout bands of wood. It may be remembered that on the eve of S. George's day there used not to be a Saxon farm in Transylvania which had not the gates of the yard decorated with branches of wild rose bushes in order to keep out the witches.[41] Since other thorny shrubs were also utilized in this way, the idea originally seems to have been that the evil visitants would get caught in the briars if they attempted to climb through, but this precaution became at least partially obscured and certain magical properties were ascribed to the wild rose of itself.

In the district of Teleorman, on the third day after a death, when people go to the house of mourning in order to burn incense they carry with them nine spindles, and these they thrust deep into the grave. Should the vampire rise he would be pierced by their sharp points. Another method is to take tow, to scatter it upon the grave, and to set fire to it there, for it is believed that the occupant will scarce venture through the flames. Sometimes the anathema of a priest will confine the vampire in his tomb.

In the Romanați district the vampire is stripped and the naked carrion thrust into a stout bag. The clothes and cerements are sprinkled with holy water, replaced in the coffin which is secured and again buried in the grave. The body is taken away to the forest. The heart is first cut out, and then it is hacked piecemeal limb from limb and each gobbet

burned in a great fire. Last of all the heart is flung into the
flames and those who have assisted come near so that they
shall be fumigated with the smoke. But all must be consumed, every shred of flesh, every bone. The veriest scrap
if left would be enough to enable the vampire again to mater-
ialize. Occasionally the ashes of the heart are collected,
mingled with water and given to sick people as a powerful
potion.

At Zârneşti after a female vampire had been exhumed great
iron forks were driven through the heart, eyes, and breast
after which the body was buried at a considerable depth, face
downwards.

In Mehedinti it was once thought a sufficient precaution if
the body was carried far away to some remote spot among
the mountains and there totally abandoned. But such a
method in practice was rarely used, and indeed was seldom
found effectual. It is not to be compared with the Greek
method of transporting the body to some lonely island, for
in the latter case this is done precisely because the vampire is
unable to cross the waters of the sea.

It is held to be imperative that the vampire should be
traced to his lair and destroyed at the very first opportunity.
If he is sufficiently cunning to avoid detection so long at the
end of seven years he will become a man again, and then he
will be able to pass into another country, or at any rate to a
new district, where another language is spoken. He will marry
and have children, and these after they die will all go to swell
the vampire host.

In Roumania as in Greece and other lands the vampire
first attacks his own household and even the animals belonging
to his family. Yet he will return in the night and talk with
them ; he may even help with the housework, fetch and carry,
cleave wood and bring it home from a considerable distance.
Female vampires persistently return to their children. Sometimes, however, he will be destructive, break dishes, upset
jars of water, cause a veritable racket, and abominably plague
the whole house. However, whether he be busily helpful or
whether he prove a bane all the inhabitants will quickly die
off, and even the cattle will fall victims to some strange disease.
The village priest is then generally requested to read certain
prayers over the graves, but if the horrid molestations persist

more drastic measures must speedily be taken. In order precisely to discover which is the tomb that is the source of these fatal distresses a white stallion is led to the cemetery, and the grave over which he refuses to pass, but at the side of which he stands still, shivering with fright and neighing wildly, contains the vampire. In the same way a gander will not walk over the vampire's grave. The body must then be exhumed and if the notable marks of vampirism are found it can be dealt with in the traditional manner.

It may be noted that if the relations of a vampire have died the monster will be found in his coffin full and foggy as a great leech, his mouth gaping wide and slobbered with rank gouts of fresh crimson blood. If he has only been destructive of pots and pans and eaten what he could find in the larder the mouth will be covered with maize meal. It is believed that very often the vampire will resist when his body is disinterred and utter hideous yells to scare those who are employed upon the business, but if they pluck up good courage and if the priest be there the monster cannot harm them.

In Roumania at certain times during the year when their power is at its height special precautions must be taken against the attacks of the vampire. The two particular periods in a year when the vampire is most active are S. Andrew's Eve and S. George's Eve. There exist, however, many variants of this idea in different districts. Thus in some localities they are said to be most troublesome just before Easter ; in Mihalcea their operations are confined to the period between S. Andrews Eve and the Epiphany ; in Siret they are given a longer term since they are free to plague living folk from S. Andrew's Day until the Transfiguration, or in some cases from S. George's Day until the feast of S. John.

Generally, however, the particular precautions to safeguard a house or a village are taken on the last day of the year, before Easter Sunday, before S. Andrew's Day and on the eve of S. George. Throughout the whole of Eastern Europe, indeed, the feast of S. George, 23 April, is one of the most important celebrations of the whole year and it has become the occasion of numberless observances and rites which can barely be glanced at here. S. George is the patron or protector of England, Antioch, Bavaria, Venice, Constantinople, Friedberg, Genoa, Gronsfeld, Haguenau, Keldra, Leuchtenberg, Molsheim,

Ochsenhausen, Ratisbon, Rechheim, Ueberlingen, Ulm, Vige-
vano, of Serbia, Saxony, Russia, and of numberless other
countries and towns.[42] S. George, "le très-loyal Chevalier
de la Chrétienneté," has always been honoured in the East as
"The Great Martyr," and one of the first churches erected by
Constantine, after his profession of Christianity, was in honour
of this saint. He is the especial patron of cattle, horses and
wolves, and it may not untruly be said that among the herds-
men and shepherds of Eastern Europe the feast of S. George,
who will protect their flocks from the ravages of wild beasts
has a national, one might almost write an international as well
as an ecclesiastical character. At the same time upon the
eve of the saint the power of vampires, witches and every
evil thing is at its height. Among the Ruthenians of Bukowina
and Galicia the farmer's wife gathers great branches of thorn
to lay on the threshold of her house and every door is painted
with a cross in tar to protect it from the witches. The Huzuls
kindle large bonfires for their houses for the same reason
whilst throughout Transylvania, Walachia and Bulgaria
precautions of various kinds are similarly taken. The South
Slavs favour bundles of thistles which are placed on the fence,
the windows and the doors to prevent the entry of any evil
thing. On the morrow, 23 April, the house is garlanded with
flowers, chaplets of roses decorate the stalls and the
horns of the cows are wreathed with blossom in honour of the
saint. Until quite recent years in Swabia all the church bells
used to be kept ringing a merry chime from nightfall until
dawn on the day of the festival. This no doubt was often taken
to be merely the due ushering in of the celebrations, but
originally it had a further signification, for in those parts it
was believed that no vampire and no witch can come within
the sound of a church bell. Although unfortunately, in many
cases as in England,[43] owing to the blameworthy coldness and
neglect of the authorities, the cultus of S. George cannot be
said to be flourishing or popular, yet in some places the saint
is still particularly honoured and it is sad to think that the
solemn celebrations which attracted pilgrims from far and near
to Ostrotta in Poland and Ertringen in Bavaria have lost
much of their popularity.

In Roumania upon these particular days when the vampire
is most malicious the country folk anoint the windows with

garlic, they tie bundles of garlic on the door and in the cow sheds. All lights throughout the house must be extinguished and it is well that every utensil should be turned topsy-turvy. Pious people will pass the whole night in prayer, and even those who have not this devotion do their best to keep awake. If a man must sleep he generally puts a knife unsheathed beneath the pillow. Nor will anyone answer if called by name, at least not until he has been summoned three times, for as in Chios, a vampire may call you once at night but cannot repeat his request, wherefore if one waits to hear the name a third time one may be well assured it is not the horrible intruder.

It is upon record that there have been from time to time in Roumania very grave outbreaks of vampirism, and in consequence of these widespread molestations the peasants, as is not surprising, more than once took the law into their own hand until they were checked by the authorities. Ureche in his *History of Roumania*, records :—" In 1801, on 12 July, the Bishop of Sigen sent a petition to the hospodar of Wallachia, requesting that he should order his provincial waywodes no longer to permit the peasants of Stroesti to disinter dead people, who had already been twice exhumed, under the idea that they were *vârcolaci*." Again in the *Biserica Orthodoxa Romana* we find : " The Archbishop Nectarie (1813-19) dispatched an official letter to all his higher clergy (protopopes) exhorting them to inquire in what districts it was thought that the dead might return as vampires. If they came upon a case of vampirism they were not to take it upon themselves immediately to cremate the corpse, but they were rather to instruct the people how to proceed according to the formal canon of the Church."

Dr. Tudor Panfile, one of the most eminent of Roumanian scholars has collected a vast number of vampire stories in *Ion Creanda*, a native periodical of peasant art and literature. Thence I take the following which must serve as typical of very many.[44]

" Some twenty or thirty years ago (from 1914) in the commune Afumati in Dolj, a certain peasant, Mărin Mirea Ociocioc, died. It was noticed that his relations also died, one after the other. A certain Badea Vrajitor (Badea the wizard) dug him up. Badea himself, going later into the forest up to the frontier on a cold wintry night, was eaten by wolves. The bones of Marin were sprinkled with wine, a church service read over them, and replaced in the grave. From that time there were no more deaths in the family.

"Some fifteen years ago, in Amărăşti, in the north of Dolj an old woman, the mother of the peasant Dinu Gheorghiţa, died. After some months the children of her eldest son began to die, one after the other, and, after that, the children of her youngest son. The sons became anxious, dug her up one night, cut her in two, and buried her again. Still the deaths did not cease. They dug her up a second time, and what did they see ? The body was whole without a wound. It was a great marvel. They took her and carried her into the forest, and put her under a great tree in a remote part of the forest. There they disembowelled her, took out her heart, from which blood was flowing, cut it in four, put it on hot cinders, and burnt it. They took the ashes and gave them to children to drink with water. They threw the body on the fire, burnt it, and buried the ashes of the body. Then the deaths ceased.

"Some twenty or thirty years ago, a cripple, an unmarried man, of Cuşmir, in the south of Mehedinţi, died. A little time after, his relations began to die, or to fall ill. They complained that a leg was drying up. This happened in several places. What could it be ? ' Perhaps it is the cripple ; let us dig him up.' They dug him up one Saturday night, and found him as red as red, and all drawn up into a corner of the grave. They cut him open, and took the customary measures. They took out the heart and liver, burnt them on red-hot cinders, and gave the ashes to his sister and other relations, who were ill. They drank them with water, and regained their health.

"In the Cuşmir, another family began to show very frequent deaths, and suspicion fell on a certain old man, dead long ago. When they dug him up, they found him sitting up like a Turk, and as red as red, just like fire ; for had he not eaten up nearly the whole of a family of strong, young men. When they tried to get him out he resisted, unclean and horrible. They gave him some blows with an axe, they got him out, but they could not cut him with a knife. They took a scythe and an axe, cut out his heart and liver, burnt them, and gave them to the sick folk to drink. They drank, and regained their health. The old man was reburied, and the deaths ceased.

" In Văguileşti, in Mehedinţi, there was a peasant Dimitriu Vaideanu, of Transilvanian origin, who had married a wife in Văguileşti and settled there. His children died one after the other ; seven died within a few months of birth, and some bigger children had died as well. People began to wonder what the cause of all this could be. They took counsel together, and resolved to take a white horse to the cemetery one night, and see if it would pass over all the graves of the wife's relations. This they did, and the horse jumped over all the graves, until it came to the grave of the mother-in-law, Joana Marta, who had been a witch, renowned far and wide. Then the horse stood still, beating the earth with its feet, neighing and snorting, unable to step over the grave. Probably there was something unholy there. At night Dimitriu and his son took candles and went to dig up the grave. They were seized with horror at what they saw. There she was, sitting like a Turk, with long hair falling over her face, with all her skin red, and with finger nails frightfully long. They got together brushwood, shavings, and bits of old crosses, they poured wine on her, they put in straw and set fire to the whole. Then they shovelled the earth back and went home."

To multiply similar relations of peasant anas and local fable throughout Eastern Europe would be no difficult but a somewhat superfluous task. It is well to consider the more serious side of tradition, and accordingly the following account of the Bulgarian beliefs as given by St. Clair and Brophy in their *Twelve Years' Study of the Eastern Question in Bulgaria*[45] will not be impertinent here. " By far the most curious superstition in Bulgaria is that of the Vampire, a tradition which is common to all countries of Slavonic origin, but is now to be found in its original loathsomeness only in these provinces. In Dalmatia and Albania, whence the knowledge of this superstition was first imported into Europe, and which were consequently, though wrongly, considered as its mother-countries, the Vampire has been disfigured by poetical embellishments, and has become a mere theatrical being—tricked out in all the tinsel of modern fancy. The Dalmatian youth who, after confessing himself and receiving the Holy Communion as if in preparation for death, plunges a consecrated poniard into the heart of the Vampire slumbering in his tomb ; and the supernaturally beautiful

Vampire himself, who sucks the life-blood of sleeping maidens, has never been imagined by the people, but fabricated, or at least dressed up, by romancers of the sensational school.

"When that factitious poetry, born from the ashes of a people whose nationality is extinct, and from which civilization has reaped its harvest, replaces the harsh, severe, even terrible poetry which is the offspring of the uncultivated courage or fear of a young and vigorous humanity, legendary lore becomes weak, doubtful, and theatrical. Thus, as in a ballad said to be antique, we recognize a forgery by the smoothness of its rhythm and the nicety of its rhythm ; so, when the superstitions of a people naturally uneducated and savaged are distinguished by traits of religion or of sentiment, we trace the defacing hand of the Church or the poet.

" In Dalmatia the Vampire is now no more than a shadow, in which no one believes, or at best in which people pretend to believe ;[46] just as a London Scottish volunteer will assure you of his firm faith in the Kelpie and Brounie of Sir Walter Scott, or will endeavour to convince you that he wears a kilt from choice and not for effect. Between the conventional Vampire and the true horror of Slavonic superstition there is as much difference as between the Highland chief who kicked away the ball of snow from under his son's head, reproaching him with southron effiminacy in needing the luxury of a pillow, and the kilted cockney sportsman who shoots down tame deer in an enclosure.

" In Poland the Roman Catholic clergy have laid hold upon this superstition as a means of making war upon the great enemy of the Church, and there the Vampire is merely a corpse possessed by the Evil Spirit,[47] and no longer the true Vampire of the ancient Slavonians. In Bulgaria we find the brute in its original and disgusting form ; it is no longer a dead body possessed by a demon, but a soul in revolt against the inevitable principle of corporeal death ; the Dalmatian poniard, blessed upon the altar, is powerless here, and its substitute is an Ilatch (literally, medicine) administered by the witch, or some other wise woman, who detects a Vampire by the hole in his tombstone or the hearth which covers him, and stuffs it up with human excrement (his favourite food) mixed with poisonous herbs.

"We will now give the unadulterated Bulgarian superstitions, merely prefacing that we ought to be well acquainted
with it, inasmuch as a servant of ours is the son of a noted
Vampire, and is doing penance during this present Lent by
neither smoking, nor drinking wine or spirits, in order to
expiate the sins of his father and to prevent himself inheriting
the propensity.

"When a man who has Vampire blood in his veins—for
this condition is not only epidemic and endemic, but heredi-
tary—or who is otherwise predisposed to become a vampire,
dies, nine days after his burial he returns to upper earth
in an æriform shape. The presence of the Vampire in this
his first condition may be easily discerned in the dark by a
succession of sparks like those from a flint and steel; in
the light, by a shadow projected upon a wall, and varying in
density according to the age of the Vampire in his career.
In this stage he is comparatively harmless, and is only able
to play the practical jokes of the German Kobold and Gnome,
of the Irish Phooka, or the English Puck; he roars in a
terrible voice, or amuses himself by calling out the inhabitants
of a cottage by the most endearing terms, and then beating
them black and blue.

"The father of our servant, Theodore, was a Vampire of
this class. One night he seized by the waist (for vampires are
capable of exercising considerable physical force) Kodja
Keraz, the *Pehlivan*, or champion wrestler, of Derekuoi,
crying out, "Now then, old Cherry Tree, see if you can throw
me." The village champion put forth all his strength, but
the Vampire was so heavy that Kodja Keraz broke his own
jaw in throwing the invisible being who was crushing him
to death.

"At the time of this occurrence, five years ago, our village
was so infested with Vampires that the inhabitants were
forced to assemble together in two or three houses, to burn
candles all night, and to watch by turns, in order to avoid
the assaults of the Obours, who lit up the streets with their
sparkles, and of whom the most enterprising threw their
shadows on the walls of the room where the peasants were
dying of fear; whilst others howled, shrieked, and swore
outside the door, entered the abandoned houses, spat blood
into the flour, turned everything topsy-turvy, and smeared

the whole place, even the pictures of the saints, with cow-dung. Happily for Derekuoi, Vola's mother, an old lady suspected for a turn for witchcraft, discovered the Ilatch we have already mentioned, laid the troublesome and troubled spirits, and since then the village has been free from these unpleasant supernatural visitations.

"When the Bulgarian Vampire has finished a forty days' apprenticeship to the realm of shadows, he rises from his tomb in bodily form, and is able to pass himself off as a human being, living honestly and naturally. Thirty years since a stranger arrived in this village, established himself, and married a wife with whom he lived on very good terms, she making but one complaint, that her husband absented himself from the conjugal roof every night and all night. It was soon remarked that (although scavengers were, and are, utterly unknown in Bulgaria) a great deal of scavengers' work was done at night by some unseen being, and that when one branch of this industry was exhausted, the dead horses and buffaloes which lay about the streets were devoured by invisible teeth, much to the prejudice of the village dogs, then the mysterious mouth drained the blood of all cattle that happened to be in any way sickly. These occurrences, and the testimony of the wife, caused the stranger to be suspected of Vampirism ; he was examined, found to have only one nostril, and upon this irrefragable evidence was condemned to death. In executing this sentence, our villagers did not think it necessary to send for the priest, to confess themselves, or to take consecrated halters or daggers ; they just tied their man hand and foot, led him to a hill a little outside Derekuoi, lit a big fire of wait-a-bit thorns, and burned him alive.

"There is yet another method of abolishing a Vampire—that of *bottling* him. There are certain persons who make a profession of this ; and their mode of procedure is as follows : The sorcerer, armed with a picture of some saint, lies in ambush until he sees the Vampire pass, when he pursues him with his *Eikon ;* the poor Obour takes refuge in a tree or on the roof of a house, but his persecutor follows him up with the talisman, driving him away from all shelter, in the direction of a bottle specially prepared, in which is placed some of the Vampire's favourite food. Having no other resource, he enters this prison, and is immediately fastened down with a cork, on the interior of which is a fragment of the *Eikon*. The bottle is then thrown into the fire, and the Vampire disappears for ever. This method is curious, as showing the grossly material view of the soul taken by the Bulgarians, who imagine that it is a sort of chemical compound destructible by heat (like sulphuretted hydrogen), in the same manner that they suppose the souls of the dead to have appetites, and to feed after the manner of living beings, 'in the place where they are.'

"To finish the story of the Bulgarian Vampire, we have merely to state that here he does not seem to have that peculiar appetite for human blood which is generally supposed to form his distinguishing and most terrible characteristics, only requiring it when his resources of coarser food are exhausted."

Although I have quoted this account at length I would point out that often the writers have gone astray, not so much perhaps in the presentation of facts as in their interpretation of these. Their scepticism sets ill upon them, and, as all scepticism, is very fallible—yet I have chosen to cite them fairly rather than to emend.

In a note (p. 32) they say : "Since commencing this chapter (III), we have learned that the village of Dervishkuoi, six hours from here, is just now haunted by a Vampire. He appears with a companion who was suppressed by means of the usual remedy, but this one seems to be proof against poison, and as he will shortly have completed his fortieth day as a shadow, the villagers are in terrible alarm lest he should appear as flesh and blood." The allusion to a period of forty days has been fully considered and explained in the previous chapter which deals with the Vampire in modern Greece. It is plain that the writers here fail to appreciate this important point, and indeed although they have set forth a certain number of facts, valuable in themselves, they appear incapable of regarding the subject from the philosophical or even traditional point of view.

The belief that spirits and evil entities could be enclosed in vessels of glass would appear to be of Oriental origin,[48] and amongst other fantasies to have been introduced into Spain by the Morisco. Owing to the notorious trial for witchcraft of Doctor Eugenio Torralda in 1531, the Grand Inquisitor,

Don Alfonso Manriquez promulgated certain articles detailing various offences connected with demonolatory which every good Christian was bound to denounce to the Holy Office, and among these appears the following inquiry : " If any person made or caused to be made mirrors, rings, phials of glass or other vessels in order thereby to control or therein to contain some spirit who should reply to his demands and aid his projects," such a one must be delated to the proper ecclesiastical authorities.

It will be remembered that in *El Diabolo Coxuelo* by Luis Velez de Guevara, which romance was first printed in 1641, the hero Don Cleofas having by chance entered the chamber of an astrologer delivers from a bottle wherein he had been confined by potent charms *El Diabolo Coxuelo* who proves grateful and richly rewards his liberator. The situation will be at once recognized by all as having been used by Le Sage in his *Le Diable Boiteux*, which is so amply conveyed from his Spanish predecessor.

So far as I am aware there is no other country save Bulgaria where it is supposed that a Vampire can be imprisoned in this manner, and even in Bulgaria it cannot be the real Vampire, the dead body returned from the grave, but rather some vampirish wraith which they imagine can be trapped in this manner. There is reason to suppose that this local superstition comes from the Turks, and this, indeed, seems borne out by its very crudity. There does, indeed, exist a belief in Vampires among the Turks, but the Turkish Vampire is almost entirely to be identified with the ghoul, which monster has already been sufficiently considered. Among the people who are grossly materialistic many barbarous horrors are ignorantly believed, and there are corresponding methods, paynim and uncouth, for defending themselves against the goblins and devils which are so very present to them.

It is not too much to say that terrible though he may be in Christian countries the Vampire, when a material reality, may be baffled and destroyed, but upon passing beyond the pale of Christianity the unhappy people become the sport and the prey of fiends and cacodemons who so far from being exorcized and banished are rather attracted by the cantrips and abracadabra of their warlocks and voodoo professors of darkest necromancy.

NOTES. CHAPTER V

[1] The Emperor Maurice was murdered at Chalcedon in 602, when he was succeeded by the centurian Phocas who had revolted against him. There is a study by Adamek, *Beitrage zur Geschichte des Kaisers Mauricius*, Graz, 1891.

[2] His chief work is a chronicle of the reign of the Emperor Maurice, in eight books, from the death of Tiberius II and the accession of Maurice in 582 down to the murder of the latter. Ed. by Bekker, Bonn, 1834.

[3] He lived during the second half of the eighth century, and the early part of the ninth. In consequence of his resistance to the Iconoclasts he was banished by the tyrant Leo the Armenian to the island of Samothrace, where he died in 818. The *Chronicon* commences with the accession of Diocletian in 277 and concludes in 811. It was edited by De Boor, Leipzig 1883, and may also be found in the Collections of the Byzantine writers Paris, 1655, folio ; and Venice, 1729, folio.

[4] Edited by Hase, Paris, 1818 ; and by Migne, 1863.

[5] Born 25 July, 975 ; died 1 December, 1018. Dithmar's original manuscript, with corrections and additions made by himself, is still preserved at Dresden. A facsimile edition of it was prepared by L. Schmidt, Dresden, 1905. The chronicle was also published by Kurze in *Scriptores Rerum Germanicarum*, Hanover, 1889 ; and by Lappenberg in *Monumenta Germaniæ Historiæ Scriptorum*, III, 733-871, whence it was reprinted in Migne, *Patres Latini*, CXXXIX, 1183-1422. A German translation was made by Laurent, Berlin, 1848 ; reprinted Leipzig, 1892.

[6] Cosmas was born about 1045 at Prague, and died there, 21 October, 1125. His *Cronica* consists of three books ; the first brings the narrative to 1038, the second to 1092, and the third to 1125. The work has been repeatedly edited ; Freher, *Scriptores rerum bohemicarum*, Hanover, 1602, 1607, and 1620 ; Mencke, *Scriptores rerum Germanicarum*, Leipzig, 1728, vol. I ; Pelzl and Dobrowsky, *Scriptores rerum bohemicarum*, Prague, 1783 ; Koepke, *Monumenta Germaniæ Historiæ Scriptorum*, Hanover, 1851, vol. IX. It is also to be found in Migne, *Patres Latini*, CLXVI ; Emler and Tomek, *Fontes rerum bohemicarum*, Prague, 1874, vol. II.

[7] One may recall the episode in the Fourth Voyage of Sindbad the Sailor. *Le Livre des Mille Nuits et Une Nuit :* La trois cent troisième nuit et la trois cent quatrième nuit ; traduction de Dr. J. C. Mardrus, tome VI, Paris, 1901, pp. 140-153.

[8] Ibn Fozlan's narrative was published in 1823 by the Russian Academy of Sciences, with a German translation by C. M. Frahn. Rasmussun had previously translated it into Danish, and an English rendering of his version appeared in the Fourth volume of *Blackwood's Magazine*.

[9] Adolf Bastian, *Der Mensch in der Geschichte*, Leipzig, 1860, II, p. 328.

[10] A. Wuttke, *Deutscher Aberglaube*, 736. Klemm, *Culturgeschichte*, II, p. 101.

[11] Servius on Vergil, *Aeneid*, Ed. G. Thilo and H. Hagen. Leipzig, 1881, I, p. 186. Charles Rogers, *Social Life in Scotland*, Edinburgh, 1884-1886, I, p. 161. F. Schmidt, *Sitten und Gebrauche in Thuringen*, p. 94. The Rev. William Ellis, *Polynesian Researches*, Second Edition, London, 1832-1836, IV, p. 361). (*Cf.* Captain James Cook's, *Voyages*, London, 1809, p. 149 *sqq.*). Mungo Park, *Travels in the Interior Districts of Africa*. Fifth Edition, London, 1807, p. 414.

[12] *Russian Folk-Tales*, London, 1873, pp. 320-322.

[13] III. Chapter xxvi.

[14] Afanasief : *Poeticheskiya Vozzryeniya Slavyan na Peirodu*, III, 558. Translated by Ralston, *Songs of the Russian People*, pp. 411-12.

[15] Afanasief. V, pp. 142-4. Ralston, *op. cit.*, pp. 309-311. The tale is from the Tambof Government.

[16] Afanasief. V, pp. 324-5. Ralston, p. 312.

[17] The crowing of the cock disperses all phantasms of the night and dissolves enchantments. So Prudentius sings :

> Ferunt uagantes Dæmonas
> Lætas tenebras noctium
> Gallo canente exterritos
> Sparsim timere et credere.

The sabbats of witches concluded at cock-crow, and a witch named Latoma confessed to Nicolas Remy that this bird is the most hateful of all to sorcerers. See my *History of Witchcraft*, pp. 117-118.

[18] Afanasief, VI, pp. 321-2. Ralston, pp. 313-14.

[19] Afanasief, V, pp. 144-7. Ralston, pp. 314-18. This story is from the Tambof Government.

[20] *Op. cit.*, p. 318.

[21] London, Chapman and Hall, 1854, pp. 190-191.

[22] *Ion Creanga*, vol. iv, p. 202.

[23] In *Superstitions anciennes et modernes*, 2 tom, folio, Amsterdam, 1733-36, (I, l.xvi, p. 107) we have : " On me disoit, il y a quelque tems que les septiemes filles avoient le privilege de gucrir les mules aux talons. Mais ce rare privilege ne subsiste que dans l'imagination des personnes qui veulent railler, non plus qui celin de guerir les louppes, lequel ou attribue aux enfants posthumes, et à la main d'un Bourreau fraischement revenu de faire quelque execution de mort." In Devonshire the power to heal is attributed to a seventh daughter ; see *Transactions of the Devonshire Association*, ix, 93 ; also *Notes and Queries*, VII, i, 6, 91, and 475. James Kelly, *Scottish Proverbs*, London, 1721, has : " Or why in England the King cures the Struma by stroking, and why the Seventh Son in Scotland ; whether his Temperate complexion conveys a balsom and sucks out the corrupting principles by a frequent warm sanative contact ; or whether the parents of the seventh child put forth a more eminent virtue to his production than to all the rest as being the certain meridian and height to which their vigour ascends, and from that forth have a gradual declining into a feebleness of the body and its production." Arthur Mitchell in his *Superstitions of the Highlands and Islands of Scotland*, 1862, records : " In the island of Lewis, the seventh son of a seventh son in curing the King's evil by laying on of hands, gives the patient a sixpenny-piece with a hole in it, through which a string is passed, to wear round the neck. Should this be taken off, a return of the malady may be looked for." The Epilogue, spoken by Doctor Hughball (and Perigrine), to Brome's comedy, *The Antipodes*, acted at Salisbury Court in 1638 ; quarto 1640 ; commences thus :

> Whether my cure be perfect yet or no,
> It lies not in my doctor-ship to know.
> Your approbation may more raise the man,
> Then all the Colledge of physitians can ;
> And more health from your faire hands may be wonne,
> Then by the stroakings of the seaventh sonne.

[24] There is a vestige of such practices among the mountaineers on the north-west coast of New Guinea. F. S. A. de Clercq, " De Westen Noord-kust van Nederlandsch Nieuw-Guinea," *Tijdschrift van het kon. Nederlandsch Aardrijkskundig Genootschap*, Tweede Serie, x (1893), p. 199.

[25] F. Müller, *Beitrag zur Geschichte des Hexenglaubens und Hexenprozesses in Siebenbürgen.* Brunswick, 1854.

[26] Friebrich S. Krauss, *Volksglaube und religiöser Brauch der Südslaven.* Munster, i, W., 1890, p. 112.

[27] J. D. Holzmayer, " Osiliana." *Verhandlungen der Gelehrten Estnischen Gesellschaft zu Dorpat*, vii (Dorpat, 1872), No. 2, p. 53.

[28] P. Einhorn, " Wiederlegunge der Abgötterey ; der ander Theil." Riga, 1627. Reprinted in *Scriptores rerum Liuonicarum*, ii, 645. Riga and Leipzig, 1848.

[29] Alfred de Nore, *Coutumes, Mythes et Traditions des provinces de France*, Paris and Lyons, 1846, p. 88.

[30] W. Woodville Rockhill, "Notes on some of the Laws, Customs, and Superstitions of Korea," *The American Anthropologist*, iv, p. 183. Washington, 1891.

[31] Nelson Annandale, "Primitive Beliefs and Customs of the Patani Fishermen," *Fasciculi Malayenses, Anthropology*, Part I, April, 1903, p. 94.

[32] *Panjab Notes and Queries*, iii, p. 116.

[33] H. von Wlislocki, *Volksglaube und Volksbrauch der Siebenbürger Sachsen*, Berlin, 1893, p. 167.

[34] Richard Andree, *Braunschweiger Volkskunde*, Brunswick, 1896; p. 266.

[35] G. A. Wilken, "Het amimisme bij de volken van den Indischen Archipel," *De Indische Gids*, June, 1884, p. 940. This article was separately reprinted at Leyden in the following year.

[36] Hugh Miller, *My Schools and Schoolmasters*, Edinburgh, 1854; Chapter vi, pp. 106 *sqq.*

[37] Anton Birlinger, *Volksthümliches aus Schwaben*, Freiburg im Breisgau, 1861-62; I, 303.

[38] Eugen Mogk, "Sitten und Gebrauche im Kreislauf des Jahres," in R. Wuttke's *Sachsiche Volkskunde*, Dresden, 1901, Second Edition, p. 318.

[39] Mrs. Agnes Murgoçi, "The Vampire in Rumania," *Folk-Lore*, xxxvii, no. 4; pp. 320-21.

[40] Mrs. Murgoçi, *op. cit.*, p. 321.

[41] As quoted by Mrs. Murgoçi, *op. cit.*, p. 335.

[42] Josef Haltrich, *Zur Volkskunde der Siebenburger Sachsen*, Vienna, 1885, p. 281.

[43] C. D. Frick, *De S. Georgio*, Lipsiæ, 1683; Neuius, *De equite S. Georgio*, Tubingen, 1716; and Joachim Mantzelm, *De Georgiis . . . claris*, Gustrouiæ, 1712; amongst many other authorities.

[44] As early as 1222 the national synod of Oxford ordered S. George's Day to be kept as a lesser holiday. In 1415 the Constitution of Archbishop Chichele raised S. George's Day to the rank of one of the chief feasts of the year in England and prescribed that it should be observed with the same solemnity as Christmas Day itself. In England during the seventeenth and eighteenth centuries S. George's Day remained a Holiday of Obligation.

[45] *Ion Creanga*, vol. VII, 1914, p. 165. These particular stories were collected by N. I. Dumitrascu. I give them from the version of Mrs. Murgoçi.

[46] London, 1877, pp. 29-33. The book is a revised edition of a *Residence in Bulgaria*, written in 1866-67 and published in 1869.

[47] It is almost superfluous to say that this is wholly incorrect. The Vampire tradition still prevails in Dalmatia.

[48] This again is wholly mistaken. The authors, perhaps naturally enough, have no knowledge of the terrible facts of possession, and write unwittingly and somewhat flippantly.

[49] See my *Geography of Witchcraft*, pp. 603-605, and the corresponding notes.

INDEX